COMMUNICATING IN SMALL GROUPS

Principles and Practices

Fifth Edition

Steven A. Beebe

Southwest Texas State University

John T. Masterson

University of Miami

LONGMAN

An imprint of Addison Wesley Longman, Inc.

New York • Reading, Massachusetts • Menlo Park, California • Harlow, England
Don Mills, Ontario • Sydney • Mexico City • Madrid • Amsterdam

Acquisitions Editor: Deirdre Cavanaugh
Editorial Assistant: Kwon Chong
Project Coordination and Text Design: York Production Services
Cover Designer: Kay Petronio
Photo Researcher: Julie Tesser
Electronic Production Manager: Valerie Zaborski
Manufacturing Manager: Helene G. Landers
Electronic Page Makeup: York Production Services
Printer and Binder: R. R. Donnelley & Sons Company
Cover Printer: The Lehigh Press, Inc.

For permission to use copyrighted material, grateful acknowledgment is made to the copyright holders on pp. 363, which are hereby made part of this copyright page.

Library of Congress Cataloging-in-Publication Data

Beebe, Steven A., 1950–
    Communicating in small groups: principles and practices / Steven A. Beebe,
John T. Masterson. — 5th ed.
      p. cm.
    Includes index.
    ISBN 0-673-98080-4
    1. Small groups.   2. Communication in small groups.   3. Groups relations training.
I. Masterson, John T., 1946– . II. Title.
HM133.B43   1996
302.3'4—dc20   96–2588
                                               CIP

ISBN 0-673-98080-4

345678910—DOC—999897

CONTENTS

93215

CHAPTER THREE

CHAPTER FOUR

CHAPTER FIVE

CHAPTER SIX

CHAPTER SEVEN

CHAPTER EIGHT

CHAPTER NINE

CHAPTER TEN

CHAPTER ELEVEN

APPENDIX

PREFACE

e are pleased that the first four editions of *Communicating in Small Groups: Principles and Practices* continue to be praised and widely used both by teachers and by students. Our goal for over 15 years has been to present a digest of essential principles and practices that are relevant, practical, and useful, yet based on both classic and cutting-edge research. We appreciate the opportunity to continue our partnership with those of you who teach group communication.

This book is written to serve as the primary text for a college-level course. Instructors of such courses have many options in selecting a text. Some texts adopt a primarily theoretical perspective. But presenting theory without helping students apply principles can result in informed yet unskilled group members. Other texts emphasize skills to the exclusion of theoretical frameworks. While students often clamor for techniques and skills to enhance their ability to work with others, such approaches do not give students principles to guide their newfound applications. Skills alone will not give students inventive options in managing the multiple challenges and opportunities of collaborating with others. The fundamental premise of the fifth edition of this book remains the same as in earlier editions: Effective group communication requires knowledge of both the principles that help us explain and predict group communication, and the practices that foster application. As in previous editions, we draw on a variety of theoretical perspectives to achieve our goal. Our philosophy is that a singular theoretical perspective does not adequately introduce students to the multitude of paradigms that are used to help unravel the mysteries of group communication, teamwork, and collaboration.

We have designed our text to provide learning options both for teacher and for students. In our fifth edition, we continue to distill major conclusions in review boxes that help students clinch key ideas. Our refined "Putting Principles into Practice" section at the end of each chapter makes an even greater attempt to answer the "So what?" question about the principles and practices we have identified. Improved and updated pedagogical features such as chapter objectives, a glossary, discussion questions, chapter-end activities, case studies, and exercises are integral parts of our partnership with instructors in teaching group communication principles and practices and providing opportunities for students to think critically about them.

While retaining the lively, engaging writing style that students have appreciated in previous editions, we have updated several content areas throughout the book and included new references to the best small group communication research conclusions that we could find.

Changes in this edition are evident from Chapter 1 through our concluding chapter. For example, we begin the book with a new discussion of communication to anchor our definition of small group communication. Chapter 1 also includes a new discussion of individualism and collectivism and of the essential elements of a competent small group communicator. In Chapter 2 we have added a new discussion of symbolic convergence theory; we also draw students' attention to the effect new technology is having on group deliberations. In fact, we refer throughout the book to the role of such technologies as e-mail, video conferences, and other media. Another even more prominent theme is the effects of culture, gender, and human diversity on group deliberations. We have included new information about culture and gender differences in the chapters that discuss group relationships, nonverbal communication, conflict, leadership, and other areas in which new research conclusions are helping us understand the role of these factors on collaboration and teamwork. Other new additions or substantive revisions include:

- An explicit acknowledgment that group communication may occur even when people are not meeting face to face; this reflects the increased prominence of technology linking people in collaborate deliberations.
- A new perspective for distinguishing between primary and secondary groups.
- More explicit qualification of research conclusions that are primarily applicable to North Americans.
- Crisp, brief, yet interesting new examples sprinkled throughout the text to illustrate key principles.
- A new discussion of high- and low-context, and high- and low-contact cultures and group communication.
- Expanded discussion of the use of technology and electronic data bases as sources of information needed for group discussion.
- A new discussion of how to avoid reasoning fallacies when solving problems and making decisions in groups.
- Revised discussion of group problem-solving and decision-making approaches.
- A new framework for balancing group structure and interaction when presenting prescriptive methods of enhancing group performance.
- A new integration of problem solving steps and tools in Chapter 8.
- A new discussion in Chapter 9 of how to deal with difficult group members, as well as more explicit suggestions for managing pseudo-, simple-, and ego-conflict.
- The latest research conclusions about leadership in small groups.
- Recent research applications of gender and leadership in small groups.
- A revised approach to discussing applications of group principles and practices in organizations in Chapter 11.
- A simple, yet powerful perspective for understanding and improving group meetings.
- Additional material about the role of small groups in achieving quality products and services.
- Expanded coverage of teamwork theory and applications throughout the text.
- Revised and expanded instructor's manual.

We are grateful to the many individuals who reviewed earlier editions of the book and offered excellent revision suggestions. This is an improved book because the following people offered constructive and detailed commentary about our work:

Pat Calder, Los Angeles Valley College

Deborah Chasteen, Mercer University

Thomas Droessler, Owens Community College

Ruth M. Guzley, California State University, Chico

Robert D. Harrison, Gallaudet University

Barbara J. Holmes, University of Colorado, Denver

Joseph M. Mazza, Central Missouri State University

David Natharius, California State University, Fresno

Nan Peck, Northern Virginia Community College

We have again been blessed by a skilled and professional editorial support team at Addison Wesley in preparing this new edition. Our acquisitions editor, Cynthia Biron, was a strong supporter of our work. We look forward to working with Diedre Cavanaugh, our new editor at Addison Wesley. Our development editor, Leslie Taggart, provided outstanding editorial leadership in keeping two busy authors on track and on target by managing a multitude of editorial details and by her prose-polishing skill. Julie Tesser, our Addison Wesley art and photo researcher, did an excellent job of selecting new visual images to enliven the text and keep it contemporary and visually appealing. Kwon Chong, editorial assistant at Addison Wesley, helped us manage many of the logistical needs we had in producing this volume. We also thank our colleagues and students at Southwest Texas State University and the University of Miami for their assistance, support, and suggestions. Stephanie Ludwig and Russ Wittrup at Southwest Texas State University offered helpful feedback that shaped several of our discussions of theory and skills. Maria Kharcheva, research assistant at Southwest Texas State, helped locate research sources and track down details. Manuscript typist Rhonda Brooks and administrative assistant Sue Hall, both at Southwest Texas State, again provided outstanding support. We also want to acknowledge the expertise of our friends and colleagues Dennis and Laurie Romig of Performance Resources, Inc., in Austin, Texas, for their knowledge and practical insight about groups and teams. Their management-consultant experience helped anchor our research conclusions with practical applications, especially in our discussions of problem solving, teamwork, meetings, and conflict.

At the University of Miami, assistant to the vice provost Nely Li has provided her usual high level of administrative support. Our colleague Valerie Manno Giroux and her students gave us many suggestions and helpful criticism of the fourth edition. Law student Diamela del Castillo offered encouragement, feedback, and her prodigious library research talents. One of us could not have made it through this revision without her. Thank you, Dee.

Finally, as in our previous editions, we offer our appreciation and thanks to our families—our most important small groups—who continue to teach us about teamwork and collaboration. John and Noah Masterson have grown up, graduated from college, and moved out into the world. Nancy Masterson, after three decades with her husband, continues as his greatest love, his best friend, and most respected critic.

Mark and Matt Beebe were infants when the first edition was written. They are now growing into mature individuals who continue to teach their father about communication. Susan Beebe has been an integral part of the editorial and author team in this and every previous edition. She is again acknowledged for her considerable gift of working with words and her encouragement, support, and love of her spouse who works with words.

Steven A. Beebe
John T. Masterson

CHAPTER
O·N·E

An Introduction to Small Group Communication

After studying this chapter, you will be able to:

- Define communication.
- Define small group communication.
- Explain the importance of studying small group communication.
- List and describe the advantages and disadvantages of working with others in small groups.

- Compare and contrast primary and secondary groups.
- Describe differences between individualistic and collectivistic cultures.
- Identify the three elements of becoming a competent small group communicator.

*U*sing a variety of research methods, communication scholars, sociologists, psychologists, and anthropologists have reached a similar conclusion about humankind: We are social creatures. We need to establish meaningful relationships with others. We need to associate with others in groups. We are reared in family groups. We are educated in groups. We worship in groups. We are entertained in groups. We work in groups. When an important problem arises, we seek others' advice and meet with problem-solving and decision-making groups in order to help find answers to important issues.

This book is about groups. More specifically, it is about communication in small groups.

"Why study small group communication?" You have probably already asked yourself that question. Or maybe you have asked, "What can a systematic study of small group communication do for me? How will it help me with my career? Will it really help me be a better committee member? Will studying small group communication improve my interpersonal relationships with my family and my friends?"

Studying small group communication may help you in many ways, but the main purpose of this book is to help you become a better communicator in the context of a small group. The book will strive to give you both a broad understanding of group communication processes and practical advice to help you become a more effective small group participant. Note that the book will primarily deal with **task-oriented small groups**—groups with a specific objective to achieve, information to share, a problem to solve, or a decision to make.

To frame our study of small group communication, we will examine two fundamental concepts. We will first explain assumptions about human communication and then zero in on a definition of small group communication.

WHAT IS COMMUNICATION?

This book will focus on communication that occurs in a group. One scholar, discussing the importance of communication to an organization, describes it as:

the lifeblood . . .

the glue that binds . . .

the oil that smooths . . .

the thread that ties . . .

the force that pervades . . .

the binding agent that cements all relationships.[1]

FIGURE 1.1   THE SHANNON-WEAVER MODEL

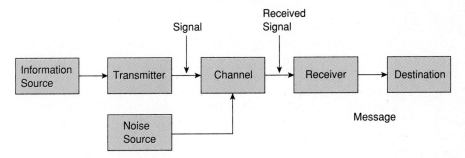

The Shannon-Weaver model. (From *The Mathematical Theory of Communication* by Claude E. Shannon and Warren Weaver. University of Illinois Press, 1949. Reprinted by permission.)

These metaphors apply to small groups as well as to large corporations. Regardless of a group's size, its members must be able to talk, listen, and respond to one another. They must be able to communicate effectively and appropriately to achieve their goals.

What is this powerful, pervasive process called communication? Reduced to its essence, **communication** is the process of acting on information.[2] Someone does or says something, and there is a response in action, word, or thought. Throughout the past five decades, our understanding of the nature of communication has evolved from viewing it as a simple action-and-reaction exchange to a more complex, simultaneous, transactive process. Next we will examine the evolving meaning of the term *communication*.[3]

COMMUNICATION AS ACTION: TRANSFER OF INFORMATION

"But I told you what I wanted!" Such expressions of exasperation assume that if you send a message someone will receive it. An early conception viewed the communication process as:

who (sender)

says what (message)

in what channel (medium)

to whom (receiver)

with what effect.[4]

While this notion is clear and straightforward, it has a fundamental flaw: Communication is rarely, if ever, as simple as "what we put in is what we get out." Figure 1.1 shows an early model of communication which represents it as a linear, input-output process.

While this model depicts most critical elements of the process, it may nonetheless perpetuate the myth that information is communication. It is a

FIGURE 1.2   FEEDBACK

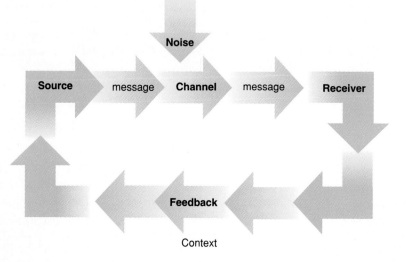

misconception to believe that communication has occurred simply because someone has said something to someone else. A response, or feedback to the message, is an essential aspect of the communication process.

COMMUNICATION AS INTERACTION: EXCHANGE OF INFORMATION

Feedback is the response to a message. When you communicate, someone may respond, perhaps with a frown or a smile, or maybe by saying something about your message. Feedback can be intentional (when you congratulate your child on successfully learning to ride a bicycle) or unintentional (when you yawn at a boring story). Your response can be verbal ("I really like your idea") or nonverbal (you frown when someone disagrees with your point.) Figure 1.2 depicts communication as an interactive process, or action and reaction. Feedback, or a response, is now included in the process.

But just because feedback is included in the model does not mean that the communication is effective. **Noise,** either in the channel or in the mind of the receiver, may contribute to an inaccurate understanding of the message intended. To be truly effective, communication should achieve three goals. First, the message should be understood; the receiver should comprehend it as encoded. Second, the communication should achieve the intended effect. If the receiver understands the message but does not take the requested action, the communication is still less than effective. Third, communication must be ethical.[5] The communicator should not coerce the listener to respond to a message. Nor should he or she lie or knowingly use false information to achieve an intended effect.

FIGURE 1.3   COMMUNICATION AS SIMULTANEOUS TRANSACTION

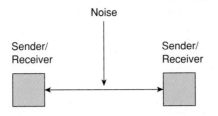

COMMUNICATION AS TRANSACTION: SIMULTANEOUS MESSAGE CREATION

Today scholars view communication as a **transactive process**—one in which messages are sent and received simultaneously. As you talk to someone, you respond to both verbal and nonverbal messages. For example, if you are telling a joke and your listener breaks eye contact or exhibits a glassy-eyed stare, you know that he or she is bored even before you get to the punchline. Figure 1.3 illustrates the communication-as-transaction approach with arrows that indicate a constant and simultaneous process of message creation. Our definition of communication as acting upon information is still accurate. The key addition is that when we communicate with another person, especially in a face-to-face setting—the context for most small group meetings—the transactive nature of communication means that messages are simultaneously being responded to. Even if you remain silent or nod off to sleep, your nonverbal message provides information to others about your emotions. The transactive nature of communication suggests that you cannot *not* communicate.

Viewing communication as a simultaneous, transactive process is especially important to our understanding of small group communication. It is unlikely that all members of a small group will be talking at the same time (although sometimes they do). Nevertheless, just being in one another's presence means that both verbal and nonverbal feedback are occurring, making group communication a transactive process of message creation.

WHAT IS SMALL GROUP COMMUNICATION?

Consider these situations:

As the nation becomes more frustrated with a seemingly skyrocketing national debt, the president of the United States meets with the administration's chief economic advisers to discuss possible solutions.

The Amalgamated Cable-TV Company is considering making a takeover bid for a fiber optics company. The chief executive officer calls company executives together to examine the virtues and pitfalls of the possible merger.

To prepare for the final exam in your algebra class, you and several class members meet three nights each week to study.

Each of these three examples involves a group of people meeting for a specific purpose. And as they communicate with one another, they are communicating transactively; they are simultaneously responding to one another as they express ideas, information, and opinions. Although the groups' purposes are quite different in these three scenarios, these groups share something in common—something that distinguishes them from a cluster of people waiting for a bus or riding in an elevator, for example. Just what is that "something"? What are the characteristics that make a group a group? We define **small group communication** as interaction among a small group of people who share a common purpose or goal, who feel a sense of belonging to the group, and who exert influence on one another. Next, we will examine this definition more closely.

A SMALL GROUP OF PEOPLE

A group includes at least three people; two people are usually referred to as a **dyad.** The addition of a third person immediately adds an element of increased complexity and uncertainty to the transactive communication process. The probability increases that two will form a coalition against one. And although the dynamics of group roles, norms, power, status, and leadership are also present in two-person transactions, they become increasingly important in affecting the outcome of the transaction when three or more people are communicating.

If at least three people are required for a small group, what is the maximum number it may have and still be considered small? Scholars do not agree on a specific number. However, having more than 12 people (some say 13, others say 20) in a group significantly decreases individual members' interaction. The larger the group, the less influence each individual has on the group and the more likely that subgroups will develop. With 20 or more people, the communication more closely resembles a public-speaking situation, when one person addresses an audience, providing less opportunity for all members to participate freely. The larger the group, the more likely that group members will become passive rather than actively involved in the discussion.

MEETING WITH A COMMON PURPOSE

The President's economic advisers, the Amalgamated Cable TV Company, and your algebra study group have one thing in common—their members have a specific purpose for meeting. They share a concern for the objectives of the group. While a group of people waiting for a bus or riding in an elevator may share the goal of transportation, they do not have the same *collective* goal. Their individual destinations are different. Their primary concerns are for themselves, not for others. As soon as their individual goals are realized, they leave the bus or elevator. On the other hand, a goal keeps a committee or discussion group together until that goal is realized. Many groups fail to remain together because they never identify their common purpose. While participants in small groups may have somewhat different motives for their membership, a common purpose cements the group together.

Feeling a Sense of Belonging

Not only do group members need a mutual concern to unite them, but they also need to feel that they belong to the group. Commuters waiting for a bus probably do not feel part of a collective effort. Members of a small group, however, need to have a sense of *identity* with the group; they should be able to feel that it is *their* group.

Exerting Influence

In a small group, the behavior of one group member affects that of others. Group members can influence one another even when not meeting face to face. While an overwhelming majority of small group communication still involves meeting with others live and in person, more and more small group transactions occur in mediated settings. In this age of telephone conference calls, fax machines, video teleconferences, Internet correspondence, and electronic mail, communicating over a great distance has become increasingly easy. There is some evidence that groups linked together only by e-mail or a computer network can generate more and better ideas than groups that meet face to face.[6] Such communication may, nonetheless, be hindered by sluggish feedback or delayed replies, which are not a problem when meeting in person. And while more ideas may be generated in a media meeting, complex problems and relationship issues are better handled in person than on the Internet or another computer or media network.[7] In most cases, in-person communication affords the best opportunity to clarify meaning and resolve uncertainty and misunderstanding.

Mediated group communication using the latest technology may be an *efficient* way of exchanging data and basic information, but it is less *effective* for groups trying to manage conflict or deal with other relationship issues. Usually group members meeting face to face exert influence upon one another, but evidence suggests that technology is affecting the way we work in groups and teams. Throughout this book, we will refer to the growing body of research that explains how technology both helps and hinders group deliberations. With or without technology, however, group members influence others and are influenced by others.

In summary, small group communication is defined as interaction among a small group of people who share a common purpose or goal, who feel a sense of belonging to the group, and who exert influence on one another. Usually group members interact in face-to-face situations. Sometimes, however, a group of people collaborate even when not present in the same room.

WHY LEARN ABOUT SMALL GROUPS?

Besides defining small group communication, one of this book's first objectives is to help you understand the value of studying the principles of effective communication in a small group. Consider these reasons for learning about small groups.

1. *You spend a significant portion of your time working in small groups.* Stop reading for just a moment and count how many different groups you are involved in this week. What is your total? Perhaps you thought of only one or two groups you currently belong to, such as a committee or a work group. But did you consider your friends? How about fraternities, sororities, or religious groups? Your family? If you are employed, did you consider the groups you participate in while on the job?

Human beings need to socialize. We have a need to congregate, to associate with others. Unless you are a hermit living in an isolated cave, you communicate with others in groups. Chances are, you will continue to do so. Work groups, social groups, educational groups and family groups occupy a significant portion of our communication time. While this book will emphasize small groups that exist for the purpose of making decisions, solving problems, and sharing information, it will also discuss many principles that are applicable to most of the groups in which you participate.

2. *You need to understand how groups make decisions and solve problems.* You may not consider many of the groups you belong to as decision-making or problem-solving groups. You join some groups just for the fun of socializing and being with others. You may think that problem solving or decision making occurs only in groups with a very specific task, but even in social groups problems arise and decisions need to be made. This book will discuss various approaches to group problem solving and decision making. An increased understanding of what happens when people make decisions in groups should improve your ability to arrive at better decisions and, consequently, enhance your enjoyment of working in a group.

3. *You can reduce the uncertainty and anxiety you may have about working with others in small groups.* You often fear what you do not understand. Your first day on a new job provokes fear and anxiety; you are not sure what to expect. You probably experience some uncertainty on your first day in a new

class or at a new school. Often, anxiety and uncertainty can so inhibit you that you do not make the most of your situation, whether it is a new job, a new class, or any kind of new group. Most colleges and universities have orientation programs to help reduce your uncertainty about your new environment. On a new job, you are usually given time to learn the ropes, and you may go through extensive training programs to help you do a better job. Learning the principles of small group communication and applying specific suggestions for improving its quality can reduce (but not necessarily eliminate) some of the uncertainty and discomfort you may feel working with others in small groups. It helps to know what to expect. Armed with communication theory and skills, you should be in a better position to explain and predict what happens when people communicate in small groups.

4. *You will better understand your own communication behavior.* After participating in a small group discussion, have you ever asked yourself, "Now why did I say that?" or said "I don't know why I feel so tense and uncomfortable in this group"? Have you ever wondered why you always seem to disagree with someone or why you are not an effective committee leader? Studying small group communication should help you answer these questions. This book will discuss relationships and leadership, as well as nonverbal communication, conflict management, and reasons for joining groups. As you work with others, a knowledge of small group communication principles and theory will expand your understanding of your own role within the groups to which you belong.

5. *You can help groups in which you participate function more effectively.* Mounting evidence indicates that many group meetings are poorly run. It has been estimated that over half the productivity of the billions of hours that Americans spend in meetings is wasted. One company estimated that it lost $71 million a year because of inept management of meetings. Another study reported that one-third of the chief executive officers of the companies studied thought meetings were of "marginal value or not worth the time."[8] While one course in small group communication cannot cure all the problems that plague group meetings, learning about effective group principles and practices can make a difference.

Individuals trained in small group communication have the opportunity to improve many of the group situations in which they find themselves. Because most groups are not run effectively, skillfully, or diplomatically, you will stand out as a valuable member of any group. While you do not need to announce your expertise to the group or use other heavy-handed approaches, you can use your skills subtly and helpfully to nudge the group into functioning effectively.

REVIEW BOX

Why Learn about Small Groups?

1. You spend much time working in groups.
2. You can better understand how groups make effective decisions and skillfully solve problems.
3. You can reduce your uncertainty and anxiety about working with others in groups.
4. You will better understand your own behavior when working with others in groups.
5. You can help make groups function more effectively.

ADVANTAGES AND DISADVANTAGES OF WORKING IN SMALL GROUPS

"What's so great about working in groups?" mutters an exasperated member of the student entertainment committee after spending two hours in a committee meeting. "I could have solved the problem in 15 minutes. Why do we have to spend two hours rehashing old information?"

"I'm really looking forward to our committee meeting this evening," says an enthusiastic member of an ecology group. "There is always such a great spirit of unity and cohesiveness during each meeting. Even though we sometimes disagree, each group member really seems to respect the ideas and opinions of the others. I think it's because we really enjoy working together as a group."

What are your feelings about working in groups? Maybe you dread attending group meetings. Perhaps you agree with the observation that a committee is a group that keeps minutes but wastes hours. You may believe that groups bumble and stumble along until they reach some sort of compromise—a compromise with which no one is pleased. "To be effective," said one committee member, "a committee should be made up of three people. But to get anything done, one member should be sick and another absent."

Conversely, you could be one of those people who enjoys group work. You may relish the challenge of trying to solve problems, make decisions, and accomplish tasks while working with others. If you're lucky, you've had more pleasant than unpleasant encounters with group work, but most likely you've had both.

People can easily become disgruntled with a group if it does not meet their expectations of how a good group should function. An important purpose of this book is to help you appreciate the advantages of working with other people; as many advantages as there are, you will also encounter problems that may lead to frustration and anxiety. By understanding both the advantages and the potential pitfalls of working in groups, you will form more realistic expectations about small group work.[9]

Some people view groups as a cure-all for complex problems. If they need a solution to a problem, they form a group or committee. The work of small groups can result in good solutions, sound decisions, and well-executed projects. Some situations and problems, however, are best not handled by a group at all.

ADVANTAGES

1. *Groups have greater information resources than individuals do.* Because of the variety of backgrounds and experiences that individuals bring to a group, the group as a whole has more information and ideas from which to

seek solutions to a problem than one person would have alone. With more information available, the group is more likely to discuss all sides of an issue and is also more likely to arrive at a better solution.[10]

2. *Groups can employ a greater number of creative problem-solving methods.* Research on groups generally supports the maxim that "two heads are better than one" when it comes to solving problems.[11] Groups usually make better decisions than individuals working alone, because groups have more approaches to or methods of solving a specific problem. A group of people with various backgrounds, experiences, and resources can more creatively consider ways to solve a problem than one person can.

3. *Working in groups fosters improved learning and comprehension of ideas discussed.* Imagine that your history professor announces that the final exam next week is going to be comprehensive. History is not your best subject. You realize you need help. What do you do? You may form a study group with other classmates. Your decision to study with a group of people is wise; education theorists claim that when you take an active role in the learning process your comprehension of information is improved. If you studied for the exam by yourself, you would not have the benefit of asking and answering questions posed by other study group members. By discussing a subject with a group, you learn more and improve your comprehension of the subject.

4. *Members' satisfaction with the group decision increases because they participate in the problem-solving process.* Group problem solving provides an opportunity for group members to participate in making decisions and achieving the group goal. Several research studies suggest that individuals who help solve problems in a group are more committed to the solution and better satisfied with their participation in the group than if they weren't involved in the discussion.

5. *Group members gain a better understanding of themselves as they interact with others.* Working in groups helps you gain a more accurate picture of how others see you. The feedback you receive makes you aware of personal characteristics that are not known to you but that are known to others. Whether the interaction is advantageous or disadvantageous depends largely on how you respond to the feedback others provide. If someone tells you that you are obnoxious and difficult to work with, you may respond by ignoring the comment, disagreeing with the observation, or examining your behavior to see if the criticism is justified. By becoming sensitive to feedback, you can better understand yourself (or at least better understand how others perceive you) than you would if you worked alone. Group interaction and feedback can be useful in helping you examine your interper-

sonal behavior and in deciding whether you want to change your communication style.

DISADVANTAGES

While working in small groups can produce positive results, problems sometimes occur when people congregate. Perhaps you have heard the sentiment that committees are groups of the uninformed assigned by the unwilling to do the unnecessary. Consider some of the disadvantages of working in groups. Identifying these potential problems can help you avoid them.

1. *Group members may pressure others to conform to the majority opinion.* Most people do not like conflict; they generally try to avoid it. Some people believe that in an effective group, members readily reach agreement. But this tendency to avoid controversy in relationships can affect the quality of a group decision. What is wrong with group members reaching agreement? Nothing, unless they are agreeing to conform to the majority opinion or even to the leader's opinion. Group members may agree on a bad solution just to avoid conflict. Social psychologist Irving Janis calls this phenomenon **groupthink**—when groups agree primarily in order to avoid conflict.[12] Chapter 9 discusses conflict in small groups, talks about groupthink in more detail, and suggests how to avoid it.

2. *An individual group member may dominate the discussion.* In some groups it seems as if one person must run the show. That member wants to make the decisions and, when all is said and done, insists that his or her position on the issue is the best one. "Well," you might say, "if this person wants to do all the work, that's fine with me. I won't complain. It sure will be a lot easier for me." Yes, if you permit a member or two to dominate the group, you may do less work yourself, but then you forfeit the greater availability of knowledge and more creative approaches that come with full participation. Other members may not feel satisfied because they too feel alienated from the decision making. If they do not enjoy working on the project, the group will suffer from their reduced input.

Try to use the domineering member's enthusiasm to the group's advantage. If an individual tries to monopolize the discussion, other group members should channel that interest more constructively. The talkative member, for example, could be given a special research assignment. Of course, if the domineering member continues to monopolize the discussion, other group members may have to confront that person and suggest that others be given an opportunity to present their views.

3. *Some group members may rely too much on others to get the job done.*

"Charlie is a hard worker. He'll see that the job is done right."

"Ayako seems to really like taking charge. She is doing such a good job. The group really doesn't need me."

"No one will miss me if I don't show up for the meeting this afternoon. There will be enough people to do the work."

Statements like these occur when group members are not aware of each individual's importance in the group. A danger of working in groups is that individuals may be tempted to rely on others rather than pitch in and help. Working together distributes the responsibility of accomplishing a task. Spreading the responsibility among all group members should be an advantage of group work. However, when some group members allow others to carry the work load, problems can develop. Just because you are part of a group does not mean that you can get lost in the crowd. Your input is needed. Do not abdicate your responsibility to another group member. To avoid this problem, try to encourage less-talkative group members to contribute to the discussion. Also, make sure each person knows the goals and objectives of the group. Encouraging each member to attend every meeting helps, too. Poor attendance at group meetings is a sure sign that members are falling into the "let Charlie do it" syndrome. Finally, see that each person knows and fulfills his or her specific responsibilities to the group.

4. *Working with others in a group takes longer than working alone.* For many people, one of the major frustrations about group work is the time it takes to accomplish tasks. Not only does a group have to find a time and place where everyone can meet (sometimes a serious problem in itself), but a group simply requires more time to define, analyze, research, and solve problems than do individuals working alone. It takes time for people to talk and listen to others. Still, such input usually results in a better solution. You have to remind yourself and the group, "If we want a better solution, it is going to take time, patience, and understanding." And, as you've heard, time is money! One researcher estimates that one two-hour meeting attended by 20 executives would cost the equivalent of a week's salary for one of them.[13]

If you determine that solving problems in groups takes too much time, you may decide that problems requiring an immediate decision may be better handled by individuals. In the heat of battle, commanders usually do not call for a committee meeting of all their troops. True, the troops may be better satisfied with a decision that they have participated in making, but the obvious need for a quick decision overrides any advantages that may be gained from meeting as a group. Thus, though small group communication can be extremely effective, you should also know when it may be more efficient to solve problems individually. Remember that solving problems in groups requires more time.

REVIEW BOX

Advantages and Disadvantages of Working in Groups

Advantages:

> Groups have more information.
>
> Groups are often more creative.
>
> Working in groups improves learning.
>
> Group members are more satisfied if they participate in the process.
>
> Group members learn about themselves.

Disadvantages:

> Group members may pressure others to conform.
>
> Someone may dominate the discussion.
>
> Members may rely too much on others and not do their part.
>
> Group work takes more time than working individually.

TYPES OF SMALL GROUPS

So far you have read about the key characteristics of small groups, the importance of studying small group communication, and several advantages and disadvantages of working in groups. Besides understanding what a small group is and why you should study it, you need to keep in mind that small group communication can range from a relatively unstructured, spontaneous discussion of an issue to a more formal, planned presentation.

Groups are formed for several reasons. As you will find in Chapter 3, some groups originate to fulfill our basic needs for association and community. Others are formed to solve a specific problem, to make a decision, or to gather information.

To give you an idea of the variety and purposes of our association with others in groups, we will discuss the role of both primary and secondary groups.

PRIMARY GROUPS

A **primary group** is a group whose main purpose is to fulfill the basic need to associate with others. Your family provides one of the best illustrations of a primary group. In "The Death of the Hired Man," poet Robert Frost mused, "Home is the place where, when you have to go there/They have to take you in." Family communication usually does not follow a structured agenda; family conversation is informal. Conversation is also informal within other primary groups, such as informal cliques of friends or workers who interact over an extended period of time. Primary group members associate with one another for the joy of community—to fulfill the basic human need to be social.

The main task of the primary group is to perpetuate the group so that members can continue to enjoy one another's companionship. Because people want to maintain these ties, they may be eager to conform to the behavior of the group. Teenagers who embrace the latest style in clothing or music often do so not only because they genuinely enjoy what is in vogue but also because they need to fit in with their peers. Primary groups do not meet regularly to make decisions unless a meeting is necessary to perpetuate the social patterns of the group. As with any group, some members may assert more influence than others. The key reward of belonging to a primary group, however, is simply the satisfaction of being a member.

SECONDARY GROUPS

Secondary groups exist to accomplish a task or achieve a goal. Most of the groups you belong to at work or school are secondary groups. You are not involved in a committee or a class group assignment just for fun or to meet your social need for belonging (even though you may enjoy the group and make friends with other group members). The main reason you join secondary groups is to get something done. Next we will identify several different kinds of secondary groups to which you may belong at some point in your life.

Problem-Solving Group   A **problem-solving group** exists to overcome some unsatisfactory situation or obstacles to achieving a goal. Many, if not most, groups in business and industry are problem-solving groups. The most common problem that for-profit organizations face is finding a way to make more money. Chapters 7 and 8 will review principles and suggestions for improving your group problem-solving ability.

Decision-Making Group   The task of a **decision-making group** is to make a choice among several alternatives. The group must identify what the possible choices are, discuss the consequences of the choices, and then select the alternative that best meets a need or achieves the goal of the group or parent organization. A search committee that screens applicants for a job has the task of making a decision. The group must select one person from among the many alternatives available. A city council that must decide where to build a new airport looks at the alternatives recommended by a consulting firm. The council's job is to choose one site from the several that are recommended.

As we will discuss in Chapter 7, decision making is usually a part of the problem-solving process. Groups that have a problem to solve usually must identify several possible solutions and decide on the one that best solves the

In small groups individuals have access to more information and resources to help them in solving a problem than they would have working alone.

problem. While all group problem solving involves making decisions, not all group decision making solves a problem. In Chapter 11 we will apply principles and strategies to enhance both decision making and problem solving in organizational settings.

Study Group   As a student you are no doubt familiar with **study groups.** The main goal of these groups is to gather information and learn new ideas. We have already noted that one advantage of participating in a group is that you learn by being involved in a discussion. A study group also has the advantage of having access to more information and a wider variety of ideas through the contribution of different individuals.

Therapy Group   A **therapy group,** also called an *encounter group* or *T-group,* strives to provide treatment for group members' personal problems. Such groups are led by professionals who are trained to help members overcome, or at least manage, individual problems in a group setting. Group therapy takes advantage of the self-understanding that members gain as they communicate with one another. Members also learn how they are perceived by others. By participating in a therapy group, people with similar problems can benefit from how others have learned to cope. Groups such as Weight Watchers and Alcoholics Anonymous also provide positive reinforcement when members have achieved their goals. By experiencing therapy with others, members of a T-group take advantage of the greater knowledge and information available to the group.

Committee   A **committee** is a group of people who are elected or appointed for a wide range of purposes. Some committees are formed to solve problems. Others are appointed to make a decision or simply to gather information so that another group, team, or committee can make a decision. Some committee members are appointed to a **standing committee** (one that remains active for an extended time period); others serve on an **ad hoc committee** (one that disbands when its special task has been completed). Like many other people, you may react negatively to serving on a committee. Committee work is often regarded as time-consuming, tedious, and ineffective—except in increasing the sale of aspirin! Perhaps you have heard some of these sentiments about committees:

> A committee is a group that keeps minutes but wastes hours.
>
> A committee is a way of postponing a decision.
>
> A committee is a group of people who individually can do nothing and who collectively decide nothing can be done.

While frustration with committees is commonplace, you do *not* have to be doomed to have a negative experience when working with others in a committee. Throughout this text we review principles and skills of group communication than can help you enhance the quality of committee meetings. In Chapter 11 we will provide specific tips for chairing and participating in meetings.

REVIEW BOX

Types of Small Groups

GROUP TYPE	GROUP PURPOSE	EXAMPLES
Primary group	To fill the basic need to associate with others	Family Close friends
Secondary group	To accomplish a task or achieve a goal	Problem-solving group Decision-making group Study group Therapy group Committees

ME VERSUS *WE:* AN OBSTACLE
TO COLLABORATION IN GROUPS AND TEAMS

The personal pronouns *I, me,* and *my* represent a primary stumbling block to our collaboration with others in small groups. Most North Americans champion individual achievement over collective group or team accomplishment. Researchers describe our tendency to focus on individual accomplishment as **individualism.** According to Geert Hofstede, individualism is the "emotional independence from groups, organizations, or other collectivities."[14] Individualistic cultures value individual recognition more than group or team recognition. There is also a strong pull to self-actualize; to be all that you can be as an individual. The United States, Great Britain, and Australia usually top the list of countries in which individual rights and accomplishment are valued over collective achievement.

By contrast, **collectivistic** cultures are those in which group or team achievement is valued more than individual achievement. People from Asian countries such as Japan, China, and Taiwan tend to value collaboration and collective achievement more than those from individualistic cultures. Venezuela, Colombia, and Pakistan are other countries in which people score high on a collective approach to work methods.[15] In collective cultures, *we* is more important than *me*. While collectivistic cultures usually think of a group as the primary unit in society, individualistic cultures think about the individual.[16]

As you might guess, people from individualistic cultures tend to find it more challenging to collaborate in group projects than do people from collectivistic cultures. Table 1.1 contrasts individualistic and collectivistic approaches to working in small groups.

If you and members of your group or team operate from an individualistic cultural perspective, it will be more challenging to develop collaborative approaches to solve problems, make decisions, and accomplish the work of the group. We are not suggesting that you totally abandon your cultural value of individualism. But being aware of individualistic group-member tendencies explains why working in groups can be frustrating and time consuming.

One of the most important strategies for overcoming a focus on individual concerns is for a group or team to develop what one research team calls a "clear and elevating goal" that the entire group can support.[17] Without an overarching group goal, individual agendas are likely to be more important than the group agenda. The goal should be one that excites the group and fosters a team approach rather than an individual approach. Groups, teams, and meetings are here to stay. From the outset of our study of small group communication, it is important to understand the general perspectives that group members hold toward group work and to identify strategies for improving group performance.

TABLE 1.1   INDIVIDUALISM AND COLLECTIVISM IN SMALL GROUPS

INDIVIDUALISTIC ASSUMPTIONS	COLLECTIVISTIC ASSUMPTIONS
The most effective decisons are made by individuals.	The most effective decisions are made by teams.
Planning should be centralized by the leaders.	Planning is best done by all concerned.
Individuals should be rewarded.	Groups or teams should be rewarded.
Individuals work primarily for themselves.	Individuals work primarily for the team.
Healthy competition between colleagues is more important than teamwork.	Teamwork is more important than competition.
Meetings are mainly for sharing information with individuals.	Meetings are mainly for making group or team decisions.
To get something accomplished, you should work with individuals.	To get something accomplished, you should work with the whole group or team.
A key objective in group meetings is to advance your own ideas.	A key objective in group meetings is to to reach consensus or agreement.
Team meetings should be controlled by the leader or chair.	Team meetings are for each team member to bring up what they want.
Group or team meetings are often a waste of time.	Group or team meetings are the best way to achieve a quality goal.

Adapted from: John Mole, *Mind Your Manners: Managing Business Cultures in Europe.* London: Nicholas Brealey Publishing Limited, 1995.

BECOMING A COMPETENT SMALL GROUP COMMUNICATOR

In the chapters ahead, we offer principles and skills designed to enhance your competence as a member of a small group. A **competent group communicator** is one who is able to interact appropriately and effectively with others in small groups. One model suggests that there are four levels of attaining competence at any skill or set of skills. This model can be applied to becoming a competent group communicator.

First, many communicators in small groups exhibit *unconscious incompetence;* they are unaware that they are ineffective or that they behave in inappropriate ways. The group member who talks too much or tries to bully oth-

To work together effectively individuals will need to develop common goals and a collective focus rather than only pursue individual goals.

ers to get his or her way may not be aware of behaving inappropriately. Or someone who offers little encouragement and seeks only to criticize others may think that he or she is being helpful; in reality such insensitive behavior is destructive. These interpersonally inept individuals may be oblivious to the needs of others.

The second level of competence is called *conscious incompetence*. Consciously incompetent individuals are aware that they lack the abilities to function effectively, but they simply do not know how to behave appropriately. After reading a chapter or two of this book, you may become aware of some skills you need to polish in order to improve your effectiveness. Students who take a driver's education course at first may be overwhelmed with the amount of information and number of skills they need to master in order to drive a car safely. They become aware of how much they do not know. Eventually, however, they master what at first seemed intimidating. In learning about groups, our goal is not to overwhelm you with what you do not know but to identify skills and principles that can enhance your competence.

The third level of competence, *conscious competence,* occurs when the communicator understands the effective or appropriate behavior but is not yet completely comfortable with adopting it. The individual has to work mindfully and with some effort, at being competent. When you took your first solo drive around the block, you probably were thinking about the numerous behaviors, skills, and information you needed to navigate in traffic. Similarly, when you try to use a structured problem-solving agenda during a group meeting, it may seem uncomfortable at first. Even though you are communicating effectively, it may seem unusually awkward.

You know you are truly competent at a skill when you reach the level of *unconscious competence.* When you no longer need to consciously tick off each step of the skill-performance process, you know you have become more comfortable; the skill is now part of your "natural" behavior. For example, when driving along an interstate highway, you sometimes may not be aware of exactly where you are; you may have been lost in your thoughts even while you were successfully keeping the car in the correct lane and traveling at the speed limit. Momentarily you were unconsciously competent in employing your driving skills. Another example is tying your shoes; it is a skill that takes no great concentration or conscious effort but one that you perform as needed. We are not suggesting that the ultimate goal is mindlessly to apply principles of group communication skills. We are suggesting, however, that as you develop practice in using these skills, you will become more comfortable and develop a greater ease in adapting skills and practices to your own style and personality.

Scholars who have studied how to enhance communication competence suggest that three elements are necessary to become truly competent. A competent communicator needs to be *motivated* to behave competently, *knowledgeable* about communication principles, and *skilled* to put the knowledge into action.[18] Phrased as a mathematical formula it would look like this:

$$\text{Competence} = \text{Motivation} + \text{Knowledge} + \text{Skill}.$$

Next we will examine each of these elements and consider how they fit together to enhance group-member performance.

MOTIVATION

Motivation is an internal drive to achieve a goal. If you are motivated to become a competent small group communicator, you probably have an understanding of the benefits or advantages of working with others in groups. Members of a football, basketball, or other sports team are usually motivated to win the game. A group of investors in the stock market are undoubtedly motivated to make money from their investments. Perhaps you

REVIEW BOX

Levels of Small Group Competence

LEVELS OF COMPETENCE	DESCRIPTION	EXPLANATION
Unconscious incompetence	We don't know that we don't know.	We are not aware that we are unskilled in communicating in small groups.
Conscious incompetence	We know that we don't know.	We become aware of our incompetence as group communicators.
Conscious competence	We know how to perform a skill yet must think and work consciously to perform it.	We understand how to communicate in small groups; we can effectively perform when we consciously try to put what we know into action.
Unconscious competence	Our performance of a skill becomes second nature to us.	We have developed a natural and comfortable style of working with others in small groups.

have been part of a group where you were motivated to do a good job but others were not so inspired. An unevenly motivated group or team will find it more challenging to achieve the goal of the group than a uniformly well-motivated group. One objective we have in writing this book is to help you see the benefits and advantages of team or group collaboration. Seeing those advantages and developing a realistic attitude toward being successful in groups and teams are important elements in the competence equation.

KNOWLEDGE

Just *wanting* to interact effectively and appropriately does not make you competent; you need to know principles and concepts that can lead to competent group performance. Early chapters in the book describe several principles and theories that will help you better understand, predict, and manage group processes. Why are you a member of certain groups? How does your role in groups develop? How do issues of power and status affect whom you talk to and who talks to you? How can you develop an effective group climate? We will discuss these and other questions.

Later chapters in the book focus on principles that can help you work with others to summarize and present information, solve problems, and

To be effective, groups such as this management team should be motivated to work together, be knowledgeable about group principles, and be skilled group communicators.

make decisions. These chapters are designed to help you get work done effectively and efficiently. How do groups make decisions? What do groups need to know to help their deliberations seem more focused and less chaotic? How can groups best manage the disagreements that inevitably will occur? How can leaders lead effectively? What principles and theories can help groups and teams in organizations to be more effective? Answers to these questions will help you gain the knowledge you need to become a competent group communicator.

SKILL

But even if you are motivated to be an effective group member and can ace a test on the principles, concepts, and theories of small group communication, you also need to be able to translate your wealth of information and desire to be effective into meaningful action. You need to have mastered group communication skills. At the end of each chapter, we offer specific suggestions for putting principles into practice. Chapter-end activities will give you a chance to try out skills and apply principles in group settings. You also will probably have an opportunity to apply your skills in several group activities. It is a myth that skills are all you need to become an effective group

---

REVIEW BOX

Elements of Small Group Competence

ELEMENTS	DESCRIPTION	EXAMPLES
Motivation	An internal drive to achieve a goal	Wanting to get an "A" on a group project Wanting to win an award Wanting the satisfaction of doing a job well
Knowledge	Information, principles, concepts, and theories that help to explain and predict behavior	Understanding group roles Understanding theories of group problem solving
Skills	Behaviors that lead to the accomplishment of a desired goal	Listening skills Leadership skills Problem-analysis skills

---

member. An individual may possess skills but still lack the knowledge of how, when, and why to apply the skills. Similarly, a highly motivated group member can be disruptive to the group if motivation is not coupled with an understanding of how groups work and the skills necessary to communicate with sensitivity.

A competent communicator has the knowledge and skill and is also motivated to work well with others. Robert Fulghum suggested that he learned everything he needed to know about getting along with others and accomplishing tasks effectively while he was in kindergarten. This book is designed to add to what you learned both in kindergarten and later in your life in order to help you become a competent group member.

PUTTING PRINCIPLE INTO PRACTICE

Groups are an integral part of society. This chapter has explained the importance of studying small group communication. To help summarize how you can apply some of the principles of groups, consider these suggestions:

- Work in small groups to benefit from the knowledge and information that others have but that you lack.
- Work in small groups to take advantage of other members' creative approaches to problem solving and decision making.

- When you want to improve your understanding and comprehension of a subject or issue, form a discussion group and talk about the topic with others.
- If it is important to be satisfied with decisions that affect you, work in small groups so that you can participate in making decisions. You will be more likely to support a decision if you have had an opportunity to contribute to the discussion.
- You can usually learn something about yourself when you work with others in small groups.
- Try not to let others pressure you to conform to the group's majority opinion just for the sake of agreement.
- Do not let one or two members of a small group dominate the discussion. If they do, you lose many of the advantages of working in groups.
- Avoid the trap of relying too much on other group members. Assume your fair share of the responsibility for getting things done.
- You will probably be less frustrated if you realize that groups take more time to work together to accomplish a task than you do when you work alone.
- If you are conscious of the specific behaviors needed to participate in a small group discussion you can employ them more efficiently.
- As a competent small group member you must be motivated, knowledgable, and skilled.

PRACTICE

GET-ACQUAINTED ACTIVITIES

The following activities are designed to help you get to know your classmates better. These discussion starters can be used in most small group situations.

Activity 1: If you were in a gift shop, what kind of gift would you buy for the various members of your group to make them feel good about themselves as well as about you? Share with the group. React to the gifts others give you. Try to be honest. Would the gifts really make you feel good about yourself? About them?

Activity 2: Describe the kind of house or apartment you think each member now lives in or may live in later. If group members are not married, what kind of mates would the members choose? How would they rear their children? What kind of work would they do? What hobbies would they have? How would they entertain themselves? Share with the group. React to others' perceptions of you.

Activity 3: Each member can give a short talk about himself or herself.

Activity 4: Describe to the group what your name means to you.

Activity 5: If members of the group could change their names and be someone else, who do you think they would choose to be? You may select well-known figures from the past or the present or characters from plays or novels. Share with the group. React to others' insights of you. Would you really like to be such a person?

Activity 6: Take turns describing what you do least well. Then take turns describing what you do best.

Activity 7: Try to picture each member of the group at age eight or nine. What kind of person was he or she? Aggressive? Shy? A leader? A follower? It may help to close your eyes and develop a mental image of the person. Share with the group.

Activity 8: Each member of the group should draw or symbolize his or her family tree. Explain how you see yourself in comparison to your mother, father, brother, sister, son, daughter, etc.

Activity 9: Each member of the group should draw or symbolize his or her lifeline. Use symbols and pictures to illustrate your life; depict where you have been and where you think you are going.

AGREE-DISAGREE STATEMENTS

Read each statement once. Mark whether you agree (A) or disagree (D) with each statement. Take five or six minutes to do this.[19]

_____   1. A primary concern of all group members should be to establish an atmosphere in which all feel free to express their opinions.

_____   2. In a group with a strong leader, an individual is able to achieve greater personal security than in a leaderless group.

_____   3. Often individuals who are part of working groups should do what they think is right regardless of what the groups decide to do.

_____   4. It is sometimes necessary to use autocratic methods to obtain democratic objectives.

_____   5. Sometimes it is necessary to push people in the direction you think is right, even if they object.

_____   6. It is sometimes necessary to ignore the feelings of others in order to reach a group decision.

_____   7. When leaders are doing their best, one should not openly criticize or find fault with their conduct.

_____   8. Democracy has no place in a military organization, an air task force, or an infantry squad when actually in battle.

_____   9. Much time is wasted talking when everybody in the group has to be considered before making a decision.

_____   10. Almost any job that can be done by a committee can be done better by having one individual responsible for the job.

_____   11. By the time most people reach maturity, it is almost impossible for them to increase their skills in group participation.

After you have marked the above statements, form small groups and try to agree or disagree unanimously with each statement. Try especially to find reasons for differences of opinion. If your group cannot reach agreement or disagreement, you may change the wording in any statement to promote unanimity.

ICE BREAKER ACTIVITY: TRUE OR FALSE

Tell three things about yourself, but one of them should not be true. Group members should try to guess which one of the things you have disclosed about yourself is not accurate. After all group members have made their guesses, tell them which piece of information you shared was false. Group members can then discuss how they form impressions of one another.

GROUP COMMUNICATION JOURNAL

Keep a journal in which you describe, analyze, and evaluate your interactions with others in small groups during the semester. After each group activity, assignment, or case study, record your analysis of the group interaction. Consider organizing your journal entries this way:

1. *Describe what happened.* Make brief notes identifying what occurred during your group meeting.
2. *Analyze what happened.* Cite principles and research from your text to help you interpret why your group behaved as it did.
3. *Evaluate what happened.* What did the group do well? What could your group have done to improve its performance? What could you have done to improve the group?

Keep your entries in a notebook. Your instructor may collect your journal from time to time to assess your ability to describe, analyze, and evaluate your group experiences.

NOTES

1. Gerald M. Goldhaber, *Organizational Communication*, 6th ed. (Dubuque, Iowa: Wm. C. Brown, 1993), 5.
2. Frank E.X. Dance and Carl Larson. *Speech Communication: Concepts and Behavior* (New York: Holt, Rinehart & Winston, 1972).
3. Our discussion of the evolution of communication is based on a discussion found in: Steven A. Beebe, Susan J. Beebe, and Mark V. Redmon, *Interpersonal Communication: Relating to Others* (Boston: Allyn & Bacon, 1996).
4. H. Lasswell, "The Structure and Function of Communication in Society," in *The Communication of Ideas*, ed. L. Bryson (New York: Institute for Religious and Social Studies, 1948), 37.

5. John T. Masterson, Steven A. Beebe and Norman H. Watson. *Invitation to Effective Speech Communication* (Glenview, IL: Scott, Foresman and Company, 1989).

6. See: Starr Roxanne Hiltz, Murray Turoff, and Kenneth Johnson, "Experiments in Group Decision Making, 3: Disinhibition, Deindividuation, and Group Process in Pen Name and Real Name Computer Conference," *Decision Support Systems* 5 (June 1989):217–32.

7. P.L. McLeod and J.K. Liker, "Electronic Meeting Systems: Evidence from a Low Structure Environment," *Information Systems Research* 3 (1992): 195–223.

8. Roger K. Mosvick and Robert B. Nelson, *We've Got to Start Meeting Like This!* (Glenview, Ill.: Scott, Foresman, 1987).

9. The discussion of the advantages and disadvantages of working in small groups is based, in part, on Norman R.F. Maier, "Assets and Liabilities in Group Problem Solving: The Need for an Integrative Function," *Psychological Review* 74 (1967): 239–49. Also see Michael Argyle, *Cooperation: The Basis of Sociability* (London: Routledge, 1991).

10. Robert A. Cooke and John A. Kernaghan, "Estimating the Difference between Group versus Individual Performance on Problem-Solving Tasks," *Group & Organizational Studies* 12, no. 3 (September 1987): 319–42.

11. Ibid.

12. Irving L. Janis, "Groupthink," *Psychology Today* 5 (November 1971): 43–46, 74–76.

13. Donaleson R. Forsyth, *An Introduction to Group Dynamics* (Monterey, Calif.: Brooks/Cole, 1983), 424.

14. Geert Hofstede, *Culture's Consequences: International Differences in Work-Related Values* (Beverly Hills, Calif.: Sage, 1980), 221.

15. Ibid.

16. In addition to the work of Hofstede, also see: John A. Wagner III and Michale K. Moch, "Individualism-Collectivism: Concept and Measure," *Group & Organizational Studies* 11 (September 1986): 280–304; Harry C. Triandis, Christopher McCusker, and C. Harry Hui, "Multimethod Probes of Individualism and Collectivism," *Journal of Personality and Social Psychology* 59 (1990): 1006–20; C. Harry Hui, "Measurement of Individualism-Collectivism," *Journal of Research in Personality* 22 (1988): 17–36; Charles R. Bantz, "Cultural Diversity and Group Cross-Cultural Team Research, *Journal of Applied Communication Research* (February 1993): 1–20; Mitchell R. Hammer and Judith N. Martin, "The Effects of Cross-Cultural Training on American Managers in a Japanese-American Joint Venture," *Journal of Applied Communication Research* (May 1992): 161–82.

17. C. Larson and F. LaFasto, *Teamwork: What Must Go Right/What Can Go Wrong* (Beverly Hills, Calif.: Sage, 1989).

18. B. H. Spitzberg, "Communication Competence as Knowledge, Skill, and Impression." *Communication Education* 32 (1983): 323–29.

19. Developed by Alvin Goldberg, University of Denver.

CHAPTER
T·W·O

Small Group Communication Theory

After studying this chapter, you will be able to:

- Discuss the nature and functions of theory and theory construction.

- Explain the relevance of theory to the study of small group communication.

- Discuss five general theories that apply to small group communication.

- Explain the model of small group communication presented in this chapter.

- Identify some of the components of small group communication.

"Well, it sounds good in theory, but in reality. . . ."

"Theoretically speaking. . . ."

"Yes, but that's only a theory."

*T*heory. It is a word people encounter almost daily in their casual conversations, in classrooms, and on news broadcasts. They discuss and evaluate theories of evolution, the theory of relativity, quantum theory, social exchange theory, continental drift theory. Fictitious criminal investigators on television develop theories about what took place at a crime scene. Psychologists and parents create theories of personality development and theories of childrearing (in fact, there are practically as many theories of childrearing as there are parents). In short, theories abound—some are simple, some complex; some are formal, some informal; some are scientific, some unscientific. Yet few people take the time to think about what theory is. What are theories? Where do they come from? How are they built? What do people do with them after they've got them?

Many people are intimidated by the word *theory*. To them, studying theory is an esoteric activity that has no relevance except for the scientist or the academician. Today's students are interested in relevant, practical kinds of knowledge, and sometimes they seem to assume that theory is neither relevant nor practical. Dance and Larson disagree, claiming that "theorizing is a very basic form of human activity."[1] Theory is *very* practical. Theorizing helps to explain or predict the events in people's lives. On a rudimentary level people theorize when they reflect on their past experiences and make decisions based on these experiences. Theory, then, has two basic functions: to explain and to predict. These functions are discussed more fully later in the chapter.

This chapter examines some of the central issues of group communication theory. First, we will discuss the nature of theory and the theory-building process. Second, we will turn our attention to the relevance and practicality of theory in the study of small group communication. Third, we will discuss five theoretical perspectives for the study of small groups. Finally, we will present a theoretical model of small group communication.

THE NATURE OF THEORY AND THE THEORY-BUILDING PROCESS

Theories are very practical. Suppose, for example, that you do your weekly grocery shopping every Thursday after your late afternoon class. When you arrive at the store you are pleased to see that several checkout lanes are open with no waiting at any of them. "Ah," you say, "I'll be out of here in short order." With your cart before you, you proceed up one aisle and down the next. To your dismay, you notice that each time you pass the checkout lanes, the lines have grown. By the time you have filled your cart, at least six people are waiting in each lane. You now have a 20-minute wait at the checkout.

If the situation described above were to occur once, you would probably curse your luck or chalk it up to fate. If you find, however, that the same events occur each time you visit the market, you begin to see a consistency in your observations that goes beyond luck or fate. In noticing this consistency, you take the first step in building a theory. You have observed a *phenomenon*. You have witnessed a *repeated pattern* of events for which you feel there must be some *explanation*. So you ponder the situation. In your mind you organize all of the facts available to you: the time of your arrival, the condition of the checkout lanes when you entered the store each time, and the length of the lines when you completed your shopping. Lo and behold, you discover that you have been arriving at the store at approximately 4:45 each afternoon and reaching the checkout lanes about 25 minutes later. You conclude that between the time you arrive and the time you depart, thousands of workers head for home, some of them stopping off at the store on the way. *Voilà*—you have a theory. You have organized your information to explain the phenomenon.

Assuming that your theory is accurate, it is now very useful for you. Having *explained* the phenomenon, you may now reasonably *predict* that under the same set of circumstances, events within the phenomenon will recur. In other words, if you continue to do your weekly shopping after your late class on Thursday, you will repeatedly be faced with long checkout lines. Given this knowledge, you can adapt your behavior accordingly, perhaps by doing your shopping earlier or later in the day.

On a more personal level, your theory about yourself—your **self-concept**—influences the choices you make throughout the day. You tend to do things that you see as being consistent (predictable) with your self-concept. In essence, this self-concept or "self-theory" serves to explain you to yourself, thereby allowing you to predict your behavior and to successfully select realistic goals. This is theory at its most personal and pervasive.

Theory building is a common, natural process of human communication. You notice consistencies in your experience and examine relationships among the consistencies. You then build an explanation of the phenomenon that allows you to predict future events and, in some cases, to exercise some control over situations. Some theories, of course, are very elaborate and formal, but even in these the fundamental features of explanation and prediction can be seen. In George Kelly's definition of theory we find reference to these features:

> A theory may be considered as a way of binding together a multitude of facts so that one may comprehend them all at once. When

the theory enables us to make reasonably precise predictions, one may call it scientific.[2]

Theory is crucial to the study of small group communication. The explanatory power of good theory helps make sense of the processes involved when people interact with others in a group. The predictive precision of theory allows people to anticipate probable outcomes of various types of communicative behavior in the group. Armed with this type of knowledge, people can adjust their own communicative behavior to help make group work more effective and rewarding.

THEORY: A PRACTICAL APPROACH TO GROUP COMMUNICATION

Theory, both formal and informal, helps people make intelligent decisions about how to conduct themselves. Working in small groups is no exception. Everyone brings a set of theories to small group meetings—theories about oneself, about other group members, and about groups in general. Once in the group, people regulate their behavior according to these theories. They behave in ways consistent with their self-concepts. They deal with others in the group according to their previous impressions (theories) of them. If they believe (theorize) that groups are essentially ineffectual, that "a camel is a horse designed by a committee" or that "if you really want something done, do it yourself," then they probably will act accordingly and their prophecy will be fulfilled. If, on the other hand, they come to the group convinced that groups are capable of working effectively, and if they know how to make the group work, they will behave very differently and contribute much more to the group's effectiveness.

EXPLANATORY FUNCTION

To be practical, theories of small group communication must suggest ways in which participants can make group discussion more efficient and rewarding. The **explanatory function** of theory is important in this regard. If people understand why some groups are effective while others are not, or why certain styles of **leadership** are appropriate in some situations but not in others, then they are better prepared to diagnose the needs of their own groups. Studying theories of group interaction can help people understand that process and the ways in which different facets of it are related.

PREDICTIVE FUNCTION

While people derive satisfaction from understanding a process, the **predictive function** of theory is even more useful for them. Consider the hypothetical situation that follows:

A CASE STUDY

The dean of student affairs at your college has become sensitive about reports from students that the activities scheduled for orientation week each year are silly. Specifically, students have been reacting to two of the dean's favorite activities at the first orientation mixer—a pass-the-orange-under-your-chin race and a find-your-own-shoes-in-the-middle-of-the-room relay race. Students claim to feel undignified during these activities. They feel they are being treated more as children than as adults. Bewildered, the dean remembers how much the Class of '75 enjoyed these activities and is at a loss about what to do. Therefore, the dean has appointed a group of students to investigate the matter. You are one of those students.

The committee is composed mostly of juniors and seniors. The dean thinks they have been around long enough to know the ropes. As president-elect of next year's sophomore class, you are the youngest of the six committee members. The chairperson is a graduating senior.

You arrive at the first meeting ready to work. The committee is to plan activities that are "more closely aligned with the needs of today's college men and women." You are excited about being a part of a decision-making process that will have a real effect. To your dismay, the other members of the group seem to disregard their task and spend the meeting discussing the prospects for the basketball team, hardly mentioning orientation week activities for next fall. You leave the meeting confused but hopeful that the next meeting will be more fruitful. You resolve to take a more active role and to try to steer the meeting more toward the committee's task.

At the second meeting, you suggest that the committee really should discuss orientation week. Members concur, then make jokes about past orientation week activities. When the chairperson makes no effort to keep the group on the track, you feel overwhelmed and bewildered.

Many theories, if you were familiar with them, might help you understand what is going on in this group—leadership theories, theories of group growth and development, problem-solving theories, various theories of interpersonal interaction, and so on. Basing your observations on theory, you might say, for example, that your inferior status as the youngest committee member reduces your ability to influence the group process. You might also say that the chairperson's leadership style is inappropriate to the task and situation. You might say that every group goes through an orientation period and that the time spent on trivia is a necessary part of the group process.

All of these theories might be correct to a degree. At least you have a way of describing your group experience systematically. However, you have not met the test of practicality. While understanding that a process is satisfying, the more important question is what do you *do* with your understanding? Once you know something about group communication, how do you use what you know to help the group function more effectively?

In medicine a diagnosis is useless unless it suggests some course of treatment. Nevertheless, diagnosis—explanation—is a necessary first step. *Understanding* the process leads toward ways of *improving* the process, and herein lies the usefulness of the predictive quality of theory. By understanding a specific group and group communication in general, and by being aware of the alternative behaviors that are possible, you can use theory to select behaviors that will help you achieve the goal of your group. In other words, if you can reasonably predict that certain outcomes will follow certain types of communication, you can regulate your behavior to achieve the most desirable results. If, in the example of the dean's advisory committee, participants know that a necessary interpersonal orientation period is coming to a close and that some task-oriented statements will help the group achieve its goal, they can choose to make such statements. In this way, theory *informs* communicative behavior in small groups. Group members no longer behave randomly; they behave with understanding and purpose.

Some theories presented in this book explain small group phenomena. These descriptive theories are referred to as **process theories.** Other theories, called **method theories,** take a prescriptive approach to small group communication. These how-to theories are particularly useful in establishing formats for solving problems and resolving conflicts in a group. Both types of theories add to the knowledge and skills that can make you a more effective communicator. Central to your effectiveness as a communicator, is the ability to use words, which is the subject of the next section.

THE PURPOSE OF COMMUNICATION IN SMALL GROUPS: REDUCING UNCERTAINTY

A group cannot function without words; **communication** is the vehicle that allows a group to move toward its goals. Words call into being the realities, or potential realities, that they represent. Thus, a verbal description of an idea for a new product at a manufacturing company's board meeting creates a vision of that product for board members. Presented effectively, the description may result in new or changed attitudes and behaviors; the idea may be adopted. Words, then, have the power to create new realities and change attitudes; they are immensely powerful tools. While this may seem obvious, it is a truth that often goes unnoticed. People spend so much of each day speaking, listening, reading, and writing that language seems commonplace to them. It is not. Through language people unravel the immense complexity that is their world. With language, we build the theories that reduce our uncertainty.

UNCERTAINTY

Dean Barnlund and others have proposed that the aim of speech communication is to reduce uncertainty.[3] According to this principle, speech communication organizes and makes sense out of all the sights, sounds, odors, tastes, and sensations in the environment. As Barnlund states, "Communication occurs any time meaning is assigned to an internal or external stimulus."[4] Thus, when people arrive at a meeting room and begin to shiver, the sensation brings to their minds the word *cold*. Within themselves, or on an *intrapersonal level*, they have reduced uncertainty about the nature of an experience. The room is too cold. Giving verbal expression to an experience organizes and clarifies that experience.

At the *interpersonal level* of speech communication, the reduction-of-uncertainty principle is even more clearly evident. As you get to know someone, you progressively discover what it is that makes that person unique. You reduce uncertainty about him or her. By developing an explanation of that person's behavior, you can predict how he or she is likely to respond to future communication and events. You base your predictions on what you know about the person's beliefs, attitudes, values, and personality. In essence, you build a theory that allows you to explain another person's behavior, to predict that person's future responses, and to control your own communicative behavior accordingly. In other words, theories help reduce people's uncertainty about others.

COMPLEXITY

Getting to know someone is a process of progressively reducing uncertainty—and a lot of uncertainty exists, especially at the outset of a relationship. Think back to your first day at college or to your first day in group communication class. You were probably surrounded by many unfamiliar faces. At times such as these, you feel tentative and think "What am I doing here?" and "Who are all of these other people?" Your feelings of uncertainty soar. You encounter a person you find attractive in the cafeteria line. You say, "Hi! Are you new? What do you think of school so far?" This takes a bit of courage because you do not know what kind of response you will get. So you are hesitant. You make small talk and look for signs in the other person's behavior that might indicate whether that person desires further communication. You communicate, observe the response, and base further communication on your interpretation of that response. This is a complex process, particularly because both individuals communicate, observe, respond, and interpret simultaneously!

The complexity of the process creates uncertainty. Many communication theorists have noted that whenever an individual communicates with another person at least six people are involved: (1) who you think you are, (2) who you think the other person is, (3) who you think the other person thinks

TABLE 2.1   INCREASE IN POTENTIAL RELATIONSHIPS WITH AN INCREASE IN GROUP SIZE

SIZE OF GROUP	NUMBER OF RELATIONSHIPS
2	1
3	6
4	25
5	90
6	301
7	966

Reprinted from "A Quantitative Analysis of Intragroup Relationships" by William M. Kephart, *American Journal of Sociology* 60 (1950), by permission of The University of Chicago Press.

you are, (4) who the other person thinks he or she is, (5) who the other person thinks you are, and (6) who the other person thinks you think he or she is. All six of these people influence and are influenced by the communication—a very complex matter indeed, and one that contributes to people's uncertainty about interpersonal relationships. Nevertheless, people persist in communicating and find that, on the interpersonal level, communication reduces their uncertainty about others.

SMALL GROUPS: MORE COMPLEXITY AND MORE UNCERTAINTY

If six people are involved when two people interact, how many are involved when eight people interact? Mathematically inclined readers probably already know that the numbers grow exponentially rather than arithmetically with the addition of each new member to a group. (See Table 2.1) When eight people interact, literally thousands of factors influence communication and are influenced by it—factors such as "who I think Ted thinks Rosa thinks Amit is" or "who I think Lourdes thinks Tom thinks I am."

Fortunately, people don't consciously think about all of these factors all of the time. They would be horribly debilitated if they did so. Nevertheless, these dynamics subtly influence people whenever they interact. The number of factors influencing people interacting in groups is staggering.

THEORETICAL PERSPECTIVES FOR THE STUDY OF SMALL GROUP COMMUNICATION

Thus far this chapter has discussed the nature of theory and its relationship to effective small group communication. It has pointed out that uncertainty and complexity are pervasive characteristics of small groups, while speech communication is the driving force that moves groups toward their goals.

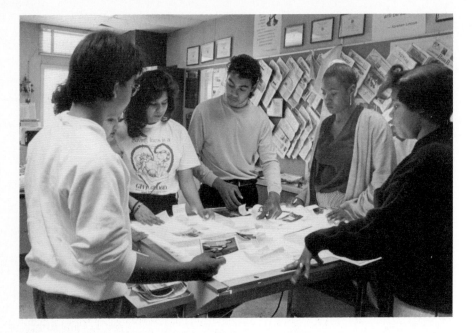

Theories reduce uncertainty and guide our behavior in groups.

Small group communication theory attempts to explain and predict small group phenomena. Given the complexity of the process and the number of variables that affect small group communication, no single theory can account for all of the variables involved, nor can one theory systematically relate the variables to one another. Therefore, a number of approaches to group communication theory have emerged in recent years. Each seeks to explain and predict group behavior while focusing on different facets of the group process. Five of these theoretical perspectives are described briefly here: social exchange theory, rules theory, systems theory, symbolic convergence theory, and structuration theory.

SOCIAL EXCHANGE THEORY

Social exchange theory is a simple but powerful attempt to explain human behavior in terms that sound like a blend of behavioral psychology and economic theory. According to this theory, relationships can be described in terms of their rewards and costs, profits and losses. Rewards are pleasurable outcomes associated with particular behaviors; costs include such things as mental effort, anxiety, or even embarrassment.[5] Profit equals rewards minus costs; as long as rewards exceed costs, a relationship remains attractive.

Rewards and costs can take many forms in a group. As we will see more clearly in Chapter 3, fellowship, job satisfaction, achievement, status, and

Small group communication is governed by shared rules.

meeting personal needs and goals are all rewards that groups provide. On the other hand, group work takes time and effort and may be frustrating—all forms of cost. Social exchange theory predicts that as long as rewards exceed costs—that is, as long as group membership is profitable—group membership will continue to be attractive.

Small group variables such as **cohesiveness** and productivity are directly related to how rewarding the group experience is to its members. The basics of social exchange theory are useful in their descriptiveness. Keep them in mind as you read the remaining chapters and as you observe working groups.

RULES THEORY

Rules theory assumes that for successful communication to take place, interactants must share rules that structure communicative behavior. The rules of grammar that order words in a logical sequence are one example. However, people of a particular culture also share rules about how to greet others, how to take turns speaking, and how to be insulting or sarcastic.

Susan Shimanoff defines a rule as "a followable prescription that indicates what behavior is obligated, preferred, or prohibited in certain contexts."[6] By definition, a rule must be *followable*. This implies that people have a choice about whether or not to follow a rule. If they had no choice, they would be conforming to a law of nature, not a rule. A rule is also *prescriptive;* that is, failure to conform may result in some form of penalty, such as criticism or social ridicule. Furthermore, a rule dictates behavior. It tells people what to do or what not to do, but it does not dictate how people should think, feel, or interpret.[7] Finally, a rule is *contextual.* While some rules are relatively stable (such as the rule that says one should apologize for stepping on someone's toe), others vary from one situation to another. Rules also vary across cultures—a factor to consider in any multicultural group.

In groups, rules indicate which behaviors are appropriate or inappropriate. They apply to behaviors that the group wishes to encourage or discourage. Shimanoff suggests that most "rules can be classified in one of seven categories: (1) who says, (2) what, (3) to whom, (4) when, (5) with what duration and frequency, (6) through what medium, and (7) by what decision-procedure." In the literature of group theory and research, rules are usually referred to as *norms*.[8]

In groups, norms are powerful determinants of behavior, but it is behavior that determines norms! For example, a committee chairperson's "call to order," appointment of a recording secretary, and request for a motion and a second to get a topic "on the floor," is likely to establish parliamentary procedure as the norm of that committee, whether appropriate or not. Once established, group norms direct the group's activities. Understanding rules theory and its application to small groups can help you to encourage norms that are productive and to avoid those that are dysfunctional.

SYSTEMS THEORY

Perhaps the most prevalent approach to small group communication is that of systems theory. In many respects, systems theory represents the most promising perspective on small group communication because it is flexible enough to encompass the vast array of variables that influence small group interaction.

One way to approach the concept of **system** is to think of your own body. The various organs of your body make up systems (digestive, nervous, circulatory) that, in turn, make up the larger system: you, yourself. Each organ depends on the proper functioning of other organs: a change in one part of the system causes changes in the rest of the system. Furthermore, the physiological system cannot be isolated from the environment that surrounds it; to maintain the proper functioning of your physiological systems, you must adjust to changes outside of the body. A decrease in oxygen at a higher elevation will cause you to breathe more rapidly, a rise in temperature will make you perspire, and so forth. In other words, your body is an *open* system composed of interdependent elements. It receives *input* from the environment (food, air, water), *processes* that input (digestion and oxygenation), and yields an *output* (elimination of waste materials, such as carbon dioxide). Like the human body, a small group is an open system—composed of interdependent variables—that receives input, processes the input, and yields an output.

Openness to Environment   A group does not operate in isolation; it is continually affected by interactions with its environment. New members may join, and former members may leave; demands from other organizations may alter the group's goals. Even the climate may affect the group's ability to work.

Interdependence   The various components of the group process are interrelated in such a way that a change in one component will alter the relationships among all other components. A shift in cohesiveness can change the group's productivity level. The loss of a group member or the addition of a new member effects a change felt throughout the system. **Interdependence** in the small group makes the study of small group communication so fascinating and so difficult: None of the variables involved may be understood properly in isolation.

Input Variables   By viewing them as parts of subsystems, the variables of small group communication can be categorized according to the systems theory concept of input, process, and output. Input variables in the small group system include such things as group members and group resources, among them funds, tools, knowledge, purposes, relationships to other groups or organizations, and the physical environment.[9]

Process Variables   These variables relate to the procedures that the group follows to reach its goals. Many of these variables are represented in the model in the next section.

Output Variables   Output variables, the outcomes of the group process, range from solutions and decisions to personal growth and satisfaction.

Although systems theory does not explain small group phenomena, it serves as a useful organizational strategy. It also reminds us that a full understanding of group communication involves the broader contexts or environments in which groups operate. All of the theories identified in this section are incomplete pictures of human behavior. Each does, however, provide insight into the maze of forces that affect small group communication.

The next theory focuses on the relationship between communication and the type of task before a group.

SYMBOLIC CONVERGENCE THEORY

If you consider your closest interpersonal relationships, you can probably remember a point at which the relationship took on a life of its own. You might describe it as when two acquaintances became friends: the relation-

Small groups can be viewed as open systems comprising interdependent variables that include input, process, and output such as this quilt.

ship took on an identity based on your experiences together and your shared stories and visions of those experiences. Perhaps you develop "inside" or private jokes that have meaning only for the two of you.

Communication scholar Ernest Bormann has noted that groups take on this kind of shared personality as well. The **symbolic convergence theory** of communication explains how certain types of communication function to shape a group's identity and culture, which in turn influence other dynamics such as norms, roles, and decision-making. Over time groups develop a collective consciousness with shared emotions, motives, and meanings.[10]

This group consciousness, Bormann says, evolves through group members, sharing group fantasies or stories. Within this theory, **fantasy** does not mean something not grounded in reality. Rather, it has a technical meaning: the creative and imaginative shared interpretation of events that fulfills a group psychological or rhetorical need.[11] A psychological or rhetorical need can include such things as a need to take a break from work, to release tension, or to metaphorically deal with an issue facing the group. A fantasy is usually introduced as a story that captures the imagination of the group and momentarily takes the group away from the specific issue under discussion.

In groups, as in almost all forms of human endeavor, we can discern two levels of reality: what actually happens and our interpretations and beliefs about what happens. What remains in our memories and what guides our subsequent behavior is the latter.

If, for example, you are in a group discussing how to reduce cheating and other forms of academic dishonesty and a group member says "Hey, did anyone see the Tonight Show last night? They had a guy who won the national lying championship. He was so funny. He has been able to talk his way into getting photographed with the President of the United States." Another group member chimes in and says, "Yea, I saw that. I had an uncle who used to tell whoppers. He once convinced my Aunt that he had won a million dollars in the lottery." Yet another group member says, "My brother is always playing practical jokes on my mom." Before you know it, the pace of conversation has quickened and other group members are telling stories about people who love to play practical jokes. A **fantasy theme** consists of the common or related content of the stories the group tells. In addition, the fantasy of one group member leads to a **fantasy chain**—a string of connected stories that revolve around a common theme. These fantasy chains help the group develop a shared sense of identity just as the unique stories and experiences you experience with a close friend help give your relationship a unique identity. Usually a fantasy chain includes all of the elements you would find in any well-told story. There are often elements of conflict, heroes, villains, and a plot that gives shape of the story.

By being mindful of the fantasies or stories that develop in a group, you can gain insight into what the group values. What may seem like "off task" behavior, such as talking about TV programs, movies, or events seemingly unrelated to the group's agenda, can be beneficial in giving the group a sense of identity. Noting the common themes of the group's fantasy (such as who the villains are in the stories or who wins or loses in the story) can also give you insight about a group's values and culture. And fantasies may be a way for groups to deal with sensitive issues in an indirect way.

The power of symbolic convergence theory is that it points out that groups, like individuals, have unique "personalities," cultures, or an identity built on shared symbolic representations related to the group and that these cultures evolve through the adoption of fantasy themes or group stories. A group's identity converges through these shared fantasies. Just as we try to understand an individual's behavior by taking into account "what sort of person she is," we must do the same for groups. Reflecting upon the stories a group tells, which may at first seem off the topic, can give you insight into a group's personality, culture, values, and identify.

STRUCTURATION THEORY

Another contemporary theoretical approach to help us understand how people behave in small groups is offered by Anthony Giddens[12] and further advanced by communication researcher Marshall Scott Poole and his colleagues.[13] Structuration theory provides a general framework that explains how people use rules and resources to interact in a social system. According to Poole, structuration explains how groups produce and reproduce social systems through group members' use of rules and resources in interaction. At first glance, this concept may seem complicated because of abstract terms;[14] however, we have already talked about two important terms in the definition; however—rules and systems.

A system, as you recall, is composed of many interdependent elements. Rules are explicit or implied prescriptions that affect how people behave in a group (system). "Don't talk while others are talking" and "Don't leave the meeting until the boss says everyone is dismissed" are examples of rules. These rules determine how the group structures itself and performs tasks, and how group members talk to one another. Structuration theory suggests that when we join a new group we use rules we learned in other groups to structure our behavior. For example, when you walked into your first college class, you probably drew on your experiences as a high school student to know how to act. But groups also create their own rules and resources to determine what is appropriate and inappropriate. You learned that a college class is similar to but not exactly like high school. You also know that different classes have different rules or structure; some classes have informal rules, while others have more formal ones. One teacher may deduct points for lack of attendance while another teacher may not take roll at all. Structuration explains how we use rules based on past and immediate experiences to help us describe how group members interact in a system. How those communication rules are organized is based on factors both internal and external to the group. Structuration theory helps explain why and how groups develop the rules and behavior patterns that they adopt.

REVIEW BOX

Theoretical Perspectives for the Study of Small Group Communication

1. **Social exchange theory:** Groups remain attractive to their members so long as the rewards of group membership exceed the costs.
2. **Rules theory:** For successful communication to take place, group members must share followable, prescriptive rules that structure their interaction.
3. **Systems theory:** The small group is an open system of interdependent elements, employing input variables and process variables to yield output.
4. **Symbolic convergence theory:** The development of a group consciousness and identity through the sharing of fantasies or stories which are often chained together and have a common theme.
5. **Structural theory:** People use rules and resources in interaction to structure social systems.

NEW TECHNOLOGIES AND SMALL GROUP COMMUNICATION THEORY

Like movable type, telegraph, and the telephone before them, new information technologies are changing the way we live by restructuring how we communicate. Many group decisions in businesses and organizations are already computer-assisted. Electronic messaging, teleconferencing, and store-and-forward facilities smooth the flow of communication, even among participants who are often not face-to-face. The term **Group Decision Support System** (GDSS) refers to any "computer-based information system used to support intellectual collaborative work."[15] GDSSs include technological support for agenda setting, rules for discussion such as parliamentary procedure, and communication technologies that allow multiple users to interact simultaneously.

We have only begun to imagine how these new technologies will affect group decision making over time. For now, though, we can consider them in light of some of the theories discussed above. For example, the use of technology can heighten or diminish the rewards and costs associated with group communication as viewed through social exchange theory. From a rules perspective, technologies impose their own sets of prescriptions for behavior that must be followed in order for successful communication to occur. As input and process variables within a system, GDSSs reshape group interaction as well as the resulting output variables. Depending on group members' reactions to technology, GDSSs can serve as the referents for group fantasy themes and become part of the group's shared reality.

Structuration theory is perhaps best suited to understanding the impact of technologies on groups. This theory shows that communication technologies such as GDSS can be understood as structures—rules and resources.[16] Thus, theory can inform the development of such technologies insofar as they are *social* technologies.[17] Technology does not necessarily result in any particular group outcome; it is how the group works technology into its interaction that has the impact.

New technologies will increasingly reshape how groups make decisions and solve problems. The use of technology in both personal and organizational communication can provide greater structure and thus keep a group on task. We will discuss the impact of technology on groups and teams in organizational settings in Chapter 11.

A DESCRIPTIVE APPROACH TO SMALL GROUP COMMUNICATION

A model that takes into account all the possible sender, receiver, and message variables in a small group would be hopelessly complicated even before it could be designed to include other variables central to the study of

FIGURE 2.1   CONSTELLATION OF VARIABLES IN SMALL GROUP
COMMUNICATION

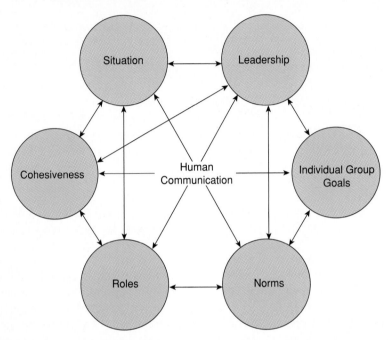

small group communication. Students must, then, settle for a less comprehensive model but one that suggests the features and relationships critical to
an understanding of small group communication.

Figure 2.1 represents such a descriptive model. This framework depicts
small group communication as a constellation of variables, each related to
every other. Communication—what you say and how you say it—establishes and maintains the relationships among these essential variables.
Chapters 3, 4 and 10 present an in-depth discussion of these variables; for
now, note the brief discussion that follows.

Communication   At its essence, communication is the process of acting on
information. Human communication comprises what people say, how they
say it, and to whom they say it. This is the primary object of study in small
group communication research.

Leadership   In Chapter 1, part of the definition of small group communication concerned mutual influence. Leadership refers to behavior that exerts
influence upon the group.

Goals   All groups have goals. A goal may be to provide therapy for members, to complete some designated task, or simply to have a good time. Indi-

vidual group members also have goals. Often individual goals complement the group goal; sometimes, though, they do not.

Norms   Norms are rules that establish which behaviors are permitted or encouraged within the group and which are forbidden or discouraged. Every group, from your family to the President's Cabinet, develops and maintains norms or rules. Some norms are formal, such as when a group must use parliamentary procedure. Others are informal, such as the fact that a group always begins meetings fifteen minutes late.

Roles   Roles are sets of expectations people hold for themselves and for others in a given context. People play different roles in different groups. Researchers have identified several roles that need to be filled in order for a small group to reach maximum satisfaction and productivity.

Cohesiveness   Cohesiveness is the degree of attraction group members feel toward one another and toward the group. Feelings of loyalty help unite the group.

Situation   The context in which group communication occurs is of paramount importance. The task is significant, but many other important situational variables exist, such as group size, the physical arrangement of group members, the location or setting, the group's purpose, even the amount of stress placed on the group by time constraints or other internal or external pressures. We will examine each of these situational variables later in the book.

Small group communication theory seeks to explain the relationships among these and other variables and to make predictions based on such explanations. Thus, the theories presented in this book help eliminate most of the complexity and uncertainty that surface at every level of group interaction.

PUTTING PRINCIPLE INTO PRACTICE

The theories discussed throughout this book explain consistencies in communicative behavior that researchers have observed within small groups. If you can attain a theoretical grasp of small group communication, you can more successfully predict and control behavior.

As you observe groups of which you are a member, keep the following in mind:

- Theories provide explanations of behaviors that allow us to predict the likely consequences of various actions. Use the theories discussed in this chapter to help predict the probable consequences of various actions.
- One descriptive model for small group interaction is composed of seven variables: communication, leadership, goals, norms, roles, cohesiveness,

and situation. Use these categories to help structure your thinking about groups.

- Social exchange theory describes how satisfaction with a group relates to the relationship between the rewards and costs of group membership. Do a simple cost/benefit analysis to help you understand group members' behaviors.
- Systems theory can help you organize your observations into input variables, process variables, and output variables. Its primary application to small group communication is as an organizational strategy. Use systems theory to help you understand how your group's system relates to individual systems within it and the broader systems of which it is a part.
- Symbolic convergence theory reminds us that groups, like individuals, have personalities which we must understand and adapt to in order to be most effective. Explore the ways in which your group's "personality" relates to other variables such as rules, roles, and decision-making.
- Structuration theory directs us to the power of rules and resources to structure interaction and outcomes. Identify existing rules and resources in order to enhance your influence in any group.

As you read the rest of the book, continue to seek ways to apply what you're learning. The practicality of our theories is measured only by how we can use them to be more effective group leaders, members, and scholars.

PRACTICE

1. Make a list of informal theories you have about an ordinary day (e.g., Professor X is boring, I'm afraid of speaking in class, etc.). On what basis did you formulate these theories? How do they affect your behavior? What might cause you to alter them?
2. Make a list of your beliefs about working in small groups. How do these beliefs affect your behavior in small groups?
3. Based on your experience in groups and the descriptive approach presented in this chapter, predict how changes in one facet of small group communication would affect the other facets.
4. What areas of uncertainty can you identify within the small group context? How does communication function to reduce uncertainty in these areas?
5. The purpose of small group communication theory is to explain and predict small group phenomena. This exercise attempts to relate the theories discussed in this chapter (i.e., social exchange theory, rules theory, systems theory, symbolic convergence theory, structuration theory) to

specific group communication situations so that you may more clearly understand how theory explains everyday communication.

A. The class will break into groups of five to seven members.
B. Each group will discuss the theories identified in this chapter until all feel that they understand the central ideas in each theory.
C. Then, consider the following situations:

An engineering research and development team for an automobile manufacturer
The committee in the case study near the beginning of the chapter
A jury
A group of students working on a class project
A family

What are the characteristics of each that make that situation unlike the others?

D. Relate the theories to the situations. Do certain theories seem better suited to explain different situations? Why or why not? What are the strengths and weaknesses of each theory?
E. Relate your findings to the group communication model shown in Figure 2.1. What aspects of the model relate most clearly to the situations and theories you have discussed?
F. What conclusions can you derive from these analyses? Report these conclusions to the class.

NOTES

1. Frank E. X. Dance and Carl E. Larson, *The Functions of Human Communication: A Theoretical Approach* (New York: Holt, Rinehart & Winston, 1976), 4.
2. George A. Kelly, *A Theory of Personality: The Psychology of Personal Constructs* (New York: Norton, 1963), 18.
3. Dean Barnlund, *Interpersonal Communication: Survey and Studies* (Boston: Houghton Mifflin, 1968).
4. Dean Barnlund, "Toward a Meaning Centered Philosophy of Communication," in Johnson et al. (eds.), *Nothing Never Happens* (Beverly Hills Calif.: Glencoe Press, 1974), 213.
5. Stephen W. Littlejohn, *Theories of Human Communication,* 5th ed. (Belmont, Calif.: Wadsworth, 1989).
6. Susan B. Shimanoff, *Communication Rules: Theory and Research* (Beverly Hills: Sage Publications, 1980), p. 57.
7. Littlejohn, *Theories of Human Communication,* 63.
8. Susan B. Shimanoff, "Group Interaction via Communication Rules," in Robert S. Cathcart and Larry A. Samovar (eds.), *Small Group Communication: A Reader,* 6th ed. (Dubuque, Iowa: Wm. C. Brown, 1992).
9. John K. Brilhart, *Effective Group Discussion,* 8th ed. (Dubuque, Iowa: Wm. C. Brown, 1995), 26.
10. Ernest Bormann, "Symbolic Convergence Theory and Communication in Group Decision Making," in R.Y. Hirokawa and M.S. Poole (eds.), *Communication and Group Decision Making* (Beverly Hills: Sage Publications, 1986).

11. Ibid., 221.

12. See Anthony Giddens, *New Rules of Sociological Method*, 2nd ed. (Palo Alto, Calif.: Stanford University Press, 1993), and Anthony Giddens, *Studies in Social and Political Theory* (New York: Basic Books, 1979).

13. Marshall Scott Poole, David R. Seibold, and Robert D. McPhee, "A Structurational Approach to Theory Building in Group Decision-Making Research," in R. Y. Hirokawa and M. S. Poole (eds.), *Communication and Group Decision Making* (Beverly Hills Calif.: Sage Publications, 1986).

14. Ibid.

15. Leonard M. Jessup and Joseph S. Valacich (eds.), *Group Support Systems* (New York: Macmillan, 1992).

16. M. Scott Poole and Michele H. Jackson, "Communication Theory and Group Support Systems" in Leonard M. Jessup and Joseph S. Valacich (eds.), *Group Support Systems* (New York: Macmillan, 1992).

17. M. Scott Poole and G. L. DeSanctis, "A Study of Influence in Computer-Mediated Group Decision Making," *MIS Quarterly* 12 (1988):625–44.

CHAPTER
T·H·R·E·E

Group Formation

After studying this chapter, you will be able to:

- Discuss two classification systems of interpersonal needs and describe how they relate to group formation.

- Explain the potential conflict between individual goals and group goals.

- Suggest ways of establishing mutuality of concern in a work group.

- Identify and explain four factors that are elements of interpersonal attraction.

- Identify and describe three factors in group attraction.

- Facilitate a group's movement through the initial stages of its formation.

- Apply your knowledge of group formation toward greater effectiveness as a communicator.

*A*re you considering or being considered for membership in any particular group right now? A fraternal organization? A sports club? A political action group? Are you thinking about getting married? Granted, a marriage starts with only two people, but it has a way of becoming a group of three or more.

To which groups do you already belong? Can you identify a circle of friends you might refer to as "your group"? Do you belong to clubs? Teams? You can probably generate a rather long list of groups that you either belonged to in the past or are involved with in the present. From the moment you are born into your first group—your family—you belong to a succession of groups. Some are formally organized, some are loosely structured; some you choose, others you are assigned to. But *membership in groups does not happen randomly.* Groups meet specific needs and perform special functions. To understand group formation, then, requires that you examine the needs and functions around which groups form.

Upon learning of the plans for this book, a friend remarked. "I don't know how you can even stand to think about it. I hate committee work. I'll do anything I can to avoid working in groups. I'd rather do things my own way." This fairly prevalent attitude toward groups ignores the pervasive influence that groups have on people's lives (discussed in Chapter 1). When asked if there wasn't at least one group in his life that provided him with some pleasure, the friend faltered, "There is my bowling team . . . and, come to think of it, I enjoyed working with a group of political strategists in the last election. My religion and human rights discussion group at the church is pretty interesting, . . . and of course there is my family." He added, "But there's a difference between *those* groups and the committees I have to serve on as part of my job." Although this person might be in the wrong job, groups people choose to belong to differ from those to which they are assigned. Even the groups and committees people are assigned to at work or in school are the result of choices they have made. Professors do not enjoy every university committee on which they serve, but these committees are a part of the larger group that they *did* choose—the academic community. You may not have selected the group you work with in class, but you *did* select that class. Therefore, it is safe to say that all of the groups people belong to reflect *personal decisions.* Some groups they chose directly; others resulted from prior choices they made.

WHY DO PEOPLE JOIN GROUPS?

Understanding the many reasons that draw people to groups can help explain the complexity of small group interaction. Groups are many things to many people. To one member of a committee, the group's problem is an exciting vehicle toward greater self-understanding. To another member, it is merely an uninteresting but necessary obstacle on the way to reaching a personal goal. These individuals differ dramatically in their motivation for join-ing the group and in their commitment and contribution to it. This chapter will first examine the needs and goals that lead individuals to join small groups; then it will explore the impact of these needs and goals on small group communication.

The answer to the question "Why do people join groups?" has many di-mensions. These dimensions can be placed into several broad categories: (1) **interpersonal needs,** (2) individual goals, (3) group goals, (4) interpersonal attraction, and (5) group attraction.

INTERPERSONAL NEEDS

Maslow's Theory

Abraham Maslow asserts that all humans have basic needs and that these needs can be arranged in a hierarchy; that is, people do not concern them-selves with higher-level needs until lower-level needs are satisfied.[1] Maslow termed the two levels of needs at the bottom of the hierarchy *physiological needs* and *safety needs.* People's physiological needs are for air, water, and food. Their safety needs are for security and protection. Maslow called these two levels *survival needs;* satisfaction of these needs is necessary for basic hu-man existence. During childhood years, the family satisfies these needs.

Once survival needs are fulfilled, the higher-level needs that Maslow called *psychological needs*—the need to belong, the need for esteem, and the need for self-actualization—become more important. These needs may af-fect people's group memberships throughout their lives. See Figure 3.1 to understand how interpersonal needs form a hierarchy.

Figure 3.1   MASLOW'S NEED HIERARCHY

Belongingness Need Maslow posits that once people have satisfied their basic survival, physiological, and safety needs, they turn their attention to a social or belongingness need. People need to feel that they are a part of some group. Here again, the family provides a sense of belonging for children, but as they get older they begin to look outside the family to satisfy this need. Peer groups gain special importance during adolescence. At that time, people's need for affiliation is at its strongest.

Esteem Need Once people have developed a sense of belonging, Maslow says that they have a need for respect or esteem. They need to feel not only that they are accepted, but also that they are worthwhile and valued by others.

Self-Actualization Need Finally, Maslow says that people have a need for self-actualization. This need differs from the first four needs. The former needs Maslow calls *deficiency needs* because individuals perceive them as a void to fill by drawing on the resources of other people. Maslow calls self-actualization a *being* need. It involves people trying to be all that they can be and living life to its fullest. They are ready to function as autonomous beings, operating independently in quest of their own full potential. They no longer need groups to take care of their deficiencies; instead, they need groups in which to find and express their wholeness. While this need level is, perhaps, the most difficult to grasp conceptually, Maslow's hierarchy is consistent: People need groups to satisfy interpersonal needs. People also clearly differ from one another in their motivations for joining groups. Their differing motivations may be reflected in their communicative behavior in the group. Those who simply want to belong may interact differently from those who need the group's esteem and respect. The higher we move up Maslow's hierarchy, the greater is the importance of communication in our need satisfaction.[2]

REVIEW BOX

Maslow's Hierarchy of Interpersonal Needs

Survival Needs

Physiological needs: The fundamental needs for air, water, and food

Safety needs: The needs for security and protection

Psychological Needs

Belongingness need: The need to feel part of some group

Esteem need: The need to feel worthwhile and valued by others

Self-actualization need: The need to realize one's full potential: groups are seen as arenas for expressing personal wholeness rather than means for making up deficiencies

SCHUTZ'S THEORY

In an elaborate theory of interpersonal behavior, William Schutz suggests that three basic human needs influence individuals as they form and interact in groups: **inclusion, control,** and **affection.**[3] Individuals' needs vary, but groups often provide them settings in which such needs can be satisfied.

Inclusion Need   Just as Maslow postulates in his belongingness need, Schutz says people join groups to fulfill their need for inclusion. They need to be recognized as unique individuals and need to feel understood. When people try to understand someone it implies that the individual is worthy of their time and effort. In this respect, Schutz's inclusion need is related to Maslow's esteem need.

Control Need   The need for control is a need for status and power. People need to have some control over themselves, and others, and sometimes to give others some control over them, such as when they seek guidance and direction.

Affection Need   The need for affection drives people to give and receive emotional warmth and closeness.

In a broad sense, groups are more than collections of people with common goals; they are arenas in which individual needs are satisfied or frustrated. Schutz asserts that people join groups to satisfy needs for inclusion, control, and affection and that these needs influence group process throughout the life of the group. He has observed that in the initial stages of group formation, communication aims primarily toward inclusion needs. Group members are friendly but cautious as they try to evaluate one another and try to be accepted by other members. As the group develops, control needs become more evident: members contest issues and vie for leadership. Schutz observes that as conflicts are resolved, people turn toward affection needs. Members characteristically express positive feelings in this phase. The progression, Schutz says, is cyclical.

Continuing Cycle of Group Process   From Schutz's perspective, group formation is a process not limited to the initial coming together of the group. Rather, formation patterns repeat themselves as the group develops over time. Group decision-making involves a series of smaller decisions on the way toward achieving the group's primary goal. For example, a group of engineers planning a bridge must make decisions about the location and frequency of their meetings as well as the design and materials for the bridge. A group progresses through developmental phases throughout its life (as will be discussed in Chapter 7), and this cyclical pattern of formation and reformation occurs whenever the group approaches each new meeting and each new decision. If this process could be visualized, it might look something akin to a large jellyfish moving through the water. The jellyfish floats in the water in a relatively disorganized state until it needs to move forward: then it organizes itself, contracts, and propels itself through the water until it

People cluster in groups to meet interpersonal needs and goals.

returns to a restful, less organized state. Group process moves through a similar series of contractions until it reaches its ultimate goal.

A group is defined, in part, by a common purpose. Within that purpose are several smaller goals. As a group reaches each of these goals, it momentarily loses a bit of its definition until a new goal replaces the old. As people accomplish each new goal, they begin a new cycle of inclusion, control, and affection behaviors. Following is an example:

HARV: Well, it's been hard, but we've finally found a date for the banquet that we can all agree on.

JUANITA: For sure. For a while I thought we'd never agree, but I think we've made the best decision now.

BETSY: Yeah. We're over the major hurdle. Feels good, doesn't it?

PHIL: Amen. We're organized now and ready to go for it! This is getting to be fun.
(*Laughter, followed by a pause*)

JUANITA: Well, here we are. What do we do next?

PHIL: I guess we ought to talk about the theme and the speakers.

HARV: Hold on there! The speakers are irrelevant if no one is there to hear them. We've got to talk first about how we're going to publicize.

PHIL: C'mon. Harv. How can we publicize if we don't even have a theme?

BETSY: Here we go again.

People often form groups simply because they enjoy the same activities, as do the crew members of the racing yacht shown here.

In this example you can see the end of one cycle and the beginning of the next. Members expressed positive feelings about the group and its accomplishments and halted a little in their conversation before regrouping for another attack on a new facet of their problem. The sense of cohesiveness peaks during the affection phase and then falls off, only to rebuild around the next task. Like the jellyfish, which coordinates its process around its task of propulsion, the small group does not end up back where it started. The whole process moves forward. To say that the phases are cyclical, then, is somewhat misleading. Certain types of communicative behaviors recur, but the whole process moves forward. Frank E. X. Dance captured the essence of this process when he described human communication as being like a helix.[4] Like a bedspring, the helix is both linear and circular. It turns in on itself and yet always moves forward. Seen in this light, group formation does not cease but pulses throughout the life of the group.

INDIVIDUAL GOALS

Theories of interpersonal needs provide some of the psychological bases for group formation. So, too, do individual goals. Goals have a more tangible and obvious effect on people's selection of group memberships. What is it

---

REVIEW BOX

Schutz's Theory

Individuals join groups, in part, to satisfy their needs for inclusion, control, and affection.

- They want to be recognized and feel included. They also have needs to share and include others in their activities.
- People have varying needs to control or to be controlled that groups can satisfy.
- Individuals satisfy their affection needs through giving and receiving emotional support in groups.

Groups pass through observable, cyclical phases of inclusion, control, and affection.

---

that you want out of life? Prestige? Status? Power? Anonymity? Recreation? Education? Personal growth? In other words, what goals do you have that exist apart from any particular group membership?

Individual goals are instrumental in determining which groups people join. Obviously, if people enjoy arranging flowers and wish to improve their skills, they may join garden clubs. If personal growth is an aim, people will join a T-group. If they desire status and power, they will seek a group that they think will bring such status and power. Sometimes the prestige associated with a particular group is enough to make membership attractive to some people. This is often a motivation for joining a particular sorority or fraternity. Whatever their individual goals may be, people bring those goals with them when they join groups.

GROUP GOALS

Group goals are identifiable goals that transcend the group members' individual goals. Certain professional and fraternal organizations serve community needs. For example, the Lions Club is well known for its contributions toward finding cures for eye diseases and preventing blindness. Individual members have many different goals for joining the club: the chance to rub elbows with other professionals from the community, camaraderie and fellowship, the prestige of membership, the sense of belonging, or a genuine interest in serving the community. While individual goals may vary, the group goal takes precedence over them.

Of course, somewhere along the way an individual or small group of individuals proposed the group goals, which suggests some initial commonality of purpose among individual goals. Once individuals adopt group goals, however, their individual goals are superseded. The many needs and goals that individuals bring to small groups may be incompatible with the group's goal. This is a potential source of problems in small group communication. Consider the following situation:

A CASE STUDY

The First Church of Roseville has a building and grounds committee. This committee, charged with overseeing the regular maintenance and upkeep of the church building and surrounding property, makes sure that the lawns are mowed, the hedges trimmed, the furnace maintained, the roof patched, and so forth. The committee consists of the following members:

Roberto Bomblast. Roberto has been an accountant for a local firm for twenty-three years. He has always felt that his firm has never given him a chance to show his true leadership ability. He sees this committee, of which he is chairperson, as his big chance to prove himself and show the world what a truly fine administrator he is. He has another ulterior motive: He wants very much to be the new part-time business manager for the church when "Old George," the present manager, dies or becomes too senile to do the job. This committee, then, is Roberto's stepping-stone to greatness.

Marmalade. No one is sure of Marmalade's real name. He was found ten years ago wandering around the sanctuary saying, "Wow . . . wow . . . wowwwww . . . wowwwwwwwwww." The church members took him under their wing, and he has been sweeping floors and doing other odd jobs around the church since then. The pastor thought it would "do Marmalade some good" to get involved with a responsible committee, so he assigned him to this one.

Latasha Greene. Latasha is a young attorney who joined the church last year because she enjoys its outstanding music program. She has been dismayed, though, to find church governance dominated by white males. "What decade are we in?" she wonders "Don't they know it's the nineties?" She is continually annoyed when men like Roberto Bomblast and Thurman Jester act as if they are in charge of everything.

Merry Midwest. In all of her forty-seven years, Merry has not been outside of her home state. She loves her country, her state, her community, her home, and her family. She especially loves her church because of the sense of warmth and community she feels there. She has served on every committee in the church, and when she is not serving on a committee she misses a sense of community. Merry has high needs for inclusion. She is pleased to be on this committee.

Thurman Jester. Ever since his vacation trip to Dallas, Thurman wears a white belt and off-white shoes to work every day (and strongly urges his employees at the insurance office to do the same). He is committed to keeping up with the trendsetters, and Dallas, he feels, is where trends are set. Thurman was also impressed by a 40-foot neon cross he spotted outside a church in Dallas. Thurman is highly motivated by control needs.

Imagine that this group has come together for its first monthly meeting, that the church custodian has just resigned, and that the roof of the church leaks. The group's goal is to maintain the building and grounds. All of the members are, to some degree, committed to the goal. However, this commitment means different things to different members. An individual need or goal shapes each person's perception of what the group should be doing. Group members are aware of their personal goals, but most members are not aware that their behavior is motivated by desires to satisfy interpersonal needs. Merry Midwest may interpret her own behavior as a desire to serve, while her underlying, unconscious motive may be her need for inclusion. Thurman Jester wants to put a neon cross outside the church, but he may not be aware of his need to control others.

Needs and goals influence individuals' perceptions of group members and the group's task. Some individual goals are likely to overlap with group goals, while other individual goals will emerge from the group's focus. If a group goal is the desired end result of a group, and an individual goal is the desired end result of an individual, then individual and group goals will likely overlap in any given group. Differences between these goals may help or hinder the group. The conflict between individual and group goals is often the reason why some groups can't get off the ground.

FIGURE 3.2   GROUP GOALS VS. INDIVIDUAL GOALS AND THE NEED FOR
MUTUALITY OF CONCERN

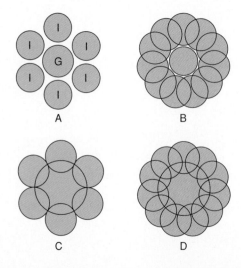

   Returning to the case of the church committee, try to imagine what the first meeting or two might be like. Each group member has a personal agenda—an individual goal—that will have a profound effect on his or her behavior in the group. Roberto seeks personal gain; Marmalade is unpredictable; Latasha wants to serve the church and be treated with the same respect afforded more experienced members; Merry just wants to feel a part of something; and Thurman wants to make his mark on the world with a 40-foot neon cross. Each of these characters will direct his or her communication in the group toward a particular goal, but none of their five goals is fully compatible with the more immediate need for fixing the leaky roof and hiring a new custodian. While all the characters have come together ostensibly for the same purpose, each has a different idea of what the group should be doing. If each member pulls in a different direction, the results could be disastrous. The group may go nowhere, and, to compound matters, each member will probably perceive the others as being uncooperative. For this reason, groups must question their members' **mutuality of concern**—the degree to which members share a concern for a group's task needs—during the initial stages of group formation.

ESTABLISHING MUTUALITY OF CONCERN[5]

When people join groups, they often assume that other group members share their commitment to the group's task. If a problem is to be solved they take for granted that others view the problem in much the same way they do. However, as in the earlier example of the building and grounds committee, each person may view the problem differently.

   Groups can also be frustrated because people bring different levels of commitment or concern to them. Suppose you have been appointed to a student government group whose task is to recommend whether your college should institute a plus/minus grading system or continue with a straight A, B, C, and D grading policy. If you are a first- or second-year student, this policy change could have a direct effect on your grade point average over your four years in college. If you are a graduating senior, a policy change would have little or no effect on you. Hence the level of concern over the problem can vary from member to member. Once again, individual goals interact with a group goal. Those affected directly by the problem will probably become more active in the group than those who are not as concerned with the problem. This can lead to needless conflict, as when some members resent having to carry the bulk of the workload.

   The degree to which members are concerned with the group's task needs to be clarified at the outset. Each group member should state clearly her or his personal needs and goals regarding the topic area. Clarifying mutuality of concern can resolve a lot of misunderstanding and avoid needless conflict.

   While individual needs and goals may bring a group together in the first place, they can also break a group apart. The success or failure of a group depends, in part, on the degree to which its goal is assumed by individuals as their own. Unsatisfied or unclarified individual needs and goals can become **hidden agendas**—private goals toward which individuals work while seeming to work toward the group goal. Such hidden agendas can be extremely disruptive to the group. Establishing mutuality of concern can help reduce this negative influence.

Culture is another important factor in balancing individual and group needs and goals. The value placed on individuality or conformity varies widely. In Japan, China, Israel, and Russia, for example, individuals tend to acquiesce to the will of the group, as a high degree of conformity is expected. As we noted in Chapter 1, North Americans and Europeans are thought to be more individualistic.[6] When all of us come to the group, our cultures—whatever they may be—come with us.

In any given situation the interaction of individual and group needs will cause one of four possible outcomes:

> (1) Individual and group needs may be so diverse that they interfere with each other with no positive effects accruing either to individuals within the group or to the group as a whole. (2) Group interaction may result in the realization of goals desired by the group as a whole, while individual needs are not met. (3) Individual needs may be realized by one or more group members to the detriment or destruction of the group. (4) Individual and group needs may blend so completely that the needs realized by the group as a whole are the same needs individuals wish to realize.[7]

In the ideal, fully integrated group this fourth alternative is realized. Mutuality of concern can merge individual and group needs and goals.

Aside from the relationships among interpersonal needs, personal goals, and group goals, two other factors have an influence on people's selection of groups: interpersonal attraction and group attraction.

INTERPERSONAL ATTRACTION

Often people are attracted to groups because they are attracted to the people who compose them. While many factors influence interpersonal attraction, four of these are especially significant: similarity, complementarity, proximity/contact/interaction, and physical attractiveness.

SIMILARITY

One of the strongest influences in interpersonal attraction is **similarity.** Remember your first day on campus? That feeling of newness, strangeness, and aloneness? You needed a friend, and with luck you found one. Who did you look for to be your friend? Did you seek out someone you perceived to be very different from you? Probably not. If the principle of similarity in interpersonal attraction applies here, you probably looked for someone to talk to who appeared to be in the same situation—another lonely newcomer, or perhaps someone dressed in a style similar to yours.

Who are your closest friends? Do you share many of the same attitudes, beliefs, and values? Do you enjoy the same activities? More than likely you do. People are often attracted to those they consider to be like them. A probable explanation for this is that similar backgrounds, beliefs, attitudes, and values make it easier to understand one another—and all people like to feel that they are understood.

One of the dangers of the similarity factor in group formation is that our tendency to be attracted to persons like ourselves may result in a group that is too homogeneous to approach a complex task effectively. Indeed, research on classroom groups found that by a two-to-one margin, students reported their worst experiences with groups they had formed themselves. Their best experiences were with groups to which professors had assigned them.[8]

COMPLEMENTARITY

In reading the previous section on similarity, some of you probably shook your heads and said, "No, that's not the way it is at all. My best friend and I are about as similar as an orchid and a fire hydrant!" No generalization is entirely true, and so it is with the principle of similarity. While there is some truth to the statement that birds of a feather flock together, it is also true that opposites attract. Thibaut and Kelley suggest that some interpersonal relationships are based primarily on similarity, while others are based on **complementarity.**[9] At times people may be attracted to others who exhibit qualities that they do not have but that they admire. While the principle of similarity seems to be the more pervasive phenomenon, everyone can cite instances of complementarity. For at least a partial explanation of attraction through complementarity, consider Schutz's theory of interpersonal needs, discussed earlier in this chapter. According to Schutz's theory, a person who has a high need to control would be most compatible with a person who has a high need to be controlled. The same would be true of needs to express and to receive inclusion and affection. These are complementary needs rather than similar needs.

PROXIMITY/CONTACT/INTERACTION

You tend to be attracted to people who are physically close to you, who live and work with you, and whom you see and talk with often. If you know that you have to live or work close to another person, you may ignore that person's less desirable traits in order to minimize potential conflict. Furthermore, proximity, contact, and interaction breed familiarity, and familiarity has a positive influence on interpersonal attraction.[10] Interaction with another person helps you get to know that other person, and through this process the two of you may uncover similarities and discover ways in which you can satisfy each other's interpersonal needs. The actual physical distance between people, then, does not influence attraction, but the interpersonal possibilities illuminated by proximity, contact, and interaction do.

PHYSICAL ATTRACTIVENESS

At least in the initial stages of interpersonal attraction, physical attractiveness influences people. If a person is physically beautiful, others tend to want to affiliate with him or her.[11] However, evidence indicates that this factor diminishes in importance over time and that—at least in North American cultures—physical beauty is more important to males than to females.[12]

In sum, people seem to be attracted to others who are likely to understand them, who can fulfill their needs, who complement their personalities, and who are physically appealing. Those individuals constitute a powerful influence on people's selection of groups.

GROUP ATTRACTION

While individuals may be attracted to a group because they are attracted to the members who compose it, they may also be attracted to the group itself. Such attraction usually focuses on the group's activities or goals, or simply on the desirability of group membership.

GROUP ACTIVITIES

Although research is not extensive in this area, it seems fairly clear that people who are interested in the same activities tend to form groups.[13] People who enjoy intellectual pursuits may join literary discussion groups. Bridge players may join bridge clubs. Beyond these obvious examples, people may be attracted to the activities of a group in a more general sense. Some may join groups simply because they enjoy going to regular meetings and joining in group discussions, regardless of the group's specific aims or goals. The structure and human contact provided by groups are potentially rewarding in and of themselves.

GROUP GOALS

Another factor that may attract people to a group is the goal to which it is dedicated. If, for example, people believe that the spread of nuclear power must be curtailed, they may join a group dedicated to making it illegal. If they are committed to preserving and protecting the natural environment, they may join American Forests, the Sierra Club, the Audubon Society, or any organization that professes a goal similar to their own.

Group attraction includes elements of attraction that have already been mentioned: similarity in interpersonal attraction and the relationship between individual and group goals.

GROUP MEMBERSHIP

Sometimes it is not a group's members, activities, or goals that attract people but membership itself. Potential members may perceive that membership in an exclusive club or honor society will bring them prestige, acceptance, or professional benefits outside of the group. For example, company officials may expect a young executive to belong to some civic group because such memberships provide good public relations for the firm.

The need for affiliation—Maslow's belongingness need and Schutz's inclusion need—can make group membership attractive. You probably know of professional committee members who move from group to group because their lives seem incomplete without some type of group membership. The need for affiliation is basic to human nature. Group membership can help satisfy that need.

PUTTING PRINCIPLE INTO PRACTICE

The dynamic interrelatedness of all of the variables that affect small group processes makes the study of small group communication challenging and exciting. As you continue through the rest of this book, it is important that you retain what you have previously learned. Only when you have fit all of the puzzle pieces together can you see a clear picture of small group communication.

This chapter has zoomed in on one part of the puzzle: those needs and goals that motivate people to join groups and that influence their behavior within those groups. In the initial stages of group development, uncertainty is at its peak—uncertainty about the group, about its goals, and about people's place in it. How you communicate at this sensitive stage of group development provides the basis for future interaction. As you join new groups, keep in mind the following:

- At the first meeting of any new group, you may feel anxious. Members are often uncertain who the others are, what each person's role is to be, and what to say to whom. At this stage, share a little information about yourself and encourage others to do the same. Many group leaders will ask the members to say a few words about themselves. This strategy breaks the ice and provides some familiarity on which to base further discussion. In short, it reduces people's uncertainty and helps them relax.

- Sometimes you do not choose the groups you belong to, but are assigned to them, perhaps by a teacher, a supervisor, or an employer.

REVIEW BOX

Factors in Interpersonal Attraction

FACTORS	DEFINITION	NOTES/COMMENTS
Similarity	The degree to which two persons are alike	You tend to like people who resemble you in their thinking and experiences; it is reinforcing, and they are more likely than most to understand you.
Complementarity	The degree to which two persons are compatibly different from each other	You tend to be attracted to people who possess qualities that you admire but do not yourself possess.
Proximity, contact, and interaction	The actual, physical availability of other people	Talking with others reveals their similar and complementary traits and, thus, their attractiveness to you.
Physical attraction	The perception of physical beauty or handsomeness	Especially important in the early stages of a relationship; less important after you get to know someone.

Factors in Group Attraction

FACTORS	DEFINITION	NOTES/COMMENTS
Group activities	People interested in the same activities tend to group together	The mere structure and human contact of group activities may provide rewards.
Group goals	Attraction based on mutually shared goals	Civic groups, the PTA, and environmental groups are examples.
Group membership	Attraction based on the rewards of membership per se	Membership is often seen as having prestige or status.

When you are assigned to a group, look carefully at the group's goal. Then assess the resources that you can bring to accomplishing that goal. Evaluate the benefits that you can derive from the experience. Decide what your level of commitment is to the goal and the group. Talk about it with the group, and begin establishing mutuality of concern.

- When you join a new group, ask yourself what attracts you to it: "Why am *I* a part of this group? What do *I* want to accomplish here? What are *my* goals? What do I *want* from these people . . . and what can I *give* to them?" Never assume that everyone in your group shares your level of commitment to the group and its task. Clarify this potential uncertainty by telling the group openly and honestly how you feel about the group and its task, with the clear expectation that others will do the same.

- You may find that you are attracted to a group only because you are attracted to its members. If that is so, think twice before you join. When a group is dedicated to a common purpose, its members will probably resent someone being there for purely social reasons.

In sum, people are attracted to groups for different reasons and join groups to satisfy a variety of needs. An understanding of these factors in group formation should guide your communicative behavior in groups.

PRACTICE

1. Select two groups in which you are an active member—a study group, a club, or your family, for example. Considering each group, indicate below the importance to you of the various factors in group formation. What attracts you to these groups? What are their rewards? Use a scale of one to five, one being "very important" and five being "not at all important to me."

	GROUP 1	GROUP 2
Interpersonal Needs		
Inclusion	_____	_____
Control	_____	_____
Affection	_____	_____
Interpersonal attraction		
Proximity	_____	_____
Similarity	_____	_____
Complementarity	_____	_____
Physical attraction	_____	_____
Group attraction		
Group activities	_____	_____
Group goals	_____	_____
Group membership	_____	_____

Compare your ratings of the two groups. Do you now have a better understanding of the roles these groups play in your life?

2. Study the diagrams in Figure 3.2C. For each, create an example where individual or group goals converge or diverge. Discuss the dynamics and probable outcomes of each situation.

3. Make a list of the groups you are affiliated with. For each one, identify its members, its activities, and its goals. Then note your individual goals in regard to each group. Examine the results. What is your primary attraction to each group? Are your individual goals compatible with the group's goals? Do you have any hidden agendas? Do your answers to these questions explain any of your attitudes about or behaviors within these groups?

4. Role-play the scenario outlined in the First Church case study. Observe the relationships between individual and group goals. Then, discuss strategies to help the group approach its task more effectively.

5. Observe a videotaped group discussion. Periodically stop the tape and identify the phase of the group's cycle (inclusion, control, affection) the group is operating in. What are the verbal and nonverbal cues that lead you to this conclusion? Continue the tape and note the group's strategies for passing from one phase into the next. Can you observe any differences in the members' communicative behavior as the group repeats the cycle?

NOTES

1. Abraham Maslow, *Toward a Psychology of Being,* 2nd ed., (Princeton, N.J.: Van Nostrand, 1982).

2. Don Stacks, Mark Hickson III, and Sidney R. Hill. Jr., *Introduction to Communication Theory* (Chicago: Holt, Rinehart & Winston, 1991).

3. William Schutz. *The Interpersonal Underworld* (Palo Alto, Calif.: Science & Behavior Books, 1958).

4. Frank E. X. Dance, "A Helical Model of Communication," in *Human Communication Theory* (New York: Holt, Rinehart & Winston, 1967), 294–98.

5. For a full discussion of mutuality of concern, see Bobby Patton and Kim Giffin, *Decision-Making Group Interaction,* 3rd ed. (New York: HarperCollins, 1990), 118–19.

6. L. Mann, "Cross Cultural Studies of Small Groups," in H. Triandis (ed.), *Handbook of Cross-cultural Psychology,* vol. 5 (Boston: Allyn & Bacon).

7. Charles S. Palazzo. "The Social Group: Definitions," in Robert S. Cathcart and Larry A. Samovar (eds.), *Small Group Communication: A Reader,* 5th ed. (Dubuque, Iowa: Wm. C. Brown, 1988), 11–12.

8. Susan Brown Feichtner and Elaine Actis Davis, "Why Some Groups Fail: A Survey of Students' Experiences with Learning Groups," *The Organizational Behavior Teaching Review* 9: 75–88.

9. John Thibaut and Harold Kelley, *The Social Psychology of Groups* (New Brunswick, N.J.: Transaction Publishing, 1986).

10. Robert Zajonc, "Attitudinal Effects of Mere Exposure," *Journal of Personality and Social Psychology* 9 (1968): 1–29.

11. Marvin Shaw, *Group Dynamics: The Psychology of Small Group Behavior* (New York: McGraw-Hill, 1981), 93.

12. D. Krebs and A. A. Adinolf, "Physical Attractiveness, Social Relations, and Personality Style," *Journal of Personality and Social Psychology* 31 (1975): 245–53.

13. Shaw, *Group Dynamics*, 85.

CHAPTER
F·O·U·R

Relating to Others in Small Groups

After studying this chapter, you will be able to:

- Describe how an individual develops and defines self-concept.

- Identify the task, maintenance, and individual roles that group members assume.

- Identify several group norms that often develop in small group discussions.

- Recognize and adjust to cultural differences in group communication.

- Describe several effects of status differences on small group communication.

- Describe how power affects relationships in small groups.

- Identify factors that foster trusting relationships with others.

- Apply guidelines for appropriate self-disclosure in small groups.

- Describe how relationships develop over time among group members.

*D*o you consider yourself to be a leader or a follower in small group meetings? Do you usually talk a lot or a little when you serve on a committee? Do you think you are a good or mediocre group member? Perhaps your answers depend on the quality of your relationships with others in the group.

Relationships refer to the feelings, roles, norms, status, and trust that both affect and reflect the quality of communication between you and others. If the members of your group are old friends, your relationships with them will obviously be different than if you have just met for the first time. Have you served on a committee with three or four other people that you felt were much better qualified than you were to contribute to the discussion? Your feeling of inferiority undoubtedly affected your relationship with the other group members. In small groups, and in other communication contexts as well, the quality of interpersonal relationships often determines what people say to one another.

Relational communication theorists assert that every message people communicate to one another has both a content dimension and a relationship dimension. The content dimension of a message includes the specific information conveyed to someone. The relationship dimension refers to message cues that provide hints about whether you like or dislike the person with whom you are communicating. For example, the formality of their language and nonverbal cues provide important information about the relationship between two individuals having a conversation. Whether you are giving a public speech, talking with your spouse, or communicating with another member of a small group, you are providing information about the feelings you have toward your listener as well as about *ideas* and *thoughts.*

This chapter will emphasize the communication elements that affect the quality of the relationships you establish with other group members. Specifically, it will concentrate on five variables that have an important effect on the relationships you establish with others in small groups: the roles you assume, the norms or standards the group develops, the status differences that impact the group's productivity, the power some members have, and the trust that improves group performance.

ROLES

Stop reading this chapter for just a moment, and reflect on the question, "Who are you?" A simple question, you probably think. Perhaps you took little time to answer it. Maybe you responded by saying your name. Maybe you said you are a student—a label that summarizes your current status. Ask yourself the question again. Get a pencil and write ten different responses.

WHO ARE YOU?

1. I am_____
2. I am_____
3. I am_____
4. I am_____
5. I am_____
6. I am_____
7. I am_____
8. I am_____
9. I am_____
10. I am_____

Some of you may have had little trouble coming up with a detailed profile of who you think you are. Others, however, may have had more difficulty labeling multiple aspects of your **self-concept.** As you relate to others in small groups, your concept of self—who you think you are—affects your communication and relationships with other group members. In addition, your self-perception will have an impact on how others relate to you.

In trying to reduce the uncertainty that occurs when they communicate in groups, people quickly assess the behaviors of others. They assign others roles, or sets of expectations. For example, Gloria seems like a leader: She usually takes charge and delegates responsibility. On the other hand, Hank doesn't talk much. He will probably follow the recommendations of others rather than introduce ideas of his own—or at least this is the behavior others expect of him. In a small group, roles result from: (1) people's expectations about their own behavior—their *self-concepts,* (2) the perceptions others have about individuals' positions in the group, and (3) people's actual behavior as they interact with others. Since their self-concepts largely determine the roles people assume in small groups, it is important to understand how self-concepts develop—how people come to learn who they think they are.

SELF-CONCEPT DEVELOPMENT: GENDER, CULTURE, AND ROLE FORMATION

How do you know who you are? Why did you respond as you did when you were asked to consider the question, "Who are you?" A number of factors influence your self-concept. First, other people influence who you think you are. Your parents gave you your name. Perhaps a teacher once told you that you were good in art, and consequently you think of yourself as artistic. Maybe your music teacher or your brother or sister told you that you cannot sing very well. Because you believed that person, you may now view yourself as not being very musically inclined. Thus, you listen to others, especially those whose opinions you respect, to help shape your self-concept.

One important part of everyone's self-concept is *gender*.[1] Whether you have experienced life as male or female affects your communication with others. While it is natural to assume that there are communication differences based on aspects of gender defined biologically, recent research suggests that the psychological aspects of gender may be at least as important a variable.[2] While psychologically a person can be placed anywhere on a scale ranging from stereotypically female, through androgynous, to stereotypically male, the important point to remember is that psychological gender affects our behavior in groups.[3]

Another important component of self-concept is *culture of origin*. Different cultures foster different beliefs and attitudes about communication, status, nonverbal behavior, and all of the interpersonal dynamics discussed throughout this book. The development of selfhood takes place very differently from culture to culture. For example, Japanese and North American social lives flow from different premises. In Japan, the group or the collective is the measure of all things but in the West—and in the Unites States in particular—the individual is the measure and arbiter of all things.[4] Many North Americans prize the image of the "rugged individualist"; the Japanese, on the other hand, view this image as suggestive of egotism and insensitivity. To the Japanese, the line where self ends and others begin is far less clearly defined than it is for most North Americans.

Culture influences self-concept and thus such behaviors as the willingness to communicate in a group.[5] There is ample evidence that individuals from different cultures interpret situations and concepts very differently from one another.[6] Therefore, understanding cultural differences is essential to understanding behavior in small groups.

The various groups with which one affiliates also helps to define one's self-concept. If you are attending college now, you may describe yourself as a student. If you are a member of a fraternity or sorority, you may consider that that association sets you apart from others. Your religious affiliation, your political party, and your membership in civic and social organizations all contribute to the way you perceive yourself.

You also learn who you are by simply observing and interpreting your own behavior. Just before leaving your dorm, house, or apartment, you may look in the mirror to see if your hair is okay and if your clothes are wrinkle-free. You try to see yourself as others will see you. You stand back and look at yourself, almost as if you were looking at someone else, evaluating what you see and forming an impression of who you are. Of course, as both the observer and the observed, your impressions are subject to bias. You may be too critical in evaluating who you are. Your high expectations for your own behavior, when compared with your perceptions of your actions, may give you a distorted view. For example, you may want to be a great opera singer, yet your only opportunity to sing comes in the shower. Even though you may have an excellent voice, your expectations have not been fulfilled, so you tell others that you are not a very good singer. The contradiction between your expectations and your actual experiences affects your self-concept and self-worth.

DIVERSITY OF ROLES IN SMALL GROUPS

As a member of a small group, you bring with you the perceptions, expectations, and experiences you have had with other people. Your self-expectations thus provide a foundation for the roles you will assume in a group. Yet your role is also worked out between you and the other group members. As noted by Brown and Keller, "At the heart of every relationship lie the self-images of the persons involved, each created by interaction with the other."[7] As you interact with others, they form impressions of you and your abilities. As they reward you for your actions in the group, you learn what abilities and behaviors they will reinforce. These abilities and behaviors may, in turn, become part of your self-concept. Consider the following example:

> Mohammed has long had an interest in physics and nuclear energy. When his small group in the group communication class considers a discussion of peaceful uses of nuclear energy, Mohammed is enthusiastically supportive. Other group members soon recognize Mohammed's knowledge and interest in the subject. Mohammed enjoys providing resources and information for the group, soon emerging as the group member who provides most of the information and coordinates the group's research efforts. It is a role he enjoys, and the rest of the group appreciates his contributions.

Mohammed's role as an initiator of ideas, a contributor of information, and a coordinator of research resulted from his interest and ability (which were reflected in his self-concept). The group's need and desire to have him serve as a leader also helped determine his role.

People assume roles because of their interests and abilities and because of the needs and expectations of the rest of the group. At times, however, some roles are formally assigned to group members. When police officers arrive on the scene of an accident, bystanders do not generally question their leadership roles. In a task-oriented small group, a member may be assigned the role of secretary, which includes specific duties and responsibilities. A chairperson may be elected to coordinate the meeting and delegate responsibilities. Assigning responsibilities and specific roles reduces uncertainty. A group can sometimes get on with its task more efficiently if some roles are assigned. Of course, even if a person has been elected or assigned the role of chairperson, the group may reject his or her leadership in favor of that of another member who may better meet the needs of the group.

The kinds of roles discussed so far are **task roles**—they help accomplish a group's task. There are also two other kinds of roles. **Maintenance roles** define a group's social atmosphere. A member who tries to maintain a peaceful, harmonious group climate by mediating disagreements and re-solving conflicts performs a maintenance function. **Individual roles** call at-tention to individual contributions and tend to be counterproductive to the overall group effort. Someone who is more interested in seeking personal recognition than in promoting the general benefit of the group is adopting an individual role.

Benne and Sheats have compiled a comprehensive list of possible roles that individual group members can assume.[8] Perhaps you can identify the var-ious roles you have assumed while participating in small group discussions.

GROUP TASK ROLES

Initiator-contributor	Proposes new ideas or approaches to group problem solving; may suggest a different approach to procedure or organizing the problem-solving task
Information seeker	Asks for clarification of suggestions; also asks for facts or other information that may help the group deal with the issues at hand
Opinion seeker	Asks for a clarification of the values and opinions ex-pressed by other group members
Information giver	Provides facts, examples, statistics, and other evidence that pertains to the problem the group is attempting to solve
Opinion giver	Offers beliefs or opinions about the ideas under discus-sion
Elaborator	Provides examples based upon his or her experience or the experience of others that help to show how an idea or suggestion would work if the group accepted a par-ticular course of action
Coordinator	Tries to clarify and note relationships among the ideas and suggestions that have been provided by others
Orienter	Attempts to summarize what has occurred and tries to keep the group focused on the task at hand
Evaluator-critic	Makes an effort to judge the evidence and conclusions that the group suggests
Energizer	Tries to spur the group to action and attempts to moti-vate and stimulate the group to greater productivity.
Procedural technician	Helps the group achieve its goal by performing tasks such as distributing papers, rearranging the seating, or running errands for the group
Recorder	Writes down suggestions and ideas of others; makes a record of the group's progress

GROUP BUILDING AND MAINTENANCE ROLES

Encourager	Offers praise, understanding, and acceptance of others' ideas and suggestions
Harmonizer	Mediates disagreements among group members
Compromiser	Attempts to resolve conflicts by trying to find an acceptable solution to disagreements among group members
Gatekeeper and expediter	Encourages less talkative group members to participate and tries to limit lengthy contributions of other group members
Standard setter	Helps to set standards and goals for the group
Group observer	Keeps records of the group's process and uses the information that is gathered to evaluate the group's procedures
Follower	Basically goes along with the suggestions and ideas of other group members; serves as an audience in group discussions and decision making

INDIVIDUAL ROLES

Aggressor	Destroys or deflates the status of other group members; may try to take credit for someone else's contribution
Blocker	Is generally negative, stubborn, and disagreeable without apparent reason
Recognition seeker	Seeks the spotlight by boasting and reporting on his or her personal achievements
Self-confessor	Uses the group as an audience to report personal feelings, insights, and observations
Playboy	Lacks involvement in the group's process; lack of interest may result in cynicism, nonchalance, or other behaviors that indicate lack of enthusiasm for the group
Dominator	Makes an effort to assert authority by manipulating group members or attempting to take over the entire group; may use flattery or assertive behavior to dominate the discussion
Help seeker	Tries to evoke a sympathetic response from others; often expresses insecurity or feelings of low self-worth
Special-interest pleader	Works to serve an individual need; speaks for a special group or organization that best fits his or her own biases.

In looking at the preceding list of roles, you might be tempted to label group members according to these classifications. You may have recognized

Both group task roles and group building and maintenance roles are important to a group's success.

yourself as a harmonizer or a follower and said, "Yes, that's me. That's the role I usually take." You may also have tried to classify other group members into these categories. While identifying the characteristics of roles may help you understand their nature and function in small group communication, stereotyping individuals can lock them into roles. Bormann and his colleagues have extensively studied role behavior in groups and note that participants, when asked to analyze group roles, often categorize members into roles corresponding to the category labels.[9] As you identify the roles adopted by group members, be flexible in your classifications. Realize that you and other members can assume several roles during a group discussion. In fact, a group member rarely serves only as an "encourager," "opinion seeker," or "follower." Roles are dynamic; they change as perceptions, experiences, and expectations change. An individual can assume leadership responsibilities at one meeting and play a supporting role at other meetings.

Since a role is worked out jointly between you and the group, you will no doubt find yourself assuming different roles in different groups. Perhaps a committee you belong to needs someone to serve as a procedural leader to keep the meeting in order. Because you recognize this need and no one else keeps the group organized, you may find yourself steering the group back on to the topic, making sure all members have a chance to participate. In another committee, where others serve as procedural leaders, you may be the person who comes up with new ideas. Whether consciously or not, you develop a role unique to your talents and the needs of the group. Your role, then, changes from group to group.

If you understand how group roles form and how various roles function, you will be better able to help a group achieve its purpose. For example, groups need members to perform both maintenance and task functions. Task functions help the group get the job done, and maintenance functions help the group run smoothly. If no one is performing maintenance functions, you could point this out to the group, or assume some responsibility for them. If you notice individuals hindering the group's progress because they have adopted individual roles (blocker, aggressor, recognition seeker, etc.), you could bring this to the attention of the offending group member. Explain that individual roles can make the group less efficient and can lead to conflict among members. While you cannot assume complete responsibility for distributing roles within your group, your insights can help solve some of the group's potential problems.

NORMS

You have undoubtedly seen a movie or television show about the Old West in which townspeople feared villains who had no respect for the law. According to the way movies depict history, people like Wyatt Earp were among the first to enforce the law and restore peace and order. In small groups as well as in the Old West, standards of acceptable behavior are necessary to keep peace and order. While a small group of people does not need a Wyatt Earp to enforce order, it probably does need certain norms to help its members feel comfortable with their roles and their relationships.

IDENTIFYING GROUP NORMS

Norms are rules or standards that determine what is appropriate and inappropriate behavior in a group. They establish expectations of how group members should behave. Norms reduce some of the uncertainty that occurs when people congregate. People's speech, the clothes they wear, or do not wear, and how and where they sit are all determined by group norms. Group norms also affect group-member relationships.

If you recently joined a group, how do you know what the group's norms are? One way to identify norms is to observe any repeated behavior patterns. Note, for example, any consistencies in the way people talk or dress. In identifying normative behavior in a group, consider the following questions:

1. How do group members dress?
2. What are group members' attitudes toward time (e.g., do group meetings begin and end on time? Are members often late to meetings?)?
3. What type of language is used by most group members (e.g., is swearing acceptable? is the language formal?)?
4. Do group members use humor to relieve tension?
5. Do group members formally address the group leader?
6. Is it proper to address group members by their first names?

Answering these questions will help you pinpoint a group's norms. Some groups even develop norms for developing norms. For example, members may discuss the type of clothing that will be worn to meetings or talk about what should be done with absent or tardy members.

Noting when someone breaks a rule can also reveal group norms. If a member arrives late and other members frown or grimace at that person, they probably do not approve of the violation of the norm. If, after a member uses obscene words, another member says, "I wish you wouldn't use words like that," you can be certain that for at least one person a norm has been broken. Thus, punishable offenses indicate violated norms. Often the severity of the punishment corresponds to the significance of the norm.[10] Punishment can range from subtle nonverbal expressions of disapproval (which may not even be noticed by the person expressing them) to death. The hangman's noose was commonly the ultimate punishment for those who violated the norms or laws of the Old West.

How Do Norms Develop?

Have you noticed that in some classes it is okay to say something without raising your hand, but in others the instructor has to recognize you before you speak? Raising your hand is a norm. How did different norms develop for two similar activities? At least two key reasons account for this: (1) People develop norms in new groups based on those of previous groups they have belonged to, and (2) norms develop based on what happens early in a group's existence.

Poole suggests that a group organizes itself based, in part, on norms members encountered in previous groups.[11] As we noted in Chapter 2, Poole calls this process *structuration*. Groups do things based on the ways those things were done in other groups. If many of your classmates previously had classes in which they had to raise their hands before speaking, then they will probably introduce that behavior into other groups. If enough people accept it, a norm is born—or, more accurately, a norm is reborn.

Norms also develop from the kinds of behavior that occur early in a group's development. Because of member uncertainty about how to behave when a group first meets, members are eager to learn what is acceptable be-

havior. If, for example, on the first day of class, a student raises his or her hand to respond to the instructor, and another student does the same, that norm is likely to stick. However, if several students respond without raising a hand, chances are that raising hands will not become a norm in the class.

Conforming to Group Norms

What influences how quickly and rigidly people conform to the rules and standards of the group? According to Reitan and Shaw, at least five factors affect conformity to group norms.[12]

The Individual Characteristics of the Group Members   In summarizing the research on conformity. Shaw notes that more intelligent persons are less likely to conform than less intelligent persons; women usually conform more than men, at least on traditional tasks; there is a curvilinear relationship between age and conformity; persons who generally blame themselves for what happens to them conform more than those low on self-blame; and authoritarians conform more than nonauthoritarians.[13]

Thus, group members' past experiences and unique personality characteristics influence how they conform to established norms.

The Clarity of the Norm and the Certainty of Punishment for Breaking It The more ambiguous a group norm, the less likely it is that members will conform to it. The military spells out behavior rules clearly so that little if any ambiguity remains. A new recruit is drilled on how to talk, march, salute, and eat. Failure to abide by the rules results in swift and sure corrective sanctions. Thus, the recruit quickly learns to conform. In some small groups particularly when groups first meet, members have a great deal of uncertainty about how to act. Yet as soon as rules become clear and norms are established, members will usually conform. The clearer the norms, the more likely group members will conform.

The Number of People Who Have Already Conformed to the Norm Imagine walking into a room with five or six other people. Three lines have been drawn on a blackboard. One line is clearly shorter than the other two. One by one, each person is asked which line is shortest, and each says that all the lines are the same length. Finally, it is your turn to judge which of the lines is shortest. You are perplexed because your eyes tell you that one line is definitely shorter. Yet can all the other members of your group be wrong? You answer that all of the lines are the same length—you conform. You do not want to appear odd to the other group members. Factors such as the size of a group, the number of people who agree with a certain policy, and the status of those who conform contribute to the pressure for conformity in a group.

The Quality of the Interpersonal Relationships That Have Developed in the Group A group whose members like one another and respect one another's opinions is more likely to support conformity than is a less cohesive group. Employees who like their jobs, bosses, and coworkers and take pride in their work are more likely to support group norms than those who have negative or frustrating relationships with their employers or colleagues.

The Sense of Group Identification That Members Have Developed If group members can readily identify with the goals of the group, they are more likely to conform to standards of behavior. For example, church members who support the doctrine of a church are probably going to conform to the wishes of those in leadership positions. In addition, group members who feel they will be a part of a group for some time are more likely to conform to group norms.

Although violating a group norm usually results in group disapproval and perhaps chastisement, such a violation can occasionally benefit a group. Just because members conform unanimously to a rule does not mean that the rule is beneficial. For example, if a norm of low productivity were to develop in a group, work output would be adversely affected.

CULTURE

Earlier in the chapter, we noted the powerful effect of culture on self-concept and behavior. To be effective leaders and members in multicultural groups, we must develop understanding and sensitivity to cultural differences.

A complete treatment of this subject would require volumes. Nevertheless, we can provide an introduction to get you started. We will divide cultural differences into three categories: *individualism, conversational style,* and *time.*

INDIVIDUALISM AND COLLECTIVISM

Groups often have difficulty establishing norms and roles because of cultural variations in individualism among group members. As we discussed in chapter one, in some cultures (such as the Anglo-American) individual autonomy and initiative are valued; in others (Japan, for instance) collective well-being takes precedence over individual achievement. Persons from collectivist cultures are therefore likely to view assertive individualists as self-centered, while individualists may interpret their collectivist counterparts as weak. Collectivists are more likely to conform to group norms, and to value group decisions more highly.[14]

While differences in individualism always exist in groups, these differences can be extreme in the presence of cultural diversity, resulting in low group satisfaction and productivity. To establish and maintain norms with which all members can feel comfortable, groups need to understand and be sensitive to one another's cultural expectations.

CONVERSATIONAL STYLE

Conversational norms vary by culture.[15] If not understood, these differences can cause misunderstanding, anxiety, and group conflict.

The white middle-class North American norm that has one group member quietly awaiting a turn to speak may cause him or her to wait a very long time when those from other cultures do not share that norm. People from some cultures love a good argument, while others, such as the Japanese, revere harmony and the ability to assimilate differences to build consensus.[16] Some cultures are put off by North Americans' frankness and relative lack of inhibition about sharing negative information. In Western cultures, control is exerted through speaking; in Eastern cultures, control is expressed through silence and in the outward show of reticence.[17]

The topics we address and our willingness to talk about personal matters varies by culture. While Mexicans may talk about a person's soul or spirit, such talk may make North Americans uncomfortable. Persons from Hispanic cultures often begin conversations with inquiries about one's family, even with casual acquaintances or in a business meeting. Many North Americans view family matters as too personal to be discussed casually.[18]

TIME

Thomas Fitzgerald recounts an anecdote that illustrates cultural differences in the temporal dimension. While interviewing a group of Brazilian students, Fitzgerald asked his subjects how they felt about a person who was consistently late. He was surprised to find that the students view such a person as probably more successful than those who are on time. A person of status, they reasoned, is *expected* to be late.[19]

North Americans are arguably the most timebound culture in the world. Even the Japanese view North American business people as much too driven by schedules and deadlines, which in turn interfere with the smooth development of human relationships. North Americans tend to view time as **monochronic**—linear and segmented; they value precision in time. Many other cultures, including the African-American subculture, take a more **polychronic** view. Polychronic time is partly characterized by a more *laissez-faire* attitude about what constitutes being "on time" or "late." Peoples who have a polychronic sense of time do not expect human activities to proceed like clockwork. After all, humans were here on earth long before the invention of clocks.[20]

PERSONS WITH DISABILITIES

As physical spaces are built and renovated to be increasingly accessible, full participation by persons with disabilities in all aspects of social and professional activity is finally becoming a reality. Able–bodied (or, as a friend of ours puts it, "temporarily able–bodied" individuals who have little or no experience communicating with persons with disabilities sometimes feel uncomfortable and/or do and say things that are inappropriate.

Persons with physical disabilities see themselves as members of a culture. Dawn Braithwaite offers some *do's* and *don'ts* to assist in this form of intercultural communication:

Don't assume that persons with disabilities cannot speak for themselves or do things for themselves.

Do assume they can do something unless they communicate otherwise.

Don't force your help on persons with disabilities. *Do let* them tell you if they want something, what they want, and when they want it. If a person with a disability refuses your help, don't go ahead and help anyway.

Disabilities can be viewed as cultural variables that can affect communication. Effective communication relies on our understanding of such variables.

Don't avoid communicating with persons who have disabilities simply because you are uncomfortable or unsure. *Do remember* they probably feel the same way you do.

Do treat persons with disabilities as *persons* first, recognizing that you are not dealing with a disabled person but a *person* who has a disability.[21]

Most of the research conclusions reported in this book are based on studies of the predominantly white, able-bodied, North American culture. When groups are multicultural (as is increasingly the case), the dynamics of the group will change, if only slightly. Where relevant information about cultural differences exists, we have included it in the remaining chapters of this book, with a special section on culture and nonverbal communication in Chapter 6. Remember that when cultural differences are present, the importance of interpersonal communication skills in groups increases.

STATUS

"My dad can run faster than your dad."
"Oh, yeah? Well, my dad is smarter than your dad."
"No, he's not!"

"Oh, yes he is!"
"Says who?"
"Says me. Wanna make something of it?"

Even as children people are concerned about status—who is better, brighter, and more beautiful. **Status** refers to an individual's importance. People with higher social status generally have more prestige and command more respect than do people of lower status. Many people want to talk to and talk about, see and be seen with those with high status. They are interested in the lives of high-status individuals. Fan magazines and weekly tabloid newspapers are filled with features about the famous and near famous—status achievers and status seekers. The president of the United States, television personalities, authors, and athletes often provide the names that make name-dropping the pastime of status seekers.

PRIVILEGES ACCORDED TO HIGH-STATUS GROUP MEMBERS

Most people like to be perceived as enjoying some status within a group. Because occupying a position of status fulfills a need for attention, it also builds self-respect and self-esteem. Bormann suggests that high-status positions are pleasant because

> The group makes a high-status person feel important and influential. They show him deference, listen to him, ask his advice, and often reward him with a greater share of the group's goods. He gets a bigger office, more secretaries, better furniture, more salary, a bigger car, and so forth. Even in communication-class discussion groups, the high-status members receive considerable gratification of their social and esteem needs. One of the most powerful forces drawing people into groups is the attraction of high status.[22]

Perhaps you have participated in small groups in which the status of an individual afforded him or her certain privileges that were not available to the

REVIEW BOX

Conformity to Group Norms Depends On:

- Culture
- The individual characteristics of group members
- The clarity of the norm and the certainty of punishment for breaking it
- The number of people who already conform to the norm
- The quality of interpersonal relationships in the group
- The sense of group identification members have developed

rest of the group. The chairperson of the board may have a private dining room or an executive washroom while other members must eat in the company cafeteria and use public washrooms.

EFFECTS OF STATUS DIFFERENCES

In small groups, group members' status or social rank exerts a significant effect on interpersonal relationships. Status affects who talks to whom and how often a member speaks. The status or reputation an individual has before joining a group certainly affects the role he or she assumes. In addition, norms that help groups determine how they will deal with status differences and what privileges they should allow those with greater prestige develop quickly. Several researchers have observed how status differences affect the relationships among members of a small group. Consider the following research conclusions:

1. High-status group members talk more than low-status members.[23]
2. High-status group members communicate more with other high-status members than they do with those of lower status.[24]
3. Low-status group members tend to direct their conversation to high-status group members rather than to those of lower or equal status.[25]
4. Low-status group members communicate more positive messages to high-status members than they do to those of equal or lower status.[26]
5. High-status group members are likely to have more influence on the group's decision making than low-status members.[27]
6. High-status group members usually abide by the norms of the group more than do low-status group members. (The exception to this research finding occurs when high-status members realize that they can violate group norms and receive less punishment than low-status group members would receive; thus, depending on the situation, they may violate certain group norms.)[28]
7. Group members are more likely to ignore the comments and suggestions made by low-status members than those made by high-status members.[29]
8. Low-status group members communicate more irrelevant information than do high-status members.[30]
9. High-status members are less likely to complain about their jobs or their responsibilities.[31]
10. Communication with high-status group members can replace the need for the upward movement of low-status members in the group's status hierarchy.[32]

11. High-status group members tend to talk to the entire group more than members of lower status do.[33]

12. The leader of a small group is usually the member with the highest status. (The exception to this conclusion occurs when the leader emerges because of capability and competence and not necessarily because of popularity. That kind of leader holds a lower status than does a more popular and well-liked group member.)[34]

OBSERVING STATUS DIFFERENCES TO PREDICT GROUP DYMAMICS

Knowing how status affects the relationships among group members helps you predict who will talk with whom. If you can perceive status differences, you can also predict the type of messages communicated in a small group discussion. These research conclusions suggest that the social hierarchy of a group affects group cohesiveness, group satisfaction, and even the quality of a group's solution. This knowledge is a form of power, the subject of our next section.

POWER

Sociologist Robert Bierstedt once observed that "In the entire lexicon of sociological concepts, none is more troublesome than the concept of **power.** We may say about it in general only what St. Augustine said about time, that we all know perfectly well what it is—until someone asks us."[35] While scholars debate definitions of power as well as its relationship to other variables such as status and authority, they generally agree that power, at its core, involves the ability of one person to control or influence some other person.[36] Power in a small group, then, is reflected in an individual's ability to get other members to conform to his or her wishes.

Certain group members may have more power in the group than others. Sometimes the sources of their power are clear to members, such as in groups with large status differences; but in other cases, the sources of power are not so clear. In order to map out the territory of social power in small groups, you need to look at power bases and the effects of power on group processes.

POWER BASES

Your power base in a group is the sum of the resources that you can use to control or influence others. Because no two group members have exactly the

---

REVIEW BOX

Effects of Status Differences in Groups

Group members with high status:
  Talk more
  Communicate more often with other high-status members
  Have more influence
  Generally abide by group norms
  Are less likely to be ignored
  Are less likely to complain about their responsibilities
  Talk to the entire group
  Are likely to serve in leadership roles
Group members with low status:
  Direct conversation to high-status rather than low-status members
  Communicate more positive messages to high-status members
  Are more likely to have their comments ignored
  Communicate more irrelevant information
  Talk to high-status members as a substitute for climbing the social hierarchy in the group

---

same resources, each member operates from a different power base. What are some of these power bases? French and Raven identified five power bases in their study of small groups: legitimate power, referent power, expert power, reward power, and coercive power.[37]

Legitimate power stems from a group member's ability to influence others because of being elected, appointed, or selected to exert control over a group. Legitimate power comes from occupying a position of responsibility. The principal of a school has the legitimate power to control school policy; the senators from your state have legitimate power to represent their constituents. Many of the benefits reported in the previous section for high-status group members reflect this kind of power base. A small group member who has been elected chairperson is given legitimate power to influence the group's procedures.

Referent power is the power of interpersonal attraction. Recall from Chapter 3 that people are attracted to others whom they admire and want to emulate. Put simply, people we like have more power over us than those people we do not like.

Expert power stems from a group member's ability to influence others based on the knowledge and information that the member possesses. As the saying goes, knowledge is power. Suppose you are a member of a group studying ways to improve the environment of the river in your community. If one of your group members has a Ph.D. in aquatic plant life, that person's knowledge and access to information gives him or her expert power. More than likely, that person can influence the group. However, just because a group member has knowledge does not mean that he or she will exert more influence in the group. The group must find the knowledge credible and useful.

Reward power is based on a person's ability to provide rewards for behaviors. If you are in a position to help another member gain money, status, power, acceptance, or other rewards, you will have power over that person. Of course, group members are motivated by different needs and goals. What is rewarding to one may not be rewarding to others. Reward power is effective only if a person finds the reward satisfying or valuable. Others must also believe that a person actually has the power and resources to bestow the reward.

Coercive power, the negative side of reward power, is based on the perception that another can punish you for acting or not acting in a certain way. A person's ability to demote others, reduce their salaries or benefits, force them to work overtime hours, or fire them are examples of resources that can make up this power base. Even though coercive power may achieve a desired effect, group members usually resent threats of punishment intended to make them conform. Punished group members often try to win the next round or escape from heavy-handed efforts to accomplish a group goal.

EFFECTS OF POWER ON GROUP PROCESS

Members who have power influence the group process. Whether their influence will be positive or negative depends on how wisely the members use their influence. The following principles summarize the impact of power on group deliberations:

- The struggle for power among group members can result in poor group decisions and less group cohesion.
- Members who overtly seek dominance and control over a group often focus attention on themselves rather than on achieving group goals. They typically serve as aggressors, blockers, recognition seekers, dominators, or special-interest pleaders (these individual roles were discussed earlier in this chapter). Individuals who seek power make the group less cohesive, and power struggles emphasize individual rather than group agendas.
- Group members with little power often talk less frequently in a group.
- Charles Berger observed that "persons who talk most frequently and for the longest periods of time are assumed to be the most dominant group members. In addition, persons receiving the most communication are

assumed to be most powerful."[38] While not all powerful members dominate group conversations, a relationship exists between verbal contributions to the group and influence. The exceptions to this principle are members who talk so frequently that they are ignored by the group. Cultural variations can influence this perception as well.

- Group members can lose power if other members think they use power for personal gain or to keep a group from achieving its goals.
- Group members usually expect individuals with greater power to have high-status privileges. However, if members believe that powerful members are having a detrimental effect on the group, their credibility and influence are likely to diminish. Too many perks and privileges given to some members sap a group's ability to do its job and can result in challenges to the influential group members.
- Too much power in one individual can lead to less group decision making and more autocratic decision making.
- Autocratic decision making occurs when one person with several power bases (for example, one who can reward and punish, has needed information, is well liked, and has been appointed to lead) makes a decision alone rather than with the group as a whole. Group members may not speak their minds for fear of reprisals.
- Increasing your level of activity in a group can increase your power and influence.
- Groups with equal power distribution show higher quality group communication than do groups with unequal power distribution.[39]

If you are participating in a group and sense that your influence is diminishing, try to participate more and to take an active role in helping the group achieve its goal. Volunteering to help with tasks and increasing your knowledge about group problems, issues, or decisions can also enhance your influence. If you see other group members losing influence, you can give them specific tasks that will bring them back into the group's mainstream (assuming that they are willing to accept the responsibility).

REVIEW BOX

Power Bases

TYPE OF POWER	INFLUENCE BASED ON:
Legitimate	Being elected, appointed, or selected to lead the group
Referent	Being well liked
Expert	A member's knowledge and information
Reward	Providing rewards for desired behavior
Coercive	The ability to punish another

Power and Gender

Stereotypes portray women as being more easily influenced than men and as having less power over others than their male counterparts. However, recent research tends to dispel these illusions. In Sagrestano's study, when women were placed in positions of power, they were just as likely as men to use strategies typically associated with power. Because men typically occupy roles of higher power in society, the opportunity for them to use power strategies is greater than for women. This observation led the researcher to conclude that this unequal distribution of power results in the illusion of gender differences, which are really the result of women's and men's relative social status. Thus, apparent gender differences must be understood within a context of status and power.[40]

Status and Power: A Cultural Footnote

It is important to remember that status is primarily in the eye of the beholder. Frequently status is meaningless when we cross cultural boundaries; your authors' Ph.D.s are not universally revered in a country-and-western bar. Communication scholar Marshall Singer notes that

> The Ph.D. holder and the famous athlete have acquired high status and the ability to influence their respective "constituents." Because high status—whether ascribed or acquired—depends so much on its being perceived as such, it may be the least transferable, across cultural barriers, of all the components of power we are discussing.[41]

Cultural differences in perceptions of status are revealed pointedly in the following letter. On June 17, 1744, the commissioners from Maryland and Virginia negotiated a treaty with the Indians of the Six Nations at Lancaster, Pennsylvania. The Indians were invited to send young men to William and Mary College. The next day they declined the offer as follows.

> We know that you highly esteem the kind of learning taught in those Colleges, and that the Maintenance of our young Men, while with you, would be very expensive to you. We are convinced, that you mean to do us Good by your Proposal; and we thank you heartily. But you, who are wise must know that different Nations have different Conceptions of things and you will therefore not take it amiss, if our ideas of this kind of Education happen not to be the same as yours. We have had some Experience of it. Several of our young People were formerly brought up at the Colleges of the Northern Provinces: they were instructed in all your Sciences; but, when they came back to us, they were bad Runners, ignorant of every means of living in the woods . . . neither fit for Hunters, Warriors, nor Counsellors, they were totally good for nothing.

We are, however, not the less oblig'd by your kind Offer, tho' we decline accepting it; and, to show our grateful Sense of it, if the Gentlemen of Virginia will send us a Dozen of their Sons, we will take Care of their Education, instruct them in all we know, and make Men of them.

TRUST

What do used-car salespeople, politicians, and insurance agents have in common? They are often stereotyped as people whose credibility is suspect. The untrustworthy images such people evoke are not always justified; but when people want something from you, whether it is money or a vote, you are often suspicious of the promises they make. When you trust people, you have faith that they will not try to take advantage of you and that they will be mindful of your best interests. In developing interpersonal relationships in small groups, the degree of trust you have in others affects your relationships with them. The following sections consider how trust in relationships affects group members and suggests how you can elicit more trust as you interact with others.

DEVELOPING TRUSTING RELATIONSHIPS

Why do you trust some people more than others? What is it about your closest friend that enables you to confide your most private feelings? How can group members develop trusting relationships? First, developing trusting relationships in a group takes time. Just as assuming a role in a group discussion requires time, so does developing confidence in others. Second, you base trust on the previous experiences you have had with others. You probably would not give a stranger your bank account number. You would, however, more than likely trust this number to your spouse or to a friend you have known for several years. As you communicate with other people, you gradually learn whether you can trust them. First you observe how an individual completes various tasks and responsibilities. Then you decide whether you can rely on him or her to get things done.

Trust, then, develops when you can predict how another person will behave under certain circumstances. Put another way, trust helps you reduce uncertainty as you form expectations of others. As you participate in a group, you trust those who, because of their actions and support in the past, have given you reason to believe that they will support you in the future. Group members establish trusting relationships as they develop mutual respect and as the group becomes more cohesive.

However, even time and experience cannot guarantee trust. A certain amount of risk is always involved whenever you trust another person. As Reichert suggests, "Trust is always a risk, a kind of leap in the dark. It is not based on any solid proof that the other person will not hurt you . . . trust is always a gamble."[42] Sometimes the gamble does not prove profitable. For example, if you have recently worked in a small group with several people who proved untrustworthy, you may be reluctant to trust others in future groups. Thus, your good and bad experiences in past groups affect the way in which you relate to people in future groups.

SELF-DISCLOSURE

One of the most important ways to establish and maintain trusting relationships with others is through **self-disclosure**—the deliberate communication of information about yourself to others. Self-disclosure, like trust, involves a certain degree of risk. When you reveal personal, private information, you open yourself to the possibility that others might reject you. John Powell, author of the book *why am i afraid to tell you who i am?*, says that people hesitate to disclose much about themselves because "if I tell you who I am, you may not like who I am, and it's all that I have."[43]

Self-disclosure should be timed to suit the occasion and the expectations of the individuals involved. Telling all too soon may violate what the other person expects. In Western cultures, it would not be appropriate to talk about the intimate aspects of your life (for example, your financial net worth or your romantic endeavors) when you first introduce yourself to someone. The other person may feel uncomfortable and want to terminate the relationship. Thus, when you first meet someone, you usually reveal information that is not too threatening or personal. As you establish a trusting relationship with an individual, you may feel more comfortable about discussing private feelings and concerns. Powell notes that the information you reveal about yourself often progresses through several predictable levels:

Level 5: *Cliché communication.* Standard phrases like "Hi, how are you?, Nice to see you, Beautiful weather, isn't it?," and "How's it going?" signal the desire to initiate a relationship.

Level 4: *Facts and biographical information.* You reveal nonthreatening information about yourself, such as your name, hometown, or occupation.

Level 3: *Personal attitudes and ideas.* After introducing yourself and getting down to business, you then respond to various ideas and issues, noting where you agree and disagree with others.

Level 2: *Personal feelings.* Talking about your personal feelings makes you more vulnerable than discussing attitudes and ideas, particularly when you talk about feelings regarding yourself or others.

Level 1: *Peak communication.* People seldom reach this level. Only with your closest friends or people you have known for some time will you share personal insights that may result in rejection. This level of self-disclosure takes much time and trust to develop.[44]

These five levels are merely a means of describing the self-disclosure process, so do not try to classify all of your personal communication with others into one of these categories. Such thinking may detract from an otherwise spontaneous conversation. While self-disclosure should not be used as a tool to manipulate others into trusting relationships, you should develop greater awareness of the self-disclosure process to help evaluate your relationships with others in small groups.

One researcher has described five characteristics of appropriate self-disclosure.[45] First, *self-disclosure is a function of the ongoing relationship*. This means that self-disclosure is not something you do just once; you continually share information about yourself with others.

Second, *self-disclosure is reciprocal:* When you disclose something to another person, that person will probably disclose something to you—at least, if you give him or her an opportunity. If you rarely give others a chance to talk, they probably will not respond to you. If you want to create a climate of trust in your group, you must be willing to share with others.

Third, *self-disclosure is timed to what is happening in your group*. For example, if your group is discussing where a new highway should be located, it would not be appropriate for you to talk about how much you enjoy playing with your cat. In other words, do not disclose just for the sake of disclosing. You comments should be relevant to the discussion at hand.

Fourth, *self-disclosure should deal with what is happening among the people present*. Not only should your self-disclosure be appropriate to an occasion, but it should also be appropriate for the people in your group. You need not talk about a troubled relationship if it clearly is of no concern to the others present. You may find someone who will listen to you, but if the others present have no interest in your confessions, keep them to yourself.

Finally, *self-disclosure usually moves by small increments* (i.e., it takes time). Establishing trusting relationships with others cannot be rushed. If a group of people will meet for only two or three sessions, do not feel compelled to enter into a self-disclosure session. If you ask others to disclose personal information too quickly, group members may interpret your efforts to establish trust as prying into their personal lives. While you should not disclose too much too soon, you should persevere in trying to get to know other group members. Self-disclosure is a useful way to improve relationships.

THE DEVELOPMENT OF GROUP RELATIONSHIPS OVER TIME

It takes time for relationships to develop. You experience some tension and anxiety the first time you participate in a small group. You are uncertain what your role in the group will be. The group has not met long enough for norms to develop. True, in some groups, certain standards of behavior already exist because of the common culture that group members share, but these expectations provide only skeletal guidance for behavior. Status differences among group members can also create tension. Bormann has defined this initial uneasiness as **primary tension,** which is

> the social unease and stiffness that accompanies getting acquainted. Students placed in a discussion group with strangers will experience these tensions most strongly during the opening minutes of their first meetings. The earmarks of primary tensions are extreme politeness, apparent boredom or tiredness, and considerable sighing or yawning. When members show primary tension, they speak softly and tentatively. Frequently they can think of nothing to say, and many long pauses result.[46]

Expect to find some primary tension during initial meetings. It is a normal part of group development. A group leader can minimize this tension, however, by helping members get to know one another. Get-acquainted exercises and brief statements of introduction can ease primary tension. While members of groups that meet only once might deem getting to know one another impractical, using a few minutes to break the ice and reduce some of the primary tension can help create more satisfying relationships among group members.

After a group resolves primary tension and its members become more comfortable with one another, another type of tension develops. **Secondary tension,** according to Bormann, occurs as conflicts arise and as differences of opinion emerge. Whether recognized as a personality conflict or simply as a disagreement, secondary tension surfaces when group members try to solve the problem, accomplish the task, or resolve specific issues facing the group. Secondary tension also is the result of power struggles. Secondary tension usually establishes group norms. Joking or laughing often helps manage secondary tension. However cohesive a group may be, some conflict over procedure will normally develop as relationships among members form. Chapter 7 will discuss the phases of a group's growth and development in more detail, and Chapter 9 will consider some suggestions for managing the conflict and controversy that result from secondary tension.

REVIEW BOX

Group Tension

Primary tension:	Uneasiness and uncomfortableness in getting acquainted and managing initial group uncertainty about the group task and group relationships
Secondary tension:	Tension that occurs as group members struggle for influence, develop roles and norms, and explore differences in approaching the group task

PUTTING PRINCIPLE INTO PRACTICE

Five variables affect and reflect individuals' relationships with others in small groups: roles, norms, status, power, and trust. An understanding of how these concepts affect your performance and the performance of other group members will help you explain and predict the types and quality of relationships that form in small groups. As you attempt to apply the information presented in this chapter, consider these suggestions:

ROLES

- Roles grow out of self-concept, which is based on a composite of life experiences. These experiences are influenced by gender and culture, as well as by the significant groups to which we have belonged. Work to understand your own self-concept to help understand your role in small groups.
- If no one performs important group roles, point this out to the group or assume the responsibility for performing them yourself.
- If you observe one or more group members hindering the progress of your group because they are adopting an individual group role (blocker, aggressor, recognition seeker, etc.), bring this to the attention of the group or the offending group member.
- Do not try to fit yourself or other group members into just one or two group roles. You and other group members can assume several roles during the course of a discussion.

NORMS

- Identify group norms by noting repeated patterns of behavior.
- Another way to identify group norms is by noting what kind of offenses group members punish.
- Consider the individual characteristics of group members, the clarity of norms and the certainty of punishment for breaking them, the number of people who have broken norms, the quality of relationships among group members, and the sense of group identification to help determine whether members will conform to the group norms.

CULTURE

Culturally diverse groups often have difficulty establishing satisfactory roles and norms because of differences in cultural expectations. Such groups require extra effort in group building and maintenance.

When group members do not share a common native language, some additional tactics may be necessary:[47]

- *Slow down* communication.
- *Repeat* or paraphrase when nonverbal expressions suggest that listeners do not understand.
- *Verify* common understanding by having others restate the argument or idea.
- If necessary (and possible), encourage *restatement* in the listener's native language.

Remember that cultures vary widely in conversational style as well as the appropriateness assigned to topics of conversation. Do not make the mistake of attributing such differences to impoliteness or insensitivity.

Status

- Identify the status of group members by the privileges that high-status group members receive.
- If you can spot status differences in small groups, you can predict who talks to whom.
- If you are aware of status differences, you can communicate more effectively and with greater influence.

Power

- People develop power in a group because they can provide information, expertise, rewards, and punishment; because they have been elected or appointed; or because they are well liked or have status in the group.
- Consider the possible sources of power in your group to help you understand patterns of influence.
- Work to maximize the positive sources of power for *all* group members.

Trust

- In most groups, don't expect trusting relationships to form too soon—it takes time for trust to develop.
- Self-disclosure is an important factor in developing trusting relationships with others. Self-disclosures and trust involve risk. Taking these risks with others helps them to do the same with you.

Self-Disclosure

- Do not think that self-disclosure just happens once when the group first gets together; it is a function of ongoing group relationships.
- Do not talk solely about yourself without giving other people a chance to talk about themselves.

- Appropriate self-disclosure should deal with what is happening among the persons present. Your revelations should be relevant to the discussion at hand.
- Take your time self-disclosing; appropriate self-disclosure moves by small increments.
- Use get-acquainted exercises and brief statements of introduction during the first group meeting to help manage primary tension.

PRACTICE

NORM EXERCISES

Several behaviors are listed below. For each one, indicate how appropriate or inappropriate you think it would be as a norm for your group. Write the number that shows your best estimate of how the group would feel—5 if the behavior is definitely appropriate as a norm, 4 if the behavior is somewhat appropriate, 3 if the behavior is questionable, 2 if it is somewhat inappropriate, and 1 if it is definitely inappropriate.[48]

_____ 1. Said little or nothing in most meetings.
_____ 2. Talked about the details of her sex life.
_____ 3. Brought up problems he had with others who were not in the group.
_____ 4. Kissed another group member.
_____ 5. Asked for reactions or feedback ("How do you see me in this group?").
_____ 6. Talked mostly about what was going on in the group.
_____ 7. Frequently joked.
_____ 8. Pleaded for help.
_____ 9. Challenged other members' remarks.
_____ 10. Said she was not getting anything out of being in the group.
_____ 11. Described his reactions to what was taking place in the group.
_____ 12. Highlighted opposition among ideas.
_____ 13. Formed a contract with another member about the use of each other's resources in meeting both their needs and goals.
_____ 14. Refused to be bound by a group decision.
_____ 15. Asked for the goal to be clarified.
_____ 16. Noted competition in the group and asked how it could be reduced.
_____ 17. Gave advice to other group members about what to do.
_____ 18. Interrupted a dialogue between two members.
_____ 19. Told another member that she was unlikable.
_____ 20. Was often absent.
_____ 21. Shouted with anger at another member.
_____ 22. With strong feelings, told another member how likable he was.

_____ 23. Tried to manipulate the group to get her own way.
_____ 24. Hit another group member.
_____ 25. Acted indifferently to other members.
_____ 26. Dominated the group's discussion for more than one session.
_____ 27. Encouraged other group members to react to the topic under discussion.
_____ 28. Tried to convince members of the rightness of a certain point of view.
_____ 29. Talked a lot without showing his real feelings.
_____ 30. Told the group off, saying that it was worthless.
_____ 31. Showed she had no intention of changing her behavior.
_____ 32. Resisted the suggestions of other members about procedures.
_____ 33. Commented that the decision-making procedure was not appropriate to the nature of the decision.
_____ 34. Asked that the causes of a group problem be analyzed.
_____ 35. Expressed affection for several group members.

After reacting to these items, the members of your group may think of other behavioral norms to include. Once all members have rated the group norms, the group should discuss them and decide how each affects the cohesion of the group.

GROUP ROLE INVENTORY

When you see yourself differently from the way others see you, when there is a difference between role perception and role enactment, or when your expectations of people cloud your perceptions of them, there is a potential for uncertainty, confusion, frustration, and conflict. The group role inventory was designed to help members become more aware of the roles they play and of how others perceive those roles. It is time-consuming (it takes at least 45 minutes) but worth the time and effort, particularly when a group is having trouble establishing norms. The group role inventory can also be an effective means of dealing with one or two problem members by bringing everyone's role expectations into the discussion rather than by ganging up on the troublemakers.

Objectives: To become aware of the roles you play in your group and of how others perceive your roles
Materials: Group role inventory sheet (attached)
Time: 45 minutes
Participants: Ongoing groups
Procedures: 1. Fill out group role inventory sheet.
  2. Go over the list and check the role you would like to have performed but did not perform.

>   3. Go over the list again and star (*) the role you per-
>   formed but would rather not have performed.
>
>   4. Discuss results with your group.

Application: The exercise should make members aware of how roles
are used in their groups.

GROUP ROLE INVENTORY SHEET

Who in your group, including yourself, is most likely to:

1. Take initiative, propose ideas, get things started?
2. Sit back and wait passively for others to lead?
3. Express feelings most freely, frankly, openly?
4. Keep feelings hidden, reserved, unexpressed?
5. Show understanding of other members' feelings?
6. Be wrapped up in personal concerns and not very responsive to others?
7. Interrupt others when they are speaking?
8. Daydream, be lost in private thoughts during group sessions, be "far away"?
9. Give you a feeling of encouragement, warmth, friendly interest, support?
10. Converse privately with someone else while another member is speaking to the group?
11. Talk of trivial things, engage in superficial chitchat?
12. Criticize, put people on their guard?
13. Feel superior to other members?
14. Be listened to by everyone while speaking?
15. Feel inferior to other members?
16. Contribute good ideas?
17. Contradict, disagree, argue, raise objections?
18. Sulk or withdraw when the group is displeasing?
19. Be the one you would like to have on your side if a conflict arose in the group?
20. Agree or conform with whatever is said?
21. Be missed, if absent, more than any other member?

NOTES

1. For a full discussion of gender and communication, see Julia T. Wood, *Gendered Lives: Communication, Gender and Culture* (Belmont, Calif: Wadsworth, 1993).
2. T. Veenendall and R. Braito, "Androgyny in Spouse Interaction," in L. P. Stewart and S. Ting-Toomey (eds.), *Communication, Gender, and Sex Roles in Diverse Interaction Contexts* (Norwood, N.J.: Ablex, 1987).
3. J. C. Pearson and R. West, "An Initial Investigation of the Effects of Gender on Student Questions in the Classroom: Developing a Descriptive Base," *Communication Education* 40 (1991):22–32.

4. Dean Barnlund, *Communicative Styles of Japanese and Americans: Images and Realities* (Belmont, Calif: Wadsworth, 1989).

5. J. C. McCroskey and V. P. Richmond, "Willingness to Communicate: Differing Cultural Perspectives," *The Southern Communication Journal* 56 (1990): 72–77.

6. M. L. Hecht, S. Ribeau, and J. K. Alberts, "An Afro-American Perspective on Interethnic Communication," *Communication Monographs* 56 (1989): 385–410.

7. Charles T. Brown and Paul W. Keller, *Monologue to Dialogue* (Englewood Cliffs, N.J.: Prentice-Hall, 1973), 2.

8. Kenneth D. Benne and Paul Sheats, "Functional Roles of Group Members," *Journal of Social Issues* 4 (Spring 1948): 41–49.

9. Ernest G. Bormann, *Discussion and Group Methods: Theory and Practice.* 3rd ed. (New York: Harper & Row, 1989), 209.

10. S. Schacter, "Deviation, Rejection, and Communication," *Journal of Abnormal and Social Psychology* 46 (1951): 190–207.

11. Marshall Scott Poole, "Group Communication and the Structuring Process," in Robert S. Cathcart and Larry A. Samovar (eds.), *Small Group Communication: A Reader,* 5th ed. (Dubuque, Iowa: Wm. C. Brown, 1988), 275–87.

12. H. T. Reitan and Marvin E. Shaw, "Group Membership, Sex-Composition of the Group, and Conformity Behavior," *Journal of Social Psychology* 64 (1964): 45–51.

13. Marvin Shaw, *Group Dynamics: The Psychology of Small Group Behavior* (New York: McGraw-Hill, 1981), 281.

14. Charles R. Bantz, "Cultural Diversity and Group Cross-Cultural Team Research," *Journal of Applied Communication Research* 21 (1993): 1–20.

15. T. Katriel, *Communicative Style in Cross-Cultural Perspective: Arabs and Jews in Israel.* Paper presented at the annual meeting of the Western Speech Communication Association, Sacramento, Calif, 1990.

16. Barnlund, *Communicative Styles of Japanese and Americans,* 1989.

17. Satoshi Ishii and Tom Bruneau, "Silence and Silences in Cross-Cultural Perspective: Japan and the United States," in Larry A. Samovar and Richard E. Porter (eds.), *Intercultural Communication: A Reader,* 6th ed. (Belmont, Calif: Wadsworth, 1991).

18. John Condon, ". . . So Near the United States: Notes on Communication between Mexicans and North Americans," In Samovar and Porter, (eds.), *Intercultural Communication: A Reader,* 6th ed. (Belmont, Calif.: Wadsworth, 1991).

19. Thomas K. Fitzgerald, *Metaphors of Identity: A Culture-Communication Dialogue* (Albany: State University of New York Press, 1993).

20. Condon, 11.

21. Dawn O. Braithwaite, "Viewing Persons with Disabilities as a Culture," in Larry A. Samovar and Richard E. Porter, *Interculturae Communication* (Belmont, Calif.: Wadsworth, 1991).

22. Bormann, *Discussion and Group Methods,* 215.

23. J. I. Hurwitz, A. F. Zander, and B. Hymovitch, "Some Effects of Power on the Relations among Group Members," in D. Cartwright and A. Zander (eds.), *Group Dynamics: Research and Theory* (New York: Harper & Row, 1953), pp. 483–92.

24. Ibid.

25. Ibid.

26. D. C. Barnlund and C. Harland, "Propinquity and Prestige as Determinants of Communication Networks," *Sociometry* 26 (1963):467–79.

27. Shaw, 246.

28. George C. Homans, *The Human Group* (New York: Harcourt Brace and World, 1992).

29. John K. Brilhart, *Effective Group Discussion* (Dubuque, Iowa: Wm. C. Brown, 1978), 36.

30. H. H. Kelly, "Communication in Experimentally Created Hierarchies," *Human Relations* 4 (1951): 36–56.

31. Ibid.

32. Ibid.

33. Bormann, *Discussion and Group Methods*, p. 215.

34. Ibid.

35. Robert Bierstedt, "An Analysis of Social Power," *American Sociological Review* 6 (1950):7–30.

36. Shaw, *Group Dynamics*, 294.

37. J. R. P. French and B. H. Raven, "The Bases of Social Power," in D. Cartwright and A. Zander (eds.), *Group Dynamics* (Evanston, Ill.: Row, Peterson, 1962), 607–23.

38. Charles R. Berger, "Power in the Family," in Michael Roloff and Gerald Miller (eds.), *Persuasion: New Direction in Theory and Research* (Beverly Hills, Calif.: Sage Publications, 1980), 217.

39. Marshall R. Singer, *Intercultural Communication: a Perceptual Approach* (Englewood Cliffs, N.J.: Prentice-Hall, 1987), 118.

40. Linda M. Sagrestano, "Power Strategies in Interpersonal Relationships: The Effects of Expertise and Gender," *Psychology of Women Quarterly* 16 (1992): 481–95.

41. Shu-Chu Sarrina Li, *Power and Its Relationship with Group Communication,* unpublished doctoral dissertation, University of Iowa, 1993.

42. Richard Reichert, *Self-Awareness through Group Dynamics* (Dayton, Ohio: Pflaum/Standard, 1970), 21.

43. John Powell, *why am i afraid to tell you who i am?* (Niles, Ill.: Argus Communications, 1990), 12.

44. Ibid., pp. 54–58.

45. Joseph Luft, *Of Human Interaction* (Palo Alto, Calif.: National Press, 1969), 132–33.

46. Bormann, *Discussion and Group Methods*, 181–82.

47. Adapted from Charles R. Bontz, "Cultural Diversity and Group Cross-Cultural Team Research," *Journal of Applied Communication Research* 21 (1993): 12.

48. David W. Johnson and Frank P. Johnson. *Joining Together: Group Theory and Group Skills* (Englewood Cliffs, N.J.: Prentice-Hall, 1994), 421.

CHAPTER
F·I·V·E

Improving Group Climate

After studying this chapter, you will be able to:

- Observe a group discussion and identify behaviors that contribute to a defensive or supportive group climate.

- Identify examples of confirming and disconfirming interpersonal responses.

- Explain three types of listening in small groups.

- Describe two major barriers to effective listening.

- Observe, identify, and describe at least four factors in group cohesiveness.

- Explain communication networks and their effects on group climate and individual satisfaction.

- Describe the relationships among group size, composition, and climate.

- Explain the relationship between group climate and productivity.

- Communicate in ways that are more likely to improve group climate.

*W*hat does the word *climate* call to mind? If you've taken a course in geography or meteorology or have studied weather patterns, you may think of temperature gradients, barometric pressure, and how bodies of water, latitude, ocean currents, and mountains affect the weather of a particular region. Look out your window. What is the weather like? Does today's weather make you want to curl up with a book? Go to the beach? Go skiing? Would you say that climate affects your desire to engage in certain activities? How do you feel about a cold, snowy night spent in front of a roaring fire in a cozy room?

Group climate is roughly analogous to geographical climate. A variety of factors interact to create a group feeling or atmosphere. How group members communicate, to whom they communicate, and how often they communicate influence their satisfaction as well as productivity. You may have participated in groups where there was a genuine sense of warmth, trust, camaraderie, and accomplishment. This chapter examines how people communicate in ways that help the group establish a positive climate.

A CASE STUDY

Not long ago I received a rather mysterious telephone call from a good friend. He said that he and his wife had a business proposition for me and my wife, which they would like to discuss as soon as they could. No, he really didn't want to discuss any details over the phone. When could we meet? Tuesday evening? At my place? They'd see us then.

Our curiosity piqued, we anxiously awaited the Tuesday evening rendezvous. What could our friends possibly have up their sleeves? The appointed hour arrived. Right on time, the doorbell rang. ("Unusual," we thought, "they're usually a half-hour late.") Our next surprise was that our friend George was dressed in a three-piece suit, his wife Margaret in a tailored dress. My wife and I looked at each other in our jeans, bare feet, and T-shirts, then returned our gaze to George and Margaret and asked whether they had just returned from a funeral. They laughed nervously, marched past us, and began to set up a small demonstration board on our dining room table. Turning down our offer of wine, they asked if we could begin the meeting. This was becoming stranger by the moment. My wife, Nancy, and I were beginning to feel as if we had invited insurance agents into our home even though we had gone camping, hiking, canoeing, and spent many an evening with George and Margaret over many a beer. Something didn't fit, but our curiosity was aroused so we decided to play along.

It wasn't long before the experience began to get frustrating. George and Margaret asked us what we wanted out of life. We suggested that they probably ought to have some idea of that by now—that most of our goals were inward, state-of-being kinds of goals, like having a greater awareness of ourselves and others, peace of mind, and so forth. This answer agitated our guests, who responded by suggesting that it might be nice if we never again had to worry about money. We agreed that it would, indeed, be pleasant. At this, they seemed to breathe a little more easily and proceeded to haul out charts, graphs, and illustrations which, they claimed, proved that we could double our present income in a little over a year—in our spare time, of course.

After an hour, George and Margaret were still refusing to tell us what it was we would have to sell (we'd figured out *that* much) or to whom we'd have to sell it. ("Please bear with us until the end," they said.) Something was definitely wrong. Here I was sitting in my own dining room with my wife, my friends, and a glass of wine, yet I felt as if I were back in junior high being asked to please hold all my questions until the end. I've had the same experience with life insurance and encyclopedia salespeople. They were treating us not as people, but as faceless members of that great mass of consumers whom sales manuals target and who serve as the inspiration for countless commercials in which housewives dance, sing, and extol the virtues of airtight plastic containers, soap powders, and kitchen floors that shine like new.

George and Margaret were still making their pitch. They had finally revealed the name of the company and its line of products and were now setting about the task of showing how rapidly the company had grown due to its unique marketing concepts, fine products which sell themselves (of course), and so forth. It didn't matter, I had already decided not to do it. I felt dehumanized, abused by my friends. Why hadn't they simply told us that they were involved with the company (which we had heard of long before) and that they'd like to explore the possibilities of our becoming involved as well? With friends, it would be a much more effective approach—certainly a more honest one.

The formal part of the presentation was over. They were asking for our comments and questions. I was ready. As a communication professor, I am well versed in the art of critiquing oral presentations and visual aids. I proceeded to evaluate their entire presentation, emphasizing their failure to adequately analyze their audience and to adapt their communication style accordingly. George and Margaret were shocked and hurt. They had not, they said, come into our home to be criticized. They had come in good faith with an honest proposal from which we all stood to benefit. If they had offended us, they were sorry. No, they still did not care for a glass of wine. We'd get together again sometime soon.

DEFENSIVE COMMUNICATION

Pause for a moment and ask: What was wrong with this picture? How many causes can you identify for the deterioration of the situation described in the case study? This case study illustrates many of the principles discussed in this text. Clearly, some group norms were being violated, particularly the interpersonal expectations of openness and honesty. Likewise, group roles to which all of the participants had adjusted were altered dramatically as new roles of "salesperson" and "critic" were introduced. Messages, both verbal and nonverbal, were interpreted differently (e.g., their "professional" attire seemed out of place to us). The scenario is a particularly good example of the type of communication which fosters a *defensive climate* in the small group.

A closer look at the case study reveals that from the first telephone call, information was withheld—a pattern that repeated itself throughout the entire episode. When George and Margaret arrived they were dressed in a very businesslike fashion, suggesting a change in what had become a typical pattern of interaction for the two couples. George and Margaret took *control* of the conversation. They maintained control of information and, to an extent, controlled others' choices (through limiting alternative responses). The response to George and Margaret was defensive, verbal aggression. I gave an evaluative critique of the presentation which aroused further defensiveness, hurt, and anger in a cyclical process that left old questions unanswered and new ones unasked. In short, it was a very uncomfortable and unproductive evening. The specific examples of **defensive communication** we find occurring here are *strategy, control,* and *evaluation.*

DEFENSIVE AND SUPPORTIVE CLIMATES

For several years Dr. Jack Gibb observed the communicative behavior of people in groups and identified the types of behaviors that contribute to defensive climates and supportive climates. Gibb suggests that a defensive climate is clearly counterproductive in any group.

> The person who behaves defensively, even though he also gives some attention to the common task, devotes an appreciable portion of his energy to defending himself. Besides talking about the topic, he thinks about how he appears to others, how he may be seen more favorably, how he may win, dominate, impress, or escape punishment, and/or how he may avoid or mitigate a perceived or an anticipated attack.[1]

More recent research continues to reinforce the relationship of a supportive climate to productivity.[2] The key to building a supportive climate in the group lies, of course, in communication; and in this case it is not so much *what* people communicate as *how* they communicate it. A message can be delivered in ways that evoke support or defense. Consider some examples based on Gibb's categories.

EVALUATION VERSUS DESCRIPTION

Problem solving in small groups involves generating and evaluating ideas. Unfortunately, not all ideas are perfect, and the group needs to discover this if

LITZLER

" ...AND THEN, APPARENTLY THEY STONED THE COMMITTEE CHAIRMAN. "

it is to reach the most effective decision. When someone puts forth a less-than-perfect idea, you can respond by saying, "You idiot, that's the most ridiculous idea I've heard in a decade," or you can say, "As I think through that idea and apply it to our problem, I run up against some other problems. Am I missing something?" Imagine yourself on the receiving end of the first comment. How do you feel? You have just been put down and are likely to be defensive. This is an example of evaluation (albeit an extreme one). The second response, an example of description, is much more effective and supportive. Your idea may, in fact, be terrible, but at least the second response allows you to save face. It also keeps the door open for further discussion of your idea. Quite possibly, further investigation into your bad idea may lead to a better idea.

A supportive group climate can lead to greater productivity.

In a nutshell, *evaluation* is "you" language: It directs itself to the other person's worth or the worth of that person's ideas. As a result, it can provoke much defensiveness. *Description,* on the other hand, is "I" language: It describes the speaker's thoughts about the person or idea. This type of response leads to more trust and cohesiveness in groups.

CONTROL VERSUS PROBLEM ORIENTATION

Communicative behavior that aims at controlling others can produce much defensiveness in group members. This pattern characterizes many aggressive salespeople who, quite intentionally, manipulate you into answering trivial questions that lead up to the final question of whether or not you want to buy a product. Various persuasive tactics aim at controlling behavior (as any student of television commercials can observe). Implicit in attempts to control lies the assumption that the controller knows what is good for the controllee—the "I know what's good for you" assumption. When people become aware of this attitude, they frequently get defensive.

In a group, *problem orientation* is a more effective approach. If others perceive you as a person who genuinely strives for a solution that will benefit all concerned (rather than just yourself), this perception will contribute to a supportive climate, greater cohesiveness, and increased productivity.

Communication that is spontaneous is perceived as more supportive than is communication that appears planned.

STRATEGY VERSUS SPONTANEITY

Like controlling behavior, strategy suggests manipulation. The effects of strategy on the group's climate can be seen in the case study that began this chapter. Because we perceived George and Margaret to be withholding information and acting with hidden motivations, we became defensive. We felt used and manipulated. Again, this sort of behavior places the self before the group and does not lead to the most effective solutions to group problems.

On the other hand, if others perceive you as a person who acts *spontaneously* (that is, not from hidden motivations or agendas) and as a person who immediately and honestly responds to the present situation, you are likely to contribute to creating a more supportive climate.

NEUTRALITY VERSUS EMPATHY

If you behave in a detached, uncaring fashion, as if the people in your group and the outcome of the group's process do not concern you in the least, your behavior will probably arouse defensiveness. Involvement and concern for the group task and for other group members are perceived as supportive.

SUPERIORITY VERSUS EQUALITY

If you feel superior, a small group meeting is not the place to show it. You probably know people who approach you in class after tests have been returned and ask, "What'd ya get?" Frequently these students use this question merely as a preface to showing you their superior grade. Most people think such behavior is obnoxious. It makes them feel defensive. In groups, some people preface their remarks with words such as "obviously" or point out their greater knowledge, experience, or some other attribute that makes them superior to other members. Most likely, their behavior will meet with some resistance. People create more supportive climates when they indicate a willingness to enter into participative planning with mutual trust and respect.

CERTAINTY VERSUS PROVISIONALISM

Do you know people who always have all the answers, whose ideas are truths to be defended, who are intolerant of those with the wrong (that is, different) attitudes? These highly dogmatic people are well known for the defensiveness they produce in others. The usual response is to want to prove them wrong. This behavior is counterproductive in groups. Individuals are likely to be more effective if their attitudes appear to be held *provisionally;* that is, if they appear flexible and genuinely committed to solving problems rather than to simply taking sides on issues. If people leave themselves open to new information and can admit that, from time to time, they may be wrong about something, they will be more effective group members and will help build more supportive group climates.

As a communicator, you control you own actions. Your knowledge of defensive and supportive behaviors will help you make your group work more effectively. Another area of research and application in group climate is interpersonal confirmation and disconfirmation. This research deals not with communicative behaviors that you initiate, but with the ways in which you respond to other group members.

DISCONFIRMING AND CONFIRMING RESPONSES

Group process often seems to go nowhere. Questions are left unanswered and ideas remain ignored. One of the most frequent complaints among group members is that communication in the group seems disconnected and disjointed, fostering vague feelings of uneasiness, as if the members are being disregarded.[3] Unfortunately, this is a common phenomenon and one that does not satisfy task, process, or individual needs. While attending a series of committee meetings, one observer noted that hardly anyone directly acknowledged what anyone else said. Rather, the meetings proceeded as a series of soliloquies. Not surprisingly, most group members expressed dissatisfaction with the group's process and frustration with their inability to reach decisions.

In an investigation of communication in effective and ineffective groups, Evelyn Sieburg examined the ways in which group members responded to the communicative acts of others. In this seminal study and in later work with Carl Larson, Sieburg identified several types of responses

REVIEW BOX

Defensive and Supportive Communication

DEFENSIVE COMMENTS

Evaluation: "You language"; calls into question the worth of the person.

Control: Aims at getting others to do what you want them to do.

Strategy: Planned communication; working from a "script"—for example, saying something nice before criticizing someone; a "psychological sandwich."

Neutrality: Emotional indifference; "You'll get over it."

Superiority: Attitude that you're better than the other person; "I'm okay, you're not okay."

Certainty: Taking dogmatic, rigid positions; "Don't bother me with facts, my mind is made up." Usually more interested in winning an argument than in solving a problem.

SUPPORTIVE COMMENTS

Description: "I language"; describes your own feelings and ideas.

Problem orientation: Communication aimed at solving problems: "Let's find a solution that works for both of us."

Spontaneity: Here-and-now orientation; being honest rather than planning how to manipulate.

Empathy: Emotional involvement; nonverbal behavior is important.

Equality: Communication based on mutual respect; "I'm okay, you're okay."

Provisionalism: Openness to receiving new information; showing some flexibility in the positions you take.

that she classified as *confirming* or *disconfirming*. Simply stated, **confirming responses** are those that cause people to value themselves more, while **disconfirming responses** are those that cause people to value themselves less.[4] Sieburg's identification of confirming and disconfirming responses has been one of the most salient contributions to the understanding of group climate.

Some interpersonal responses are obvious examples of confirmation and disconfirmation, such as when a person responds to another with overt praise or sharp criticism. However, group members confirm and disconfirm one another in more subtle ways. Sieburg and Larson identify some of those behaviors as follows.

DISCONFIRMING RESPONSES

1. *Impervious response.* When one speaker fails to acknowledge, even minimally, the other speaker's communicative attempt the response may be called impervious.

2. *Interrupting response.* When one speaker cuts the other speaker short or begins while the other is still speaking, the response may be called interrupting.

3. *Irrelevant response.* When one speaker responds in a way that seems unrelated to what the other has been saying, or when one speaker introduces a new topic without warning or returns to his or her earlier topic, apparently disregarding the intervening conversation, the response may be called irrelevant.

4. *Tangential response.* When one speaker acknowledges the other person's communication but immediately takes the conversation in another direction, the response may be called tangential. Occasionally, individuals exhibit what may appear to be direct responses to the other, such as "Yes, but. . . " or "Well, you may be right, but. . . ," and then respond with communicative content very different from what preceded. Responses such as these may still be called tangential.

5. *Impersonal response.* When a speaker conducts a monologue, when his or her speech communication behavior appears intellectualized and impersonal, when the speech contains few first-person statements and many generalized "you" or "one" statements—and is heavily loaded with euphemisms or clichés—the response may be called impersonal.

6. *Incoherent response.* When the speaker responds with incomplete sentences; with rambling, difficult-to-follow statements; with sentences containing much retracing or rephrasing; or with interjections such as "you know" or "I mean," the response may be called incoherent.

7. *Incongruous response.* When the speaker engages in nonvocal behavior that seems inconsistent with the vocal content, the response may be called incongruous. For example, "Who's angry? I'm not angry!" (said in a tone and volume that strongly suggest anger), or "I'm really concerned about you" (said in a tone that suggests lack of interest or disdain).

CONFIRMING RESPONSES

1. *Direct acknowledgement.* One speaker acknowledges the other's communication and reacts to it directly and verbally.

2. *Agreement about content.* One speaker reinforces information expressed by the other.

3. *Supportive response.* One speaker expresses understanding of the other, reassures the other, or tries to make the other feel better.

4. *Clarifying response.* One speaker tries to clarify the content of the other's message or attempts to clarify the other's feelings. The usual form of a clarifying response is to elicit more information, to encourage the other to say more, or to repeat in an inquiring way what was understood.

Our self esteem is affected by how others respond to us. Confirming responses cause us to value ourselves more.

5. *Expression of positive feeling.* One speaker describes his or her own positive feelings related to prior utterances of the other. For example, "Okay, now I understand what you are saying."[5]

When you perceive others' behavior as threatening to your emotional security or position in a group, your uncertainty about your role in the group increases. Individual needs are elevated to a place equal to or even greater than the group's task and process needs. If you respond defensively, you are likely to evoke further defensiveness from the rest of the group. People do not trust one another in a defensive, disconfirming climate. The realization that you cannot trust another suggests that that person's behavior is unpredictable—that you do not know for sure how he or she will respond. Such uncertainty is counterproductive in a problem-solving group. On the other hand, in a supportive, confirming climate, where mutual respect and trust prevail, you are more certain of your own well-being. This security, in turn, allows you to increase your concentration on the task and the process needs of the group.

The implication of this research for improving communicative effectiveness and thus the effectiveness of groups is this: By using confirming responses rather than disconfirming responses when communicating with other group members, people contribute toward a supportive, trustful climate and therefore promote greater group effectiveness and individual satisfaction.

LISTENING

Poor listening habits are one of the most common sources of defensiveness and disconfirmation. If you do not actively attend to what another person says, your responses will be perfunctory at best and apathetic, impervious, or tangential at worst. It is even easier to be a poor listener in groups than it is in interpersonal situations, because you do not have to respond to the speaker. After all, the others can always pick up the conversation. However, groups cannot reach their maximum effectiveness unless all members listen actively to one another.

Listening is a skill that can be improved with practice. It is an active process through which people select, attend, understand, and remember. To listen effectively, people must actively select and attend to the messages they receive. This involves filtering out the other stimuli that compete for their attention: the hunger pangs they're starting to feel, reminders of the groceries they need to pick up on the way home, curiosity about the attractive person nearby. Improving any skill takes knowledge and practice. This section will provide some knowledge. The practice is up to you. Are you listening?

TYPES OF LISTENING

Allan Glatthorn and Herbert Adams suggest that the three types of listening are hearing, analyzing, and empathizing.[6]

Hearing.   Hearing is the fundamental type of listening on which the other two types are built. "Hearing is receiving the message as sent."[7] Glatthorn and Adams point out that in order to achieve this seemingly simple objective, you must perform several complex operations. You must:

> Receive the sounds as transmitted
>
> Translate these sounds into the words and meanings that were intended
>
> Understand the relationship of those words in the sentences spoken
>
> Note the relevant nonverbal cues that reinforce the message
>
> Comprehend the entire message as intended[8]

Viewed in this way, hearing becomes a great deal more than a physiological response to stimuli. To say "I hear you" takes on new meaning.

Analyzing.   Analyzing is "discerning the purpose of the speaker and using critical or creative judgment." Analyzing is based on hearing but goes far beyond; it includes making judgments about unspoken messages, as well as the broader context in which messages were received. For example, many messages in small groups are aimed at persuading other group members. Often these messages contain emotional appeals, such as "Our group's failure to stand up in support of anti-abortion laws is tantamount to murder!"

Hearing this message is not difficult, particularly if the speaker's nonverbal behavior reinforces it. Analyzing it is a bit trickier. An appropriate response requires that you analyze the content of the message, the intent of the speaker, and the context within which the transaction takes place. You need to consider the persuasive strategy the speaker is employing, his or her degree of commitment to the issue, the nature and objectives of the group, and the probable positions other group members hold on the issue. In short, to respond with maximum effectiveness, you need to consider multiple factors instantaneously. Glatthorn and Adams claim that analyzing involves the following steps:

Hearing the message accurately

Identifying the stated purpose

Inferring the unstated purpose

Determining if a critical or creative judgment is required

Responding accordingly[9]

Empathizing.   Empathizing is the most complex and difficult type of listening. It requires concentration, a sensitivity to the emotional content of messages, an ability to see the world from the speaker's viewpoint, and a willingness to suspend judgment. Empathizing involves hearing and analyzing but again moves beyond them. It involves these steps:

Hearing the message accurately

Listening to the unstated purpose

Withholding judgment

Seeing the world from the speaker's perspective

Sensing the unspoken words

Responding with acceptance[10]

Often problems that affect a group are expressed obliquely—not in the words themselves, but in the feelings behind the words.

CINDY: You all can do whatever you want to do. I'll go along with anything.

TONI: You sound as if you're not all here tonight. Is it something you can talk about?

CINDY: Oh, I'm having some problems at home. It'll all work out, but I can't get it out of my mind. I'm sorry if I'm a little distant tonight.

FLOYD: That's okay. We understand.

Cindy has a problem that she brought with her to the group. While her problem does not affect the group directly, it can be a potential source of misunderstanding and conflict. Her seeming lack of interest in the group may be a cause for unwarranted anger:

CINDY: You all can do whatever you want. I'll go along with anything.

LOU: Dammit, Cindy, I'm not going to let you get away with that. This group needs your ideas as much as anyone's, and you just can't sit back and let us do all the work.

This insensitive response reflects Lou's failure to empathize, which results in a disconfirming response to Cindy. Toni's empathizing response in the first dialogue, however, was accepting and supporting. It promoted the group's understanding of the situation, which led to a more positive group climate.

There are many good reasons to listen effectively, among them that there is a relationship between listening and leadership: Group members perceived as poor listeners are not typically perceived as occupying leadership positions. People seen as leaders are also seen as good listeners.[11]

BARRIERS TO EFFECTIVE LISTENING

As explained earlier, listening is the process of selecting, attending, understanding, and remembering. The previous discussion suggests that this process can take place at a number of levels. To fully attend to, understand, and remember what another is saying at any of these levels requires that you overcome the common obstacles to effective listening. There are many such barriers—outside distractions, an uncomfortable chair, a headache—but the focus here will be on two prevalent and serious barriers: prejudging and rehearsing.

Prejudging the Communicator or the Communication   Sometimes you simply dislike some people or always disagree with them. You anticipate that what these people will say will be offensive, and you begin to tune them out. An example of this is many people's tendency not to listen carefully to the speeches of politicians who hold political beliefs different from their own. In a group, you must overcome the temptation to ignore those you think are boring, pedantic, or offensive. Good ideas can come from anyone, even from people you do not like. Likewise, you should not prejudge certain topics as being too complex, boring, or controversial. This can be difficult, especially when a cherished belief is criticized or when others say things about you that you might not want to hear. These are precisely the times when communication needs to be clear, open, honest, and confirming. To communicate in that way, you need to listen.

It is especially important today not to prejudge others on the basis of culture, ethnicity, or race. As far as our society has progressed, such prejudices linger.[12] In one study, college students indicated that racial stereotypes are alive and well. African Americans said that whites were "demanding" and "manipulative," while whites reported that blacks are "loud" and "ostentatious."[13] Such prejudices inhibit our ability to listen effectively and also foster defensiveness in groups.

Rehearsing a Response.   This barrier is perhaps the most difficult to overcome. It is the tendency people have to rehearse in their minds what they will say when the other person is finished. One of the reasons for this barrier is the difference between speech rate and thought rate. Most people speak at a rate of about 100 to 125 words per minute, but they have the capacity to think or listen at a rate of 400 or more words per minute! This gives them the mental time and space to wander off while keeping one ear on the speaker. The thought/speech differential is better used, though, to attend fully to what the speaker is saying—and not saying. When people learn to do this, their responses can be more spontaneous, accurate, appropriate, confirming, and supportive.

A Guide to Active Listening

Supportive, confirming communication focuses not only on verbal messages but on the emotional content of nonverbal behaviors as well. Learning to quiet one's own thoughts and to avoid prejudging others is a first step. Fully understanding others, though, involves considerable effort.

Active listening is an attempt to clarify and understand another's thoughts and feelings. To listen actively involves several steps. You need to: (1) stop, (2) look, (3) listen, (4) ask questions, (5) paraphrase content, and (6) paraphrase feelings.

Stop   Before you can effectively tune in to what someone else may be feeling, you need to stop what you are doing, eliminate as many distractions as possible, and focus fully on the other person.

Look   Now look for nonverbal clues that will help you identify how the other person is feeling. Most communication of emotion comes through nonverbal cues. The face provides important information about how a person is feeling, as do that person's voice quality, pitch, rate, volume, and use of silence. Body movement and posture clearly indicate the intensity of a person's feelings.

Listen   Listen for what another person is telling you. Even though that person may not say exactly how he or she feels, look for cues. Match verbal with nonverbal cues to decipher both the content and the emotion of the person's message. In addition, ask yourself, "How would I feel if I were in that person's position?" Try to interpret the message according to the sender's code system rather than your own.

Ask Questions   As you try to understand another person, you may need to ask some questions. Most of these will serve one of four purposes: (1) to obtain additional information ("How soon will you be ready to give your part of our presentation?"); (2) to find out how someone feels ("Are you feeling

overwhelmed by this assignment?"); (3) to ask for clarification of a word or phrase ("What do you mean when you say you didn't realize what you were getting into?"); and (4) to verify your conclusion about your partner's meaning or feeling ("Are you saying that you can't complete the project without some additional staff assistance?").

Paraphrase Content   Paraphrasing is restating in your own words what you think another person is saying. Paraphrasing is different from parroting back everything that person has said. After all, you can repeat something perfectly without understanding what it means. Rather, from time to time, quickly summarize the message another person has given you so far.

> EMILY: I think this job is too much for me; I'm not qualified to do it.
> HOWARD: You think you lack the necessary skills.

Note that at this point Howard is dealing only with the content of Emily's message. The goal of active listening, though, is to understand both the feelings and the content of another person's message.

Paraphrase Feelings   In the example above, Howard could follow his paraphrase of the content of the message with a question such as, "You're probably feeling pretty frustrated right now, aren't you?" Such a paraphrase would allow Emily either to agree with Howard's assessment or to clarify how she's feeling. For instance, she might respond, "No, I'm not frustrated. I'm just disappointed that the job's not working out."

Effective listening skills can contribute a great deal to building a supportive, cohesive group. Cohesiveness is an important factor in the life of a group and is the subject of a later section.

VERBAL DYNAMICS IN THE SMALL GROUP

The most obvious yet elusive component of small group communication is the spoken word. Words lie at the very heart of who and what people are. Their ability to represent the world symbolically gives humans the capacity to foresee events, to reflect on past experiences, to plan, to make decisions, and to consciously control their own behavior. Words are the tools with which people make sense of the world and share that sense with others.

WORDS AS BARRIERS TO COMMUNICATION

While words can empower people to create new realities and to influence attitudes and behaviors, they can also impede a process as well as facilitate it. While speech communication gives individuals access to the ideas and inner worlds of other group members, it can also—intentionally or unintentionally—set up barriers to effective communication. Words affect group climate.

If you grew up in the United States you can probably remember chanting, defensively, "Sticks and stones can break my bones but names can never hurt me." Even as you uttered these lines you knew you were using a lie to protect yourself. You often unwittingly communicate in ways that threaten and make others feel defensive. When group members feel a need to protect themselves, they shift their attention from the group's goal to their own personal goal of self-protection, thus creating a barrier to effective group process. Some more subtle but pervasive word barriers are bypassing, allness, and fact-inference confusion.

Bypassing   The meanings of the words you use seem so obvious to you that you assume those words suggest the same meanings to others. Nothing could be further from the truth. **Bypassing** takes place when two people assign different meanings to the same word. Many words are open to an almost limitless number of interpretations. Consider, for example, the words *love*, *respect*, and *communication*. You may know precisely what you mean when you say that the department's account is "seriously overdrawn," but how are others to interpret that? How serious is "seriously"?

According to some estimates, the 500 most frequently used words in the English language have over 14,000 dictionary definitions. Considering that a dictionary definition reflects only a tiny percentage of all possible meanings for a word and that people from different cultures and with different experiences interpret words differently, it is amazing that people can understand one another at all.

In groups, the problem of bypassing is compounded by the number of people involved; the possibility for multiple misunderstandings is always present. This points to the importance of good feedback among group members. Feedback is any response by listeners that lets speakers know whether they have been understood accurately. To overcome word barriers, people must understand that words are subjective. They need to check that what they understand from others is really what those others intend.

Allness   **Allness statements** are simple but untrue generalizations. You have probably heard such allness statements as "Women are smarter than men," "Men can run faster than women," and "Football players are stupid."

REVIEW BOX

A Summary of Word Barriers and Their Solutions

BARRIER	DESCRIPTION	SOLUTION
Bypassing	Occurs when the same word is used to mean two different things	Use specific language; be aware of multiple interpretations of what you say; clarify.
Allness Statements	Simple but untrue generalizations.	Don't overgeneralize; remember that all individuals are unique.
Fact-inference confusion	Mistaking a conclusion you have drawn for an observation	Clarify and analyze; learn to recognize the difference between fact and inference, and communicate the difference clearly.

These statements are convenient, but they simply are not accurate. The danger of allness statements is that you may begin to believe them and to prejudge other people unfairly based on them. Therefore, be careful not to overgeneralize; remember that each individual is unique.

Fact-Inference Confusion   **Fact-inference confusion** occurs when people respond to something as if it were something they have actually observed when, in reality, it is merely a conclusion they have drawn. While statements of fact can be made only after direct observation, inferences can be made before, during, or after an occurrence—no observation is necessary. The key distinction is that in statements of inference people can speculate about and interpret what they *think* occurred. Suppose, for example, that you heard someone comment, "Men are better than women at math." If this statement were true, it would mean that *all* men and women were tested and that the results indicated that men are better in math than women. The statement is, in reality, an inference. If the speaker is summarizing research that has investigated the issue, he or she should say "Some studies have found that. . . " rather than "It's a fact that. . . ." The first statement more accurately describes reality than does the second. Like bypassing and allness statements, fact-inference confusion can lead to inaccuracy and misunderstanding.

GROUP COHESIVENESS

If this were a textbook in introductory physics, it would define *cohesion* as the mutual attraction that holds together the elements of a body. This, of course, is a small group communication textbook, but it offers a very similar definition of **group cohesiveness.** Cohesiveness is the degree of attraction that members feel toward one another and the group. It is a feeling of deep loyalty, of "groupness," of esprit de corps, and the degree to which each individual has made the group's goal his or her own. It is a sense of belonging and a feeling of morale.[14] Cohesiveness results from the interaction of a number of variables, including group composition, individual benefits derived from the group, task effectiveness, and, first and foremost, communication.

COMPOSITION AND COHESIVENESS: BUILDING A TEAM

As noted in Chapter 3, people often join groups because they feel an attraction toward the people in that group. Factors discussed earlier, such as the similarity of group members or the degree to which group members' needs complement one another, are influential in the development of group cohesiveness.

To borrow a metaphor from the sports world, the best team has the right players at the right positions—and good coaching. Based on their size, speed, aggressiveness, reaction time, and so forth, different players are suited for different positions. So it is with groups: For maximum effectiveness, they need participants with different talents that complement one another.

Cohesiveness develops around both the task and relationship dimensions we discussed in Chapter 4. Building a group solely on the basis of similarity in interpersonal attraction (Chapter 3) predicts strong cohesiveness based on relationships but mediocrity as a task group. On the other hand, extreme diversity within a group brings stimulating perspectives to problem solving but may strain the relational aspects of group process.

Most work groups today are culturally and racially diverse in addition to reflecting a range of talents and expertise. As we noted in Chapter 4, such diversity can be a source of strength because of the multiple perspectives it brings to problem solving *if* the group can work together to minimize misunderstandings that can derive from diversity. That takes leadership.

We will discuss leadership further in Chapter 10. Chapter 11 will address team building.

INDIVIDUAL BENEFITS AND COHESIVENESS

If cohesiveness is a combination of forces that hold people in groups, clearly the aspects of membership that bring people personal satisfaction must be important. Depending on the nature of the group, its members can derive benefits of affiliation, power, affection, and prestige. People like to be with groups in which these needs are satisfied. Such groups can become important reference groups in that they allow people to validate their judgments about themselves and others.[15] An important determinant of group cohesiveness, then, is the degree to which a particular group is capable of meeting members' needs in comparison to the ability of any other group to meet those same needs. If people perceive that they derive from a group benefits that no other group could provide, their attraction toward that group will strengthen considerably. This factor partially accounts for the intense attraction most people feel toward their families or closest friends.

TASK EFFECTIVENESS AND COHESIVENESS

The relation of personal and interpersonal variables to group cohesiveness has already been discussed. The performance of the group as a whole has considerable influence as well; success fosters cohesiveness. The mutuality of concern for the group's task, which provides the focal point for working toward that task, becomes socially rewarding when the task is completed successfully. Here is another example of the interrelatedness of the task and social dimensions: Reaching a particular goal provides a common, rewarding experience for all group members. This commonality, or shared experience, further sets a group apart from other groups.

COMMUNICATION AND COHESIVENESS

None of the factors described so far is enough, in and of itself, to build a cohesive group. Rather, the interaction of these variables determines the degree of cohesiveness. Communication is the vehicle through which this interaction takes place. Through communication, individual needs are met and tasks are accomplished. In other words, "the communication networks and the messages that flow through them ultimately determine the attractiveness of the group for its members."[16]

Recall from Chapter 2 our discussion of the role of communication in creating symbolic convergence through which a cohesive group identity evolves. According to symbolic convergence theory, the group develops a unique identity through the sharing of fantasies or stories. A feeling of cohesiveness is likely to increase as group members share stories and other group members respond to those stories. A fantasy chain occurs when one story leads to another story thus creating a bond among group members and the revelation of common fantasies.

Most of this book is devoted to the study of how communication affects small group process. The earlier discussion of defensive and supportive communication, for example, suggests some ways in which people can adjust their communicative behavior to improve group cohesiveness. In addition to the *quality* of communication, the *amount* of communication in the group also affects cohesiveness. George Homans suggests: "If the frequency of interaction between two or more persons increases, the degree of their liking for one another will increase, and vice versa."[17] Free and open communication characterizes highly cohesive groups. The more people interact with one another, the more they reveal themselves to others and the more others reveal themselves to them. Through communication, people negotiate

REVIEW BOX

Suggestions for Enhancing Group Cohesiveness

EFFECTIVE GROUPS	INEFFECTIVE GROUPS
Talk about the group in terms of "we" rather than "I."	Only emphasize individual contributions of group members.
Reinforce good attendance at group meetings.	Make no effort to encourage group members to attend every meeting.
Establish and maintain group traditions (e.g., end each meeting with refreshments).	Make little or no effort to develop group traditions.
Set clear short-term as well as long-term group goals.	Avoid setting goals or establishing deadlines.
Encourage everyone in the group to participate in the group task.	Allow only the most talkative members to do most of the work.
Celebrate (e.g., have a party, go to a movie together) when the group achieves a short-term as well as a long-term goal.	Discourage group celebrations; group meetings should be all work.
Let the group reflect on its history.	Limit group discussion only to the job ahead.
Stress teamwork.	Stress individual achievement.
Encourage the development of group norms.	Discourage the group from establishing common norms.

Adapted from Ernest G. Bormann and Nancy C. Bormann, *Effective Small Group Communication* (Minneapolis: Burgess Publishing Company, 1980), 70–72.

group roles, establish goals, reveal similarities and differences, resolve conflict, and express affection. It makes sense, then, that as the frequency of communication increases, so does the group's cohesiveness. Communication is also the foundation for interpersonal trust within the group.

COMMUNICATION NETWORKS

Another influence on group climate is the **communication network,** or who talks to whom. If you think about the group meetings in which you participate, it may seem that while some people talk more than others, most of their communication is addressed to the group as a whole. Next time you are in a group, note who is talking to whom. You will find that people address relatively few comments to the group as a whole and that they direct most of what they say in groups toward specific persons. In some groups,

FIGURE 5.1   EQUAL DISTRIBUTION OF COMMUNICATION

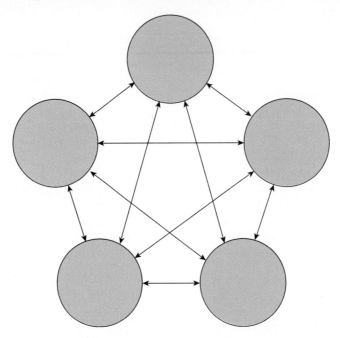

people find that communication tends to be distributed equally among group members. Figure 5.1 represents such a distribution.

In some groups, members address most comments to one central person, perhaps the designated leader or chairperson. Figure 5.2 represents this type of communicative pattern.

Other patterns may emerge. These include circular patterns, in which people talk primarily to those sitting next to them, or linear patterns, in which people communicate in a kind of chain reaction. These patterns may be built into the group from the outset, or they may emerge spontaneously. Either way, networks tend to stabilize over time. Once people establish channels of communication, they continue to use these same channels. This network of channels influences group climate as well as group productivity.

A review of research suggests that, in general, "groups in which free communication is maximized are generally more accurate in their judgments, although they may take longer to reach a decision."[18] People also tend to feel more satisfied in groups in which they participate actively. When interaction is stifled or discouraged, people have less opportunity to satisfy their needs through communication. Groups with centralized communication networks (see Figure 5.2) are certainly more efficient. That efficiency enhances group cohesiveness, but considerable evidence suggests that free and open communication networks, which include everyone in the

FIGURE 5.2   LEADER-ADDRESSED COMMUNICATION

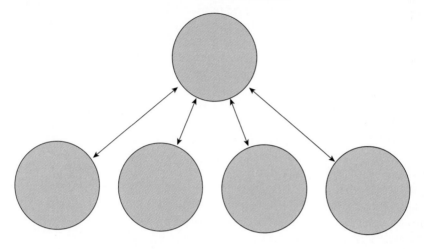

group (see Figure 5.1), are more likely to lead to more accurate group judgments as well as to more attractive group climates and greater individual satisfaction.

ANOTHER FACTOR: GROUP SIZE

In a group, there is a positive relationship between the level of people's participation and the degree of their individual satisfaction. Obviously, as the size of a group increases, the opportunity to interact with other members decreases. What size should a group be in order to achieve maximum cohesiveness and productivity? Three heads are better than one, but are twenty heads better than three?

No one knows the precise number of people that will maximize the effectiveness of your group, but some observations may provide guidance. As a group's size increases, the principle of diminishing returns sets in. Imagine a long rope attached to a heavy weight. By yourself, using all of your strength, you may not be able to move that weight. As more people join you in your effort, the weight begins to move and the task becomes easier. But as the group size increases, individuals use smaller and smaller percentages of their total strength.[19] One study found that cohesiveness is positively related to the opportunity for interaction afforded by group size: As group size increases, the opportunity for interaction decreases.[20] Cohesiveness is also related to productivity. More-cohesive groups render poorer-quality decisions as group size increases.[21] What, then, is the optimum size?

Herbert Thelen has suggested the principle of "least group size." Clearly people want groups small enough to encourage maximum participation yet large enough to generate the maximum number of ideas. Thelen says that "the group should be just large enough to include individuals with all the relevant skills for problem solutions."[22] While this principle provides no firm rule about group size, it does at least provide a guideline. In small group communication, bigger is not necessarily better. Groups of five to seven members are just about right in size. Twelve is just about the right size for a small group—if five people don't show up.

GROUP CLIMATE AND PRODUCTIVITY

Thus far this chapter has discussed many variables that affect group climate—defensive behavior, confirming and disconfirming responses, group cohesiveness, group size—and has made some suggestions about how to improve the climate of groups. As already suggested, when communication is free and open and when everyone participates, people tend to feel more attraction toward the group and consequently receive more personal satisfaction. Another reason for developing and maintaining a positive group climate is that climate affects productivity.

When a group has a trusting, open atmosphere and a high level of cohesiveness, members "do not fear the effects that disagreement and conflict in the task dimension can have on their social fabric. *Cohesive groups have strong enough social bonds to tolerate conflict.*"[23] Chapters 7 and 9 explore the function of conflict in groups. Here it is enough to say that through constructive conflict, groups deal with the difficult issues confronting them. When there is no conflict, it is usually because people do not trust one another enough to assert their individuality. Avoiding the issues does not lead to clarity concerning those issues. An absence of clarity does not help the group reach the most effective solutions.

It is a mistake to view positive group climate or group cohesiveness as a condition in which everyone is nice all the time. Quite the contrary. In a highly cohesive group, members know that they will not be rejected for their views and are therefore more willing to express them—even though expressing them may provoke disagreement. Ernest Bormann notes:

> At a point where someone in a cohesive group would say, "You're wrong!" or "I disagree!" an individual in a less cohesive group will say, "I don't understand," or "I'm confused." Members of groups with little cohesion have yet to create much of a common social reality.[24]

This common "social reality," which includes group roles and group norms, gives people the freedom to assert their individuality within a predictable context. In a cohesive group, people already know that they are accepted in the group.

Another aspect of this social reality is the degree to which group members make the group's goal their own. In highly cohesive groups, individuals personally commit themselves to the group's well-being and to accomplishing the group's task. In part, this personal commitment can be attributed to the feeling that this particular group meets people's needs better than any other group. When this is the case, as it often is in a cohesive group, people have a degree of *dependence* on the group. This dependence increases the *power* the group has over individuals. To put this in a less intimidating way, "There can be little doubt that members of a more cohesive group more readily exert influence on one another and are more readily influenced by one another."[25] These factors—personal commitment to the group, personal dependence on the group, group power over individuals within the group—come together in a positive group climate. The result is that cohesive groups work harder than those groups with little cohesiveness, regardless of outside supervision.[26]

With few exceptions, building a group climate in which cohesiveness can grow results not only in greater individual satisfaction but in greater group productivity as well.[27]

PUTTING PRINCIPLE INTO PRACTICE

Chapters 4 and 5 have focused on knowledge and skills associated with **communication competence**—communicative behavior that is both effective and appropriate in a given context. *Effectiveness,* says communication scholar Brian Spitzberg, is "the successful accomplishment of valued goals, objectives, or rewards relative to costs. *Appropriateness* means that the valued rules, norms, and expectancies of the relationship are not violated significantly."[28]

Successful group communication requires communication competence: "The competent communicator knows how and when to communicate (cognitive ability) and is able to do so (behavioral ability)."[29] This chapter has provided principles that, when put into practice, can help you to be a more competent communicator in groups.

- To the extent that you engage in supportive—rather than defensive—communication, you will foster a positive group climate in which people are free to focus their attention on the group and its task.
- If you can develop a sensitivity to your own confirming and disconfirming behaviors, you can become more confirming in your group behavior, thus contributing to a more positive group climate.
- Effective listening is crucial to maintaining a positive group climate. Only by listening attentively can people gain the understanding necessary to respond accurately, appropriately, and supportively to others. To do this, they need to overcome the barriers of prejudging and inner re-

hearsal. Listen actively. Remember to stop, look, listen, ask questions, and paraphrase.

- Cohesiveness is the result of the interaction of a number of variables, including the group's composition, individual benefits derived from the group, and task effectiveness and communication. Be aware of these factors to help foster group cohesiveness.
- If you are forming a group, include just enough people to ensure the presence of all of the relevant skills for problem solving—and no more.
- A positive group climate is essential if you are to reach your maximum potential as a working group. A trusting and open climate allows all members the freedom to be themselves: to agree or disagree, or to engage in conflict without fear of rejection. The ability of a group not only to withstand but to benefit from constructive conflict is crucial to a group's productivity. To build such a climate, learn to communicate more supportively and confirmingly: Avoid defensive, disconfirming behavior.

PRACTICE

Confirmation/Disconfirmation

In your discussion group, stage a discussion in which group members attempt to use all of the disconfirming responses listed in this chapter. Choose a familiar topic about which everyone has something to say. Have observers keep a record of the number and type of disconfirming responses and the reactions (especially nonverbal) to them. Now repeat the discussion, covering as many of the same topics as possible, but this time concentrate on using only confirming responses. Again, have observers keep records. When you have completed both rounds of discussion, have group members discuss their reactions and have observers report their findings.

Group Climate Self-Assessment

How does your behavior affect group climate? The following questions may provide some insight. Answer each question by assigning the number from the list below that most accurately describes your behavior in groups.[30]

1. Always
2. Usually
3. Frequently
4. Half the time, yes; half the time, no
5. Occasionally
6. Seldom
7. Never

_____ 1. I try to clarify the ideas of others.

_____ 2. I plan what I am going to say while others are speaking.

_____ 3. I tend to tell others when their ideas are irrelevant or inappropriate.

_____ 4. It is extremely important to me for the group to adopt my point of view.

_____ 5. My responses to others' comments are direct and supportive.

_____ 6. I express my ideas without concern for others' previous comments and personal feelings.

_____ 7. I make frequent contributions to a group discussion.

_____ 8. In a group I feel free to share my feelings about the group's task and other group members.

_____ 9. I encourage my group to confront problems as they arise.

_____ 10. I praise others for their good ideas.

Add up the numbers of your responses to determine your score. Compare your score with other group members. Discuss the results.

Variation Complete this exercise as you believe other group members would respond. To what degree do your perceptions and theirs coincide? Why are there differences?

OBSERVING COMMUNICATION NETWORKS: INTERACTION DIAGRAMS

Communication networks—who talks to whom—have an effect on group cohesiveness, leadership patterns, and group productivity. A few minutes spent observing small group interaction will show you clearly that members infrequently address the group as a whole; instead, they tend to address specific group members. An **interaction diagram** can reveal a lot about the interaction patterns in your group. It tells you who is talking to whom and how often. You can identify the most active and the most reticent members. You can pattern the relationships that form among group members. By combining an interaction diagram with a **category system,** such as the confirming and disconfirming responses described in this chapter, you can recognize the contributions each member makes to the group. Interaction diagrams are extremely useful tools. This is how to make one:

1. Draw a circle for each member of the group, arranging your circles in the same relative positions as those in which group members are seated (Figure 5.3).

2. Refer to Figure 5.3. If Nancy were to open the meeting by asking Phil for the minutes from the last meeting, you would draw an arrow from Nancy's circle to Phil's, indicating the direction and destination of

FIGURE 5.3   INTERACTION DIAGRAM

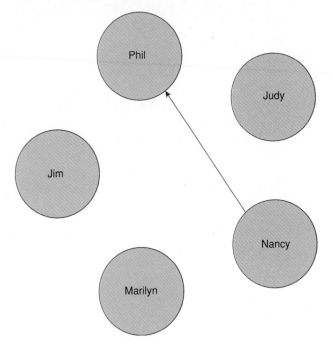

Nancy's communication. Each subsequent remark Nancy makes to Phil would then be indicated by a short crossmark at the base of the arrow.

3. Repeat this process each time someone in the group addresses someone else. If Phil were to address the minutes to Nancy, you would put an arrowhead at the other end of the line that connects the two.

4. Indicate communication addressed to the group as a whole with a line pointing away from the center of the group. Again, note subsequent remarks with crossmarks.

5. Figure 5.4 is an example of what a completed interaction diagram might look like.

If you take a few moments to examine Figure 5.4, you will see some patterns beginning to emerge. For example, Phil seems to be the most vocal member of the group. Furthermore, most members address their remarks to Phil, which suggests that they perceive Phil to be the group's leader. The frequency with which Phil addresses the group as a whole supports this observation. The amount of communication between Phil and Jim indicates a strong relationship there, perhaps that of a leader and his "lieutenant."

The interaction diagram is an easy way to describe graphically the interaction patterns in a group. Also, this method of observation can be used without seriously disrupting the regular workings of the group. By updating the interaction diagram during several meetings, you can observe

FIGURE 5.4   COMPLETED INTERACTION DIAGRAM WITH CATEGORY SYSTEM

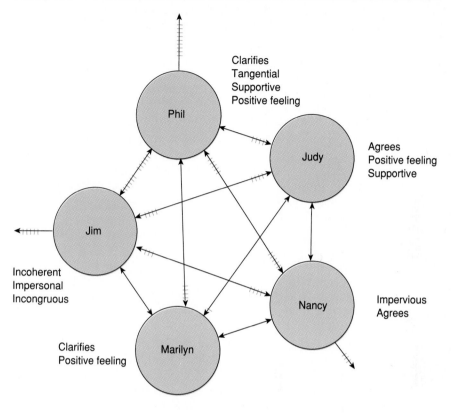

changes in group interaction. The addition of a category system to the interaction diagram renders this a most powerful descriptive tool.

FACT OR INFERENCE

Read the following three stories. Assume that all the information presented
is accurate. You can refer back to the stories whenever you wish. Next, read
the statements following each story. If the statements following the story are
true (verified by information in the story as factual), circle T for true. If the
statements are false (contrary to the information in the story), circle F for
false. If you are unable to determine whether the statements are true or false
(an inference) circle the ?.

After you have completed these three exercises individually, meet in a
small group and reach consensus as a group on the correct answers. Your
instructor will supply the correct answers to help you sort out fact from
inference.[31]

Story A   As you step onto your front porch from your living room, you observe a delivery truck approaching along the street. You see that your next-

door neighbor is backing her car from her garage into the street in the path of the approaching truck. You see the truck swerve, climb over the curbing, and come to a stop against a tree, which crumples one of its front fenders.

STATEMENTS ABOUT STORY A

1. Your next-door neighbor was backing her car into the street in the path of an approaching truck.   T F ?
2. The delivery truck was traveling at a reasonable speed.   T F ?
3. The only damage resulting from the incident was to the truck's fender.   T F ?
4. You saw the truck swerve and climb over the curbing.   T F ?
5. Your neighbor across the street was backing her car out of the garage.   T F ?
6. The truck suffered no damage.   T F ?
7. You saw the truck approaching as you stepped onto your front porch from your living room.   T F ?
8. The man who drove the delivery truck swerved and ran his truck up over a curbing.   T F ?
9. The delivery truck driver swerved in order to miss a child playing in the street.   T F ?

Story B   A man, his wife, and his sons, aged 11 and 14, drove across the country on a vacation trip in their three-year-old automobile. They started the trip on a Friday, the 13th of the month. The wife said she did not like the idea of leaving on that day, and the man laughed at her statement. In the course of the trip the following mishaps occurred:

The automobile radiator sprang a leak.

The 11-year-old boy became carsick for the first time in his life.

The wife was badly sunburned.

The man lost his fishing rod.

STATEMENTS ABOUT STORY B

1. There were fewer than two children in the family.   T F ?
2. The sedan's radiator sprang a leak.   T F ?
3. The wife really didn't mind leaving on Friday the 13th.   T F ?
4. A fishing reel was lost.   T F ?
5. The family's trip began on Friday the 13th.   T F ?
6. The 11-year-old boy lost his fishing rod.   T F ?
7. The story mentions the name of the family taking the trip.   T F ?
8. The make of the automobile in which the family made the trip was not mentioned in the story.   T F ?
9. The man laughed at his wife's fears of Friday the 13th.   T F ?

Story C   John and Betty Smith are awakened in the middle of the night by a noise coming from the direction of their living room. John Smith investigates and finds that the door opening into the garden, which he thought he had locked before going to bed, is standing wide open. Books and papers are scattered on the floor around the desk in one corner of the room.

STATEMENTS ABOUT STORY C

1. Betty Smith was awakened in the middle of the night.   T F ?
2. John Smith locked the door from his living room to his garden before going to bed.   T F ?
3. The books and papers were scattered between the time John Smith went to bed and the time he was awakened.   T F ?
4. John Smith found that the door opening into the garden was shut.   T F ?
5. John Smith did not lock the garden door.   T F ?
6. John Smith was not awakened by a noise.   T F ?
7. Nothing was missing from the room.   T F ?
8. Betty Smith was sleeping when she and her husband were awakened.   T F ?
9. The noise did not come from their garden.   T F ?
10. John Smith saw no burglar in the living room.   T F ?
11. John and Betty Smith were awakened in the middle of the night by a noise.   T F ?

NOTES

1. Jack R. Gibb, "Defensive Communication," *Journal of Communication* 11 (September 1961): 141.
2. Charles H. Tandy, "Assessing the Functions of Supportive Messages," *Communication Research* 19 (1992): 175–92.
3. Alvin Goldberg and Carl Larson, *Group Communication: Discussion Processes and Applications* (Englewood Cliffs, N.J.: Prentice-Hall, 1975), 105.
4. Evelyn Sieburg and Carl Larson, "Dimensions of Interpersonal Response." Paper delivered at the annual conference of the International Communication Association, Phoenix, April 1971, 1.
5. Goldberg and Larson, *Group Communication*, pp. 103–104.
6. Allan A. Glatthorn and Herbert R. Adams. *Listening Your Way to Management Success* (Glenview, Ill.: Scott, Foresman, 1984).
7. Ibid., 1.
8. Ibid., 2.
9. Ibid., 2.
10. Ibid., 3.
11. Curt Bechler and Scott D. Johnson, "Leadership and Listening: A study of Member Perceptions," *Small Group Research* 26 (1995): 77–85.

12. Brenda J. Allen, "Diversity and Organizational Communication," *Journal of Applied Communication Research* 23 (1995): 143–155.

13. R. Leonard and D. C. Locke, "Communication Stereotypes: Is Interracial Communication Possible?" *Journal of Black Studies* 23 (1993): 332–43.

14. Kenneth A. Bollen and Rick H. Hoyle, "Perceived Cohesion: A Conceptual and Empirical Examination," *Social Forces* 69 (1990): 479.

15. A. Paul Hare, *Handbook of Small Group Research,* 2nd ed. (New York: Free Press, 1976), p. 10.

16. Ernest G. Bormann, *Discussion and Group Methods: Theory and Practice,* 2nd ed. (New York: Harper & Row, 1975), 162–63.

17. George C. Homans, *The Human Group* (New York: Harcourt Brace, 1992).

18. Hare, *Handbook,* 343.

19. W. Moede, "Guidelines for a Psychology of Achievement," *Industrielle Psychotechnik* 4, (1927): 193–209.

20. B. Mullen, T. Anthony, E. Salas and J.E. Driskell, "Group Cohesiveness and Quality of Decision Making," *Small Group Research* 25 (1994):189–204.

21. Stanley Seashore, *Group Cohesiveness in the Industrial Work Group.* (Ann Arbor: University of Michigan Press, 1954); reprinted by Ayer Publishing, 1977.

22. Herbert A. Thelen, "Group Dynamics in Instruction: Principle of Least Group Size," *School Review* 57 (1949): 139–48.

23. Bormann, *Discussion and Group Methods,* 145.

24. Ibid., 144–45.

25. Dorwin Cartwright and Alvin Zander, *Group Dynamics: Research and Theory,* 3rd ed. (New York: Harper & Row, 1968), 104.

26. Hare, *Handbook,* 340.

27. C. Burningham and M.A. West, "Individual, Climate, and Group Interaction Processes as Predictors of Work Team Innovation," *Small Group Research* 26 (1995):106–117.

28. Brian H. Spitzberg, "Intercultural Communication Competence," in Larry A. Samovar and Richard E. Porter, *Intercultural Communication* (Belmont, Calif.: Wadsworth, 1991), 354.

29. Carolyn M. Anderson and Matthew M. Martin, "The Effects of Communication: Motives, Interaction, Involvement, and Loneliness on Satisfaction: A Model of Small Groups," *Small Group Research* 26 (1995): 119.

30. The late Norman H. Watson assisted in developing this questionnaire.

31. This exercise was developed by T. Richard Cheatham and Robert Shermer for *Oral Communication Handbook* (Warrensburg: Central Missouri State University, 1972).

CHAPTER
S·I·X

Nonverbal Group Dynamics

After studying this chapter, you will be able to:

- Explain why nonverbal communication is important to the study of groups.

- Apply research findings about nonverbal communication to small groups.

- Describe how nonverbal cues should be inter-

preted in light of gender and cultural differences.

- Identify guidelines for interpreting nonverbal communication in small groups.

*I*t was day three of Apollo XIII's mission in April of 1970. All was go-ing well for Lovell, Haise, and Swiggert, the crew of yet another United States trip to the moon, an event that for many Americans was be-coming a common occurrence. Then Mission Control heard those now fa-mous words from Commander Jim Lovell, "Houston, we have a problem." Something had gone terribly wrong. An unexplained malfunction in the oxygen tanks caused the cabin to vent precious life-sustaining oxygen into space. The astronauts and Mission Control soon learned that if a solution to the problem could not be found, the crew would not return alive.

At the first news conference following the accident, members of Mission Control faced an intensely interested press corp. A small group of officials from NASA sought to put a positive spin on the situation by claiming all was under control. But as one member of the control team later commented, "All you had to do was look at our grim faces and you knew that we had a tremendous problem." The nonverbal message of the group telegraphed the anxiety that their words were attempting to overshadow. The unspoken messages on the team's faces, the stress in their voices, and the edginess in their posture and gestures let the world know that Houston, indeed, had a serious problem. The nonverbal message, as is often the case in group meet-ings and presentations, told the real story.

Nonverbal communication is communication that creates meaning for someone other than through the use of words. In the context of a small group, this definition includes such behaviors as body posture and movement, eye contact, facial expression, seating arrangement, spatial relationships, personal appearance, use of time, and even tone of voice. While the words someone utters are not classified as nonverbal commu-nication, the pitch, quality, rate, intonation, and use of silence can speak volumes; thus vocal tone is considered part of nonverbal communica-tion.

Every message contains both content and information about relation-ships. Nonverbal messages, particularly facial expression and vocal cues, are often the prime source of information about interpersonal relationships. Thus they play important **metacommunication** functions. Metacommunica-tion literally means communication about communication. The nonverbal aspects of a message communicate information about the verbal aspects of a message.

The purposes of this chapter are: (1) to identify the importance of non-verbal communication to the study of small groups, (2) to discuss the appli-cation of research in nonverbal communication to small groups, (3) to iden-tify how culture and gender differences influence nonverbal communication in groups, and (4) to identify guidelines for interpreting nonverbal commu-nication in small groups.

THE IMPORTANCE OF NONVERBAL COMMUNICATION IN GROUPS

Have you been involved with a small group student project or served on a committee in which you felt uncomfortable or out of place? While you could not identify why you felt odd, you knew something was wrong. You felt uneasy not because of what was being said, but perhaps because of something unspoken. Maybe the apathetic facial expressions or the unenthusiastic vocal qualities exhibited by other group members bothered you. Maybe it was the room in which your meeting was held. (Was it hot and stuffy or unattractively decorated?) You may not have realized it at the time, but the nonverbal dynamics of that unexciting, uncomfortable meeting probably helped create an unproductive group climate. On the other hand, you probably can remember some small group discussions that were positive experiences because other members were sensitive to both verbal and nonverbal processes. Members' posture and eye contact may have suggested that they were involved in the discussion. Perhaps you met in a comfortable room. In short, the group meeting seemed interesting, exciting, and productive. Although not all unexciting group discussions result from poor nonverbal communication, nonverbal variables dramatically affect a group's climate and members' attitudes toward the group.

Nonverbal communication variables are important to small group communication for at least three reasons. First, group participants spend more time communicating nonverbally than they do verbally. Second, people believe nonverbal communication cues more than verbal messages. Third, people communicate emotions primarily by nonverbal cues.

1. *In groups people spend more time communicating nonverbally than they do verbally.* In a small group discussion, usually only one person speaks at a time. The rest of the members can, however, emit a host of nonverbal cues that influence group deliberations. Eye contact, facial expression, body posture and movement (some cues are controlled consciously, others are emitted less intentionally) occur even when only one person is speaking. Since group members are usually within just a few feet of one another, they can easily ob-

Eye contact, posture, and facial expressions not only provide other people cues about your thoughts and attitudes but tell them how involved or uninvolved you are in the discussion.

serve most nonverbal cues. Viewing nonverbal communication from the broadest perspective, it is safe to say that "you cannot *not* communicate."

2. *People believe nonverbal messages more than verbal messages.* Nonverbal communication affects how others interpret our messages. Nonverbal cues are so important to communication that when a verbal message (either spoken or written) contradicts a nonverbal message, people are more inclined to believe the nonverbal message. The group member who sighs and, with a sarcastic edge, says, "Oh, what a great group this is going to be," communicates just the opposite meaning of that verbal message. One researcher estimates that people communicate 65 percent of the social meaning of messages nonverbally.[1]

3. *People communicate emotions primarily by nonverbal cues.* If a group member is frustrated with the group or disenchanted with the discussion, more

than likely you will detect those feelings by observing that person's nonverbal behavior—even before the member verbalizes his or her frustration. If a member seems genuinely interested in the discussion and pleased with the group's progress, this, too, can be observed through nonverbal behavior. Albert Mehrabian and some of his colleagues devised a formula that suggests how much of the total emotional meaning of a message is based on verbal components and how much on nonverbal components.[2] According to his research, only 7 percent of the emotional meaning of a message is communicated through its verbal content. About 38 percent of the impact of the emotional content is derived from the voice (from such things as the rate, pitch, quality, and volume). The largest source of emotional meaning, 55 percent, is a speaker's facial expression. Generalizing from this formula, approximately 93 percent of emotions are communicated nonverbally. Although these percentages cannot be applied to all situations, Mehrabian's research suggests that when inconsistencies exist between people's verbalized emotional states and their true emotions, expressed nonverbally, nonverbal cues carry more clout in determining how receivers interpret speakers' emotions.

An understanding of nonverbal communication, then, is vital to even a cursory understanding of communication in general and of group communication in particular. As you become a more skillful observer of nonverbal behavior, you will understand more thoroughly the way people interact in small groups.

APPLICATIONS OF NONVERBAL COMMUNICATION RESEARCH TO SMALL GROUPS

There are relatively few research studies that have investigated nonverbal behavior in groups. Despite the unchallenged importance of nonverbal group dynamics to group discussion, researchers have found this aspect of communication difficult to observe and investigate. When group members simultaneously emit a myriad of nonverbal behaviors, it is difficult to systematically observe and interpret these cues. Nonverbal messages are considerably more ambiguous than verbal messages. No dictionary has definitive meanings for nonverbal behaviors. We suggest that you exercise caution, then, when you attempt to interpret the nonverbal behavior of other group members. Yet research conclusions about nonverbal communication in a variety of contexts does help us increase our awareness and sensitivity to the rich display of information and feelings in groups.

The following sections describe some research so that you can become more sensitive to your own nonverbal behavior and to the role nonverbal communication plays in small group discussions. Specifically, the sections will discuss the following aspects of research in nonverbal communication in small groups: (1) physical posture, movement, and gestures, (2) eye contact,

(3) facial expressions, (4) vocal cues, (5) territory and personal space, (6) personal appearance, (7) the communication environment, and (8) use of time.

POSTURE, MOVEMENT, AND GESTURES

To help you observe and analyze movement, posture, and gestures, one research team has developed an approach to categorize the major types of nonverbal movement. Paul Ekman and Wallace Friesen identified five types of behavior: (1) emblems, (2) illustrators, (3) affect displays, (4) regulators, and (5) adaptors.[3]

Emblems   **Emblems** are nonverbal cues that have specific verbal counterparts and are shared by all group members. Emblems often take the place of spoken words, letters, or numbers. Group leaders who place index fingers vertically in front of their lips use a nonverbal emblem to take the place of the words, "Shhhh, let's be quiet now." A hitchhiker's raised thumb and a soldier's salute are other examples of emblems. Group members who point to their watches to indicate that the group should get on with it because time is running out or who use their index fingers and thumbs to signify all is okay also depend on nonverbal emblems to communicate their messages.

Illustrators   **Illustrators** are nonverbal behaviors that add meaning to accompanying verbal messages. In a group you may see a gesture illustrating emphasis. For example, a group member who emphasizes a point by shaking a fist in the face of another member illustrates conviction and determination. Several researchers have observed that people synchronize many of their body movements to their speech.[4] A blink of the eyes, a nod of the head, and a shift in body posture accent spoken messages. A nonverbal illustrator might contradict what someone is saying. A group member who stares out the window with an apathetic facial expression and says, "Sure, I'm interested in working in this group," nonverbally illustrates boredom and apathy.

Affect Displays   An **affect display** is a nonverbal cue that communicates emotion. As mentioned before, the face is the primary source of emotional display. Research suggests that the body indicates the intensity of the emotion, or affect, that is being expressed. For example, the faces of group members may indicate that they are bored. If they are also slouched in their chairs, they are probably more than just moderately apathetic about the discussion. When a television game show contestant wins a new sportscar, her face tells you that she is happy, and her jumping up and down, hugging and kissing the MC, tell you the intensity of her euphoria.

Regulators   **Regulators** help control the flow of communication. They are very important to small group discussions because people rely on them to know when they should talk and when they should listen. Regulators also provide cues to when other group members want to contribute to the discussion. Eye contact, posture, gestures, facial expression, and body position all help regulate communication in a group discussion. Generally, large groups operate with a rather formal set of regulators; participants raise their hands so that the chairperson will recognize them before they speak. In a less formal discussion, group members rely on direct eye contact (to indicate that a communication channel is open), facial expression (raised eyebrows often signify a desire to talk), and gestures (such as a raised index finger) as cues to regulate the flow of communication.

Adaptors   **Adaptors** are nonverbal acts that satisfy personal needs and help people adapt to their immediate environment. Adaptors are also important for learning to get along with others and for responding to certain situations. Generally, people are not aware of most of their adaptive nonverbal behavior. Self-adaptors, for example, refer to things people do to their own bodies, like scratching, biting their nails, or twirling their hair. Researchers have noted that when people become nervous, anxious, or upset, they frequently display more self-adaptive behaviors.[5]

In addition to categorizing movement, posture, and gestures, researchers have studied whether nonverbal behavior provides clues as to whether someone is lying. Sigmund Freud said, "He that has eyes to see and ears to hear may convince himself that no mortal can keep a secret. If his lips are silent, he chatters with his fingertips; betrayal oozes out of him at every

---

REVIEW BOX

Categories of Nonverbal Communication

CATEGORY	DESCRIPTION	EXAMPLE
Emblems	Movements and gestures that replace spoken messages	Group members shake their heads to communicate "no"
Illustrators	Nonverbal behaviors that add meaning to accompany verbal communication	Group members say "it was this long," holding their hands three feet apart
Affect displays	Expressions of feeling	Frowning, smiling, grimacing, smirking
Regulators	Behaviors that control the flow of communication between people	Eye contact, raising a hand or a finger to signal you want to talk
Adaptors	Movements that satisfy personal needs and help you adapt to your environment	Scratching, yawning, adjusting your glasses

pore." Paul Ekman and W. V. Friesen found that feet and legs often reveal people's true feelings.[6] They theorized that while people consciously manipulate their facial expressions to hide deception, they are not so likely to monitor their feet. You may more readily detect anxiety, then, by observing nervous movement of people's feet and legs than by looking for clues in their faces or other areas of the body that they are more likely to control consciously. One team of researchers suggested that the following behaviors (some which involve posture, movement, and gesture), listed in order from most to least important, can provide clues as to whether someone is lying:[7]

Greater time lag in response to a question

Reduced eye contact

Increased shifts in posture

More hand/shrug emblems

More adaptors

Unfilled pauses

Less smiling

Slower speech

Higher pitch in voice

More deliberate pronunciation and articulation

Simply because a group member exhibits one or more of these nonverbal behaviors does not mean that he or she lying. While a person trying to hide something or lie may exhibit some of the cues listed above, not everyone who displays such behavior is deceptive. The ambiguity of nonverbal cues prevents you from drawing such definitive conclusions about the motives of other people based on nonverbal cues alone.

Still other researchers have attempted to identify which nonverbal cues are correlated with leadership. J. O'Connor discovered that frequent gesturing was highly correlated with individuals perceived by other members to be leaders in small groups.[8] In a follow-up study, John Baird found that group members who were thought by other members to be group leaders used shoulder and arm gestures more often.[9] While leaders may gesture more frequently than followers, it does not mean that frequent gesturing causes a person to emerge as a leader. The evidence does not suggest a cause-and-effect relationship.

Do individuals in small groups use certain nonverbal cues during their attempts to persuade others? Albert Mehrabian and M. Williams found that persuasive communicators exhibit more animated facial expressions, use more gestures to emphasize their points, and nod their heads more than do those who are less persuasive.[10] Another team of researchers found that people trying to project warm, friendly images will be more likely to smile, be less likely to fidget with their hands, and be more likely to shift their postures toward others.[11]

One team of researchers found that we rely extensively on nonverbal cues to signal when we want to speak or change topics. Typically, a group member signals topic change by leaning forward, smiling, making a head nod, shifting posture, having a foot make contact with the floor, or breaking eye contact to signal a change in the direction of thought.[12]

A final, interesting line of research into body posture and movement suggests that in social situations one synchronizes one's movements and posture to the movements, postures, and speech of others. For example, at the end or beginning of a sentence spoken by another, you may nod your head or display a facial expression to agree or disagree with the comment. W. S. Condon and others, using slow-motion films, documented a distinct relationship between facial expressions and head movements and speech.[13] A. Kendon observed that people may shift their body positions in response to verbal messages.[14] Davida Navarre and Catherine Emihovich report similar evidence that group members may respond in synchrony to the movements and postures of others.[15] These authors suggest that people, during group interactions, may adopt poses similar to those of others they like or agree with. Thus, coalitions of group members may be identified not only by their verbal agreement but also by their synchronized nonverbal behavior. It is probably more than just coincidence that group members consistently fold their arms and cross their legs in the same way. Just as religious services use singing and group litanies to establish unity and a commonality of purpose, small groups may unwittingly utilize common nonverbal behaviors to foster cohesiveness. Counselors report that they can help clients self-disclose by adopting body postures similar to those of their clients. By synchronizing body position, counselors believe they can better empathize and establish rapport with their clients. In your small group discussions, observe the similarity and dissimilarity of members' postures, positions, and gestures. Such cues may provoke interesting insights about group climate, leadership, and cohesiveness.

Collectively, the studies of body posture and movement suggest how you will be perceived by other group members in terms of status, deception, leadership, and persuasiveness.

In one of the few studies that examined nonverbal behavior in groups, Edward Mabry attempted to discover whether there are changes in group members' nonverbal behavior from one meeting to the next. After observing a group that met five times, he found that during the second and third meetings group members were more likely to have the palms of their hands in more open positions. Group members also tended to lean back more in the first and fifth sessions of their deliberations. Participants also made more direct eye contact with one another after they had met together once. What do these differences mean? Mabry's study suggests that group members' nonverbal behavior changes from one group meeting to the next. Groups do not develop a static way of behaving nonverbally; nonverbal communication may be dependent on the topic and how group members feel toward one another as they become more comfortable after meeting together over several sessions.[16]

Eye Contact

Have you ever felt uncomfortable because the person you were talking to seemed reluctant to establish eye contact? Maybe you've wondered, "Why doesn't she look at me when she's talking to me?" Perhaps you've had just the opposite experience—the person you were talking to seemed to stare constantly at you. You become uneasy in these situations because they violate norms of eye contact. While you may think that you do a pretty good job of establishing eye contact with others, researchers estimate that most people look at others only between 30 and 60 percent of the time.[17] Eye contact usually lasts less than 10 seconds.

Several factors determine when eye contact occurs. Based on a summary of the literature, Knapp provides a good review of the factors that generally encourage and discourage eye contact in interpersonal situations.[18] You are *more* likely to engage in eye contact with others when:

   You are from a culture that emphasizes visual contact in interaction

   You are physically distant from your partner

   You are discussing easy, impersonal topics

   There is nothing else to look at

   You are interested in your partner's reactions—that is, you are interpersonally involved

   You are attracted to your partner—that is, you like or love the partner

   You are trying to dominate or influence your partner

   You are an extrovert

   You have high affiliative or inclusion needs

   You are dependent on your partner (and the partner has been unresponsive)

   You are listening rather than talking

You are *less* likely to look at others when:

   You are from a culture that imposes sanctions on visual contact during interaction

   You are physically close

   You are discussing difficult, intimate topics

   You have other relevant objects, people, or backgrounds to look at

   You are not interested in your partner's reactions

   You are talking rather than listening

   You are not attracted to your partner—that is, you dislike the partner

You are an introvert

You are low on affiliative or inclusion needs

You have a mental disorder like autism, schizophrenia, and the like

You are embarrassed, ashamed, sorrowful, sad, submissive, or trying to hide something

When eye contact does occur in a small group setting, it may serve one or more important functions: (1) cognitive function, (2) monitoring function, (3) regulatory function, and (4) expressive function.[19]

Cognitive Function   This function of eye contact operates when eyes indicate thought processes. For example, some people look away when they are thinking of just the right words to say. Others look away just before they speak so that they will not be distracted by the person to whom they are talking.

Monitoring Function   Monitoring is the way you seek feedback from others when communicating with them. While addressing a small group, you determine how effectively or ineffectively you are expressing yourself by looking at group members and monitoring their feedback. If you say something that other members disagree with, you may observe a change in facial expressions, body posture, or movements. You may then decide that you need to spend more time developing and explaining your point.

Regulatory Function   Eye contact plays a vital role in regulating the back-and-forth flow of communication. You can invite interaction simply by looking at others. For example, assume the chairperson of a committee asks for volunteers for an assignment. If you do not want to be volunteered for the task, you probably will not establish eye contact with the chairperson, just as you do not establish eye contact when a teacher asks a question to which you do not know the answer. Direct eye contact may be interpreted as an open communication channel, meaning that you would not mind being called on for the answer.

Expressive Function   While eyes generally do not provide clues about specific emotions, the immediate area around the eyes provides quite a bit of information about feelings and emotions.

Eye contact or lack of it, then, reveals information about thought processes, provides feedback, regulates communication channels, and expresses emotions. In addition to these functions, eye contact may provide clues about status and leadership roles in small groups. In the next small group meeting you attend, determine who receives the most eye contact in the group. Where do group members look for information and guidance? They probably look at the group leader. If, as in many groups, several group members share leadership, participants may look toward any of those lead-

Eye contact can indicate who is paying attention and who is receiving attention.

REVIEW BOX

Functions of Eye Contact

Cognitive function	Provides cues about thought processes
Monitoring function	Seeks feedback from others
Regulatory function	Signals when the communication channel is open and closed
Expressive function	Provides information about feelings, emotions, and attitudes

ers, depending on the specific problem or level of uncertainty facing the group.

FACIAL EXPRESSION

As discussed before, the face is the most important revealer of emotions. Sometimes you can cleverly mask your emotional expressions, but the face is usually the first place you look to determine someone else's emotional state. Facial expressions are particularly significant in interpersonal and small group communication because of the close proximity of communicators to one another. You can readily detect emotions displayed on a person's

"Just a few more pages, Hansen, and we'll take a short break."

face. Even though some researchers estimate that the face can produce over 20,000 different expressions, Ekman and Friesen have identified six primary emotions displayed on it: happiness, anger, surprise, sadness, disgust, and fear.[20]

Ekman has also developed a method of identifying which areas of the face play the most important roles in communicating emotions.[21] According to his research, people communicate happiness with the area around their eyes and with smiles and raised cheeks. They reveal disgust with raised upper lips, wrinkled noses, lowered eyelids, and lowered brows. They communicate fear with the area around their eyes, but their mouths are also usually open when they are fearful. When they are angry, people are likely to lower their eyebrows and stare intensely. They communicate surprise with raised eyebrows, wide-open eyes, and often open mouths. They communicate sadness in the area around the eyes and mouth.

Facial expressions are important sources of information about a group's emotional climate, particularly if several members express similar emotions. Their faces might suggest that they are bored with the discussion or that they are interested and pleased. Remember that group members may attempt to mask their facial expressions in an effort to conceal their true feelings.

VOCAL CUES

"John," remarked a group discussion member, obviously upset, "it's not that I object to what you said; it's just the way you said it." The pitch, rate, volume, and quality of your voice (also called **paralanguage** cues) play important parts in determining the meanings of your messages. As mentioned earlier in this chapter, Mehrabian estimates that as much as 38 percent of the emotional meaning of a message is derived from vocal cues.

You can, then, make inferences about how a speaker feels about you from that individual's paralanguage cues. You may also base inferences about a person's competence and personality on vocal cues. A speaker who mispronounces words and uses "uhs" and "ums" is probably going to be perceived as less credible than a speaker who is more articulate.[22] In addition to determining how speech affects a speaker's credibility, researchers have studied the communication of emotion via vocal cues.[23]

At times you can detect emotional states from vocal cues, but as a group member you should beware of drawing improper inferences and labeling someone negatively just because of vocal cues. As this chapter has emphasized, nonverbal cues do not operate in isolation. They should be evaluated in the context of other communicative behaviors.

TERRITORIALITY AND PERSONAL SPACE

The next time you are sitting in class, note the seat you select. Even though no one instructed you to sit in the same place, chances are that you tend to sit in about the same general area, if not in the same seat, during each class. Perhaps in your family each person sits at a certain place at the table. If someone sits in your chair, you feel that your territory has been invaded and you may try to reclaim your seat.

Territoriality is a term used in the study of animal behavior to note how animals stake out and defend given areas. Humans, too, stake out and defend areas.

Understanding territoriality may help you understand certain group behaviors. For example, the readiness of group members to defend personal territory may provide insights about their attitudes toward the group and toward individual members. At the next meeting you attend, observe how members attempt to stake out territories. If the group is seated around a table, do members place objects in front of and around themselves to signify that they are claiming territory? Higher-status individuals generally attempt to claim more territory.[24] Notice how group members manipulate their posture and gestures if their space is invaded. Lower-status individuals generally permit greater territorial invasion. Note, too, how individuals claim their territory by leaving markers—such as books, papers, or a pencil—when they have to leave the group but expect to return shortly.

Several researchers have studied **small group ecology**—the consistent way in which people arrange themselves in small groups. As you interact with others in a small group, see if you can detect relationships between participants' seating arrangements and their status, their leadership roles, and the amount of communication they direct toward others. B. Stenzor found that when group members are seated in a circle, they are more likely to talk to those across from them than to those on either side.[25] Other researchers

Group members often stake out their territory with objects to mark their space.

suggest that more-dominant group members select seats at the heads of rectangular tables or select seats that maximize their opportunity to communicate with others.[26] On the other hand, people who sit at the corners of tables generally contribute the least to a discussion. Armed with this information, if you find yourself in a position to prepare the seating for a discussion or conference, you should be able to make choices to maximize group interaction. If, for example, you know that Sue (who always dominates the discussion) will be attending the next meeting, you may suggest that she sit in a corner seat rather than at the head of the table.

Did you know that an individual's position relative to other group members in a small group discussion can influence his or her chances of becoming the leader of the group? In a study by L. T. Howells and S. W. Becker, five people sat around a table, three on one side and two on the other. The researchers discovered that the participants had a greater probability of becoming leaders if they sat on the side of the table facing the three discussion members.[27] More direct eye contact with numerous group members, which can subsequently result in a greater control of the verbal communication, may explain why the two individuals who faced the other three emerged as leaders.

Additional research suggests that where you sit in a group may determine whether you initiate or receive information during deliberations. One team of researchers who observed groups of three people in snack bars, restaurants, and lounges found that more-visible group members tended to receive communication while more-centrally located members usually initiated communication.[28] Another research team came to a similar conclusion: Group members who were visually central to other group members spoke most often.[29] As noted previously, eye contact seems to be an important factor in determining who speaks, who listens, and who has the greatest opportunity to emerge as group leader.

Other researchers have discovered that such variables as stress, gender, and personality also affect how people arrange themselves in small groups. Some people prefer greater personal space when they are under stress.[30] If you know that an upcoming discussion will probably produce anxiety, hold the meeting in a room that permits members to have more freedom of movement. This will allow them to find their preferred personal distance from other group members.

Sommer found that women in North America tend to sit closer to others (whether those others are men or women) than men tend to sit to other men (i.e., men generally prefer greater personal space when sitting next to other men).[31] In a study to find out whether personality characteristics affect seating arrangements, M. Cook discovered that extroverts tend to sit across from another person more than do introverts.[32] Introverts generally prefer distance between themselves and others. Collectively, these studies suggest that people arrange themselves in small group discussions with some consistency. A discussion leader who understands seating preferences should provide a comfortable climate for small group discussions.

Personal Appearance

How long does it take to determine whether or not you like someone? Some researchers claim that within seconds after meeting another person you complete your initial judgment of whether you should continue to communicate with him or her or try to excuse yourself from the conversation. You base many of your initial impressions of others primarily on personal appearance. The way people dress, their hairstyles, weight, and height affect your communication with them.

Research suggests that women who are thought to be attractive are more effective in changing attitudes than are women thought to be less attractive.[33] In addition, more-attractive individuals are often thought by others to be more credible than less-attractive people. They are also perceived to be happier, more popular, more sociable, and more successful than are those rated as being less attractive. Even people's general shape and body size affect how they are perceived by others.[34] People with fat, round silhouettes are consistently rated as older, more old-fashioned, less good-looking, more talkative, and more good-natured. Athletic, muscular people are rated as more mature, better looking, taller, and more adventurous. Tall and thin people are rated as more ambitious, more suspicious of others, more tense and nervous, more pessimistic, and quieter. Even though the research reported here was not conducted in small groups, it is reasonable to conclude that perceived attractiveness and body type can affect how group members perceive one another. Such perceptions may have an impact on interaction, decision making, problem solving, overall group climate, and member satisfaction.

Research supports the assumption that personal appearance can affect the social influence you exert on others. As a participant in small group discussions, pay close attention to your personal appearance; the contribution you make to the group may depend on it.

Communication Environment

Five students have been assigned to work together on a project for their group communication class. Their task is to formulate a policy question and solutions to it. Their first problem is finding a place to meet. Apparently, the only available place is a small, vacated office in Smythe Hall, the oldest building on campus. No one seems happy about holding meetings in the old office, but the students are relieved to have found a place to meet. When they arrive for their first meeting, they find a dirty, musty room with peeling paint, only three hardback wooden chairs, and a gray metal desk. The ventilation is poor, and half of the light bulbs have burned out. Such a dismal environment will undoubtedly affect the group's ability to work.

People can generally comprehend information and solve problems better in a more attractive environment. Research does not suggest, however, that one environment is best for all group communication situations. The optimal environment for any group depends on its specific task as well as the needs and expectations of its members. Some students need absolute quiet to read or study, while others can be productive while listening to music. Group members or leaders should attempt to find the best environments for their group based on the group's needs and the types of tasks confronting it. Group leaders could ask members which type of environment they prefer. If a group must solve problems that require considerable thought, energy, and creativity, it might work best in a quiet, comfortable room. If a group will meet over long periods of time, comfortable chairs and pleasant decor are essential.

TIME

The memo said the meeting was to start at 10:00 AM. You arrive shortly before ten armed with your agenda, notepad, and pen, ready to participate. But at 10:00 no one has arrived except you. You check your watch and double check to make sure you are in the right place. Finally, at 10:15, a couple of people arrive; most of the group comes in by 10:20. "Oh, we don't usually start right on time," said one of the latecomers. "Most people drift in by a quarter after the hour." Attitudes toward time may not seem like a nonverbal variable, yet a group's use of time and norms that develop about deadlines and efficiency are important unspoken aspects of a group's approach to work and productivity.

As we noted in Chapter 4, some people are **monochronic.** They are most comfortable doing only one thing at a time, like to concentrate on the job at hand, are more serious and sensitive to deadlines and schedules, like to plan how to use their time, and stress the importance of starting and ending meetings on time.[35] Other people are **polychronic.** These are individuals who can do many things at once, are less enslaved by deadlines and schedules, feel that relationships are more important than producing volumes of work, frequently change plans, and are less concerned about punctuality than monochronic individuals.

The use of time and expectations about time can cause conflict and frustration if group members have widely differing perspectives. Time use and expectations vary from culture to culture.[36] People from the United States and Northern Europe tend to be more monochronic; attention to deadlines and punctuality are important. Latin Americans, Southern Europeans, and Middle Easterners are more often polychronic; they give less attention to deadlines and schedules. Western cultures tend to approach problems in a linear, step-by-step fashion. How events are structured and sequenced is important. Eastern cultures (Chinese and Japanese) approach time with a less-structured perspective. As several researchers have noted:[37]

In Western Cultures	In Eastern Cultures
Time is something to be manipulated.	Time simply exists.
The present is a way-station between the past and the future.	The present is more important than the past or future.
Time is a resource that can be saved, spent, and wasted.	Time is a limitless pool.
Time is an aspect of history rather than part of an immediate experience.	Events occur in time; they cause ripples, and the ripples subside.

One researcher found that North Americans tend to think about time as a linear progression with a definite beginning and ending and believe that only one thing can be done at a time.[38] This is consistent with the monochronic approach to time discussed earlier. People from other cultures (for example, Latin American cultures) prefer working on multiple tasks and projects at the same time. And some Southeast Asians view time as a cyclical rather than a linear phenomenon.

Even if your group does not have members from widely different cultures, you may notice that people have different approaches to time. Groups develop their own norms about time. It may be useful to explicitly discuss and clarify norms related to the group's use of time. The importance of deadlines, expectations for group productivity, and general attitudes about punctuality may need to be discussed to manage any uncertainty about time that may exist. How a group approaches time is only one nonverbal variable that is strongly influenced by cultural backgrounds. Now we will focus on other ways in which cultural differences in interpreting nonverbal messages can affect group dynamics.

CULTURE AND NONVERBAL COMMUNICATION IN SMALL GROUPS

Culture is a learned system of knowledge, behavior, attitudes, beliefs, values, and norms that is shared by a group of people.[39] We often think of cultural differences as existing between ethnic groups or nations, but they can also exist between families, organizations, or even different parts of the same country or state. When individuals of different cultures interact, it is not surprising that cultural differences interfere with effective communication. As we have noted in previous chapters, cultural differences can sometimes cause problems for group members: Culture is a difference that *makes* a difference. As we noted in our discussion of how some cultures view time, unspoken cultural differences may contribute to underlying tension in small groups.

One obvious cultural difference is language—it would be challenging indeed to participate in a group without a common language! But it can also be

> ## REVIEW BOX
>
> ### Sources of Nonverbal Cues
>
> | | |
> |---|---|
> | Posture and movement | Provide information regarding status, intensity of attitude, warmth, approval seeking, group climate, immediacy, deception |
> | Eye contact | Provides cognitive, monitoring, regulatory, and expressive functions |
> | Facial expression | Communicates emotion, especially happiness, anger, surprise, sadness, disgust, and fear |
> | Vocal cues | The pitch, rate, volume, and quality of the voice communicate emotion, credibility, and personality perceptions |
> | Territoriality | Staking out, claiming, and defending a given space |
> | Personal space | Use of individual space, which communicates power, status, and intimacy |
> | Personal appearance | Clothing, body shape, and general attractiveness influence others' perceptions and reactions |
> | Communication environment | The general attractiveness or unattractiveness of a space, which contributes to the group's productivity and overall group climate |
> | Time | Responses to deadlines, beginning and ending times, and use of time during group meeting |

challenging to work with others where there are nonverbal cultural differences. Differences in how people from different cultures respond to context and attitudes toward personal contact have a direct bearing on nonverbal communication in small groups. We will explore differences between high-context and low-context cultures as well as high-contact and low-contact cultures. We will also note examples of how cultural differences in nonverbal communication can provide insight into how people interact in small groups.

HIGH-CONTEXT AND LOW-CONTEXT CULTURES

In some cultures the surrounding context or the unspoken, nonverbal message plays a greater role than in others.[40] A **high-context culture** is one in which more emphasis is placed on nonverbal communication. In high-context cultures, the physical context is important to help communicators interpret the message. The environment, the situation, and the communicator's mood are especially significant in decoding messages. A **low-context culture** places more emphasis on verbal expression. Figure 6.1 shows cultures arranged along a continuum from high to low context.

FIGURE 6.1

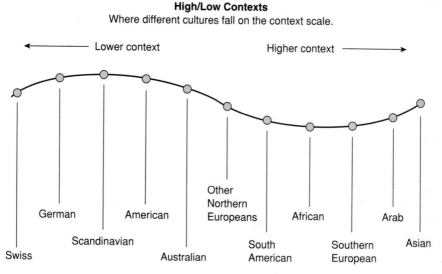

High/Low Contexts
Where different cultures fall on the context scale.

←—————— Lower context   Higher context ——————→

German   American   Other Northern Europeans   African   Arab

Scandinavian   South American   Southern European   Asian

Swiss   Australian   American   European

Low- context cultures
(Information must be provided explicitly, usually in words.)

• Less aware of nonverbal cues, environment and situation
• Lack well-developed networks
• Need detailed background information
• Tend to segment and compartmentalize information
• Control information on a "need to know" basis
• Prefer explicit and careful directions from someone who "knows"
• Knowledge is a commodity

High- context cultures
(Much information drawn from surroundings. Very little must be explicitly transferred.)

• Nonverbal important
• Information flows freely
• Physical context relied upon for information
• Environment, situation, gestures, mood all taken into account
• Maintain extensive information networks

From: Donald W. Klopf, *Intercultural Encounters: The Fundamentals of Intercultural Communication.* Englewood, Colorado: Morton Publishing Company, 1995, p. 33 and *Meeting News,* June 1993

People from high-context cultures may be more skilled in interpreting nonverbal information than people from low-context cultures. Individuals from high-context cultures may also use fewer words to express themselves. Because individuals from low-context cultures place greater emphasis on speech, they may talk more than those from high-context cultures. People from a low-context culture typically are less sensitive to the nonverbal cues, the environment, and the situation in interpreting the messages of others.[41]

In a small group, high- or low-context orientation can play a role in the amount of time a person talks and his or her sensitivity in responding to unspoken dynamics of a group's climate. Sometimes people from a high-con-

Cultural differences and similarities will influence nonverbal interaction when people communicate.

text culture will find those from a low-context culture less credible or trustworthy. Someone from a low-context culture may be more likely to make explicit requests for information by saying "Talk to me," "Give it to me straight," or "Tell it like it is." In contrast, a person from a high-context culture expects communication to be more indirect and to rely on more implicit cues.

HIGH-CONTACT AND LOW-CONTACT CULTURES

People from some cultures are more comfortable being touched or being in close proximity to others; these are said to be **high-contact cultures.** Individuals from **low-contact cultures** tend to prefer more personal space, typically have less eye contact with others and are much more uncomfortable with being touched or approached by others. Edward Hall offers the following classification of high- and low-contact cultures.[42]

HIGH-CONTACT CULTURES	**LOW-CONTACT CULTURES**
Tend to be cultures from warmer climates:	Tend to be from cooler climates:
Arab, Mediterranean, Hispanic, Indonesian, European and Middle Eastern Jews, Eastern Europeans, Russians.	Norway, Finland, Sweden, Germany, England, Japan, Anglo-Saxon Americans

Whether group members are from high- or low-contact cultures can affect preferred seating arrangements and other aspects of small group ecology that we discussed earlier. For example, some cultural groups, such as the Chinese, prefer sitting side-by-side rather than directly across from one another.[43] In Middle Eastern countries, Fathi Yousef and Nancy Briggs found that it is appropriate, if not expected, to stand close enough to someone to smell their breath.[44] North Americans usually prefer more space around them than do Latin Americans, Arabs, and Greeks.[45] Cultural differences can be found among ethnic groups within the same country. In a study conducted in the United States, whites maintained greater distances from African-Americans than whites did from other whites or than African-Americans did from whites.[46]

It may be tempting to make stereotypical inferences about all people within a given culture based on some of the research conclusions we have cited. We caution you to resist assuming that someone from a given culture will behave in a certain way simply because you have categorized him or her as from a high- or low-context, or high- or low-contact culture. Robert Shuter cautions against making broad, sweeping generalizations about a specific culture.[47] His research suggests that significant variations in nonverbal behavior exist *within* a culture. Thus, the conclusions we cite above are offered to document the existence of cultural differences and to warn that such differences may hamper effective communication in small groups.

No list of simple suggestions or techniques will help you manage the cultural differences that you will encounter in groups. However, there is a basic principle that can help: When interacting with people from a culture other than your own, note differences that you think may be culture-based and adapt accordingly. Become other-oriented. We are not suggesting that you abandon your cultural norms, traditions, and expectations—only that you become more flexible, thereby minimizing the communication distortion that cultural differences may cause. Carley Dodd suggests that if you think you have offended someone or acted inappropriately, ask the other person what you did that was wrong.[48] Being aware of and responding to cultural differences in small groups can enhance your ability to interact with others.

GENDER AND NONVERBAL COMMUNICATION IN SMALL GROUPS

Deborah Tannen's best-selling book *You Just Don't Understand* struck a responsive chord by identifying gender differences in verbal communication. Her work popularized a research conclusion that most of us already knew: Men and women have different communication patterns. There is evidence that just as there are gender differences in the way language is used, men and women differ in their use and interpretation of nonverbal behavior. Clara Mayo and Nancy Henley[49] as well as Judy Pearson[50] are among the scholars who provide excellent reviews of how males and females use and respond to nonverbal cues differently. Note some of the following conclusions that identify gender differences in sending and receiving nonverbal messages:

People of both sexes tend to move closer to women than to men.[51]

Women tend to move closer to others than do men.[52]

Men tend to have less eye contact with others than do women.[53]

Women seem to use more expressive facial expressions than do men.[54]

Men tend to use more gestures than do women.[55]

Men initiate touch more often than women.[56]

Women speak with less volume than men.[57]

Besides differing in their use of nonverbal behaviors, there is evidence that women tend to be more accurate in receiving and interpreting nonverbal messages. Why are there differences in the way males and females use and respond to nonverbal messages? Some theorize that the answer lies in physiological differences between men and women. But the leading explanation seems to focus on how we, as men and women, are socialized into society. Men typically have higher status in our culture and many other cultures throughout the world. Women seem to have learned how to respond to others' emotions. Status differences, the need for approval, and the value placed on interpersonal relationships and emotional needs are identified as differences between the sexes that may explain how males and females learn to use nonverbal cues.

The research conclusions reviewed here can help explain some of the differences in the way that men and women communicate in small groups. We emphasize, however, that these are research generalizations; do not expect all men and all women to exhibit these differences. Therefore, in your group deliberations, be cautious about always expecting to see these differences. Knowing that there are gender differences in nonverbal behavior may help you become both more flexible and tolerant when communicating with others in groups.

INTERPRETING NONVERBAL COMMUNICATION IN SMALL GROUPS

Nonverbal cues do not create meaning independently of other communication cues (e.g., message content, language style, and message organization). Also keep in mind that at this point in the development of nonverbal communication theory, there is much we do *not* know about nonverbal communication. After reading the research conclusions reported here, you may be tempted to interpret someone else's body language, but you should remember several principles when ascribing meaning to the posture and movement of others.

SOME BASIC GUIDELINES

Interpret Nonverbal Communication in Context   Just as you can misunderstand the meaning of a sentence taken out of context, so can you make an inaccurate inference about a nonverbal behavior when it is interpreted out of context. Simply because a group member sits with crossed legs and folded arms does not necessarily mean that that person does not want to communicate with others. Other variables in the communication system may be affecting the person's posture and position.

Look for Clusters of Cues   Look for a pattern of cues to help you interpret what a specific behavior means rather than considering only one gesture, expression, or use of personal space. Seek corroborating cues that can help you reach a more accurate conclusion about what a specific behavior means. Besides noting whether someone makes eye contact, also note whether there are complementary vocal cues, posture, and gestures to confirm your conclusion.

Recognize That People Respond Differently to Different Stimuli   Not all people express emotions in the same manner. It may take considerable time before you can understand the unique, idiosyncratic meaning underlying another person's specific nonverbal behaviors.

Consider Cultural and Gender Differences   Keep the person's cultural background or gender in mind when you draw an inference from his or her nonverbal behavior. As we have stressed in several places in this chapter, there are no generally held universal meanings for nonverbal behavior. Even though there is some evidence of common facial expressions across several cultures being interpreted with up to 92 percent accuracy, there are subtle as well as dramatic differences in the way nonverbal behaviors may be interpreted. In small group interactions, it is especially interesting to observe cultural differences in how people use space and territory. We'll offer additional tips for being sensitive to cultural differences in Chapter 7.

Consider Your Past Experience with Someone When Interpreting Nonverbal Cues   As you spend time working with group members, chances are that you will learn how to interpret their nonverbal cues. For example, when you first met Lee you weren't sure why he seemed so distant and aloof. His lack of eye contact suggested that he was not interested in being a productive member of the group. After you had spent several meetings getting to know him better, you realized that Lee is simply shy. He has good ideas but needs to be drawn out. Working with him convinces you that you should not make snap judgments of other group members. First impressions are not always accurate.

Look for Cues That Communicate Liking, Power, and Responsiveness Albert Mehrabian has developed a three-dimensional model that identifies how people respond to nonverbal messages. Even though this framework was not designed exclusively for small groups, his research can be useful in helping to interpret the meaning of messages. Although his conclusions cannot be applied universally, they do reflect the way many North Americans interpret nonverbal messages. His research suggests that people derive meaning from nonverbal behavior based on: (1) immediacy or liking, (2) power, and (3) responsiveness.[58]

1. *Immediacy: Behaviors that communicate liking and disliking.* As defined by Mehrabian, immediacy refers to whether people like or dislike others. The immediacy principle states that "People are drawn toward persons and things they like, evaluate highly, and prefer; and they avoid or move away from things they dislike, evaluate negatively, or do not prefer." According to Mehrabian, such nonverbal behaviors as touching, leaning forward, reducing distance and personal space, and maintaining direct eye contact can communicate liking or positive feelings. Based on the immediacy principle, group members who consistently sit closer to you, establish more eye contact with you, and, in general, are drawn to you probably like you more than group members who generally do not look at you and who regularly select seats away from you.

2. *Power: Behaviors that communicate influence and status.* People of higher status generally determine the degree of closeness permitted in their interactions. A person of higher status and influence, for example, usually is surrounded by more space. A boss who sits at the head of the table is more likely to have empty chairs around him or her; subordinates are more likely to give the boss more space. A person of higher status generally has a more relaxed body posture when interacting with a person of lower status. High-status members also tend to have less eye contact with others, a louder voice, make more expansive movements and postures, and may reflect their status by the way they dress.

3. *Responsiveness: Behaviors that communicate interest and attention.* Body movements, facial expressions and variation of vocal cues (such as pitch, rate, volume, and tone) all contribute to our perceptions of others as responsive or unresponsive. A group member who communicates energy and enthusiasm would be rated highly responsive.

Develop the Skill of Perception Checking People judge you by your behavior, not your intent. You judge others the same way—by what you see,

---

REVIEW BOX

Dimensions of Nonverbal Meaning

DIMENSION	DEFINITION	NONVERBAL CUES
Immediacy	Behaviors that signal liking, attraction, and interest	Touch, forward lean, close personal space, eye contact
Potency	Behaviors that communicate power, status, and influence	Protected space, increased distance, relaxed posture
Responsiveness	Behaviors that communicate active interactions and attention	Eye contact, varied vocal cues, animated facial expression

---

not by what they are thinking. Unless you are a mind reader, the only way to check your perception of others' nonverbal behavior is to ask them. **Perception checking** is the skill of asking someone whether your interpretation of his or her unspoken message is accurate. There are three steps to this skill. First, observe the nonverbal cues we have discussed. Next, mentally draw a conclusion about what the nonverbal behavior may mean. Finally, ask the other person if your inference was accurate.

Suppose you offer a solution to a problem your group has been discussing. After you announce your proposal, the group is silent, your colleagues break eye contact, and you see one person frown. To find out whether their nonverbal response means that your proposal has been rejected, you could ask, "Does your silence mean you don't like my idea?" You

---

REVIEW BOX

Perception Check

STEPS	FACTORS TO CONSIDER
1. Observe someone's nonverbal behavior.	What is her facial expression? Does she make eye contact? What is her posture? What is her tone of voice?
2. Mentally, consider what you think the behavior may mean.	Does she appear to be angry, sad, depressed? Is the nonverbal message contradicting the verbal message?
3. Check your perception by asking whether your interpretation is accurate.	"The expression on your face suggests you may be upset. Are you?"

could also add, "From the look on your face, you don't seem to be pleased with my suggestion." Your colleagues may say, "Oh, no. Your idea is a good one. I just need some time to think about how we could put your suggestion into action." We do not recommend that you overuse this skill. Stopping to seek confirmation of every facial expression or vocal tone would be irritating. We do suggest that you consider using this skill when you genuinely do not understand how a group member is responding to you.

These principles point to a key conclusion: Nonverbal messages are considerably more ambiguous than verbal messages. No dictionary has definitive meanings for nonverbal behaviors. Exercise caution, then, when you attempt to interpret the nonverbal behavior of other group members.

PUTTING PRINCIPLE INTO PRACTICE

This chapter has noted that nonverbal communication variables have a profound impact on small group dynamics. Group members send more messages nonverbally than they do verbally—people cannot *not* communicate.

Nonverbal cues affect the meanings of messages; individuals generally believe these cues more than they believe verbal messages. Nonverbal cues are particularly important in communicating emotions.

We have discussed several applications of nonverbal communication research to small groups. Consider the following suggestions.

BODY POSTURE, MOVEMENT, AND GESTURES

- You may be more effective in persuading others when you use eye contact, maintain a direct body orientation, and remain physically close to others.
- You can often identify high-status group members (or at least those who perceive themselves as having high status) by such nonverbal cues as relaxed postures, loud speaking voices, territorial dominance, expansive movements, and, sometimes, their keeping themselves at a distance from others.
- Someone who is lying may speak with a higher-pitched voice, use less eye contact, show less enthusiasm, shrug his or her hands more often, nod less, speak more slowly and with more errors, and adopt a less-immediate posture.
- Group leaders may gesture more than followers.
- Observing the similarity of group members' posture and gestures can reveal insights about group climate, leadership, and cohesiveness.

EYE CONTACT

- People sometimes interrupt eye contact with others because they are trying to think of the right words to say, not because they are uninterested.

- When talking with others in a small group, be sure to look at all members so that you can respond to the feedback they provide.
- You sometimes can draw a person into the conversation just by establishing direct eye contact.
- Because eye contact signals whether a communication channel is open or closed, you may be able to quiet an extremely talkative member by avoiding eye contact.
- By noting who looks at whom in a small group, you can get a good idea of who the leader is. Group members usually look at their leader more than they look at any other member (assuming that they respect their leader's ideas and opinions).

FACIAL EXPRESSION

- Look at group members' facial expressions to find out the emotional climate in the group.

VOCAL CUES

- You may find that you dislike a group member not because of what he or she says but because of that person's vocal quality, pitch, or rate of speech. People's vocal cues affect your perceptions of them.

TERRITORIALITY AND PERSONAL SPACE

- Members probably will stake out their territory or personal space early on in group gatherings.
- When group members' territories are invaded, they probably will respond nonverbally (via posture or territorial markers) to defend their territories.
- Since most small group meetings take place in what one researcher calls the "social distance category" (4 to 12 feet), a group leader should try to see that the distances between small group participants fall within this range.
- If you want to increase your interaction with a group member, sit directly across from him or her.
- If you know that a group member generally monopolizes the conversation, try to get that person to select a corner seat rather than one at the head of a conference table.
- You are more likely to emerge as a group leader if you sit so that you can establish eye contact and a direct body orientation with most of the group members.
- Since people prefer greater personal space when they are under stress, make sure that group members have plenty of territory when you know that a meeting is going to be stressful.

PERSONAL APPEARANCE

- Your personal appearance will affect the way other group members perceive you. It can also influence your ability to persuade others.

COMMUNICATION ENVIRONMENT

- Make sure that the physical environment for a group meeting is as comfortable and attractive as possible to enhance satisfaction and productivity.

TIME

- Talk with your group members about their expectations of punctuality, meeting deadlines, and work efficiency in order to avoid misunderstandings about use of time.

GENDER

- Men and women may differ in the way they interpret and send nonverbal messages; avoid assuming that all males and all females behave in a certain way.

CULTURE

- If you are communicating with someone from a high-context culture (which places more emphasis on nonverbal than verbal information), realize that your unspoken signals will be especially important in the interpretation of your message. You don't have to *say* it to say it.
- Some people prefer greater closeness (high-contact culture) while other individuals prefer less physical contact (low-contact culture); monitor your use of personal space to assess the impact that your use of territory has on others.
- Interpret nonverbal messages from both the sender's and receiver's culture.
- Become other-oriented to minimize communication distortion that may result from cultural differences.

INTERPRETING NONVERBAL BEHAVIOR

- Consider the context when making inferences about what a specific behavior may mean.
- Look for clusters of cues rather than focusing on just one nonverbal behavior when interpreting unspoken messages.

- Because not all people have the same reaction to the same situation, avoid interpreting one person's nonverbal expression in the same way as the identical expression displayed by another person.
- Factor in cultural and gender expectations that others may have when interpreting nonverbal messages.
- You will likely be more successful in interpreting nonverbal messages from people you know or have worked with over a long period of time. Therefore, be cautious when drawing a conclusion about a new acquaintance's nonverbal behavior.
- Use eye contact, posture, touch, and personal-space factors to help determine whether you are liked or disliked by others.
- Use posture, appearance, personal space, and relaxation cues to help you interpret someone's perception of his or her power and influence.
- Use eye contact, vocal cues, movement, and facial expressions to help interpret someone's interest and responsiveness toward you.
- To check your interpretation of someone's nonverbal behavior, ask whether your understanding of his or her unspoken message is accurate.

PRACTICE

RECEIVING NONVERBAL REINFORCEMENT

Pair up with another student and take turns telling each other about an important idea, feeling, or experience. Your partner should give no nonverbal indications that he or she is paying attention while you speak: no smiles, nodding of the head, "um-hums," postural orientation, facial expressions. After each of you has talked for three to five minutes, discuss what it felt like (a) to receive no nonverbal attention and (b) to give no nonverbal attention. After you discuss the importance of nonverbal communication, talk again with your partner—this time providing genuine nonverbal feedback. Your instructor will lead you in a discussion of the differences between receiving and not receiving nonverbal reinforcement.

NONVERBAL GROUP OBSERVATION

If you are working on a group project, videotape one of your group meetings or videotape your group attempting to solve a case study. Replay the videotape with the sound turned off. Or, if you don't have video equipment, simply observe a group while you are some distance from it. Focus on group members' actions, not their words.

1. Notice group members' use of emblems, illustrators, affect displays, regulators, and adaptors.
2. Observe how nonverbal cues regulate the flow of communication.

3. How do body posture and movement communicate members' status and attitudes?
4. Try to identify the four functions of eye contact in your group.
5. Do group members communicate much emotion with their faces?
6. Note relationships between territorial behavior, seating arrangement, and leadership, status, and verbal interaction in the group.
7. If your group had to meet in a special room to videotape the session, how did the change in environment affect the group?

SMALL GROUP ECOLOGY

Five people have been assigned by their instructor to work on a small group project for their group communication class. All of their meetings will take place in a room approximately 20 feet square. One large rectangular table stands in the center of the room. Several chairs are also in the room. A small circular table is shoved up into a corner.

Based on small group ecology research, what do you think would be the ideal seating arrangement for this group? Justify your arrangement with the practices and principles presented in this chapter.

Consider these personality profiles of the five members:

JULIO: He likes to be the leader. However, he usually does not pull his weight when it comes to getting a job accomplished. He likes to feel that he is in control of the group.

JANE: Jane is very intelligent, and others usually respect her opinions. However, she only participates in a discussion when she is encouraged to do so. She is very shy and does not enjoy group projects.

NELL: Nell is very outgoing. She enjoys working with people, and people enjoy working with her. She is well liked by most students.

KWON: Kwon has real leadership potential. He has a talent for organizing people and accomplishing jobs. He can be a real asset to a small group, but sometimes he must be encouraged to participate.

BARBARA: Most people do not enjoy working with Barbara because she is very pessimistic. She is intelligent and is a good researcher, but she usually does not volunteer to work unless she is encouraged by other group members.

NONVERBAL FREEZE

Before participating in the group discussion, set a timer to go off five to ten minutes into the discussion. No one should know the exact time at which the timer will sound. When it does sound, members should stop talking and freeze in position, maintaining their body orientation, facial expression, and so on. Discuss the possible meanings of the information revealed by body position and other nonverbal cues.

Nonverbal Photo Analysis

Have someone photograph your group during a deliberation. If possible, use an instant camera. After the discussion, distribute the photos for group members to analyze the nonverbal information revealed. Make observations about immediacy, power, and responsiveness cues that you can identify from the photos.

Notes

1. R. L. Birdwhistell, *Kinesics and Context* (Philadelphia: University of Pennsylvania Press, 1970).
2. Albert Mehrabian, *Nonverbal Communication* (Chicago: Aldine Atherton, 1972), 108.
3. P. Ekman and W. V. Friesen, "The Repertoire of Nonverbal Behavior: Categories, Origins, Usage, and Coding," *Semiotica* 1 (1969): 49–98.
4. W. S. Condon and W. D. Ogston, "Soundfilm Analysis of Normal and Patho-logical Behavior Patterns," *Journal of Nervous and Mental Disease* 143 (1966): 338–47.
5. P. Ekman and W. V. Friesen, "Hand Movements," *Journal of Communication* 22 (1972): 353–74.
6. Paul Ekman and W. V. Friesen, "Nonverbal Leakage and Clues to Deception," *Psychiatry* 32 (1969): 88–106.
7. Mark L. Knapp, *Nonverbal Communication in Human Interaction* (New York: Holt, Rinehart & Winston, 1978), 228.
8. J. O'Connor, "The Relationship of Kinesics and Verbal Communication to Lead-ership Perception in Small Group Discussion," unpublished Ph.D. dissertation, Indiana University, 1971.
9. John Baird, "Some Nonverbal Elements of Leadership Emergence," *Southern Speech Communication Journal* 40 (1977): 352–61; also see Laurence M. Childs et al., "Nonverbal and Verbal Communication of Leadership." Paper presented at the annual meeting of the American Psychological Association, Los Angeles, 1981.
10. Albert Mehrabian and M. Williams, "Nonverbal Concomitants of Perceived and Intended Persuasiveness," *Journal of Personality and Social Psychology* 13(1969): 37–58.
11. M. Reece and R. Whitman, "Expressive Movements, Warmth, and Verbal Rein-forcement," *Journal of Abnormal and Social Psychology* 64 (1962): 234–36.
12. Mark L. Knapp, Roderick P. Hart, Gustav W. Friedrich, and Gary Schulman, "The Rhetoric of Goodbye: Verbal and Nonverbal Correlates of Human Leave-Taking," *Speech Monographs* 40 (1975): 182–98.
13. W. S. Condon and L. W. Sander, "Neonate Movement Is Synchronized with Adult Speech: Interactional Participation and Language Acquisition," *Science* I (January 1974): 99–101; W. S. Condon and W. D. Ogston, "Soundfilm Analysis of

Normal and Pathological Behavior Patterns," *Journal of Nervous and Mental Disease* 143 (1966): 338–47.

14. A. Kendon, "Some Relationships between Body Motion and Speech: An Analysis of an Example," in A. W. Siegman and B. Pope (eds.), *Studies in Dyadic Communication* (Elmsford, N.Y.: Pergamon Press, 1972).

15. Davida Navarre and Catherine A. Emihovich, "Movement Synchrony and the Self-Analytic Group," Paper presented at the Eastern Communication Association, Boston, 1978.

16. Edward A. Mabry, "Developmental Aspects of Nonverbal Behavior in Small Group Settings," *Small Group Behavior* 20 (May 1989): 190–202.

17. M. Argyle and A. Kendon, "The Experimental Analysis of Social Performance," in L. Berkowitz (ed.), *Advances in Experimental Social Psychology* 3 (New York: Academic Press, 1967), 55–98.

18. Knapp, *Nonverbal Communication,* 313.

19. A. Kendon, "Some Functions of Gaze-Direction in Social Interaction," *Acta Psychologica* 26 (1967): 22–63.

20. P. Ekman and W. V. Friesen, *Unmasking the Face* (Englewood Cliffs, N.J.: Prentice-Hall, 1975).

21. Paul Ekman, W. V. Friesen, and S. S. Tomkins, "Facial Affect Scoring Technique: A First Validity Study," *Semiotica* 3 (1971): 37–58; Ekman and Friesen, *Unmasking the Face.*

22. K. K. Sereno and G. J. Hawkins, "The Effect of Variations in Speakers' Nonfluency upon Audience Ratings of Attitude toward the Speech Topic and Speakers' Credibility," *Speech Monographs* 34 (1967): 58–64; G. R. Miller and M. A. Hewgill, "The Effect of Variations in Nonfluency on Audience Ratings of Source Credibility," *Quarterly Journal of Speech* 50 (1964): 36–44.

23. J. R. Davitz, *The Communication of Emotional Meaning* (New York: McGraw-Hill, 1964).

24. Albert Mehrabian, "Significance of Posture and Position in the Communication of Attitude and Status Relationships," *Psychological Bulletin* 71 (1969): 363.

25. B. Stenzor, "The Spatial Factor in Face to Face Discussion Groups," *Journal of Abnormal and Social Psychology* 45 (1950): 552–55.

26. F. Strodtbeck and L. Hook, "The Social Dimensions of a Twelve Man Jury Table," *Sociometry* 36 (1973): 424–29; A. Hare and R. Bales, "Seating Position and Small Group Interaction," *Sociometry* 26 (1963): 480–86.

27. L. T. Howells and S. W. Becker, "Seating Arrangement and Leadership Emergence," *Journal of Abnormal and Social Psychology* 64 (1962): 148–50.

28. Ronald L. Michelini, Robert Passalacqua, and John Cusimano, "Effects of Seating Arrangement on Group Participation," *Journal of Social Psychology* 99 (1976): 179–86.

29. C. Harris Silverstein and David J. Stang, "Seating Position and Interaction in Triads: A Field Study," *Sociometry* (1976): 166–70.

30. M. Dosey and M. Meisels, "Personal Space and Self Protection," *Journal of Personality and Social Psychology* 11 (1969): 93–97.

31. R. Sommer, "Studies in Personal Space," *Sociometry* 22 (1959): 247–60.

32. M. Cook, "Experiments on Orientation and Proxemics," *Human Relations* 23 (1970): 61–76.

33. J. E. Singer, "The Use of Manipulative Strategies: Machiavellianism and Attractiveness," *Sociometry* 27 (1964): 128–51. J. Kelly, "Dress as Non-Verbal Communi-

cation." Paper presented to the annual conference of the American Association for Public Opinion Research, May 1969; M. Lefkowitz, R. Blake, and J. Mouton, "Status Factors in Pedestrian Violation of Traffic Signals," *Journal of Abnormal and Social Psychology* 51 (1955): 704–6; J. Mills and E. Aronson, "Opinion Change as a Function of the Communicator's Attractiveness and Desire to Influence," *Journal of Social Psychology* 1 (1965): 73–77.

34. W. H. Sheldon, *Atlas of Man: A Guide for Somatyping the Adult Male at All Ages* (New York: Harper & Row, 1954).

35. Edward T. Hall and Mildred Reed Hall, *Understanding Cultural Differences* (Yarmouth, Maine: Intercultural Press, 1989).

36. Ibid.

37. Adapted from: Donald W. Klopf, *Intercultural Encounters: The Fundamentals of Intercultural Communication* (Englewood, Colo.: Morton Publishing Company, 1995.) and Hall and Hall, *Understanding Cultural Differences*, 1989.

38. Klopf, *Intercultural Encounters*, 1995.

39. Definition based on one by A. G. Smith, ed., *Communication and Culture* (New York: Holt, Rinehart & Winston, 1966).

40. Edward T. Hall, *Beyond Culture* (Garden City, N.Y.: Doubleday, 1976).

41. Ibid.

42. Ibid.

43. Carley H. Dodd, *Dynamics of Intercultural Communication.* (Dubuque, Iowa: Wm. C. Brown, 1991).

44. Fathi Yousef and Nancy Briggs, "The Multinational Business Organization: A Schema for the Training of Overseas Personnel in Communication," *International and Intercultural Communication Annual* 2 (1975): 74–85.

45. Edward T. Hall, *The Silent Language* (New York: Anchor, 1973).

46. Melanie Booth-Butterfield and Felecia Jordan, "Communication Adaptation among Racially Homogeneous and Heterogeneous Groups," *The Southern Communication Journal* 54 (Spring 1989): 253–72.

47. Robert Shuter, "A Field Study of Nonverbal Communication in Germany, Italy, and the United States," *Communication Monographs* 44 (1977): 298–305.

48. Dodd, *Dynamics of Intercultural Communication*.

49. Clara Mayo and Nancy Henley, *Gender and Nonverbal Behavior* (New York: Springer Verlag, 1981).

50. Judy Pearson, Lynn Turner, and William Todd-Mancillas, *Gender and Communication* (Dubuque, Iowa: Wm C. Brown, 1991).

51. Gloria Leventhal and Michelle Matturro, "Differential Effects of Spatial Crowding and Sex on Behavior," *Perceptual Motor Skills* 50 (1980): 111–19.

52. Robert Sommer, "Studies in Personal Space," *Sociometry* 22 (1959): 247–60.

53. Phoebe C. Ellsworth and Linda M. Ludwig, "Visual Behavior in Social Interaction," *Journal of Communication* 22 (1972): 375–403.

54. Mehrabian, *Nonverbal Communication*.

55. Nancy M. Henley, *Body Politics: Power, Sex and Nonverbal Communication* (Englewood Cliffs, N.J.: Prentice-Hall, 1977).

56. Ibid.

57. Norman N. Markel, Joseph Long, and Thomas J. Saine, "Sex Effects in Conversational Interaction: Another Look at Male Dominance," *Human Communication Research* 2 (1976): 356–64.

58. Albert Mehrabian. *Silent Messages* (Belmont, Calif.: Wadsworth, 1972), 108.

CHAPTER
S·E·V·E·N

Small Group Decision Making and Problem Solving

After studying this chapter, you will be able to:

- Formulate a question of fact, value, or policy for a group discussion.

- Identify three criteria for a well-phased policy discussion question.

- Identify appropriate ways to use facts, examples, opinions, and statistics in group discussions.

- Identify appropriate methods for researching group discussion questions.

- Differentiate between group decision making

and group problem solving.

- Describe the elements of group decision making.

- List and describe characteristics of effective group decision makers.

- Compare and contrast descriptive, functional, and prescriptive approaches to problem solving in small groups.

- Identify the four phases of group process.

- Discuss the three types of group activity tracks.

Knowledge is power.
Not to decide is to decide.
You're either helping solve the problem or you're part of the problem.

These three statements summarize the essential reasons groups are often called upon to deliberate. Groups discuss issues to search for truth; groups make decisions; and groups solve problems. In this chapter and the next, we turn our attention to principles and strategies that provide structure and guide interaction to help groups do their work. That work often involves seeking answers to questions, making choices among several options, or circumventing vexing obstacles to solve problems.

First we present classic strategies and principles that can help any group prepare for effective discussion. How group members frame the issues they discuss and seek and use evidence are critical to the age-old quest for truth through dialogue. Second, we define group decision making, describe how groups often make decisions, and present principles that can enhance collaborative decision making. We conclude the chapter by focusing on principles of group problem solving. More research about group problem solving communication has been conducted than about any other group objective. In Chapter 8 we continue our discussion of group communication principles with a look at strategies and techniques that can help groups do their work effectively and efficiently.

PREPARING FOR GROUP DISCUSSION

The Greek philosopher Socrates believed the primary goal of dialogue and discussion was the search for truth. Today group discussion continues to be a key method of seeking answers to tough questions. Our legal system is based on a jury of men and women who, after hearing evidence, discuss whether someone is or is not guilty of a crime. In corporations, teams and task forces churn out key decisions which help shape the goals of large and small organizations alike. Community task forces are often formed to investigate issues of local concern, such as education and public safety. Regardless of a group's composition, goal, or context, its discussion will be more productive if group members have a focused goal and consider evidence and accurate information to help them accomplish their work. To prepare for deliberation, any group needs to identify their primary goal, gather information and evidence, and use that evidence to reach accurate conclusions.

FORMULATING DISCUSSION QUESTIONS

Before most scientists begin an experiment or conduct scholarly research, they have some idea of what they are looking for. Some researchers start with a *hypothesis,* a guess based on previous theory and research about what they will find in their search for new knowledge. Other investigators formulate a *research question* that provides a direction for their research. Like scientific research, problem solving seeks answers to questions. It makes sense, then, for group members to formulate a question before searching for answers. By identifying a specific question that they must answer, members can reduce some of the initial uncertainty that accompanies their discussion.

Phrasing a discussion question should be done with considerable care. It is an important part of initiating and organizing any group discussion, particularly problem-solving discussions, since the quality and specificity of a question usually determine the quality of the answer. The better a group prepares a discussion question, the more clearly articulated will be the group's goal, and the greater will be the chances for a productive and orderly discussion.

In some group discussions and conferences, the question has been predetermined. Government committees and juries exemplify such groups. But usually groups are faced with a problem or need and are responsible for formulating a specific question to guide their deliberations. There are basically three types of discussion questions: questions of fact, questions of value, and questions of policy. To help you determine which type is most appropriate for your various group discussions, we will discuss each.

QUESTIONS OF FACT

In summarizing the responsibilities of the jury during a criminal court case, the judge provides a very specific question of fact to help guide the jury in its discussion. "Your job," instructs the judge, "is to decide whether the defendant is guilty or not guilty of the charges against him." A **question of fact** asks whether something happened or did not happen; its answer determines what is true and what is false.

A question of fact can ultimately be answered by one of two responses—either "yes" or "no." (Although, of course, a yes or no response can be qualified in terms of the probability of its accuracy.) The question "Did the Twins win the World Series in 1995?" is a question of fact; either they did or they did not. "Is Russia expanding military operations in South America?" Again, the answer is either "yes" or "no," depending on the evidence. But questions of fact often appear deceptively simple. In trying to answer a question of fact, define the critical words or phrases in the question. In the preceding question, for example, what is meant by "expanding military operations"? Does it mean building new missile bases, or does it mean sending a few military advisers to a Latin American country? By reducing the ambi-

Problem solving groups must formulate their research questions carefully so that members have a clear idea of how to go about answering them.

guity of a question's meaning, a group can save considerable time in agreeing on a final answer.

Your group's objective will determine whether or not you should investigate a question of fact. If the group needs to discover what is true and what is false, then formulate a question of fact and define the key words in the question to give it greater focus and clarity. If the group needs to make a less objective value judgment or to suggest solutions to a problem, choose one of the types of questions discussed below.

QUESTIONS OF VALUE

A **question of value** generally produces a lively discussion because it concerns attitudes, beliefs, and values about what is good or bad or right or wrong. Answering a question of value is more complicated than simply determining whether an event did or did not occur. "Are Democratic presidents better leaders than Republican presidents?" is an example of a question of value. Group members' responses to this question depend on their attitudes toward Democrats and Republicans.

An **attitude** is a learned predisposition to respond to a person, object, or idea in a favorable, neutral, or unfavorable way. In essence, the attitudes you hold about your world determine whether you like or dislike what you experience and observe. A favorable attitude toward Democrats will affect your response to the value question, "Are Democratic presidents better leaders than Republican presidents?"

A **belief** is the way in which you structure what is true and false. Put another way, it is the way you structure reality. If you believe in God, you have structured your reality to assume that God exists. If you do not believe in God, you have structured your perception of what is true and false so that God is not part of your reality.

A **value** is also often defined as an enduring conception of good and bad. Your values affect your perceptions of right and wrong. A value is more resistant to change than an attitude or a belief.

What are your values? Which of your values have the most influence on your behavior? Because values are so central to how you respond in the world, you may have trouble coming up with a tidy list of your most important values. You may be able to list things you like and do not like (attitudes) or what you believe is true and not true (beliefs), but your values are sometimes difficult to identify as the guiding forces affecting your behavior. Figure 7.1 shows values in the center of the diagram to indicate that they are central to your behavior; beliefs, the next ring, are influenced by your values. Finally, you hold the attitudes you do because of what you value and what you believe to be true and false.

Understanding the differences between attitudes, beliefs, and values helps you better understand what happens when a group discusses a value question. You base your response to a value question on your own attitudes, beliefs, and values, as do other group members. If you can identify the underlying attitudes, beliefs, and values that influence the responses to a value question, you can examine and discuss them.

FIGURE 7.1   INTERRELATIONSHIP OF VALUES, BELIEFS, AND ATTITUDES

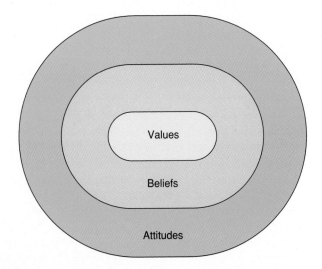

QUESTIONS OF POLICY

Most problem-solving discussions revolve around **questions of policy.** Policy questions help groups determine what course of action or policy change would enable them to solve a problem or reach a decision. "What should be done to improve the quality of education in U.S. colleges and universities?" and "What can Congress do to reduce America's trade deficit?" are examples of policy questions. These questions can be identified easily because answers to them require changes of policy or procedure. Discussion questions including phrases such as, "What should be done about. . . ?" or "What could be done to improve. . . ?" are policy questions. Most legislation in the U.S. Senate and House of Representatives is proposed in response to specific policy questions.

A well-worded policy question should imply that a specific problem must be solved. The question "What should be done about UFOs?" is not an appropriate policy question, because it does not provide enough direction to a specific problem. Do not confuse a discussion *topic* with a discussion *question.* If your group is going to discuss UFOs it has a topic, but it is not trying to solve a problem. The group could rephrase the discussion question to make it more policy-oriented: "What could be done to improve the way the government handles and investigates UFO sightings in the United States?" The rephrased question more clearly implies that there is a problem in the way the government investigates sightings of UFOs. The latter question provides clearer direction for research and analysis.

A good policy question is limited in scope. Do not try to tackle a complex problem unless your group has the time and resources to solve it. For example, a group of students was assigned the task of formulating a policy question, discussing it, and then reporting the results of the discussion to the class. The students had three weeks to analyze and suggest possible solutions to the problem they had chosen to investigate—"What should be done to deal with the federal debt?" While the question clearly implies a specific problem, its lack of focus frustrated the group. A more limited discussion question, such as, "What should be done to improve the tax base in our community?" would have been more manageable. You would do better to consider a simple, clearly worded question that can be analyzed in the time period allotted to your group than a question that would keep the U.S. Congress busy for several months or even years. On the other hand, a group should not phrase a policy discussion question so that it requires only a yes or no answer or so that it limits the group's options for solutions. Given this criterion, "Should seat belts be required by law?" is a less satisfactory policy discussion topic than "What can be done to ensure greater highway safety?"

A third important criterion is that a policy question should be controversial. It should be an important issue worth discussing. An issue is a question about which individuals disagree. If group members disagree about how to solve a problem, they should not necessarily select another issue.

Conflict, controversy, and disagreement should not always be viewed negatively. If group members agreed on how to solve a problem at the beginning of the discussion, they would have nothing to discuss. The purpose of a group discussion is to consider all alternatives and to agree on the best one. Therefore, do not reject a discussion question because other group members may hold contrasting points of view. Your discussion will be more interesting and you will probably reach a better solution if the group examines all sides of an issue.

The three types of discussion questions (fact, value, and policy) may not appear to overlap, but as one researcher has observed, group members must concern themselves with questions of fact and value when considering questions of policy.[1] They must judge evidence as true or false (question of fact). Their attitudes, beliefs, and values (questions of value) will influence the decisions they make on policy changes (questions of policy). A discussion question serves a valuable function in providing direction to group deliberations. Once groups devise discussion questions, however, they can still modify them.

Decide whether your group is considering a question of fact, value, or policy. Identifying the type of question helps you understand the dynamics of the issue under discussion. If you realize that the question "Should we legalize casino gambling?" involves value judgments, you will be less likely to condemn group members who disagree with you. Even in the face of disagreement, frustration and defensiveness can yield to understanding and compromise. Remember, too, that even though a discussion question may be clearly identified as one of fact, value, or policy, your discussion probably will include other types of questions. Once your group has a well-defined problem to discuss, members should begin researching and analyzing it.

REVIEW BOX

Three Types of Group Discussion Questions

QUESTION TYPE	DEFINITION	EXAMPLE
Question of fact	A question that asks whether something is true or false	Did the university have a freshman admission policy last year?
Question of value	A question that considers the worth or desirability of something	Is an electoral college a better system than a direct popular vote?
Question of policy	A question that considers whether a change in procedure should be made	What should be done to curtail gang violence in our community?

USING EVIDENCE IN GROUP DISCUSSION

After you formulate your discussion question, you need to define key terms and gather information on the issues it involves. Members should also know something about the four kinds of evidence available: facts, examples, opinions, and statistics. Group members who use evidence effectively make better decisions. A recent study found that the key element in swaying a jury is the quality and quantity of the evidence presented.[2]

FACTS

A *fact* is any statement proven to be true. A fact cannot be a prediction about the future, because such a statement cannot be verified; it must be a report of something that has already happened or that is happening. "It will rain tomorrow" cannot be a fact, because the statement cannot be verified. "The weather forecaster predicts rain" may be a fact if the weather forecaster has made such a prediction; the accuracy of the forecast has nothing to do with whether the statement is a fact. Ask yourself these questions to determine whether a statement is a fact:

1. Is it true?
2. Is the source reliable?
3. Are there contrary facts?

EXAMPLES

An *example* is an illustration of a particular case or incident and is most valuable when used to emphasize a fact. An example may be real or hypothetical. A real example can also be called a fact; it actually exists or has happened. A hypothetical example is of little use in proving a point but can add color and interest or help to explicate an otherwise dry or difficult factual presentation. Apply the following tests to examples:

1. Is it typical?
2. Is it significant?
3. Are there contrary examples?

OPINIONS

An *opinion* is a quoted comment. Opinions of unbiased authorities who base opinions on fact are most valuable as evidence. Like examples, opinions can dramatize a point and make it more interesting. Opinions are most effective when used in conjunction with facts or statistics. The following questions will help you determine the usefulness of opinions:

1. Is the source reliable?
2. Is the source an expert in the field?

3. Is the source free from bias?
4. Is the opinion consistent with other statements made by the same source?
5. Is the opinion characteristic of opinions held by other experts in the field?

STATISTICS

Because they cannot present dozens of facts or examples in a given time limit, people often rely on statistics. A *statistic* is simply a number: 10,000 people, 132 reported cases of child abuse, 57 Western nations. Statistics provide firm support for important points. Pay special attention, though, to the tests of statistics listed below, since statistics are probably the most frequently misgathered and misinterpreted type of evidence.

1. Is the source reliable?
2. Is the source unbiased?
3. Are the figures recent? Do they apply to the time period in question?
4. How were the statistics drawn? If from a sample, is the sample representative of the total population? Is the sample big enough to be reliable?
5. Does the statistic actually measure what it is supposed to measure?
6. Are there contrary statistics?

Once you have located and collected your evidence, keep in mind a couple of guidelines for applying it effectively. First, never take evidence out of context. Even if you find a statement that seems to be exactly the evidence you need, do not use it if the next sentence following it says something like, "However, this idea has recently been proved false." Second, try to gather and utilize evidence from as many sources as possible. Finally, use many different types of evidence to support a point.

FINDING EVIDENCE FOR GROUP DISCUSSION

How do you go about finding the evidence you need? Your group will probably seek information by heading for the library and using the numerous electronic data bases now available to access facts, examples, opinions, and statistics. Many of you will be able to retrieve evidence from your home if you have a personal computer and a modem. Through the Internet, World Wide Web, and other on-line services, you can access volumes of information useful to your group's deliberation. If you are investigating a local or campus issue, or if you want to assess local opinions and attitudes about your discussion question, you may decide to conduct a survey. We will briefly touch upon both of these traditional approaches to gathering evidence.

USING THE LIBRARY AND ELECTRONIC RESOURCES

You undoubtedly already know how to go about finding information in your library. While some libraries still have the traditional card catalog to help you find books, most libraries today have computer-assisted indexes of both books and periodicals. Check to see if your library has facilities for you to conduct computer searches of scholarly journals through the Educational Resources Information Center (ERIC), business journals through the ABI/Inform, or general works through the *Readers' Guide to Periodical Literature.* Do not overlook other useful sources of information that your library may have, such as collections of government documents or audiovisual materials.

In addition to the books and journals in the physical space in your library, a wealth of information exists in cyberspace—the network of information in computers stored around the world. Started as a network of only four computers in 1969, today the Internet consists of over 10,000 computer networks and is used by millions of people in virtually every country in the world. To access this vast depository of information, you need a computer, a telephone line, and software that lets your computer "talk" with other computers. Your college library will have the hardware and software you need if you do not own a computer.

The Internet can be a challenging place in which to navigate. The multitude of networks and subnetworks make it difficult to know where to go to get what you need. If you are not yet electronically literate, your college librarian or perhaps a member of your group can help you gather information from this valuable source. Some menu-driven systems, such as Gopher, Archie, Netscape, Java, the Wide Area Information Server (WAIS), and Mosaic are especially user friendly for locating data.

If using electronic resources is a new experience for you, be sure to allow ample time to gather what you need. Another challenge in gathering data electronically is deciding which data are relevant to your question. While you can now access hundreds of libraries and end up with a ream of documents, the *volume* of information is not nearly as important as your ability to *use* the information you gather. Use the tests of evidence presented earlier to help you wade through the evidence you retrieve.

DEVELOPING A SURVEY

If you are investigating a local campus or community problem, you may need to conduct a survey to describe the attitudes, beliefs, values, or behavior of people affected by the problem you are solving. Surveys can also help a group understand the seriousness of a problem or its probable causes, effects, and symptoms.

J. W. Bowers and John Courtwright suggest that anyone attempting to conduct a survey faces common problems, including: (1) developing clear, unbiased questions, (2) selecting a large enough sample to be representative of the entire population being sampled, (3) writing a questionnaire so that it is clear to the reader and efficient for the interviewer, (4) deciding on whether to interview people face-to-face, over the phone, or by mail; (5) making sure that the questionnaire will answer the questions that need answers, and (6) testing the clarity of the questionnaire by administering a pilot study or mini-survey.[3]

First, the group must determine a survey's objectives. What does the group want to know that it does not know now? Once a group determines its objectives, it can then decide how best to ask questions that will give clear answers. **Open-ended questions,** such as essay questions, permit respondents to answer freely without any constraints. **Closed-ended questions** ask respondents to choose answers from among several responses supplied by the interviewer. Examples of closed-ended questions include multiple-choice and true-false questions and questions that require respondents to rank items of importance or indicate agreement or disagreement. The answers to closed-ended questions can be more easily tabulated, but open-ended questions allow for a wide range of responses. The type of questions your group asks depends on what you want to know.

After developing and organizing questions, you need to decide on a survey method. If you primarily ask open-ended questions, it may be best to conduct face-to-face interviews so that you can probe and clarify respondents' answers. Interviewing requires listening and recording skills. If you have the time and resources, you may want to mail questionnaires. Including a self-addressed stamped envelope with each questionnaire improves your response rate. You can also stop people on campus or in your community to have them respond to a brief written questionnaire (Make sure you have permission to do this from whoever owns the property on which you distribute questionnaires.) In addition, most universities have rules about conducting research on campus. If you are working on a class project, consult your instructor before making final decisions about survey methods and distribution.

Before administering your questionnaire, survey a very small sample to make sure your questionnaire is clear. Have your instructor or other members of your class examine its format and wording to see that it makes sense. This step can save you time, energy, money, and embarrassment.

An example of an open-ended question is the following: "What are your feelings about increasing property taxes to support local schools and other services?" Examples of closed-ended questions include the following:

1. Are you in favor of raising property taxes?
    _____Yes   _____No
2. Local property taxes should be increased to support our local school. Circle your response.
    Strongly agree   Agree   Undecided   Disagree   Strongly disagree
3. Select the statement that most closely reflects your feelings about tax increases.

a. Property taxes should be increased to support local schools.

b. Property taxes should not be increased to support local schools.

c. I am uncertain whether property taxes should be increased to support local schools.

d. Taxes other than the property tax should be increased to support local schools; indicate which taxes should be increased to support local schools.

4. Rank the following sources of potential tax revenue increases to support local schools from most desirable (1) to least desirable (6).

_____ Property tax   _____ Cigarette tax

_____ Sales tax   _____ Alcohol tax

_____ Gasoline tax   _____ Income tax

Once you have designed and tested a questionnaire, you must make sure that you survey a broad sample of people to justify your conclusions. If, for example, you want to know if students support a 5 percent increase in university tuition, it would not be wise to ask only graduating seniors. A random sample of the entire student population at your school would provide the best basis for making a decision about the acceptability of a tuition increase. You would also need to ask enough people to gauge the attitude of your entire student body. If you survey only 20 students out of 15,000, you have a greater potential for error.

GROUP DECISION MAKING: CHOOSING AMONG ALTERNATIVES

One of the critical tasks groups are called upon to do is make decisions. **Decision making** involves choosing from among several alternatives. For example, in deciding which college or university to attend, you probably considered several choices. Perhaps you started by gathering information about 15 or 20 schools and then narrowed the alternatives as you considered the advantages and disadvantages of each institution. Eventually you narrowed your choice to two and made a final decision. Groups make decisions in essentially the same way. In this section we will consider the elements, methods, and characteristics of group decision making and also examine some of the obstacles that keep groups from making high-quality decisions.

ELEMENTS OF GROUP DECISION MAKING

According to two researchers, group decision making usually follows a predictable pattern.[4] Groups tend to make better decisions if the pattern is explicitly identified so that the group can structure its discussion. Group decision making includes the following steps.[5]

1. *The group assesses the present situation.* A group analyzes a situation based on available information and realizes that it needs to make a decision. For example, the board of directors of an airline trying to decide whether to lower fares looks at competitors' fares and the number of passengers those competitors transport each day.

2. *The group either identifies alternatives or identifies group goals.* After assessing the current situation the group usually does one of two things. Based on its needs, a group either identifies its objectives or begins to identify alternative courses of action. A group uncertain about its task usually identifies objectives; if its goal is clear, a group begins to identify alternatives or choices.

3. *The group identifies positive and negative consequences of alternatives.* The greater the number of alternatives a group generates, the greater the likelihood that it will make a good decision. Poor decisions usually occur when a group fails to generate enough good possible choices. A group must do more, however, than identify alternatives; it should also assess the positive and negative implications of each alternative before making a decision. What are the implications of lowering airfares by 10 percent? The number of passengers might increase. But if a lower fare is not properly advertised and no additional passengers fly with the airline, profits could decrease 10 percent.

4. *The group selects the alternative (makes a decision).* The alternative selected should potentially have a maximum positive outcome with minimal negative consequences. A group is more likely to select the best alternative if it has carefully assessed the situation, considered group goals, identified several choices and noted the positive and negative implications of each.

METHODS OF GROUP DECISION MAKING

After the alternatives have been narrowed and weighed, what methods can groups use to make a decision? Knowing these methods can give you and your group options to consider when a decision needs to be made.[6]

Decisions by Experts in Groups   One person in a group may seem to be the best informed about the issue, and members can turn to this person to make the choice. This expert may or may not be a group's designated leader. Deferring to an expert from within a group may be an efficient way to make a decision, but without adequate discussion, the group may not be satisfied with the outcome.

Decisions by Experts outside Groups   A group may decide that none of its members has the credibility, knowledge, or wisdom to make a decision, and it may feel unable or unwilling to do so. Members can turn to someone outside the group, someone with authority to make a decision. While an outside expert may make a fine decision, a group that gives up its decision-making power to one person loses the advantages of the greater input and variety of approaches that come from being a group in the first place.

Averaging Individual Rankings or Ratings   Group members can be asked to rank or rate possible alternatives. After the group averages the rankings or ratings, it selects the alternative with the highest average. This method of making decisions can be useful to start discussions and to see where the group stands on an issue. However, it is not the best way to make a decision, since it does not take full advantage of the give-and-take of group discussion.

Random Choice   Sometimes groups become so frustrated that they make no decisions. They resort to coin tosses or other random approaches. These methods are not recommended for groups that take their decision making seriously. Groups that resort to random methods usually are desperate.

Majority Vote   This is the most often used method of group decision making. Majority rule can be swift and efficient but can also leave an unsatisfied minority. Unless it allots time for discussing an issue, a group may sacrifice decision quality and group cohesiveness for efficiency.

Decision by Minority   Sometimes a minority of group members makes a decision. The minority may yell the loudest or threaten to create problems for the group unless it gets its way. Members may ask, "Does anyone have any objections?" and, if no one answers immediately, consider the decision to be made. Minority members whose decision is adopted may temporarily rejoice, but over time the group will have difficulty implementing a decision that is not widely accepted.

Decision by Consensus   Consensus occurs when all group members agree on a course of action. This method is time-consuming and difficult, but members are usually satisfied with the decision. If group members must also implement the solution, this method works well. To reach a decision by consensus, group members must listen and respond to individual viewpoints and manage conflicts that arise. Consensus is facilitated when group members are able to do such things as remain focused on the goal, emphasize areas of agreement, and combine or eliminate alternatives identified by the group. Several suggestions for reaching consensus and managing group conflict are identified in Chapter 9.

All of these methods of group decision making have one element in common: Group members select the best choice from available alternatives. Problem solving, on the other hand, involves making many decisions during the process of overcoming an obstacle. The group has a goal it wants to achieve, but it cannot do so unless the obstacle is removed or managed.

All decision making involves assessing a situation, identifying alternative solutions and their positive and negative consequences, and selecting the best alternative.

OBSTACLES TO QUALITY GROUP DECISION MAKING

Perhaps you have heard the saying that a camel is a horse that was designed by a committee. Groups sometimes make foolish decisions. Knowing some of the typical pitfalls groups encounter when choosing among alternatives can help your group avoid them. Consider the following obstacles.[7]

1. *The group fails to accurately analyze the present situation.* If a group improperly analyzes its current situation, it are likely to make a bad decision. To analyze something is to break it down into smaller parts. Having too little evidence—or none—is one of the reasons groups sometimes fail to analyze the present situation accurately. Even if group members do have ample evidence, it may be defective if they have not applied the proper tests of evidence, which we discussed earlier.

2. *The group fails to establish a clear and appropriate goal.* A group that has not clearly spelled out what it hopes to accomplish by making a decision has no way to assess the effectiveness of the decision. It will be more difficult for you to select the right college or university if you do not know what your major will be or what your future plans are.

3. *The group fails to identify the positive and negative consequences of the alternatives.* A group that is so eager to make a decision that it does not take time to consider the pros and cons of its actions is setting itself up to

make a bad decision. A critical error ineffective groups make is failing to consider the consequences of their decision *before* they make it.[8]

4. *The group has bad information.* G.I.G.O. is an acronym that most computer programmers know. It means "garbage in, garbage out." If a group has flawed or outdated evidence, the decision will also be flawed.[9]

5. *The group is not able to draw an accurate conclusion from the data they have.* Just having information does not mean the group will use it well. **Reasoning** is the process of drawing conclusions from information. Flawed reasoning, like flawed data, can contribute to a bad decision. Groups should avoid such reasoning fallacies as those described below.

Causal Fallacy   This fallacy is the inappropriate assumption that one event is the cause of another event. It is also called *post hoc, ergo propter hoc*, which is Latin for "after this, therefore, because of this." Saying "The stock market went down because of the terrible heat wave in the Midwest" is an example of suggesting without proper evidence that one event caused another.

Hasty Generalization   Drawing a conclusion with too little or no evidence is known as a hasty generalization. One example is: "We don't need to spend more money on music education in our schools; my son listens to classical music at home, and so can other students."

Attacking the Person, Not the Argument   This fallacy is also called *ad hominem*, Latin for "to the man." Saying, "We know he can't have any good ideas; anyone educated in another country surely must have inferior knowledge" is an example of attacking the person, not the soundness of the argument advanced.

Either/or   Another type of flawed reasoning is oversimplifying the options by saying we must do either X or Y. "We can either raise taxes and have better schools or do nothing and have inferior education." This is an either/or oversimplification.

GROUP PROBLEM SOLVING: OVERCOMING OBSTACLES TO ACHIEVE A GOAL

The board of directors of a multinational corporation, a Band Booster fund-raising committee, and a group of students doing a project for a group communication class all have something in common—they have problems to solve. Have you ever been involved in group problem solving and thought to yourself, "If I weren't working in this silly group, I could be more productive"? Despite the frustrations of group work, a small group of people has the potential of arriving at a better solution than do individuals working

---

REVIEW BOX

Comparing Effective and Ineffective Group Decision Making

EFFECTIVE GROUP DECISION MAKING	INEFFECTIVE GROUP DECISION MAKING
Accurately assesses the present situation	Improperly analyzes the present situation
Establishes clear and appropriate group goals	Does not establish clear and appropriate group goals
Accurately identifies positive and negative consequences of decision alternatives	Fails to identify enough positive and negative consequences of decision alternatives
Has accurate information	Works from too little information or faulty information
Draws reasonable conclusions from available information	Is unable to draw accurate conclusions from the information available

---

alone. As we noted in Chapter 1, groups have more information and more creative approaches to surmounting obstacles, which results in a higher-quality decision.

Problem solving is the process of overcoming obstacles to achieve a goal, while decision making involves making a choice from among alternatives. Problem solving usually requires a group to make many decisions or choices as it identifies a problem and determines how to solve it.

A problem consists of three elements: an undesirable existing situation, a goal someone wishes to achieve, and obstacles that keep that person from achieving his or her goal.[10] Group problem solving is a group's effort to eliminate or manage the obstacles that keep it from achieving its objective.

Like decision making, problem solving begins with assessing the present situation. What's wrong with what is happening now? Almost every problem can be phrased in terms of something you want more of or less of. Problems often can be boiled down to such things as lack of time, money, information, or agreement. For example, a school board that decides a district needs a new high school yet realizes it lacks the money for one has a problem: The district has too many students for existing facilities. The board needs fewer students or more space. The goal the board wants to achieve is quality education for all district students. The board cannot achieve this goal with the existing undesirable situation. The obstacles that keep the board from reaching its goal include lack of classroom space and lack of money to build more space. Every problem can be identified by noting its three elements: the undesirable present, the group goal, and the obstacles to achieving it.

> ## REVIEW BOX
>
> ### Three Elements of a Problem
>
> *Undesirable present:* Something is wrong with the way things are.
> *Goal:* What the group want to achieve.
> *Obstacles:* Something keeps a group from achieving its goal.

A group must first decide on its purpose. Sometimes a group forms for a specific task. For example, the president of the local Jaycees may appoint a committee to organize a Fourth of July celebration. Another group decides on its specific purpose only after the group is formed. Several neighbors may congregate because they are concerned about improving their neighborhood, but they decide what they want to do for their neighborhood only after they meet. Eventually, they may agree that they have a shared problem (such as a lack of security or lowered property values) that needs to be solved.

If a group decides that its function is to solve a specific problem, it must define the problem. For some groups, defining a problem is easy; for others, agreeing on the exact nature of a problem will take considerable time and debate.

After deciding on a purpose and defining a problem, a group continues to gather data, analyze the problem, and generate alternatives to try to solve it. In a group of four or five people, each of whom has different values, attitudes, and beliefs, problem solving can create uncertainty. Each person attempts to solve the problem based on his or her individual problem-solving strategy. No two group members will approach the problem from the same perspective. Sensing this disparity in approaches, each group member may become uncertain about his or her own strategy, while not really understanding anyone else's. It takes patience, understanding, and effective communication to help relieve this uncertainty.

THREE APPROACHES TO GROUP PROBLEM SOLVING

Thus far we have defined group decision making and problem solving, noted, the obstacles to and the characteristics of effective group decisions, described how to formulate discussion questions, and examined how to use evidence effectively. We will now examine three different approaches to the study of group problem solving: (1) **descriptive,** which focuses on how groups solve problems; (2) **functional,** which identifies key communicative behaviors that contribute to effective problem solving; and (3) **prescriptive,** which recommends specific agendas and techniques to improve group performance. In this chapter we will discuss the descriptive and functional approaches to group problem solving; we will introduce the prescriptive approach here but reserve a detailed discussion of it for Chapter 8.

DESCRIPTIVE

When you describe something, you use words to categorize, classify, and clarify your subject. A descriptive approach to group problem solving identifies how groups *do* solve problems, not how they *should* solve problems. As B. Aubrey Fisher notes, ". . . a descriptive approach involves observing actual groups interacting . . . [and] seeks to describe the interactive process that is common to those groups."[11] Most of the conclusions about groups drawn from a descriptive approach stem from research that seeks to identify typical patterns and behaviors most groups experience.

A descriptive approach does not offer specific guidelines and techniques for solving problems in groups; rather, it outlines how most groups go about solving problems. Fisher makes two assumptions about the descriptive approach: (1) There is a "natural" or normal process of group problem solving, and (2) a group will follow a normal problem-solving approach unless some external authority interferes with its freedom to solve its problem (e.g., an agenda is handed to the group or a strong-willed group leader dictates how the group should approach its task).[12] One of the most fruitful areas of research from a descriptive perspective seeks to identify the normal phases or cycles that groups experience when solving problems.

Describing Group Phases.   "Don't worry, Mom, I'm just going through a phase." Think back. Does this sound like something you may have said at one time? Apparently you were trying to alleviate your mother's concern by assuring her that your behavior was not at all uncommon and that it surely would pass in time. Implicit here is an assumption that individuals pass through several identifiable developmental stages, each of which leads to the next. Problem-solving groups, like individuals, go through several stages. Understanding these stages, you can learn to communicate in ways that expedite a group's passage from one stage to the next.

Several researchers have attempted to identify the phases of a problem-solving group. They have observed and recorded who speaks to whom and have categorized the comments group members exchange. Even though for the past 50 years researchers have used various labels to describe these phases they have reached similar conclusions. Table 7.1 illustrates the general pattern.[13]

Of the research on developmental phases of groups, Fisher's is the most significant for small group communication. He focused primarily on what was said throughout the development of his test groups. We use his termi-

TABLE 7.1   SUMMARY OF LITERATURE ON GROUP PHASES

	PHASE 1	PHASE 2	PHASE 3	PHASE 4
Fisher (1970, 1974)	Orientation	Conflict	Emergence	Reinforcement
Thelen and Dickerman (1949)	Forming	Conflict	Harmony	Productivity
Bennis and Shepard (1956, 1961)	Dependence	Inter-dependence	Focused Work	Productivity
Tuckman (1965)	Forming	Storming	Norming	Performing
Bales and Strodbeck (1951)	Orientation		Evaluation	Control
Schutz (1958)	Inclusion		Control	Affection

From *Interpersonal Communication: An Introduction* by Stewart L. Tubbs and Sylvia Moss. Copyright © 1974, 1977 and 1978. Reprinted by permission of McGraw-Hill, Inc.

nology in the following sections. See Table 7.1 to compare these terms to the terms other researchers use.

Phase 1: Orientation   In the first phase of small group interaction "group members break the ice and begin to establish a common basis for functioning."[14] Speech communication during this phase tends to be oriented toward members getting to know one another, sharing backgrounds, and tentatively approaching the group's task. You are not likely to say anything that might prompt the rest of the group to reject you. Fisher noted that "more ambiguous comments . . . are contained in Phase 1 than in any other phase except the third, which is also characterized by ambiguity."[15]

The research on the **orientation phase** suggests that your communication is directed at orienting yourself toward others as well as to the group's task, which can also be said about the other phases. What sets this phase apart from the others is the degree to which the social dimension is emphasized and the tentative, careful way in which the task dimension is approached.

Even the most efficient, task-motivated group will spend some time socializing and getting acquainted. Do not underestimate the importance of this type of interaction. Interpersonal trust—an essential ingredient for an effective working environment—does not happen all at once. You begin slowly, with small talk, to determine whether it is safe to move on to deeper levels of interaction. The orientation phase, then, develops trust and group cohesiveness, which are important for the group's survival in the second phase—conflict.

Phase 2: Conflict   During the orientation phase, group members begin to form opinions about their own positions in the group and about the group's task. By the second phase they start asserting these opinions. They have tested the water in the first phase and now are ready to jump in. On the process, or social, level, this is a period in which individuals compete for status in the group. Two or more potential leaders may emerge, with the support for each dividing the group into camps. In a decision-making or problem-solving group, this division is reflected along the task dimension as well. During the first phase, members are hesitant to speak about the group's task, but in the second phase they begin to assert their individuality and respond favorably or unfavorably to the direction the group is taking. With such polarization of attitudes, disagreement or conflict naturally results.[16]

Communication during the **conflict phase** is characterized by persuasive attempts at changing others' opinions and reinforcing one's own position. Some participants relish the idea of a good argument, while others see conflict as something to avoid at all cost. Avoiding conflict, however, means avoiding issues relevant and even crucial to the group's success. Just as individuals need to assert their own points of view, so do groups need to investigate all relevant alternatives in order to select the best solutions.

The conflict phase is necessary at both the task and the process dimensions of small group communication. Through conflict, you begin to identify the task issues that confront the group and clarify your own and others' roles. This clarification leads toward greater predictability, less uncertainty, and the establishment of group norms.

Phase 3: Emergence   In Phase 3, new patterns of communication indicate a group's emergence from the conflict phase. If a group is going to function as a cohesive unit, it must resolve the conflict of Phase 2. Though conflict is still a part of Phase 3, what sets the **emergence phase** apart from the preceding conflict phase is the way in which members deal with conflict. This shift is most apparent in the reappearance of ambiguity in task-related statements.

Think of a time when a group adopted a course of action that you had at first opposed. Did you support the group decision in the end? If so, you had to change your attitude along the way. How did that take place? Can you identify a time when you suddenly turned against your former position? Probably not. The change most likely was gradual. If you argue strongly for a position in Phase 2, you have a hard time letting go of that position all at once. Your ego simply will not stand for it. At the same time, you may feel a need to pull the group back together. Task and process dimensions are interwoven at this stage. While the group is divided, there is also clarity. Leadership patterns and roles have been established, the issues and problems confronting the group have been identified, and the need to settle differences and reach consensus has become apparent. Ambiguity appears to be the means by which you can comfortably shift your position toward group consensus.

Fisher noted that ambiguity in the third phase functions very differently from the way it does in the first phase. During the orientation phase, ambiguity serves as a tentative (and, therefore, safe) expression of attitudes.

> This explanation of ambiguity is not appropriate to the third phase...; groups are no longer searching for attitude direction. This direction was plotted in the orientation phase and debated in the conflict phase. In the third phase, task direction is no longer an issue.... Ambiguity ... functions in the third phase as a form of modified dissent. That is, the group members proceed to change their attitudes from disfavor to favor of the decision proposals through the mediation of ambiguity.[17]

In the emergence phase, then, a group settles on norms and moves toward consensus via ambiguous statements that gradually modify dissenting positions. Such ambiguous statements might take the form of qualifiers or reservations to the previous position: "I still would like to see our company merge with the Elector Electronics Corporation, but maybe we could consider a merger later in the year. Such a merger may be more appropriate next fall." Such a statement allows you to save face and still allows the group to reach consensus.

Phase 4: Reinforcement   A spirit of unity characterizes the final phase of group interaction. In the preceding three phases, group members struggle through getting acquainted, building cohesiveness, expressing individuality, competing for status, and arguing over issues. The group eventually emerges from those struggles with a sense of direction, consensus of opinion, and a feeling of group identity. Not surprisingly, then, the fourth phase is characterized by positive feelings toward the group and its decisions. Finally, members feel a genuine sense of accomplishment!

Reinforcement predominates in communication:

JIM: I may have been against it at first, but I've finally seen the light. We're going in the right direction now.

MARILYN: Yes, but don't shortchange your contribution, Jim. If you hadn't opposed it so vehemently, we never would have developed the idea so fully.

Fisher noted that ambiguous and unfavorable comments all but disappear in the fourth phase, being replaced by uniformly favorable comments and reinforcement. At this time, all of the hassle of group decision making and problem solving seems worthwhile. The group is at its most cohesive, individual satisfaction and sense of achievement are high, and uncertainty is at a low. Furthermore, it is a time when one finds oneself in a new group with new problems.

A group in its initial stages of development is very different from that same group in its final phase. This metamorphosis can be followed and charted by carefully observing the communicative behavior of group members. Groups, like individuals, struggle through childhood and adolescence on their way to maturity.

The Process Nature of Group Phases   Even though it may appear from the discussion that a group goes through four neat phases of development in a predictable way, group deliberations are seldom that orderly. In reality, a group may go through the four phases for *each* issue that comes before it. For example, the first issue may be "What is the purpose of this group?" A group will probably spend some time getting oriented to this task, conflict may follow as members learn about the objectives each person has, and, after discussion, a general consensus may emerge about the group's purpose. Finally, members may assure one another that their purpose has been developed clearly.

Perhaps the next issue to come before the group is "How will we organize our work—should we have subcommittees?" Again, the members may go through orientation, conflict, emergence, and reinforcement. Since group discussions tend to hop from topic to topic, a group may get bogged down in conflict, abandon the issue, and move to another issue. Groups may move through phases for each issue, or they may get sidetracked and abandon discussions about an issue.

Marshall Poole suggests that the phases of group problem solving, like any complex process, do not have clear-cut divisions.[18] Rather than describing group decision making as a sequence of four distinct stages, Poole builds on Fisher's research by suggesting that groups engage in three types of **activity tracks** that do not necessarily follow logical step-by-step patterns. The three types of activities that Poole believes best describe group interaction are: (1) **task process activities,** (2) **relational activities,** and (3) **topical focus.**[19] Task process activities are "those activities the group enacts to manage its task,"[20] such as analyzing a problem, becoming oriented to the issues of a problem, establishing criteria, and evaluating proposed solutions. Answering such questions as, "What's the problem here?" "How can we better understand the problem?" and "How effective will our solution be?" are examples of task process activities.

Verbal or nonverbal communication that indicates who is liked and disliked can be categorized as relational activity. Relational activities are "activities that reflect or manage relationships among group members as these relate to the group's work."[21] As noted in Chapter 4, communication has both a task and a relationship dimension. Relational activities are communication behaviors that sustain or damage interpersonal relationships among group members. Criticism, conflict, praise, and encouragement help group members understand their relationships with one another. Relational activities also affect a group's working climate.

The third type of activity, topical focus, deals with the "general themes, major issues, or arguments of concern to the group at a given point in the discussion."[22] Ernest Bormann and other researchers have noted that groups often focus their conversations on given themes or topics which serve as the actual agendas for the groups.[23] This third type of activity, then, deals with major topics that do not relate to a group's specific task or to member relationships.

These three activity tracks, as Poole calls them, do not all develop at the same rate or according to the same pattern. Some groups may spend a considerable portion of their time developing relationships before discussing their tasks in great detail. On the other hand, task-oriented groups often devote considerable energy to completing their tasks, letting relationships play minor roles in group deliberations. Groups switch activity tracks at various **breakpoints,** which occur as groups switch topics, adjourn, or schedule planning periods. Another type of breakpoint, called a *delay,* occurs because of group conflict or inability to reach consensus. Whereas groups may expect and schedule some breakpoints, they usually do not schedule delays. Poole notes, "depending on the nature of the delay and the mood of the group, [a] breakpoint can signal the start of a difficulty or a highly creative period."[24] A disruption, the third type of breakpoint, results from a major conflict or a realization that a group may not be able to complete its task. A group must be flexible to manage disruption.

Poole's analysis of group phases and group activity emphasizes the process nature of group communication rather than assuming that groups proceed through a linear, step-by-step approach. While several researchers have documented chronological phases in a group's decision-making efforts, a group's communication can also be described by the three activities of task process, relational activity, and topical focus. A descriptive approach to group communication can help you better understand and explain why certain types of statements are made in groups and how a group develops over time. With an understanding of the process, you should be in a better position to evaluate and improve your participation in group meetings.

FUNCTIONAL

While the descriptive approach assumes that you can identify how groups solve problems and describes the phases and activities of groups, the functional approach suggests that, to be effective, groups and group members should perform certain communication functions. Certain conditions must be satisfied for a group to effectively achieve its task. Groups are effective, argue functional theorists, not because members follow certain prescribed procedures but because they perform vital behaviors.[25]

The primary way researchers have identified the functions of effective problem solving is by examining the behaviors of both effective and ineffective groups. Certain types of communication and critical thinking happen in effective groups that do not usually occur when groups do not solve problems well.

What are these key functions? Randy Hirokawa and Kathryn Rost propose that effective group members are **vigilant thinkers.** Vigilant thinkers are critical thinkers. They pay attention to the *process* of how problems are solved rather than only the techniques used to solve a problem. Being a critical thinker and vigilantly assessing, evaluating, and scrutinizing ideas and solutions is an essential function of people who communicate in small groups. According to Hirokawa and Rost, there are four key questions that effective groups address: (1) Does something in the present situation need to be changed? (2) What goal does the group want to achieve? (3) What choices does the group have that will help achieve the goal? (4) What are the positive and negative implications of the choices?[26] Even though these issues are usually addressed in the order listed, some groups may not follow this order.[27] But if one of these crucial functions is not performed, research suggests that the group will be less likely to reach an effective solution.

Kevin Barge suggests that the following functions are essential for an effective problem-solving group. Group members should: (1) network with others within and outside the group to gather effective information; (2) acquire the skill of **data splitting**—that is, analyze information effectively; (3) generate and evaluate solutions, and (4) manage their relationships effectively by means of listening, feedback, and negotiation skills.[28]

The vigilant thinking functions suggested by Hirokawa and his colleagues as well as Barge are similar to those suggested by Irving Janis: Gather accurate information, analyze the information, draw reasonable conclusions from the data, generate solutions, evaluate the costs and risks of the solutions, and select the best one.[29]

Communication Functions of Effective Group Problem Solvers   The functional perspective assumes that groups will make a higher-quality decision if group members analyze information appropriately, generate an ample number of ideas, evaluate information and solutions, and remain sensitive to others. Note the following specific communication functions that are considered essential to effective problem solving from a functional perspective.[30]

Analysis Function   Group members who effectively analyze information and ideas have the following characteristics:

- *They see the problem from a variety of viewpoints.* One often looks at a problem as it affects oneself. A skilled problem solver considers how the problem affects others, too, and is able to think about an issue from other people's vantage points.
- *They gather data and research issues.* Good problem solvers do not rely on their own opinions. They spend time in the library or develop surveys to gather information and others' opinions about an issue.
- *They use evidence effectively to reach a valid conclusion.* Beyond just collecting evidence, a good problem solver needs to know how to use evidence to reach a conclusion.
- *They ask appropriate questions.* One big problem groups have is keeping the discussion focused on the issues. Members often bounce from one

idea or topic to the next. Good problem solvers know this and use questions to help keep the group moving toward its goal. Questions such as "Where are we now?" or "What's the next step in solving our problem?" or "Aren't we getting off the track here?" can help the group get back to the task.

Idea Generation Function   An essential aspect of a well-functioning problem-solving group is group members who are creative and inventive, who find ways to keep ideas flowing.

- *Search for many alternatives or solutions to a problem.* Effective groups are not content to have just one or two approaches to a problem. Many solutions are identified which may help overcome the obstacles keeping the group from reaching its goal.
- *Make high-quality statements to the group.* What are high-quality statements? According to several researchers, high-quality statements are precise rather than rambling and abstract. They are also consistent with previous evidence, relevant to the topic under discussion, and act to positively reinforce the comments of other group members.[31]
- *Take a vacation from a problem to revitalize the group.* If the group gets bogged down and cannot reach agreement, postpone further discussion if possible. Sometimes you get a burst of creativity when you are not even thinking about a problem.[32] Have you ever had an idea come to you while you were jogging, driving a car, or taking a shower? Give your mind a chance to work on the problem by giving yourself a break from agonizing over a solution.

Evaluative Function   Being able to separate good ideas from bad ideas is a critical function of a good problem-solving group.

- *Evaluate the opinions and assumptions of others.* Do not just accept another person's conclusion or opinion at face value. One study found that groups that reach better solutions include members who take the time to test the assumptions of others. While you should not attack another person's credibility, all opinions and assumptions need to be supported by evidence. A group that tactfully examines the basis for an opinion can determine whether the opinion is valid.
- *Test solutions to see if they meet preestablished criteria.* Criteria are standards for acceptable solutions. Such criteria as "It should be within the budget" and "It should be implemented within six months" are important to problem solving. If a group has generated criteria for a solution, a good problem solver reminds the group what the criteria are and evaluates possible solutions according to standards previously identified.

Personal Sensitivity Function   As we have emphasized throughout the book, groups have both a task and a relationship dimension. Members of

successfully functioning teams or groups are other-oriented, empathic, and sensitive to the needs of others.

- *Be concerned for both the group task and the feelings of others.* Being too task-oriented is not good for the overall group climate. As discussed in Chapter 5, sensitivity to the feelings of others can enhance the group climate and foster a supportive, rather than a defensive, approach to achieving a group goal.
- *Listen to minority arguments and opinions.* It is always tempting to disregard the voice of a lone dissenter. That individual may, however, have a

REVIEW BOX

Functions of Effective and Ineffective Group Problem Solvers

FUNCTIONS	CHARACTERISTICS OF AN EFFECTIVE GROUP PROBLEM SOLVER	CHARACTERISTICS OF AN INEFFECTIVE GROUP PROBLEM SOLVER
Analysis functions	Seeing the problem from a variety of viewpoints	Seeing the problem only from one's own viewpoint
	Gathering data and researching the issues	Failing to research the problem or gather data
	Knowing how to use evidence to reach a valid conclusion	Not knowing how to use evidence
	Asking appropriate questions	Asking inappropriate questions
Idea-generation functions	Searching for many solutions to a problem	Ceasing to search for a solution after one is identified
	Making high-quality statements	Making low-quality statements
	Taking a vacation from the problem to revitalize the group	Continuing to work even after the group is exhausted
Evaluation functions	Evaluating the opinions and assumptions of others	Never examining or evaluating others' opinions or assumptions
	Testing proposed solutions to see if they meet pre-established criteria	Not matching proposed solutions against preestablished criteria
Personal sensitivity functions	Concern for both the group task and the feelings of others	Lack of concern for the feelings of others; focusing only on the task
	Listening to minority arguments	Not listening to dissenting viewpoints; lack of tolerance for the ideas of others

brilliant idea or a legitimate complaint about the majority point of view. Assume that all ideas have merit; do not discount ideas because they come from members who are not supporting the majority at the moment.

PRESCRIPTIVE

We have examined the descriptive and functional approaches to problem solving, discussing how groups make decisions and identifying communication functions that are crucial to effective group problem solving. A third approach, the prescriptive, identifies specific agendas and techniques that help a group perform effectively.

When the doctor gives you a prescription, he or she is telling you to do something very specific: take a measured dose of a particular medicine to treat your medical problem. A prescriptive approach to problem solving is based on the assumption that groups need more than a general understanding of how groups solve problems or what the key functions of group communication are. The prescriptive approach offers specific suggestions for structuring a group's problem-solving agenda for solving problems. Prescriptive approaches invite group members to perform certain behaviors in a specific order to achieve a group goal. Fisher describes the prescriptive approach as providing ". . . guidelines, a road map, to assist the group in achieving consensus. A prescriptive approach is based on an assumed 'ideal' process."[33]

According to Fisher, there are two assumptions that underlie the prescriptive approach to problem solving: (1) Group members are consistently rational, and (2) the prescribed agenda or set of techniques will result in a better solution.

The descriptive approach to group problem solving and decision making helps a group understand *how* groups usually solve problems. The functional approach identifies key communicative behaviors that should be performed to enhance the group's effectiveness. The prescriptive approach offers specific recommendations for sequencing certain types of communication in a group. Which approach is best? Some scholars advocate the descriptive approach, pointing out that it does not constrain a group from its normal or natural process. Some people reject the prescriptive approach as being too rigid. Others suggest that groups should consciously perform key functions to maximize effectiveness. Yet others contend that the prescriptive approach gives a group needed structure for solving problems. Working in groups often results in uncertainty and ambiguity.[34]

Arthur VanGundy categorizes problems as either structured or unstructured.[35] An unstructured problem is one in which we have little information; there is high uncertainty. The more unstructured the problem, the greater the need for a prescriptive technique of gathering and analyzing information to solve the problem. Thus, a prescriptive problem-solving method helps reduce the uncertainty that groups experience when they try to solve a problem. VanGundy has identified over 70 techniques that help provide structure to the problem-solving process.

One study suggests that leaders who give the group a structure by setting goals, monitoring time, and providing suggestions about procedure enhance the group's perceived effectiveness.[36] Clearly each approach has its unique advantages. Draw on all three approaches to help you be an effective problem-solving group participant. It is useful to understand how groups solve problems and perform key functions, as well as to be acquainted with some techniques of organizing an agenda for problem-solving discussions.

If the task is very simple, a group may not need a cumbersome, predetermined set of prescriptions. Research suggests, however, that if the task is complex (as many group tasks are) specific guidelines and procedures will help the group work more effectively.[37]

In this chapter, we have emphasized descriptive and functional perspectives. In Chapter 8, we will describe in more detail prescriptive approaches, formats, and techniques to give you some options in structuring group problem solving.

CULTURAL ASSUMPTIONS ABOUT GROUP PROBLEM SOLVING AND DECISION MAKING

As we conclude this chapter, we remind you that our assumptions about the descriptions, functions, and prescriptions of group problem solving and decision making should be filtered through the cultural perspective group members may hold. As we noted in Chapter 1, some cultures assume an individualistic approach to accomplishing work (notably in the United States, Great Britain, and Northern Europe) while other cultures assume a collaborative or collectivistic mind set (such as Asian cultures).

One researcher has categorized and contrasted the assumptions North Americans hold toward decision making, compared with Japanese assumptions. Table 7.2 summarizes those assumptions.

Although Table 7.2 summarizes differences between only two cultures, it illustrates the point that you can't always assume your approach to working with others in groups to solve problems and make decisions will be compatible with approaches others may have. You need not travel abroad to experience different cultural perspectives. In the United States you are likely to encounter individuals with a wide range of cultural and ethnic traditions. Even within regions of the United States there are differences in approaches and assumptions group members may hold toward collective problem solving, collaboration, and teamwork.

What are strategies to bridge these cultural differences you will undoubtedly encounter? Consider the following suggestions:[39]

1. *Develop Mindfulness.* To be mindful is to be consciously aware of cultural differences and to note that there are differences between your assumptions and the assumptions of others.[40] Consciously say to yourself, "These group members may have a different assumption about how to accomplish this task. Before I impose my strategies on them, I'll listen and make sure I understand what they are saying."

2. *Be Flexible.* Realize that you may have to adapt and change according to the perceptions and assumptions others hold.

TABLE 7.2   NORTH AMERICAN AND JAPANESE DECISION-MAKING ASSUMP-TIONS COMPARED

NORTH AMERICAN	JAPANESE
Individual leader often assumed to take control and direct the group.	Group leader assumes role of facilitator and shares responsibility for accomplishing the task.
Makes decisions quickly yet sometimes slow in implementing decisions.	Takes longer to make decisions, but implements decisions quickly.
More likely to reach a decision by either an individual recommendation or a majority vote.	More likely to make decisions by consensus.
Assumes a rational approach to solving problems and making decisions.	More likely to assume an intuitive approach to reaching group harmony.
More likely to directly confront problems in managing conflict.	Less likely to be direct in dealing with problems and managing conflict.
More likely to rely upon one expect for information.	Less likely to rely upon one expert for information; seeks information from several sources.

Summarized from: Teruyuki Kume. "Managerial Attitudes Toward Decision-Making: North American and Japan: In *Communication, Culture and Organizational Processes,* edited by William B. Gudykunst, Lea P. Stewart, and Stella Ting-Toomey. Newbury Park, CA: Sage, 1985.

3. *Tolerate Uncertainty and Ambiguity.* Working with others from a culture or cultures different from you own is bound to create a certain amount of uncertainty and confusion. Being patient and tolerant will help you manage cultural differences when collaborating with others.

4. *Resist Stereotyping Others and Making Negative Judgments about Others.* Ethnocentrism is the assumption that your cultural heritage is superior to others'. As we learned in Chapter 5 when discussing group climate, evaluating others and assuming superiority typically leads to defensiveness.

5. *Ask Questions.* One way to learn about the assumptions others hold is to simply ask them what some of their preferences are for establishing norms and ground rules. An essential element in the development of any effective team is developing common ground rules; this can best be accomplished by asking others how they best work and solve problems.

6. *Be Other-Oriented.* Empathy and sensitivity to others is a key to bridging cultural differences. Although simply considering an issue from some-

one else's point of view will not eliminate the difference, it will help enhance understanding. One of the seven habits of Stephen Covey nicely summarizes this principle: Seek to understand before being understood.[41]

PUTTING PRINCIPLE INTO PRACTICE

If you understand how groups go about the task of solving problems, you will be better able to manage the problem-solving process in small groups. The following suggestions should help you apply the concepts presented in this chapter.

FORMULATING DISCUSSION QUESTIONS

To focus and direct the deliberations of your group, formulate a discussion question.

- If your group is trying to decide whether something is true or false or whether something did or did not occur, formulate a question of fact.
- If your group is trying to decide whether one idea or approach to an issue is better than another, formulate a question of value.
- If your group is trying to develop a solution to a problem, formulate a question of policy.

GROUP DECISION MAKING

- Start the decision-making process by accurately assessing the present situation.
- Establish clear and appropriate group goals to frame the decision-making objective.
- Identify positive and negative consequences of the alternatives identified.
- Ensure that group members have accurate information.
- Determine whether group members are drawing reasonable conclusions for the information that is available.

GROUP PROBLEM SOLVING

- With other group members, answer the question: "What do we want more or less of?" Analyze the problem by identifying: (1) the undesirable present, (2) your goal, and (3) obstacles that may keep you from achieving the goal.
- Give all group members the opportunity to help formulate appropriate group goals.

- Even when the first proposed solution seems reasonable or workable, examine other alternatives.
- Effective problem solvers:

  Are vigilant thinkers; they appropriately analyze information and data.

  Generate creative ideas; they search for many high quality solutions.

  Evaluate ideas and solutions; they examine the costs and benefits of solutions.

  Are sensitive to others; they are concerned for both the task and the feelings of other group members.

- To become a more effective problem solver, interpret and evaluate the information you collect. Do not just accept the information at face value.
- Do not let yourself be satisfied after you have generated a few potential solutions. Keep searching unless the group needs a break.

APPROACHES TO GROUP PROBLEM SOLVING

- Adopt a functional approach to group problem solving by performing the functions of effective problem solvers.
- Adopt a prescriptive approach to problem solving if your group needs the structure that a problem-solving agenda provides.
- Do not be concerned if your group takes time to orient itself to the problem-solving process. It is a normal part of group work.
- Expect some conflict and differences of opinions after a group clarifies its task and passes through the orientation phase of problem solving.
- Even though conflict may appear to impede a group's efforts to solve a problem, expect a decision to emerge after a thorough discussion and analysis of the issues.
- Do not overlook the importance of the reinforcement phase of group problem solving. Group members need a sense of accomplishment after making a decision.

BRIDGING CULTURAL DIFFERENCES

- Develop mindfulness: become consciously aware of cultural differences.
- Be flexible: be ready to adapt to the cultural expectations and traditions of others.
- Tolerate uncertainty and ambiguity: be patient when working with those who have a cultural background different from your own.
- Avoid stereotyping and making negative judgments: avoid an ethnocentric mindset that assumes your cultural traditions are superior to those of others.

- Ask questions: reduce your uncertainty by asking questions to help you and your team members develop common ground rules and norms.
- Be other-oriented: cultivate the skill of empathy and seek to understand others before forcing your ideas and opinions on others.

PRACTICE

IDENTIFYING QUESTIONS OF FACT, VALUE, AND POLICY

Read the following narrative, then identify and phrase the following questions: (1) the main discussion question, (labeled as fact, value, or policy), (2) at least one question of fact, and (3) at least one question of value.

> A new liberal divorce law has come up for discussion in the state senate. Senator Smith, who introduced the bill, has lobbied hard for it because she has found evidence to suggest that complications in the current law do not deter divorce but only result in lengthy delays and higher fees for divorce lawyers. Senator Williams also supports the new law; he was recently divorced and experienced much frustration and aggravation in the process. Senator Schwartz, on the other hand, is happily married and quite conservative; he leads opposition to the new law.

DESCRIPTION OF GROUP PROCESS

Attend a school board, city council, or other public meeting in which problems are discussed and solutions are recommended. Prepare a written analysis of the meeting by attempting to identify phases in the group's discussions. Also, try to identify examples of the three activity tracks discussed in this chapter (task process, relational, topical). In addition, provide examples of breakpoints in the discussion of the group.

EVALUATION OF GROUP DECISION MAKING

Evaluate your participation in a problem-solving or decision-making group discussion on a scale of 1 to 10, where 1 represents "no participation at all" and 10 represents "participated very well."

_____ 1. How well did the group assess the problem or decision?
_____ 2. How well did the group identify its goal?
_____ 3. How well did the group identify the positive consequences of the solutions under consideration?
_____ 4. How well did the group identify the negative consequences of the solutions under consideration?

_____ 5. Did the group draw reasonable conclusions from available information?

HURRICANE PREPAREDNESS CASE

Although you have idly watched local meteorologists track Hurricane Bruce's destructive course through the Caribbean for several days, you have not given any serious thought to the possibility that the storm might directly affect your coastal city. However, at about seven o'clock this morning, the storm suddenly veered northward, putting it on course for a direct hit. Now the National Hurricane Center in Miami has posted a Hurricane Warning for your community. Forecasters are predicting landfall in approximately 9 to 12 hours. Having taken no advance precautions, you are stunned by the amount of work you now have to do to secure your three-bedroom suburban home, which is about one-half mile from the beach. You have enough food in the house for two days. You also have one candle and a transistor radio with one weak battery. You have no other hurricane supplies, nor have you taken any hurricane precautions. Your task is to rank the following items in terms of their importance for ensuring your survival and the safety of your property. Place number 1 by the first thing you should do, 2 by the second, and so on through number 13. Please work individually on this task.

Fill your car with gas	_____
Trim your bushes and trees	_____
Fill your bathtub with water	_____
Construct hurricane shutters for your windows	_____
Buy enough food for a week	_____
Buy batteries and candles	_____
Bring in patio furniture from outside	_____
Buy dry ice	_____
Invite friends over for a hurricane party	_____
Drain your swimming pool	_____
Listen to TV and radio for further bulletins before doing anything	_____
Make sure you have an evacuation plan	_____
Stock up on charcoal and charcoal lighter for your barbecue grill	_____

After you have made your individual decisions, work in small groups with others and seek to reach consensus. Your group's task is to rank these items according to their importance.

EVALUATION OF GROUP PROBLEM SOLVING

Based upon your participation in a problem-solving group, use the following scales to evaluate your group problem-solving skills.

	Strongly Agree	Agree	Unsure	Disagree	Strongly Disagree
1. I was able to see the problem from a variety of viewpoints.					
2. I researched the issues under discussion appropriately.					
3. I evaluated the opinions and assumptions of others.					
4. I used evidence effectively to reach a valid conclusion.					
5. I was concerned for both the group task and the feelings of others.					
6. I helped to keep the discussion on track.					
7. I generated several possible alternatives or solutions to the problem.					
8. I courteously listened to minority arguments and opinions.					
9. I checked to determine if the proposed solutions met the group's preestablished criteria.					
10. If the group was not easily able to solve the problem , I encouraged members to take a break so that they could have a fresh perspective.					

STRANDED IN THE DESERT SITUATION[38]

You are a member of a geology club that is on a field trip to study unusual formations in the New Mexico desert. It is the last week in July. You have been driving over old trails, far from any road, in order to see out-of-the-way formations. At about 10:30 A.M. your club's specially equipped minibus overturns, rolls into a 20-foot ravine, and burns. The driver and professional adviser to the club are killed. The rest of you are relatively uninjured.

You know that the nearest ranch is approximately 45 miles east of where you are. There is no closer habitation. When your club does not report to its motel that evening, you will be missed. Several people know generally where you are but will not be able to pinpoint your whereabouts.

The area around you is rather rugged and dry. There is a shallow water-hole nearby, but the water is contaminated by worms, animal feces and urine, and several dead mice. Before you left you heard, from a weather report that the temperature would reach 108 degrees, making the surface temperature 128 degrees. All of you are dressed in lightweight summer clothing and all have hats and sunglasses.

While escaping from the minibus, each group member salvaged a couple of items; there are 12 items in all. Your group's task is to rank these items according to their importance to your survival, starting with 1 for the most important and proceeding to 12 for the least important.

You may assume that the number of club members is the same as the number of persons in your group and that the group has agreed to stick together.

_____ Magnetic compass

_____ A piece of heavy-duty, light-blue canvas, 20 square feet in size

_____ Book, *Plants of the Desert*

_____ Rearview mirror

_____ Large knife

_____ Flashlight

_____ One jacket per person

_____ One transparent, plastic ground cloth (6 feet by 4 feet) per person

_____ A .38-caliber loaded pistol

_____ One 2-quart plastic canteen of water per person

_____ An accurate map of the area

_____ A large box of kitchen matches

NOTES

1. Dennis S. Gouran, *Discussion: The Process of Group Decision-Making* (New York: Harper & Row, 1974), 72.
2. Ann Burnett Pettus, "The Verdict Is In: A Study of Jury Decision-Making Factors, Moment of Personal Decision, and Jury Deliberations—From the Jurors' Point of View," *Communication Quarterly* 38 (Winter 1990): 83–97.
3. John Wait Bowers and John Courtright, *Communication Research Methods* (Glenview, Ill.: Scott, Foresman, 1984).
4. Randy Y. Hirokawa and Dirk R. Scheerhorn, "Communication in Faulty Group Decision-Making," in Randy Y. Hirokawa and Marshall Scott Poole, *Communication and Group Decision-Making* (Beverly Hills, Calif.: Sage Publications, 1986), 67.
5. Ibid., 69.
6. See John K. Brilhart and Gloria Galanes, *Effective Group Discussion* (Dubuque, Iowa: Wm. C. Brown, 1992), 256; David W. Johnson and Frank P. Johnson, *Joining Together: Group Theory and Group Skills* (Englewood Cliffs, N.J.: Prentice-Hall, 1987), 99–104.
7. Hirokawa and Scheerhorn.

8. Ibid.
9. Ibid.
10. Charles H. Kepner and Benjamin B. Treogoe, *The Rational Manager* (New York: McGraw-Hill, 1965); also see Brilhart and Galanes, *Effective Group Discussion,* 232.
11. B. Aubrey Fisher, *Small Group Decision Making: Communication and the Group Process,* 2nd ed. (New York: McGraw-Hill, 1980), 132.
12. Ibid., 130.
13. Stewart L. Tubbs and Sylvia Moss, *Interpersonal Communication,* 5th ed. (New York: Random House, 1987), 270.
14. B. Aubrey Fisher, "Decision Emergence: Phases in Group Decision-Making," *Speech Monographs* 37 (1970): 60.
15. Ibid., 130–31.
16. Ibid., 61.
17. Ibid., 63.
18. Marshall Scott Poole, "Decision Development in Small Groups, III: A Multiple Sequence Model of Group Decision Development," *Communication Monographs* 50 (December 1983): 321–41.
19. Ibid., 326.
20. Ibid.
21. Ibid.
22. Ibid.
23. See Ernest G. Bormann, *Discussion and Group Methods* (New York: Harper & Row, 1975).
24. Poole, "Decision Development," 330.
25. Randy Y. Hirokawa, "Discussion Procedures and Decision-Making Performance: A Test of a Functional Perspective," *Human Communication Research* 12, no. 2 (Winter 1985): 203–24.
26. Randy Y. Hirokawa and Kathryn Rost, "Effective Group Decision-Making in Organizations: Field Test of the Vigilant Interaction Theory," *Management Communication Quarterly* 5 (1992): 267–88; Randy Y. Hirokawa, "Why Informed Groups Make Faulty Decisions: An Investigation of Possible Interaction-Based Explanations," *Small Group Behavior* 18 (1987): 3–29; Randy Y. Hirokawa, "Group Communication and Decision-Making Performance: A Continued Test of the Functional Perspective," *Human Communication Research* 14 (Summer 1988): 487–515.
27. Hirokawa, "Discussion Procedures."
28. K. Barge, *Leadership: Communication Skills for Organizations and Groups* (New York: St. Martin's Press, 1994).
29. I. L. Janis, *Victims of Groupthink* (Boston: Houghton Mifflin, 1973); I. L. Janis, *Critical Decision: Leadership in Policymaking and Crisis Management* (New York: Free Press, 1989).
30. See Randy Y. Hirokawa and Roger Pace, "A Descriptive Investigation of the Possible Communication-Based Reasons for Effective and Ineffective Group Decision Making," *Communication Monographs* 50 (December 1983): 363–79. The authors also wish to acknowledge Dennis A. Romig, Performance Resources, Inc., Austin, Texas, for his contribution to the discussion.
31. Dale G. Leathers, "Quality of Group Communication as a Determinant of Group Product," *Speech Monographs* 39 (1972): 166–73; Randy Y. Hirokawa and Dennis S. Gouran, "Facilitation of Group Communication: A Critique of Prior Research

and an Agenda for Future Research," *Management Communication Quarterly* 3 (August 1989): 71–92.

32. See Frank J. Sabatine, "Rediscovering Creativity: Unlearning Old Habits," *Mid-American Journal of Business* 4 (1989): 11–13.

33. Fisher, *Small Group Decision Making,* 130.

34. Steven A. Beebe and John T. Masterson, "Toward a Model of Small Group Communication: Applications for Teaching and Research," *Florida Speech Communication Journal* 8, no. 2 (1980): 9–15.

35. See Arthur B. VanGundy, *Techniques of Structured Problem Solving* (New York: Van Nostrand Reinhold Company, 1981), 4.

36. William E. Jurma, "Effects of Leader Structuring Style and Task Orientation Characteristics of Group Members," *Communication Monographs* 46 (1979): 282–95.

37. Susan Jarboe, "A Comparison of Input-Output, Process-Output and Input-Process-Output Models of Small Group Problem-Solving Effectiveness," *Communication Monographs* 55 (June 1988): 121–42; Randy Y. Hirokawa, "Group Communication and Decision-Making Performance."

38. Johnson and Johnson, *Joining Together,* 239.

39. This discussion of bridging cultural differences is based upon a discussion in: Steven A. Beebe, Susan J. Beebe, and Mark V. Redmond, *Interpersonal Communication: Relating To Others* (Boston: Allyn and Bacon, 1996).

40. See: William B. Gudykunst, *Bridging Differences: Effective Intergroup Communication* (Newbury Park, CA: Sage, 1991).

41. Stephen R. Covey, *The 7 Habits of Highly Effective People* (New York: Simon & Schuster. 1989).

CHAPTER
E·I·G·H·T

Small Group Problem-Solving Techniques

After studying this chapter, you will be able to:

- Use the steps and tools of reflective thinking to solve a problem in a small group discussion.

- Apply brainstorming to a problem-solving group discussion.

- Apply the ideal-solution problem-solving method to a group discussion.

- Apply the single-question problem-solving approach to a group discussion.

- Determine which problem-solving approach is most suitable for a given group discussion.

*I*magine that you are the chairperson of a committee appointed to improve the quality of education in your community. Students' scores on standard achievement tests have declined in the past two years. School administrators complain that they do not have the funds to develop new programs or to hire more teachers. Your committee must develop a plan to deal with the problem. The last chapter introduced three approaches to problem solving: descriptive, prescriptive, and functional. As committee chairperson, you could adopt a descriptive problem-solving approach by cluing in group members on some of the processes that groups experience when trying to solve problems. Although giving your committee an understanding of the process may be beneficial, you feel you need to provide more structure to help the group efficiently organize its approach to solving the problem. You could, then, approach your task from a functional perspective by ensuring that critical elements of problem solving are introduced in your discussion.

There is, as we have indicated, a third approach. This chapter identifies some *prescriptive* approaches to problem solving that may help you organize a group's problem-solving attempts. There is no one best way to solve problems in groups. Each group is unique, as is each group member. No single prescriptive problem-solving formula always works. Yet there is evidence that guiding a group through a structured agenda can enhance its effectiveness.[1]

This chapter will give you several suggestions for solving problems in groups, one of which should meet your group's need at any given time.

AN OVERVIEW OF PRESCRIPTIVE PROBLEM-SOLVING STRATEGIES

There are a vast number of specific strategies and techniques that can help you facilitate group problem solving. Table 8.1 presents a summary of several prescriptive problem-solving models.[2] As you can see, there are some activities that are common among almost all of them. Most include references to five key elements: (1) identify and define the problem, (2) analyze the problem, (3) identify possible solutions, (4) select the best solution, and (5) implement the solution. These steps outline the primary way most scientists in any discipline go about finding answers to puzzling questions. We will examine the origin of these steps as well as why they continue to be used to structure group problem-solving discussion.

TABLE 8.1   A COMPARISON OF PROBLEM-SOLVING STEPS

	Albert	Brilhart-Galanes	Brilhart-Jochem	Crosby	Dewar	Dewey	Gouran	Hirokawa-Scheerhorn	Ingle	Kepner-Trego	Larson	Lewin	Maier	Napier-Gershenfeld	Polya	Ross	VanGundy	Wright
Ventilation																		●
Establish goals										●								●
Identify problem		●	●		●	●	●	●	●		●	●		●				
Understand problem		●												●	●			
Clarify problem																		●
Fix problem				●														
Limit problem		●				●												
Define problem	●			●	●	●				●		●			●	●		
Analyze problem	●	●	●		●	●	●	●	●	●	●	●	●	●	●	●		●
Identify cause				●						●		●						
Identify alternatives						●	●	●		●				●			●	
Correct cause				●						●								
Evaluate correction				●														
Gather information	●																	
Establish criteria			●												●			●
Identify ideal solution								●			●							
Identify what could be changed										●								
Identify a plan															●			
Evaluate problem to implement solution													●					
Brainstorm solutions		●																
Select best solution	●	●			●	●	●	●	●			●		●		●	●	●
Identify/Analyze strengths/weaknesses of solutions			●				●			●			●				●	●
Evaluate solution		●								●			●		●	●		●	●
Implement solution		●	●			●				●			●		●	●		●	●
Test/Evaluate solution						●			●	●			●					

From Steven A. Beebe and Dennis A. Romig (1990) *Problem Solving.* Austin, Texas: Performance Resources, Inc. Reprinted by permission.

The Origin of Prescriptive Problem-Solving Strategies

In 1910, philosopher and educator John Dewey, in his book *How We Think*, identified the steps most people follow to solve problems. According to Dewey, a reflective thinker considered these key questions:[3]

1. What is the "felt difficulty" or concern?
2. Where is it located, and how is it defined?
3. What are possible solutions to the felt difficulty?
4. What are logical reasons that support the solution?
5. What additional testing and observation need to be done to confirm the validity of the solution?

These five steps should look familiar. They are very close to the critical elements found in most of the prescriptive techniques in Table 8.1. Even though Dewey did not focus specifically on small groups, the steps he outlined, called **reflective thinking,** have been used by many groups as a way to structure the problem-solving process. As new courses in group discussion were being designed in the 1920s and 1930s, teachers and authors adapted Dewey's framework as a standard agenda that could be used to tackle any problem-solving group discussion. One of the first texts to adapt these steps explicitly was published by J.H. McBurney and K.G. Hance in 1939.[4] Soon other scholars began making similar references to this sequence, and, as you can see, it has become a standard agenda for structuring group problem solving.

The Importance of Structuring Problem-Solving Discussion

Communicating with others in small groups to solve a problem is often a messy and disorganized process. Even though we noted that some researchers have identified distinct phases in the course of a group's deliberation (orientation, conflict, emergence, reinforcement), others find that group discussion often bounces from person to person and can be an inefficient, time-consuming process. And as we discussed in Chapter 2, groups also develop fantasy themes which can trigger a chain of stories—some that are related to the group's task and some that are not. Although these stories and group fantasies are important to a group's identity, extended off task "storytelling" can have a negative effect on the group's productivity.

To counteract the messiness of group interaction, group researchers have suggested that an agenda be used to structure the discussion. The purpose of an agenda is to help keep the discussion on track, not to stifle group interaction or consciousness raising. Robert Bales found that most task-oriented groups spend a little over 60 percent of their time talking about the task and almost 40 percent of their time talking about social, relational, or maintenance matters.[5] An agenda ensures that the time spent talking about the task is on target.

Of the approaches to structuring discussion included in Table 8.1, which method seems to be the best? Many of the sequences have not been tested empirically. Among those sequences that have been compared in controlled studies, no single method seems to work best all of the time. One powerful conclusion, however, emerges from the research: *Any method of structuring group problem solving is better than no method at all.*[6]

Groups need structure because of their members' relatively short attentions spans and the uncertainty that results from both the relationships among group members and the group's definition of the task. In separate studies, researchers found that groups shift topics about once a minute.[7] As noted in the last chapter, Poole argues that group members consider task process, relational concerns, and topical shifts with varying degrees of attention. Thus, groups benefit from an agenda that helps reduce uncertainty by keeping the discussion focused on their task. And one research study found that some members need more structure than others. Group members who have a preference for using more rigid procedures arrived at higher-quality decisions than if they used a less-structured approach to organizing their discussion.[8]

Many of the prescriptive agendas incorporate the key functions that seem to enhance group effectiveness, as discussed in the last chapter. Think of the various steps and tools in this chapter as a way to impose a common structure on a group's deliberation. Without that structure, a group is more likely to wobble, waste time, and be less productive.

Can a group have too much structure? The answer is yes. Perhaps you have been to a meeting that was more like listening to someone give a speech. An overly structured group discussion occurs if one person—sometimes the designated leader but sometimes not—talks too much, which minimizes group interaction. As Figure 8.1 suggests, the goal is to find the right balance between structure and interaction. Some research studies suggest that groups which used networked computers to share information (a highly structured situation) generated lots of ideas but had difficulty reaching a decision.[9] A less-structured, face-to-face situation was better for discussing alternatives and reaching a final decision. The techniques we review in this chapter are designed to focus the discussion but still permit the interaction that helps the group achieve its goals.

FIGURE 8.1   THE BALANCE BETWEEN STRUCTURE AND INTERACTION

Structure	Interaction
Agendas	Give-and-take discussion
Problem-solving steps	Reaction to members' contributions

REFLECTIVE THINKING: THE TRADITIONAL APPROACH TO GROUP PROBLEM SOLVING

Some researchers and numerous group communication textbooks recommend reflective thinking (or one of its many variations) as the standard agenda which should be used to organize or structure group problem solving. However, many group communication theorists today believe that it is more useful as a description of the way some people solve problems than as an ideal pattern for all groups to solve problems. We describe the following five steps along with tools which can provide even more structure as a general model to assist you and your groups in organizing the sometimes uncertain and fractious process of problem solving. The five steps we present here are not intended to be a one-size-fits-all approach that groups should use in solving every problem. They do, however, provide a logical, rational way of structuring group interaction.

STEP 1: IDENTIFY AND DEFINE THE PROBLEM

Perhaps you have heard the saying "A problem well stated is a problem half solved." A group first has to recognize that a problem exists. This may be the group's biggest obstacle. Before a PTA fund-raising committee can effectively consider suggestions for raising money, members must recognize that a need exists. Many groups do not bother to verbalize the problem facing them; each person merely begins by offering solutions to remedy the problem. A group must clearly and succinctly agree on the problem facing it. The problem should be limited so that members know its scope and size. After members identify and limit it, they should define key terms in light of the problem under consideration, so that they have a common understanding of the problem. For example, one student group recently decided to solve the problem of student apathy on campus. The students phrased their problem as a question: "What can be done to alleviate student apathy on campus?" They had identified a problem, but they soon discovered that they needed to decide what they meant by the word *apathy*. Does it mean poor attendance at football games? Does it mean a sparse showing at the recent fund-raising activity, "Hit Your Professor with a Pie"? After additional efforts to define the key word, they decided to limit their problem to low attendance at events sponsored by the student activities committee. With a clearer focus on their problem, they were ready to continue with the problem-solving process.

Consider the following questions when attempting to identify and define a problem for group deliberations:

1. What is the specific problem the group is concerned about?
2. What obstacles are keeping the group from its goal?
3. Is the question the group is trying to answer clear?
4. What terms, concepts, or ideas need to be defined?

5. Who is harmed by the problem?
6. When do the harmful effects of the problem occur?

Tools for Defining the Problem   In addition to using these questions to identify and define the problem, two tools or techniques that provide even more structure—the is/is not technique and the Journalist's Six Questions—may be useful when your group needs "super" structure to clarify and define the problem.

1. *Is/is not.* The **is/is not analysis** is a way to ensure that a group is, in fact, investigating a problem and not just a symptom of the problem.[10] Early in a group's deliberation group members consider such questions as: What is the area or object with the problem? What is not the area or object with the problem? Where does the problem occur? Where does the problem not occur? The accompanying chart includes other is/is not questions that can help give the group the structure it needs to clearly identify and define a problem. To use this technique, you could ask group members to use the chart to focus on the specific problem under consideration. Members could first write down their answers and then share their responses one at a time. Having group members write before speaking is a way to help further structure their comments.

For example, one group was attempting to investigate the declining standardized test scores that were occurring in one elementary school in their community. They thought the problem they were trying to solve was inadequate teaching which resulted in lowered scores. But when the group used the is/is not technique to identify when and where the problem is and is not observed, they discovered that the low test scores only occurred in three classrooms, which were in the same wing of the building and all controlled by the same air conditioning systems. On further investigation, they realized that the air conditioning units were not functioning, resulting in uncomfortable classrooms and, in turn, affecting student performance on the examinations. The problem changed from trying to eliminate bad teaching to changing the air conditioning system. The is/is not technique is a way to identify and define the problem rather than the symptoms of the problem.

Is/Is Not Analysis

	Is	Is Not
What	What is the area or object with the problem?	What is not the area or object with the problem?
Symptoms	What are the symptoms of the problem?	What are not the symptoms of the problem?
When	When is the problem observed?	When is the problem not observed?
Where	Where does the problem occur?	Where does the problem not occur?
Who	Who is affected by the problem?	Who is not affected by the problem?

2. *Journalist's Six Questions.* Most news reporters are taught to quickly identify the key facts when writing a news story or broadcasting a news event. The key elements of almost any newsworthy story can be captured by addressing six questions: who?, what?, when?, where?, why?, and how? Using these five W's and an H can help a group quickly structure how a problem is defined. Group members could be given a worksheet like the accompanying example and instructed to come to a meeting, having first attempted to answer these six questions.[11] The group could then pool the results and be well on the way to analyzing the problem. Or, the group could brainstorm answers to these questions while the group leader records the responses on a flip chart or chalkboard.

Journalist's Six Questions

Who?	
What?	
When?	
Where?	
Why?	
How?	

STEP 2: ANALYZE THE PROBLEM

Ray Kroc, the founder of McDonald's, was fond of saying that nothing is particularly hard if you divide it into small jobs. To analyze a problem is to break a problem into causes, effects, symptoms, and subproblems. During the analysis phase of group problem solving, members need to research and investigate the problem. In analyzing the problem, a group may wish to consider the following questions:

1. What is the history of the problem? How long has it existed?
2. How serious is the problem?
3. What are the causes of the problem?
4. What are the effects of the problem?
5. What are the symptoms of the problem?
6. What methods does the group already have for dealing with the problem?
7. What are the limitations of those methods?
8. How much freedom does the group have in gathering information and attempting to solve the problem?
9. What obstacles keep the group from achieving the goal?

10. Can the problem be divided into subproblems for definition and analysis?

Another element in the analysis step of the reflective-thinking process is to formulate criteria for an acceptable solution. **Criteria** are standards or goals for acceptable solutions. Formulating such criteria may prevent future uncertainties and misunderstandings and may help your group sort through proposed solutions to arrive at the best possible one. Many groups begin listing solutions before they have properly analyzed problems or identified adequate criteria. If you adhere to the reflective-thinking format, you will identify criteria before offering possible solutions. In listing criteria for a solution, you may wish to consider the following questions:

1. What goal are we trying to achieve?
2. What are the minimum requirements of an acceptable solution?
3. Which criteria are the most important?
4. How should the group use the criteria to evaluate the suggested solutions?

Sample criteria for a solution may include the following:

1. The solution should be inexpensive.
2. The solution should be implemented as soon as possible.
3. The solution should be agreed on by all of the group members.

Tools for Analyzing the Problem   Groups may need help in breaking a problem down into its subcomponents. Two techniques that can help a group sort out factors contributing to the problem are force field analysis and 6M analysis. Both of these techniques can help a group focus on data and facts rather than vague impressions of what may be causing the problem.

1. *Force field analysis.* This technique is based on assumptions of Kurt Lewin, often called the father of group dynamics.[12] To use force field analysis, the group needs to have a clear statement of its goal. This goal can be stated in terms of what the group wants more of or less of (for example, "We need more money, more time, or less interference from others"). The group analyzes the goal by noting what driving forces make it likely to be achieved and what restraining forces make it unlikely to be achieved.

Follow these steps to complete the action chart on page 222.[13]

1. Identify the goal, objective, or target the group is trying to achieve (e.g., more money, fewer errors).
2. On the right side of the chart, list all of the restraining forces: those forces that currently keep the group from achieving its goal.
3. On the left side of the chart, list all of the driving forces: those forces that currently help the group achieve its goal.
4. The group now decides whether to do one of three things. First, it could increase the driving forces. Second, it could decrease the restraining

FIGURE 8.2   FORCE FIELD ANALYSIS

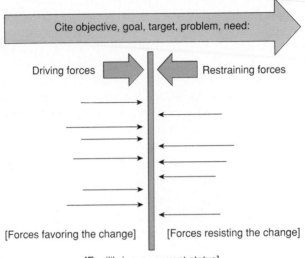

From: *The Winning Trainer* by Julius E. Eitington. Copyright © 1989 by Gulf Publishing Company, Houston, TX. Used with permission. All rights reserved.

forces. Or, third, it could increase selected driving forces and decrease those restraining forces over which the group has control.

After the group has sorted through the facts and identified the driving and restraining forces, it will more likely be able to focus on the essential causes of the problem rather than on the problem's symptoms.

Say, for example, you are working in a group that has the goal of increasing teamwork and collaboration among faculty and students. Driving forces—or those forces that favor the likelihood that teamwork will increase—include such factors as: faculty members who are motivated to work with students, students who also want to work with faculty, an existing training program that teaches teamwork and collaboration skills to both students and faculty. These and other driving forces could be included on the left-hand side of the force field chart. Restraining forces—or those forces that work against achieving the goal of increased collaboration—include: current lack of knowledge of teamwork principles, the negative attitudes of a small but vocal group of faculty members who want to use more individual approaches to education, and the lack of a tradition of collaboration. These obstacles are listed on the right side of the chart. Ideally, the group should work together on the force field analysis diagram by using a flip chart or projecting the chart using an overhead projector. After generating additional driving and restraining forces, the group then turns its attention to the question, "What can be done to increase the driving forces and decrease the restraining forces?" The group's force field analysis of the problem can provide new insights for overcoming the obstacles and achieving the goal.

2. *6M analysis.* Another tool for analysis is called 6M analysis.[14] Using a worksheet or chart like the one below, group members examine the problem defined from the following six points of view: (1) manpower (human resources)—does the problem stem from having too few or too many people involved? (2) machinery—is equipment the cause of the problem? (3) methods—are things being done wrong to create the problem? (4) materials—is lack of tangible things causing the problem? (5) money—is too little (or too much) money causing the problem? (6) minutes—is too little or too much time causing the problem? These six Ms can serve as a useful template to help analyze problem causes.

6M Analysis

Difficulty (Problem, Obstacle)	Manpower (Human Resources)	Machinery	Methods	Materials	Money	Minutes

STEP 3: GENERATE SEVERAL POSSIBLE SOLUTIONS

After analyzing a problem and selecting criteria for a solution, the group should begin to list possible solutions in tentative, hypothetical terms. Many groups suggest a variety of possible solutions without evaluating them. We will discuss how to use brainstorming as a way to generate several solutions later in the chapter.

STEP 4: SELECT THE BEST SOLUTION(S)

After a group has compiled a list of possible solutions to a problem, it should be ready to select the best solution. How do you narrow down a long list of proposed solutions? One way is to refer to the criteria proposed during the analysis stage of the discussion and consider each tentative solution in light of these criteria. The group should decide which proposed solution or combination of solutions best meets its criteria. Our discussion of how to facilitate consensus, presented in Chapter 9, offers several strategies for narrowing the number of options in seeking the best solution to a problem. The following questions may be helpful in analyzing the proposed solutions:

1. What are the advantages of each solution?
2. Are there any disadvantages to the solution? Do the disadvantages outweigh the advantages?
3. What would be the long-term effects and short-term effects of this solution if it were adopted?
4. Would the solution really solve the problem?
5. Does the solution conform to the criteria formulated by the group?
6. Should the group modify the criteria?

If group members agree, the criteria for a best solution may need to be changed or modified.[15]

Tools for Evaluating the Solutions In addition to asking questions to guide discussion of the solutions or alternatives that the group has identified, the following tools can provide additional ways of focusing or structuring discussion.

1. *Analyze the pros and cons.* One of the most consistent findings of functional communication researchers is that when a groups weigh the positive and negative outcomes of solutions they will make a better decision.[16] One method of facilitating such a discussion is to make a T-chart like the one shown here to evaluate solution pros and cons. A T-chart gets its name from that fact that when you draw a large "T" on a board or flip chart, you can list "Pros" on one side of the middle line and "Cons" on the others side. If the group is large and you want to make sure everyone participates, you can have members first silently write down pros and cons (or the risks and benefits) and then share their responses with the group. If, for example, a group were trying to decide whether to purchase a new piece of property, one side of the center line might list positive aspects, such as: good investment, property values increasing, good location, etc. On the other side of the "T" would be negative implications of the purchase, such as: it will reduce our cash flow, it will increase property taxes, expensive lawyer fees, etc. A thorough look at pros and cons can help a group consider alternatives before it makes a final decision.

T-Chart

Pros	Cons

2. *Average rankings and ratings.* It is usually easier for a group to identify possible solutions than it is to narrow the list of alternatives and select the best solution. If a group has many solutions to evaluate, one way to narrow the list is to ask group members to either rank or rate the solutions and then average the rankings or ratings to see which solutions emerge as the most and least popular. Ranking or rating should be done *after* a group has discussed of the pros and cons of the solutions. Ranking solutions works best if you have no more than five to seven solutions; group members often have a difficult time ranking more than seven items. If you have a very long list of solutions—a dozen or more—you may ask the group members to rank their top five choices, assigning a rank of 1 to their top choice, 2 to their next choice, and so on.

Besides ranking solutions, group members could also assign a rating score to each solution. Each solution could be rated on a five-point scale, with a rating of 1 being a very positive evaluation and 5 being a negative evaluation. Even a long list of 20 or more potential solutions could be rated. Averages for each solution could be calculated, and the highest rated solutions could be discussed again by the entire group.

STEP 5: TEST AND IMPLEMENT THE SOLUTION

Group members should be confident that the proposed solution is valid— that is, that it will solve the problem. After a group selects the best solution, it must determine how the solution can be put into effect. You may wish to consider the following questions:

1. How can the group get public approval and support for its proposed solution?
2. What specific steps are necessary to implement the solution?
3. How can the group evaluate the success of its problem-solving efforts?

In many groups, those who choose a solution are not the same people who will implement it. If this is the case, members who select the solution should clearly explain why they selected it to members who will put the solution into practice. If they can demonstrate that the group went through an orderly process to solve the problem, they usually can convince others that their solution is valid.

Tools for Implementing A Solution   1. *Action Chart.* An **action chart** is a grid that lists the tasks that need to be done and identifies who will be responsible for each task. Such a chart is based on more elaborate diagrams and procedures, such as a PERT diagram. PERT stands for Program Review and Evaluation Technique and was originally developed by the United States Navy in the late 1950s to assist with the production of the Polaris missile program.[17] The action chart presented on page 222 was developed by using the following steps:

1. Identify the project goal.
2. Identify the activities needed to complete the project.
3. Identify the sequence of activities (what should be done first, second, third, etc.)
4. Estimate the amount of time it should take to complete each task.
5. Determine which group members should be responsible for each task.
6. Develop a chart that shows the relationships among the tasks, times, people, and sequence of events that are needed to accomplish the project.

One of the reasons solutions do not get implemented is that there is uncertainty about who should do what. An action chart provides needed structure to reduce this uncertainty. The following story illustrates the problem.

This is a story about four people: Everybody, Somebody, Anybody, and Nobody. There was an important job to be done and Everybody was asked to do it. Everybody was sure Somebody would do it. Anybody could have done it, but Nobody did it. Somebody got angry about that because it was Everybody's job. Everybody thought Anybody could do it, but Nobody realized that Everybody wouldn't do it. It ended up that Everybody blamed Somebody when actually Nobody asked Anybody.

An action chart helps to ensure that everybody is aware of what needs to be done and reduces the risk that nobody will do anything.

An Action Chart

Names									
Ken	●		●			●	●		●
Darryl			●			●			
Steve				●		●			
Janice				●		●		●	
Carl					●	●	●	●	
Assign-ment	Conduct needs assess-ment	Write behavioral objectives	Develop training content outline	Write training facilitator guide	Develop audio-visual resources	Conduct training pilot test	Conduct training for client	Analyze evalu-ation data
Week	Week 1		Week 2		Week 3		Week 4	
Day	Monday	Friday	Monday	Friday	Monday	Friday	Monday	Friday

2. *Flow chart.* A **flowchart** is a step-by-step diagram of a multistep process. One group was charged with improving the way textbooks were ordered for college classes. The chart on page 224 shows how the group described the essential steps involved in selecting, ordering, and purchasing a text. Flowcharts can help a group see whether the sequence of procedures they have identified to solve a problem are practical and fit together. A flowchart can also help your group work through logistics and identify practical problems of moving from an idea's conception to its implementation. Like

an action plan, a flowchart is a way to give structure to group thought. Flowcharts can be simple, like our example, or very complex like those computer programmers use to identify sophisticated computer programs.

How detailed does a flowchart need to be? The level of detail needed depends on the needs of the group. We caution you, however, not to make the flowchart so detailed that your goal becomes developing a flowchart rather than describing and implementing a process. Use a flowchart as a tool to make sure all group members have a clear understanding of the critical parts of a more complex process.

APPLYING REFLECTIVE THINKING TO YOUR GROUP

Reflective thinking suggests that groups work best when their discussions are organized rather than disorganized or random. Remember that you should use reflective thinking as a guide, not as an exact formula for solving every problem. As noted earlier, several group communication researchers have discovered that groups do not necessarily solve problems in a linear, step-by-step process.[18] The process by which groups solve problems goes through several phases of growth and development as members interact.[19] Reflective thinking is most useful in helping groups understand the phases of problem solving. As Ernest Bormann has noted, "Difficulties arise when [group] participants demand rationality from a group throughout its deliberations."[20] To add flexibility to the reflective-thinking steps, a group may return to an earlier problem-solving step to help clarify the discussion. For example, after researching and analyzing a problem, a group may decide to define it a little differently than it had been defined previously. Perhaps after carefully trying to apply criteria to select the best solution, a group may decide that it needs to revise the criteria. Reflective thinking can serve as a general guide to the problem-solving process. Randy Hirokawa's research suggests that a systematic approach to group problem solving and decision making is better than no organized approach at all.[21]

In trying to apply reflective thinking to group problem solving, consider the following suggestions.

1. *Clearly identify the problem you are trying to solve.* Make sure that you are not just discussing a topic. For example, one group decided to discuss the quality of the U.S. Justice system. The group selected a topic area, but it did not identify a problem. It should have focused clearly on a specific problem, such as "How can we improve the quality of the judicial system in the United States?" or "What should be done to improve the education and training of lawyers in the United States?"

2. *Phrase the problem as a question to help guide group discussion.* Identifying your group's problem as a question adds focus and direction to your deliberations. When formulating a problem-solving discussion question, keep in mind the guidelines discussed in Chapter 7.

FIGURE 8.3   PROCESS: ORDERING A TEXTBOOK

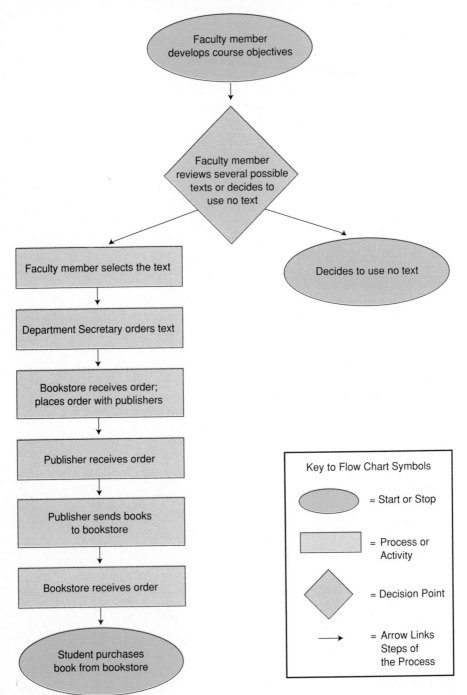

REVIEW BOX

Reflective Thinking

1. Identify and define the problem.
2. Analyze the problem.
3. Generate several possible solutions.
4. Select the best solution(s) from among the alternatives.
5. Test and implement the solution(s).

---

3. *Do not start suggesting solutions until you have analyzed the problem.* Many group communication researchers agree that until your group has researched the problem, you may not have enough information and specific facts to reach the best solution.[22] You will be tempted to think of solutions to your problem almost as soon as you have identified it. By deferring the search for a solution, you will gain a greater understanding of the causes, effects, and symptoms of the problem.

4. *In the definition and analysis steps of reflective thinking, do not confuse the causes of the problem with its symptoms.* A fever and headache are symptoms and not necessarily causes of a patient's ill health. The cause may be a cold or flu virus or a number of other things. A doctor tries to identify the cause of symptoms by running tests and analyzing a patient's medical history. In other words, a doctor needs to define, analyze, and solve a problem. You should try to clarify the differences between the causes and the symptoms (effects) of a problem. Perhaps your only goal is to alleviate the symptoms. However, you can better understand what your group is trying to accomplish if you can distinguish causes and symptoms.

5. *Constantly evaluate your group's problem-solving method.* For many years the only problem-solving method suggested to group discussion classes was reflective thinking. Some communication theorists suggest, however, that for certain types of problems alternative problem-solving methods work just as well, if not better, than reflective thinking. The remainder of this chapter will discuss some of these other problem-solving strategies.

BRAINSTORMING: A CREATIVE APPROACH TO GENERATING IDEAS FOR PROBLEM SOLVING

Imagine that your employer assigns you to a task force whose goal is to increase the productivity of your small manufacturing company. Phrased as a question, the problem is, "What can be done to increase efficiency and pro-

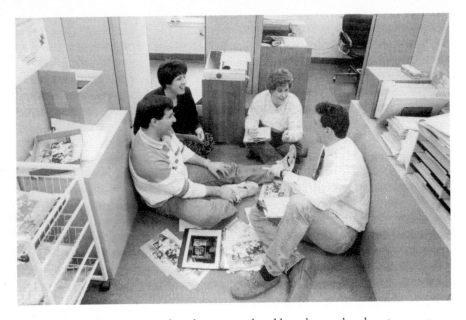

A group may be more creative when they are comfortable and in a relaxed environment.

ductivity for our company?" Your group is supposed to come up with ideas to help solve the problem. Assume that your boss has clearly identified the problem for the group and has provided you with several documents analyzing the problem in some detail. Your group may decide that reflective thinking, which focuses on identifying and analyzing problems, may not be the best process to follow. Your group needs innovative ideas and creative, original solutions. Perhaps your group could benefit from brainstorming.

Brainstorming is a problem-solving approach designed to help a group generate several creative solutions to a problem. It was first developed by Alex Osborn, an advertising executive who felt the need for a problem-solving technique that instead of evaluating and criticizing ideas would focus instead on developing imaginative and innovative solutions.[23] Brainstorming has been used by businesses, committees, and government agencies to improve the quality of group decision making. Although it can be used in several phases of many group discussions, it may be most useful if a group needs original ideas or has trouble coming up with any ideas at all. Research suggests that group members who are trained to use creative approaches to problem solving participate more, produce more ideas, are less critical of others, are generally more supportive, and use humor more often than individuals who are not trained to brainstorm.[24]

What enhances group creativity? Listing many ideas, breaking out of traditional thinking, identifying seemingly wild and far-out ideas, building on the ideas of others, and initially withholding evaluation all contribute to group creativity.

BRAINSTORMING STEPS

Here is a step-by-step description of how brainstorming works:

1. *Select a specific problem that needs solving.* Be sure that all group members can identify and clearly define the problem.
2. *Group members should temporarily put aside all judgments and evaluations.* The key to brainstorming is ruling out all criticism and evaluation. Osborn makes these suggestions:
   - Acquire a "try anything" attitude.
   - Avoid criticism, which can stifle creativity.
   - Remember that all ideas are thought-starters.
   - Today's criticism may kill future ideas.
3. *After group members have a clear understanding of the problem and know the brainstorming ground rules, tell them to think of as many possible solutions to the problem as they can.* Consider the following suggestions:
   - The wilder the ideas, the better.
   - It is easier to tame ideas down than to think ideas up.
   - Think out loud and mention unusual ideas.
   - Someone's wild idea may trigger a good solution from another person in the group.
4. *Make sure that the group understands that "piggybacking" off someone's idea is useful.* Combine ideas; add to previous ideas. Adopt this philosophy: Once an idea is contributed to the group, no one owns it. It belongs to the group and anyone can modify it.
5. *Have someone record all of the ideas mentioned.* Ideas could be recorded on a chalkboard or an overhead projector so that each group member can see them. You could also tape-record your discussions.
6. *Some groups evaluate ideas at later sessions.* Consider these suggestions:
   - Approach each idea positively, and give it a fair trial.
   - Try to make ideas workable.
   - If only a few of the ideas generated by a group are useful, the session has been successful.

NOMINAL GROUP TECHNIQUE: USING SILENT BRAINSTORMING TO GENERATE IDEAS

Nominal group technique (NGT) is a procedure that uses some of the same principles and methods of brainstorming but has members generate ideas individually before sharing them with the group. Nominal group technique gets its name from the principle that the group is nominal (in name only), in the sense that members work on problems individually rather than during sustained group interaction. This technique uses silent brainstorming to

REVIEW BOX

Brainstorming

1. Select a problem that requires creative solutions.
2. Tell group members to withhold judgments and evaluations.
3. Ask the group to generate as many solutions as possible.
4. Tell the group it is okay to piggyback off someone else's idea.
5. Have someone record the ideas generated.
6. Evaluate the ideas when the time allotted for brainstorming has elapsed.

LITZLER

"TELL ME AGAIN, THE DIFFERENCE BETWEEN A BRAIN-
STORM 'WARNING' AND A BRAINSTORM 'WATCH.'"

overcome some of the disadvantages researchers have discovered in exclusively verbal brainstorming. When one person talks during a group discussion (or if several people talk), other members stop and listen to the ideas presented.[25] Researchers also found that people work more diligently if they have an individual assignment than if they have a group assignment.[26] As we noted in Chapter 1, a disadvantage of group work is that it spreads responsibility, thereby increasing the probability that some group members will shirk their responsibilities and not participate. Several studies suggest that sometimes when using group brainstorming, group members' creative talents seem to be restricted by the presence of others. Group members may generate more ideas if members first work alone and then regroup. After they reconvene as a unit, the entire group can modify, elaborate on, and evaluate ideas. Even before a group meets for the first time, you could describe a problem and ask group members to brainstorm individually before assembling. A new twist: If group members are linked by a networked computer system, conduct the brainstorming session through electronic mail before meeting face-to-face. We will present some of the advantages and disadvantages of using technology in group discussion in Chapter 11.

Nominal group technique is a way to add structure to the brainstorming process. The following steps summarize how to use NGT:

1. Make sure all group members understand the problem under consideration. Each member should be able to define and analyze the problem.
2. Working individually, group members write down possible solutions to the problem.
3. Group members report the solutions they have identified to the entire group one at a time. Each idea should be noted on a chart, chalkboard, or overhead projector for all group members to see.
4. Group members discuss the ideas gathered, not to advocate for one idea over another but to make sure that all of the ideas are clear.
5. After discussing all proposed solutions, each group member ranks the solutions. Or, if the list of solutions is long, the group members can rank the five solutions they like best. The results are tabulated.
6. The entire group now discusses the results of the rankings. If the first round of ranking is inconclusive or the group is not comfortable with the results, the options can be ranked again after additional discussion. Research suggests that using this organized method of gathering and evaluating information results in better solutions than if the group attacks a problem in a disorganized fashion.[27] One researcher has found that nominal group technique works better than other prescriptive approaches such as reflective thinking.[28]

This individual method of idea generation and evaluation has the advantage of involving all group members in deliberations. It can be useful if some group members are unwilling or uncomfortable in making contributions because of status differences in the group. Also, alternating group discussion with individual deliberation can be useful in groups plagued by conflict and tension.

Both brainstorming and nominal group technique can be used at any phase of the problem-solving process. For example, you could combine nominal group technique with force field analysis by asking group members to silently brainstorm driving and restraining forces toward group goal attainment. Or you could ask members to brainstorm possible causes or symptoms of the problem during problem analysis. When seeking strategies to implement a solution, again, you could use brainstorming or NGT to generate possible strategies.

APPLYING BRAINSTORMING TO YOUR GROUP

While you should now understand how brainstorming works, you may still have some questions about how you can apply this method of creative problem solving to your group discussions. Consider the following suggestions:

1. *Do not make the time limit for brainstorming too short.* Recent research suggests that groups that are given only a short time for brainstorming (four minutes) can be very productive, but not as creative as groups that have a longer time for brainstorming.[29] If you are brainstorming orally, do not worry about a little silence while people are thinking. If you are using silent brainstorming (Nominal Group Technique), it is okay if people are not writing furiously during the entire brainstorming period.

2. *Be certain that each group member understands the specific problem that the group is trying to solve.* A problem must be clearly defined and understood and must also be limited in size and scope. A broad, vaguely worded problem must be clarified before a group attempts to identify possible solutions.

3. *Brainstorming works best as part of an overall problem-solving strategy.* As with reflective thinking, group members need to define and analyze the problem under consideration, provided that it has not already been identified for them. One difference between a creative problem-solving method like brainstorming and traditional reflective thinking is that those using the former method apply criteria for solutions after they generate possible solutions. Otherwise, criteria may put a damper on group creativity. Instead of developing solutions according to established criteria, members evaluate solutions after they are developed.

4. *Make sure that each group member follows the brainstorming rules.* Brainstorming will be most effective if group members stop criticizing and evaluating ideas. Do not forget that group members can criticize nonverbally through tone of voice, facial expression, or posture. Everyone in the group must feel completely free to communicate ideas that may solve the problem. What should you do if a few members just cannot stop evaluating the ideas that are suggested? You may have to: (1) remind them courteously to follow the rules, (2) ask them to be quiet, (3) ask them to record the ideas of others, or (4) ask them to leave the group.

5. *If you are serving as the group's leader, try to draw less-talkative group members into the discussion and compliment them when they come up with good ideas.* Call people by name: "Curt, you look like you've got some good ideas. What do you suggest?" You can also compliment the entire group when members are doing a good job of generating ideas: "Good job, group! We've got 30 ideas so far. Let's see if we can come up with 30 more."

6. *Set aside a definite amount of time for brainstorming.* Decide, as a group, how much time you want to devote to brainstorming. As we have discussed, be sure to give yourself plenty—it is better to have too much time than too little. You may want to set a goal for a certain number of ideas that should be recorded: "We'll stop brainstorming when we get 60 ideas."

7. *Consider a technique called* **reverse brainstorming.**[30] Ask group members to brainstorm ideas or solutions that would make the problem worse. After generating a list that would increase the problem, consider the implications of doing the opposite of what was identified.

8. *Use the* **rolestorming**[31] *method.* Ask each group member to assume roles. If you are focusing on a problem in your community, ask group members to assume the role of the mayor, superintendent of schools, or city manager. If it is a government problem, have them imagine that they are the governor, a member of the legislature, or even the president of the United States. Brainstorming in this new role may help unlock ideas and increase group creativity.

9. *Tell the group what will happen with the ideas and suggestions that are generated.*[32] Do not just finish the brainstorming session with a long list of ideas that may be shelved. Perhaps a subcommittee can be formed to combine ideas and eliminate obvious overlapping suggestions. The subgroup might also be asked to evaluate the ideas or determine which ideas need further exploration or more information.

10. *Make sure your group needs a creative problem-solving format.* Brainstorming can help generate ideas, but if your group does not have a lot of time to devote to it, a simpler, more conventional problem-solving method (such as reflective thinking) may be best. But do not avoid brainstorming when it may be useful as part of an overall problem-solving plan (e.g., it can be used to generate possible solutions in the third step of the reflective-thinking format).

Some researchers believe that five people is an ideal size for a brainstorming group. If the group is too large, members may feel too inhibited to contribute creative ideas. Therefore, make sure that brainstorming is the problem-solving format your group needs.

QUESTION-ORIENTED APPROACHES TO PROBLEM SOLVING

As discussed earlier, a group adopts a problem-solving format mainly to organize its deliberations and reach its goal more efficiently. Thus far, the chapter has discussed a traditional problem-solving format (reflective think-

REVIEW BOX

Traditional Problem-Solving Steps and Techniques

STEPS	TECHNIQUES
Identify and define the problem	Is/is not analysis Journalist's six questions Gather data
Analyze the problem	Is/is not analysis 6M analysis Journalist's six questions Force field analysis Develop criteria Identify history, causes, effects, symptoms, goals, obstacles
Generate several possible solutions	Brainstorm Rolestorm Reverse brainstorm Nominal group technique
Select the best solution(s)	Compare pros and cons Apply solutions to criteria Appoint a subgroup Combine alternatives Average rankings and ratings
Test and implement the solution	Identify implementation steps Develop a group action plan (who does what when) Develop a flow chart

ing) and a method of generating creative ideas (brainstorming). A third approach to problem solving requires groups to consider a series of questions to keep them oriented toward their goal. Two such approaches, discussed in the following sections, can help groups develop strategies for solving problems. Both formats have groups consider series of questions to help identify the critical issues that they need to resolve. The questions also provide an orderly sequence of thought to help groups formulate the best possible solutions. After you study both of these formats, the chapter will offer some specific suggestions for applying these approaches to your group discussions.

IDEAL-SOLUTION FORMAT

Obviously, problem-solving groups want to identify the best solutions to problems. In the **ideal-solution format,** groups answer questions designed to help them identify ideal solutions. Alvin Goldberg and Carl Larson have devised the following agenda of questions:

1. Do all members agree on the nature of the problem?
2. What would be the ideal solution from the point of view of all parties involved in the problem?
3. What conditions within the problem could be changed so that the ideal solution might be achieved?
4. Of the solutions available, which one best approximates the ideal solution?[33]

These questions help groups recognize the barriers that the problems under consideration have created. The questions also encourage groups to analyze their problem's cause and to evaluate proposed solutions. The advantage of the ideal-solution format over other problem-solving approaches is its simplicity. Group members simply consider each of the questions listed previously, one at a time. One expert recommends the ideal-solution format for discussions that involve people with varied interests; this format works best when acceptance of a solution is important.[34] The format enables group members to see the problem from several viewpoints in their search for the best solution.

While the ideal-solution format is similar to reflective thinking, its chief value is that it uses questions to help a group systematically identify and analyze a problem, pinpoint the best possible solution, and formulate specific methods for achieving a solution. Like the other problem-solving formats presented in this chapter, it helps a group—particularly one with varying viewpoints and experiences—to focus on a problem and devise ways to solve it.

SINGLE-QUESTION FORMAT

Like the ideal-solution format, the **single-question format** requires considering answers to a series of questions designed to guide the group toward a best solution. Goldberg and Larson suggest that the answers to the following five questions can help a group achieve its goal:

1. What is the question whose answer the group needs to know in order to accomplish its purpose?
2. What subquestions must be answered before the group can answer the single question it has formulated?
3. Does the group have sufficient information to answer the subquestions confidently? (If yes, answer them. If no, continue below.)
4. What are the most reasonable answers to the subquestions?
5. Assuming that the answers to the subquestions are correct, what is the best solution to the problem?[35]

A key difference between the single-question format and the ideal-solution format is that the former requires a group to formulate a question to help obtain the information needed to solve a problem. The single-question format also helps a group to identify and resolve issues that must be confronted before it can reach a solution. As Goldberg and Larson note, "An assumption of the single-question form seems to be that issues must be resolved, however tentatively."[36] Thus, the single-question format would probably work best if a group is capable of reaching reasonable agreement on the issues and agreeing on how the issues can be resolved. A group characterized by conflict and contention would probably not find the single-question approach productive.

The success of the single-question format depends on a group's agreeing on the subissues before trying to agree on the major issues. If you are working with a group that has difficulty reaching agreement, the single-question format may not be the best approach. The group may become bogged down arguing about trivial matters while the major issues go unanswered. Decide whether your group will be able to reach agreement on the minor issues before you decide to use the single-question format. If your group cannot reach agreement, either the ideal-solution format or reflective-thinking format may be a better method of organizing your group's deliberations.

APPLYING QUESTION-ORIENTED APPROACHES TO YOUR GROUP

You may have noticed some similarities among the single-question, the ideal-solution, and the reflective-thinking formats. All of these approaches suggest that a group should begin its deliberations by trying to define the problem or attempting to formulate a question that will focus the discussion. After a group zeroes in on key issues, members next must analyze the problem. The ideal-solution format suggests that the group formulate criteria to direct its search for a solution, while the single-question format asks a group to identify and answer subquestions to help formulate a solution.

By guiding groups toward their goals with questions, the ideal-solution and single-question formats help groups agree on minor issues before they try to agree on solutions to problems. Carl Larson tried to find out whether an ideal-solution format, single-question format, reflective-thinking format, or no format at all would produce better solutions.[37] His study indicates that ideal-solution and single-question formats generated better solutions than did the reflective-thinking approach. All three approaches fared better than no approach at all. While just one laboratory study does not prove that the single-question and ideal-solution formats are superior to the reflective-thinking format, it does suggest that under certain conditions goal-oriented approaches may have certain advantages. In Larson's study, when groups were given alternatives and told to choose the best solution to a problem, their discussions lasted only about 20 minutes. Thus, by considering specific questions, members were able to solve problems efficiently. Norman Maier also concluded that a problem-solving approach

Recording group members ideas on a flip chart can help provide necessary structure when the group is trying to solve a problem.

that has a group consider minor issues before major issues can improve group decisions.[38] Clearly, theorists need to conduct additional research before they can prescribe specific formulas to ensure efficiency in group problem solving.

If you are going to lead a group discussion, the following suggestions may help you apply the ideal-solution and single-question approaches to problem solving:

1. *If you are going to use the ideal-solution or single-question approach, provide group members with copies of the questions that will guide their discussion.* Since these approaches rely on a series of questions to guide discussion, you can reduce some of the uncertainty that occurs by making sure that each person has a copy of the questions. Tell the group to use the questions as a guide.

2. *Explain why you are using the format you have selected.* Most groups are willing to go along with a particular discussion agenda, especially if you give them reasons for having selected a specific approach. Tell the group that considering specific questions in a developmental format can keep the discussion on track. If your group has a specified time period in which to meet, you can explain that using questions to guide the discussion can help make the discussion more efficient.

3. *Keep the discussion focused on the specific question under consideration.* If you have provided copies of the questions for either the ideal-solution or single-question format, some group members may be tempted to skip a question or may want to discuss an unrelated issue. You may have to help the group focus on one question at a time. Several studies suggest that groups with members who try to keep participants aware of the pertinent issues by summarizing the discussion and requesting clarification have a good chance of agreeing on a solution and of being satisfied with their discussion.[39]

PUTTING PRINCIPLE INTO PRACTICE

In this chapter we discussed several prescriptive approaches that a group can use to solve a problem. Groups often need some plan or structure to help their members define, analyze, and solve a problem. We described four different kinds of problem-solving formats: (1) reflective thinking, (2) brainstorming, (3) ideal solution, and (4) single question. Review the following suggestions for applying these problem-solving approaches to the groups in which you participate.

REFLECTIVE THINKING

- To help your group define and limit a problem, phrase it as a question.
- Do not start suggesting solutions until your group has thoroughly analyzed a problem.
- Consider using tools such as is/is not analysis, force field analysis, journalist's six questions, and 6M analysis to help your group analyze the problem.
- Formulate criteria for a good solution before you begin suggesting solutions.
- Use brainstorming to help your group generate possible solutions.
- If the other group members agree, you may need to change the criteria you have selected during the analysis phase of reflective thinking.
- Make sure that reflective thinking is the best method for your group; another problem-solving approach may work better.
- To help make sure that everyone knows and follows through on his or her assignment, consider using an action chart or a flowchart.

BRAINSTORMING

- Make sure all group members understand the ground rules for brainstorming. Do not evaluate solutions until you have finished brainstorming.
- If group members do not follow the brainstorming rules, you may have to: (1) restate the rules, (2) ask them to keep quiet, (3) ask them to record the ideas of others, or (4) ask them to leave the group.

- If brainstorming does not work, consider having each member of the group work individually.
- Try to draw less-talkative group members into the discussion; compliment members when they come up with good ideas.
- Set aside a definite amount of time for brainstorming.
- Make certain that brainstorming is the best problem-solving approach for your group.

IDEAL SOLUTION AND SINGLE QUESTION

- If you are the leader of the group, tell the group why you have selected either the ideal-solution format or the single-question approach to problem solving.
- Use the ideal-solution format to help the group come to an agreement on the nature of the problem.
- Use the single-question format if you are sure that your group is capable of agreeing on the issues and on how they can be resolved.
- Provide members with copies of the questions used in the ideal-solution format or the single-question format; this will help to keep your discussion on track.
- Remind group members to address only those questions and issues that are relevant to the discussion.

A CASE STUDY

THE COMPANY LAYOFF[40]

You are one of the managers of a department store in your community. You have just been informed by your supervisor that one of your employees will have to be laid off due to company cut-backs. You are now meeting with your managerial colleagues to decide which employee will be chosen. All employees listed work full-time, and all work the same number of hours. There is one formal rule you have to follow: *The basis for laying a person off must be a job-related reason.* Please make the *best* decision you can with the limited information you are given. Be prepared to discuss the reasoning behind your group's decision.

LIST OF EMPLOYEES

Masha   Aged 33, married, with two children, Masha has worked for the company for *five* years. She loves her job and works with little or no supervision. You have considered giving her a promotion when the opportunity arises. Other people go to Masha when they have questions, because she trains

	well. She has been going to school part time to get a management degree and will graduate in another year.
Bob	Aged 49, divorced, with one child, Bob has worked with the company for 22 years. He keeps to himself but always gets work done. You never have to give Bob instructions, because he knows his job so well. Others in the department call him "Pop" because he seems to parent everyone and is well liked. He really adds a great deal of stability to your department. He does not want to change his job at all because he is happy. You put Bob in charge in your absence.
Trent	Aged 19, single, a Navajo, Trent just began working for your company *11 months* ago. He went to an accelerated school as a child and started college when he was 15 years old. He has since graduated with a business degree and shows promise of going far in your company. He is already the best salesperson in your department. Most people get along with him well. Because he is new, Trent needs a lot of training, but his sales are worth your extra time.
Madeline	Madeline is 25, married, and three months pregnant. She transferred to your store only *last month* but has over three years total experience in the company. You have not been very well satisfied with her attendance because she is calling in sick a lot. However, she is the only person that you feel you can give your most difficult tasks to, because she is very thorough. She also has had more customer compliments than any other person in your department.
Catrina	Catrina is 40, single, has three children, and is a recovering alcoholic. She fulfills a very necessary function in your department by doing maintenance work, which no one else really has time for. Catrina is efficient and is never late; however, she does not really associate with the others. She has worked with the company for over *10 years*, but she cannot read or write; it is likely that this is one of the few places she could find work.
Antonio	Aged 27, single, with no children, Antonio has worked for *two years* in your department and, in that time, has won three awards for creating outstanding merchandise displays (the heart and soul of retail). He is your most conscientious worker and keeps your department looking great. You have wondered, though, whether he comes to work under the influence of drugs. Several customers have complained about poor grooming habits and language he used toward them. In the last month, however, he has made significant improvements.

Please Pass the Problem

You will be placed in a group with five to seven other people. Each person in your group should write a brief description of a problem that you are currently facing. It could be related to work, school, or home. Consider writing your problem in terms of what you want more of or less of. For example, "I'd like to have more free time to spend with my family," or "I'd like to have a better work schedule so that I don't have to go to work on weekends." After each person has written one problem statement, pass your problem statement to the person on your right. Each group member should take a few moments to offer comments, questions, or suggestions about the problem. Continue exchanging problems until your problem statement returns to you. Examine the comments and observations your group members have made. Analyze the types of suggestions. Did they help you define the problem? Were there more comments about solutions than analyzing the problem? How helpful were the suggestions? Discuss the activity in terms of how individuals often first react when they encounter a problem in a group.

Using Problem-Solving Agendas

As a class, identify a problem that needs to be solved. It could be a university, local, state, or national problem. Then divide into groups of five or six members. Each group should attempt to solve the problem using a different problem-solving format. After the groups have deliberated, have one member from each summarize how the problem-solving format worked for the group. Which format was the easiest to use? Did some groups take more time than others to solve the problem? Did the problem-solving format help or hinder the group's effort to solve the problem? Note other differences and similarities in the groups' problem-solving process.

Exercise: Creativity

Solving this problem requires creativity. The class should divide into groups of three. Each group's assignment is to connect all nine dots with only four straight and connected lines.[41]

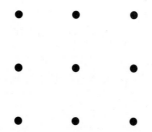

LOSING YOUR JOB

Your group represents a family with a take-home income of $43,200. You hear through the grapevine at work that because of organizational restructuring your entire department will be laid off within four months. It is probable that you will be without your monthly salary check in the very near future. You do have skills that could lead to income from consulting. You have $3,000 in a bank savings account and a $5,000 stock portfolio, but you also have $1,500 charged to your credit cards. Because of the nature of your job, you pay the IRS quarterly rather than in monthly payroll deductions. You have the following monthly budget:

30-year fixed mortgage	$1000
Food	$600
Bank-financed car payment	$300
Clothing and personal items	$400
Miscellaneous	$500
College savings fund	$200
Pension fund	$300
Medical bills	$300

You are sure you will get a good job recommendation from your boss, yet it may take you four to six months to find work at a comparable salary. Rank the following strategies from the most- to least-important actions you should take immediately to prepare for the impending loss of your income.

A. Change your mortgage from a 30-year to a 15-year term.   _____
B. Start a dramatic increase in your savings plan by reevaluating
     your budget.   _____
C. Transfer your car bank loan to a home equity loan.   _____
D. Pay off charge cards.   _____
E. Borrow more money from the bank.   _____
F. Charge most of your food and living expenses to your credit
     card to help you save.   _____
G. Quit adding money to your pension plan now.   _____
H. Switch investments from stocks into a money market fund.   _____
I.   Skip your next IRS payment.   _____
J.   Increase your purchases of items you find on sale such as
     clothes and food.   _____
K. Start your own consulting practice.   _____
L. Use this opportunity to go back to school to get retrained
     for a higher-paying job.   _____

EVALUATION OF GROUP PROBLEM SOLVING

Use the following scales to assess your skills in applying problem-solving agendas to group deliberations.

	Strongly Agree	Agree	Unsure	Disagree	Strongly Disagree
1. I helped the group identify the specific problem it was trying to solve.					
2. I helped phrase the problem as a question to guide the group's discussion.					
3. I analyzed the problem thoroughly before suggesting possible solutions.					
4. I was able to distinguish clearly between causes of the problem and symptoms of the problem.					
5. I evaluated the problem-solving approach the group used to determine if it was the best way to organize the discussion.					

POSTDECISION REACTION

Evaluate your reactions to participating in a small group problem-solving or decision-making activity on a scale of 1 to 10, where 1 represents "very satisfied" and 10 represents "not at all satisfied."

_____ 1. I was satisfied with my individual contribution to the group task.

_____ 2. I was satisfied with my individual skill in helping group members feel comfortable in participating in the group.

_____ 3. I was satisfied with the way other group members helped to complete the group's task.

_____ 4. I was satisfied with the way other group members helped to make group members feel comfortable in participating in the discussion.

POSTMEETING GROUP EVALUATION

Use the following questions to evaluate your group discussion. Compare your evaluation with those of other group members.

1. Identify effective uses of group communication skills in today's discussion.
2. Identify the weaknesses in today's discussion.
3. Identify ways in which the group meeting could be improved.

NOTES

1. John K. Brilhart and Lurene M. Jochem, "Effects of Different Patterns on Outcomes of Problem-Solving Discussion," *Journal of Applied Psychology* 48 (1964): 174–79; William E. Jurma, "Effects of Leader Structuring Style and Task Orientation Characteristics of Group Members," *Communication Monographs* 49 (1979): 282–95; Susan Jarboe, "A Comparison of Input-Output, Process-Output, and Input-Process-Output Models of Small Group Problem-Solving Effectiveness," *Communication Monographs* 55 (June 1988): 121–42.

2. John K. Brilhart and Gloria J. Galanes, *Effective Group Discussion* (Dubuque, Iowa: Wm. C. Brown, 1992); John F. Cragan and David W. Wright, *Communication in Small Group Discussions* (St. Paul: West Publishing Company, 1986); John K. Brilhart and L. M. Jochem, "Effects of Different Patterns on Outcomes of Problem-Solving Discussion," *Journal of Applied Psychology* 48 (1964): 175–79; John Dewey, *How We Think;* (Boston: D. C. Heath, 1910); R. C. Huseman, "The Role of the Nominal Group in Small Group Communication," in R. C. Huseman, C. M. Logue, and D. L. Freshley (eds.), *Readings in Interpersonal and Organizational Communication,* 3rd ed. (Boston: Holbrook Press, 1977), pp. 493–507; Carl E. Larson, "Forms of Analysis and Small Group Problem Solving," *Speech Monographs* 36 (1969): 452–55; Norman R. F. Maier, *Problem Solving and Creativity in Individuals and Groups* (Belmont, Calif.: Brooks/Cole, 1970); James H. McBurney and Kenneth G. Hance, *The Principles and Methods of Discussion* (New York: Harper and Brothers, 1939); Raymond S. Ross, *Speech Communication: Fundamentals and Practice* (New York: McGraw-Hill, 1974); David W. Wright, *Small Group Communication: An Introduction* (Dubuque, Iowa: Kendall/Hunt, 1975); Charles H. Kepner and Benjamin B. Tregoe, *The Rational Manager* (New York: McGraw-Hill, 1965); Philip B. Crosby, *The Quality Is Free: The Art of Making Quality Certain* (New York: New American Library, 1979); Sud Ingle, *Quality Circles Master Guide: Increasing Productivity with People Power* (Englewood Cliffs, N.J.: Prentice-Hall, 1982); Kenneth J. Albert, *How to Solve Business Problems* (New York: McGraw-Hill, 1978); Donald L. Dewar, *Quality Circle Leader Manual and Instructional Guide* (Red Bluff, Calif.: Quality Circle Institute, 1980); Dennis S. Gouran, *Discussion: The Process of Group Decision-Making* (New York: Harper & Row, 1974); Arthur B. VanGundy, *Techniques of Structured Problem Solving* (New York: Van Nostrand Reinhold, 1981).

3. Dewey, *How We Think;* also see R. Victor Harnack, "John Dewey and Discussion," *Western Speech* 32 (Spring 1969): 137–149.

4. J. H. McBurney and K. G. Hance, *The Principles and Methods of Discussion* (New York: Harper & Brothers, 1939).

5. Robert F. Bales, Interaction Process Analysis. Chicago: University of Chicago Press, 1976.

6. Dennis S. Gouran, Candace Brown, and David R. Henry, "Behavioral Correlates of Perceptions of Quality in Decision-Making Discussion," *Communication Mono-*

graphs 45 (1978): 60–65; Linda L. Putnam, "Preference for Procedural Order in Task-Oriented Small Groups," *Communication Monographs* 46 (1979): 193–218; also see VanGundy, *Techniques of Structured Problem Solving;* B. J. Broome and L. Fulbright "A Multistage Influence Model of Barriers to Group Problem Solving: Participant-Generated Agenda for Small Group Research," *Small Group Research* 26 (1995): 25–55; J. P. Klubuilt and P. F. Green, *The Team-Based Problem Solver* (Burr Ridge, Ill: Irwin, 1994).

7. David M. Berg, "A Descriptive Analysis of the Distribution and Duration of Themes Discussed by Task-Oriented Small Groups," *Speech Monographs* 34 (1967): 172–75; also see Ernest G. Bormann and Nancy C. Bormann, *Effective Small Group Communication,* 2nd ed. (Minneapolis: Burgess Publishing Company, 1976), 132. Marshall Scott Poole, "Decision Development in Small Groups III: A Multiple Sequence Model of Group Decision Development," *Communication Monographs* 50 (1983): 321–41.

8. R. Y. Hiokawa, R. Ice, and J. Cook, "Preference for Procedural Order, Discussion Structure and Group Decision Performance," *Communication Quarterly* 36 (Summer 1988): 217–26.

9. See: S. R. Hiltz, K. Johnson, and M. Turoff, "Experiments in Group Decision Making: Communication Process and Outcome in Face-to-Face versus Computerized Conferences, *Human Communication Research* 13 (Winter 1986): 225–52.

10. See Charles H. Kepner and Benjamin B. Tregoe, *The Rational Manager* (New York: McGraw-Hill, 1965); our application of is/is not analysis is based on Dennis A. Romig and Laurie J. Romig, *Structured Teamwork® Guide* (Austin, Tex.: Performance Resources, Inc., 1990).

11. This discussion of journalist's six questions is based on a discussion by Julius E. Eitington, *The Winning Trainer* (Houston: Gulf Publishing Company, 1989), 157.

12. Kurt Lewin, "Frontiers in Group Dynamics," *Human Relations* 1 (1947): 5–42.

13. Eitington, *The Winning Trainer,* 158.

14. Ibid.

15. For evidence to support this modification of the reflective-thinking pattern, see John K. Brilhart, "An Experimental Comparison of Three Techniques for Communicating a Problem-Solving Pattern to Members of a Discussion Group," *Speech Monographs* 33 (1966): 168–77.

16. Randy Y. Hirokawa, "Why Informed Groups Make Faulty Decisions: An Investigation of Possible Interaction-Based Explanations," *Small Group Behavior* 18 (1987): 3–29; Randy Y. Hirokawa, "Group Communication and Decision-Making Performance: A Continued Test of the Functional Perspective" *Human Communication Research,* 14 (1985): 487–515; Randy Y. Hirokawa and Kathryn Rost, "Effective Group Decision-Making in Organizations: Field Test of the Vigilant Interaction Theory," *Management Communication Quarterly* 5 (1992): 267–88.

17. Federal Electric Coporation, *A Programmed Introduction to PERT* (New York: John Wiley & Sons, 1963).

18. For example, see Robert F. Bales and Fred L. Strodtbeck, "Phases in Group Problem-Solving," *Journal of Abnormal and Social Psychology* 46 (1951): 485–95; Thomas M. Schiedel and Laura Crowell, "Idea Development in Small Groups," *Quarterly Journal of Speech* 50 (1964): 140–45; B. Aubrey Fisher, "Decision Emergence: Phases in Group Decision-Making," *Speech Monographs* 37 (1970): 53–66; and Poole, "Decision Development."

19. Chapter 7 discusses in detail the phases of a group's growth and development.

20. Ernest G. Bormann, *Discussion and Group Methods: Theory and Practice,* 2nd ed. (New York: Harper & Row, 1975), 282.

21. Randy Y. Hirokawa, "Consensus Group Decision-Making, Quality of Decision and Group Satisfaction: An Attempt to Sort 'Fact' from 'Fiction'," *Central States Speech Journal* 33 (1982): 407–15; Randy Y. Hirokawa, "Why Informed Groups Make Faulty Decisions: An Investigation of Possible Interaction-Based Explanations," *Small Group Behavior* 18 (1987): 3–29.

22. Norman R. F. Maier, *Problem-Solving and Discussions and Conferences* (New York: McGraw-Hill, 1963), 123.

23. Alex F. Osborn, *Applied Imagination* (New York: Charles Scribner's Sons, 1962).

24. Roger L. Firestien, "Effects of Creative Problem Solving Training on Communication Behaviors in Small Groups," *Small Group Research* 21 (November 1990): 507–21.

25. Andre L. Delberg, Andrew H. Van de Ven, and David H. Gustafson, *Group Techniques for Program Planning: A Guide to Nominal Group and Delphi Procesies* (Glenview, Ill. Scott, Foresman, 1975), 7–16.

26. Gerry Philipsen, Anthony Mulac, and David Dietrich, "The Effects of Social Interaction on Group Generation of Ideas," *Communication Monographs* 46 (June 1979): 119–25; Fredric M. Jablin, "Cultivating Imagination: Factors That Enhance and Inhibit Creativity in Brainstorming Groups," *Human Communication Research* 7, no. 3 (Spring 1981): 245–58; Susan Jarboe, "A Comparison of Input-Output, Process-Output, and Input-Process-Output Models of Small Group Problem Solving Effectiveness," *Communication Monographs* 55 (June 1988). Incorporating individual or silent brainstorming into the traditional brainstorming approach emerges from the nominal group technique suggested by Andre L. Delbecq, Andrew H. Van de Ven, and David H. Gustafson, *Group Techniques for Program Planning: A Guide to Nominal Group and Delphi Processes* (Glenview, Ill.: Scott, Foresman, 1975), 7–16; also see Susan Jarboe, "Enhancing Creativity in Groups: Theoretical Boundaries and Pragmatic Limitations." Paper presented at the 77th annual meeting of the Speech Communication Association, Atlanta, Georgia, November 1, 1991.

    See Fred M.Jablin and David R. Seibold, "Implications for Problem-Solving Groups of Empirical Research on 'Brainstorming': A Critical Review of the Literature," *Southwestern Speech Communication Journal* 43 (1978): 327–56; Gerry Philipsen, Anthony Mulac, and David Dietrich, "The Effects of Social Interaction on Group Generation of Ideas," *Communication Monographs* 46 (June 1979): 119–25. Also see Arthur B. VanGundy, *Techniques of Structured Problem Solving* (New York: Van Nostrand Reinhold, 1981).

27. D. H. Gustafson, R. K. Shukla, A. Delbecq, and G. W. Walster, "A Comparative Study of Differences in Subjective Likelihood Estimates Made by Individuals, Interacting Groups, Delphi Groups and Nominal Groups," *Organizational Behavior and Human Performance* 9 (1973): 280–91; VanGundy, *Techniques of Structured Problem Solving.*

28. Jarboe, "A Comparison of Input-Output, Process-Output, and Input-Process-Output Models."

29. J. R. Kelly and S. J. Karau, "Entrainment of Creativity in Small Groups," *Small Group Research* 24 (May 1993): 179–98.

30. Eitington, *Winning Trainer.*

31. Ibid.

32. Romig and Romig, *Structured Teamwork® Guide.*

33. Alvin A. Goldberg and Carl E. Larson, *Group Communication: Discussion Processes and Applications* (Englewood Cliffs, N.J.: Prentice-Hall, 1975), p. 149.
34. Goldberg and Larson, *Group Communication,* 150.
35. Ibid.
36. Ibid.
37. Carl E. Larson, "Forms of Analysis and Small Group Problem-Solving," *Speech Monographs* 36 (1969): 452–55.
38. Norman R. F. Maier, "An Experimental Test of the Effect of Training on Discussion Leadership," *Human Relations* 6 (1953): 166–73.
39. Dennis G. Gouran, "Variables Related to Consensus in Group Discussions of Questions of Policy," *Speech Monographs* 36 (1969): 385–391; Thomas J. Knutson, "An Experimental Study of the Effects of Orientation Behavior on Small Group Consensus," *Speech Monographs* 39 (1972): 159–65; John A. Kline, "Orientation and Group Consensus," *Central States Speech Journal* 23 (1972): 44–47; Steven A. Beebe, "Orientation as a Determinant of Group Consensus and Satisfaction," *Resources in Education* 13 (October 1978): 19–25.
40. This activity was developed by Russ Wittrup, Department of Speech Communication, Southwest Texas State University.
41. This activity was adapted from E. E. Scannell and J. W. Newstrom, *More Games Trainers Play* (New York: McGraw Hill, 1994).

CHAPTER
N·I·N·E

Conflict Management in Small Groups

After studying this chapter, you will be able to:

- Explain why conflict occurs in small groups.

- Describe the negative impact that conflict has on group communication.

- List three myths about conflict.

- Identify strategies for managing different types of conflict.

- Describe four conflict management principles.

- Define the concept of groupthink.

- Identify six symptoms of groupthink.

- Apply techniques for reducing groupthink.

- Define *consensus*.

- Apply techniques for managing conflict and reaching consensus in small groups.

*T*o paraphrase a popular bumper sticker: "Conflict happens." Social psychologists and communication researchers say that people inevitably disagree when they interact. Throughout history, people have been involved in conflicts ranging from family feuds to wars. Whether groups are negotiating international trade or deciding how to repave a parking lot, their members experience conflict.

This chapter gives you some ideas about the causes of conflict and presents some strategies for managing it in small groups. You will not learn how to eliminate group conflict but to understand it and its importance in your group deliberations.

First we will define conflict and note why it occurs so often. Second, we will look at three common myths about conflict in small groups. Third, we will examine three types of conflict and offer suggestions for managing each type. Fourth, we will discuss groupthink, a phenomenon that occurs when small groups have too *little* disagreement or controversy. Finally, we will discuss consensus and offer suggestions for helping groups to reach agreement. The prime objective of this chapter is to help you understand how conflict in groups can be both useful and detrimental to group decision making.

WHAT IS CONFLICT?

Conflict occurs when members disagree over two or more options that a group can take in trying to make a decision, resolve a problem, or achieve a goal. Conflict also occurs when an individual's goal is incompatible with the goals of others. Joseph Folger and Marshall Poole define *conflict* as "the interaction of interdependent people who perceive incompatible goals and interference from each other in achieving these goals."[1]

If a group experienced no conflict, it would have little to discuss. One value of conflict is that it makes a group test and challenge ideas. Conflict can also, however, be detrimental to group interaction and group decision making. Conflict has a negative impact on a group when it (1) keeps the group from completing its task, (2) interferes with the quality of the group's decision or productivity, or (3) threatens the existence of the group.[2]

What causes conflict in groups? Why does it exist? Conflict results from differences between group members—differences in personality, perception, information, and power or influence. Because people are unique, their different attitudes, beliefs, and values will inevitably surface and cause conflict. No matter how much they try to empathize with others, people still have individual perspectives on the world. People also differ in the amount of knowledge they have on various topics. In groups, they soon realize that some members are more experienced or more widely read than others. This difference in information contributes to different attitudes. People also have different levels of power, status, and influence over others—differences that can increase conflict. People with power often try to use that power to influence others, and most do not like to be told what to do or think.

Conflict does not just "happen." You can often discern phases or stages of conflict development. As we discussed in Chapter 7, B. Aubrey Fisher found that group deliberations can be organized around four phases: orientation, conflict, emergence, and reinforcement.[3] Several researchers have discovered that the conflict phase in groups often emerges in predictable stages.[4]

Three phases of conflict have been identified. The first phase of conflict, called **interpersonal conflict,** is characterized, surprisingly, by favorable comments, few disagreements, and more vague and ambiguous statements. In this first phase, group participants may actually disagree, but they keep their disagreements to themselves. The second phase is called the **confrontation** phase. At this point, the private disagreement becomes public; group members openly disagree with others. Group members may also choose sides and form subgroups pitted against one another. They may also abruptly shift topics and use ambiguous statements to signal their disagreement. The third phase, called **substantive conflict,** is evidenced by more balanced agreement and disagreement: overt conflict decreases, and group members offer more constructive and favorable comments. While these phases are not always evident, understanding what conflict is and how it often emerges can help manage the feelings of surprise and uncertainty that sometimes accompany group conflict.

Conflict in groups can be directed either toward people (interpersonal conflict), ideas (task conflict), or both people and ideas. One research team found that conflict often occurs because of perceived inequity; if we think someone has more resources or is getting more than his or her fair share, conflict often results.[5] When the conflict is directed toward people, we often first try to manage the conflict by avoiding the individual or the topic of conflict. If the conflict is more task-centered, we usually first try more integrative approaches by seeking solutions that are agreeable to all parties.

MYTHS ABOUT CONFLICT

People often have misconceptions about the role of conflict in groups because they think that conflict is bad and should be avoided. With higher rates of divorce, crime, and international political tensions, it is understandable that people view conflict negatively. The following sections will examine some of the feelings you may have about conflict and determine whether a different attitude can improve the quality of your group discussions.[6]

Myth 1: In Group Discussions, Conflict Should Be Avoided at All Costs

Do you feel uncomfortable when conflicts occur in a group? You may believe that groups should not experience conflict, that conflict is unnatural, or that if people express conflicting points of view, you should try to squelch disagreement. Conflict, however, is a natural by-product of communication; unless participants in your group share the same attitudes, beliefs, and values (an unlikely situation), there will be some conflict. Several researchers have discovered that conflict is an important, indeed useful, part of group communication.[7] Members who believe that conflict is unhealthy become frustrated when conflict erupts in a group. They should realize that conflict probably will occur and that it is a natural and healthy part of group communication.

A recent study suggests that when conflict occurs, group members are often challenged to research issues in greater detail and learn more about the issues under discussion.[8] In the end, conflict can enhance learning and spur more in-depth analysis.

Myth 2: All Conflict Occurs Because People Do Not Understand One Another   Have you ever been in a heated disagreement with someone and then shouted, "You just don't understand me!"? You easily assume that conflict occurs because another person does not understand your position. Not all conflict occurs because of misunderstandings, however. You may believe that if others really understood you, they would agree with you. As Robert Doolittle observed,

> . . . many conflicts result from more than mere misunderstandings. Indeed, some of the most serious conflicts occur among individuals and groups who understand each other very well but who strongly disagree.[9]

Conflict can result from not understanding another group member's message, but some conflicts intensify when that person clarifies his or her point.

Myth 3: All Conflict Can Be Resolved   Perhaps you consider yourself an optimist. You like to think that problems can be solved. You may also feel that if a conflict arises, a compromise will resolve it. However, you should realize that not all conflicts can be resolved. Realistically, many disagreements are not simple. Fundamental differences between evangelist Billy Graham and atheist Madaline Murray-O'Haire would probably not be resolved easily, if at all. Some ideologies are so far apart that resolving conflicts between them is unlikely. This does not mean that whenever a conflict arises in your group, you should despair: "Oh, well, no use trying to solve this disagreement." That position also oversimplifies the conflict management process. Because some conflicts cannot be resolved, group members may have to focus on differences over which they are most likely to reach agreement.

If you find yourself arbitrating a conflict in a small group, first decide which issues are most likely to be resolved. If you assume that all conflict can be resolved just by applying the right techniques, you may become frustrated. On the other hand, you must also be wary of the self-fulfilling prophecy. If you hastily reach the conclusion that the conflict cannot be resolved, you may behave in a way that fulfills your prediction.

TYPES OF CONFLICT

Gerald Miller and Mark Steinberg have identified three common types of interpersonal conflict: pseudo-conflict, simple conflict, and ego-conflict.[10] They suggest that by identifying the type of conflict in a group, you will be better able to manage it. The following sections look at these three types of conflict in the context of a small group.

PSEUDO-CONFLICT: WHEN PEOPLE MISUNDERSTAND ONE ANOTHER

Some conflict occurs because of misunderstandings. **Pseudo-conflict** occurs when individuals agree, but, because of poor communication, appear to each other to disagree. *Pseudo* means fake or false. Thus, pseudo-conflict is conflict between people who really agree on issues but who do not understand that their differences are caused by misunderstandings or misinterpretations. "Oh, I see," said Mark after several minutes of heatedly defending a

Groups must find some means of managing conflict among members so that energy can be channeled constructively and not be allowed to degenerate into personal attacks.

position he had suggested to the group. "I just misunderstood you. I guess we really agree."

To manage pseudo-conflict, consider these strategies:

- Ask others what they mean by terms or phrases they use.
- Establish a supportive rather than defensive climate if misunderstandings occur.
- Become an active listener by using the skills we discussed in Chapter 5:

  Stop: Tune into what your partner is saying rather than your own thoughts.

  Look: Pay attention to unspoken messages and monitor the emotional climate.

  Listen: Focus on key details and link them to major ideas.

  Question: Ask appropriate questions about information or ideas that are unclear to you.

  Paraphrase content: To test your understanding, summarize your conception of what someone is saying.

  Paraphrase feelings: When appropriate, check your perception of your partner's feelings.

SIMPLE CONFLICT: WHEN PEOPLE DISAGREE ABOUT ISSUES

Simple conflict occurs when each of two individuals knows what the other wants, but neither can achieve a goal without preventing the other from achieving one. "Simple conflict involves one person saying, 'I want to do X,' and another saying, 'I want to do Y,' when X and Y are incompatible forms of behavior."[11] While the conflict may seem far from simple, it is called "simple conflict" because the issues are clear and each party understands the problem. For example, in a corporation with only a limited amount of money to invest in new-product expansion, one board member may want to invest in real estate while another wants to make capital improvements. The issue is clear; the individuals simply believe the company should take different courses of action.

When you understand what someone is saying but simply disagree with his or her point, consider using these skills:

- Clarify your perception and your partner's perception of the message.
- Keep the discussion focused on issues, not personalities
- Use facts that support your point rather than opinions or emotional arguments.
- Use a structured problem-solving approach to organize the discussion: define, analyze, identify several solutions, evaluate the solutions, select the best one.
- When appropriate, look for ways to compromise.

- Make the conflict a group concern rather than a conflict between just two people; ask others for information and data.
- If there are several issues, tackle issues one at a time; decide which issues are the most important.
- Find areas of agreement.
- If possible, postpone the decision while additional research can be conducted. Such a delay may also lessen tensions.

EGO-CONFLICT: WHEN PERSONALITIES CLASH

Of the types of conflict under discussion, the third is the most difficult to manage. **Ego-conflict** occurs when individuals become defensive about their positions because they think they are being personally attacked. Ego-conflicts are charged with emotion, and defensiveness in one individual often causes defensiveness in others. "Just because you're the chair of the group doesn't give you the right to railroad decision making," snaps Frank. "Well, you're just jealous. You think *you* should have been elected chairperson," retorts Ed. This exchange suggests that the conflict is not over a substantive issue but is over ego. When egos are involved and personalities are attacked, feedback techniques or issues clarification will not resolve conflict.

If you are trying to mediate a conflict, find issues the disagreeing parties can agree on. Identify and emphasize the common ground between them, and encourage them to describe the sequence of events that created the conflict.

The conflicting parties need to express their concerns. They should not, however, personally attack one another. As Miller and Steinberg suggest, the first thing to do in managing ego-conflict is to

> . . . give people a chance to bring out relevant concerns and then stop. The parties should not be prevented from expressing primary concerns, even if they are highly emotional, but they should be discouraged from escalating the conflict into violent personal attacks and counter attacks. When an ego-conflict looms stormily on the horizon, take control of the communication situation and let each person have his say, but do not allow either one to carry on too far.[12]

Here are additional strategies that may help manage the clash of egos:

- Encourage active listening.
- Return the discussion to the key issues under discussion.
- Try to turn the discussion into a problem to be solved rather than a conflict someone has to win.
- Seek to cool the emotional climate by lowering your voice and speaking more calmly, not in a patronizing way but in a way that signals your interest in dialogue rather than emotional argument.

- Be descriptive rather than evaluative or judgmental when discussing the issues of contention. Review our discussion of supportive and defensive communication in Chapter 5.
- Develop rules or procedures that permit differences of opinion.
- Unless it is central to the essential nature of the group, agree to disagree and return to areas of agreement.

CONFLICT AND CULTURE IN SMALL GROUPS

At the root of most conflicts are differences; differences in understanding, perception, attitudes, or preferred action. Cultural differences also can contribute to disagreement, because of different perceptions and our views of the world. Your **world view** is your fundamental outlook on reality, your place in the universe, and how you view your purpose in life.[13] For example, people from Eastern cultures (Japan, China, Taiwan) tend to view humans as one with nature; people from Western cultures (United States, Northern Europe) often see humans as having characteristics that distinguish them from nature. This one generalization is not true, of course, of all Easterners or Westerners, but it illustrates how culture—our learned system of knowledge, behavior, attitudes, beliefs, values, and norms—can have a profound effect upon our interactions with others. In small group interactions, your cultural expectations about how conflict should be managed may clash with those of someone from another culture who has different fundamental assumptions about managing or resolving differences. One study suggests that group members who are in the cultural or ethnic minority tend to talk less.[14] Unless group members are sensitive to such diminished contributions, good ideas may be lost because minority group members are reluctant to speak. Other research suggests that when there are cultural or ethnic differences in a group, a cooperative approach to managing conflict encourages quieter individuals to participate and enhances the quality of the group's discussion.[15] Two frameworks for describing cultural differences shed light on how culture can explain why some conflicts develop and fester.

INDIVIDUALISTIC AND COLLECTIVISTIC CULTURAL APPROACHES TO CONFLICT

In Chapter 1 we noted that some cultures expect and nurture a team or collective approach to working with others; more individualistic cultures, such as the United States, place greater value on individual achievement. This culturally learned difference can explain why some individuals, who place different values on the role of the individual or the team, manage conflict as they do. Stella Ting-Tomey suggests that people in individualistic cultures are more likely to use direct, confrontational methods of managing disagreements than people who value a collective or team approach to group work.[16]

REVIEW BOX

Summary of Three Conflict Types

	PSEUDO-CONFLICT	SIMPLE CONFLICT	EGO-CONFLICT
Source of conflict	Misunderstanding individuals' perceptions of the problem.	Individual disagreement over which course of action of pursue	Defense of ego: Individual believes he or she is being attacked personally.
Suggestions for managing conflict	1. Ask for clarification of perceptions. 2. Establish a supportive rather than a defensive climate. 3. Employ active listening: *Stop* *Look* *Listen* *Question* *Paraphrase content* *Paraphrase feelings*	1. Listen and clarify perceptions. 2. Make sure issues are clear to all group members. 3. Use a problem-solving approach to manage differences of opinion. 4. Keep discussion focused on the issues. 5. Use facts rather than opinions for evidence. 6. Look for alternatives or compromise positions. 7. Make the conflict a group concern rather than an individual concern. 8. Determine which conflicts are the most important to resolve. 9. If possible, postpone the decision while additional research is conducted. This delay also helps relieve tensions.	1. Let members express their concerns, but do not permit personal attacks. 2. Employ active listening. 3. Call for a cooling-off period. 4. Try to keep discussion focused on issues (simple conflict). 5. Encourage parties to be descriptive rather than evaluative and judgmental. 6. Use a problem-solving approach to manage differences of opinion. 7. Speak slowly and calmly. 8. Develop rules or procedures that create a relationship which allows for the personality difference.

She also suggests that people from collectivistic cultures, especially those who also place considerable stock in nonverbal messages, are more comfortable with nonconfrontational and indirect methods of resolving differences. She suspects this difference may be because people from individualistic cultures tend to approach problem solving from a linear perspective while people from collectivistic cultures often use a more intuitive problem-solving process. Ting-Tomey also finds that people from individualistic cultures are more likely to use facts or principles as a basis for approaching conflict, negotiation, or persuasion situations.[17] People from collectivistic cultures adopt more relationship-based messages to manage differences. It is important for individuals from collectivistic cultures to save face by not being portrayed as having lost a confrontation.

HIGH-CONTEXT AND LOW-CONTEXT CULTURAL APPROACHES TO CONFLICT

In Chapter 6 we noted that a high-context culture is one in which considerable weight is given to the context of unspoken messages. In a low-context culture, such as the United States, more emphasis is placed on words and their explicit meaning than on implicit, nonverbal cues.[18] Researchers have found that people in low-context cultures give greater importance to task or instrumental issues than do people in high-context cultures.[19] In high-context cultures, the expressive or emotional aspects of managing the conflict take on special importance. In expressive conflict the goal is often to express feelings and release tension.[20] Keeping the relationship in balance, maintaining the friendship, and managing the emotional climate often take a higher priority in a high-context culture than achieving the outcome. Here again, saving face and avoiding embarrassment for all parties are more important in high-context cultures than in low-context cultures.

A similar conclusion has been put forward about differences between the way men and women manage disagreements in North America. Women tend to emphasize expressive goals in conflict while men emphasize instrumental or task objectives.[21] Such a generalization needs to be tempered by considering each individual as unique, even though some gender patterns in conflict management styles have been observed.

In your group deliberations, knowing that culture and gender differences exist can help explain why some strategies will be more effective than others. We caution you, however, to avoid stereotyping others by cultural, national, ethnic, or gender differences alone. For example, it would be most inappropriate to draw a stereotyped conclusion that all Asians will emphasize expressive rather than instrumental objectives in conflict. But knowing that cultural differences exist can give you greater insight into why some conflict management strategies are more or less effective, depending on the preferred approach others may have for managing differences. Taking an egocentric view (assuming your perspective is correct) or ethnocentric view (assuming your cultural methods of managing conflict are superior to others) can be detrimental to effective communication.

CONFLICT MANAGEMENT STYLES

Regardless of your cultural background or the type of conflict you experience, research suggests that each of us behaves in predictable ways to manage disagreements with others. What is your conflict management style? Do you tackle conflict head on or seek ways to remove yourself from the fray? While these are only two options available for managing conflict, reduced to its essence, conflict management style often boils down to fight or flight.

R. Kilmann and K. Thomas suggest that your conflict management style is based on two factors: (1) how concerned you are for other people and (2) how concerned you are for yourself.[22] Another research team has identified three general styles for managing conflict: (1) nonconfrontational, (2) controlling, and (3) cooperative.[23]

NONCONFRONTATIONAL

Some people work hard to avoid conflict with others. They do not like to argue and would rather withdraw when someone disagrees with them. Or, if they see a conflict brewing, they take a giant step away from the potential dispute. If a group member disagrees with someone who often avoids or withdraws from conflict, the nonconfrontational person may either have no response at all or readily change his or her opinion and agree.

This style is effective at times. Avoiding an immediate attack from another group member may give you time to think of a more appropriate response rather than blurting out the first thing that comes to your mind. And agreeing with others if you are, in fact, wrong can be the best way to repair a relationship so you continue to work with another team member.

However, if your only style is to withdraw or give in, you may find that your unassertive behavior diminishes your effectiveness in group discussions. Avoiding conflict does not make the source of the problem go away; it still exists. There are times when it is in your best interest, as well as in the best interest of the group, to continue exploring options rather than capitulate quickly. If you always agree with others, you may find your ideas and suggestions being discounted.

CONTROLLING

A person who likes to control is someone who wants to get his or her way. The controlling person may seek to win others over by using constructive strategies such as marshaling facts, statistics and other evidence to persuade others. Or they may use more destructive methods—blaming others or trying to bully or coerce them. As we discussed in Chapter 5, when you attempt to control someone, he or she may become defensive. Someone who uses this approach has adopted a win-lose philosophy. He or she wants to win at the expense of someone else. If you know someone with a controlling style, or if you use this style yourself, then you have experienced both the advantages and disadvantages of competition.

Is it always inappropriate to cling to what you believe and try to convince others support your position? No. If you have information that you know is accurate and you are sure that there is only one correct answer and you have it, you may be justified in trying to make sure that others see your point of view. One of the virtues of teamwork is the likelihood that one group member has information or a creative approach that other group members do not have.

The problem occurs if you try to control others without being sensitive to their needs or rights. It also can be detrimental if your method of controlling others is to outlast or outshout other group members by threatening them or using unethical means of persuasion, such as knowingly using false information to win. When assertiveness crosses the line into aggression, most group members find the controlling styles *does not* wear well over the course of several group meetings.

Cooperative

Group members who take a cooperative approach seek solutions to problems, rather than viewing conflict as a game in which one person wins and another loses. A cooperative style balances both expressive and instrumental goals. Several research studies have found that when there are cultural differences among group members, a cooperative approach to conflict management works best.[24] Essential elements of a cooperative style include leaving personal grievances out of the discussion and describing problems without being judgmental or evaluative. A team member who adopts a cooperative approach asks "What do we *both* want?" rather than "Here's what *I* want."

Like the other two approaches we have discussed, this style has advantages and disadvantages. There may be times when initially avoiding a confrontation may help initiate a dialogue with someone. Or there may be some issues about which you may not be able to compromise or modify your method of pursuing your goals. Many, if not most conflicts, however, can benefit from being approached as problems to be solved rather than as victories to be won. As we have already noted, a cooperative approach to managing differences seems to work best if your group is culturally or ethnically diverse.[25] Given the importance of developing cooperative group communication competency, we will review cooperative conflict management principles and skills in more detail.

COOPERATIVE CONFLICT MANAGEMENT: PRINCIPLES AND SKILLS

What principles and strategies can help a group cooperatively manage conflict? No simple checklist of techniques will miraculously resolve or manage group differences. Based on several studies of what works and what does not work when managing conflict, Roger Fisher and William Ury identified four overarching conflict management principles, which we will discuss.[26]

SEPARATE THE PEOPLE FROM THE PROBLEM.

When conflict becomes personal and egos become involved, it is very difficult to develop a positive climate in which differences can be managed. As we discussed in Chapter 5, if people feel they are being evaluated and strategically manipulated, they will respond with defensiveness. In terms of sequencing events in the conflict management process, this principle suggests that it is better to deal with interpersonal issues before tackling the problem causing the conflict. Separating the person from the problem means valuing the other individual as a person, treating her as an equal, and empathizing with her feelings. A key to valuing others is to use good listening skills. It is also useful to acknowledge the other person's feelings. Emotion is the fuel of conflict. Several scholars agree that efforts to manage our feelings facilitate the conflict management process.[27]

One strategy for constructively expressing how you feel toward others in conflict is to use the approach J. Gottman and his colleagues call the X-Y-Z formula.[28] According to this method, you say "When you do X, in situation Y, I feel Z." Here's an example: "When you are 15 minutes late to our staff meetings, I feel like you don't care about us or our meetings."

When you are the recipient of someone's wrath, you could use the X-Y-Z formula to explain how being yelled at makes it difficult for you to listen effectively. Trying to understand and manage your own and others' feelings helps separate personal issues from issues of substance. Joyce Hocker and William Wilmot suggest that when you are the receiver of someone's emotional outburst, you could consider the following actions.[29]

1. Acknowledge the person's feelings.
2. Determine what specific behavior is causing the intense feelings.
3. Assess the intensity and importance of the issue.
4. Invite the other person to join you in working toward solutions.
5. Make a positive relational statement.

No technique or simple formula exists to help you manage the challenging task of separating personal from substantive issues. Using good listening skills and acknowledging how others feel as well as expressing your own feelings (without ranting and raving) is a start toward mediating challenging conflict situations.

Focus on Shared Interests.

The words to one old song begin with the advice: "Accentuate the positive. Eliminate the negative." A cooperative style is characterized by focusing on areas of agreement and what all parties have in common. If, for example, you are in a group debating the merits of whether public schools should distribute condoms, group members are more likely to have a productive discussion if they verbalize the goals and values they hold in common. A comment such as, "We all agree that we want to reduce the spread of AIDS," might be a good place to start such a discussion.

Conflict is goal-driven. The individuals embroiled in the conflict want something. Unless the goal(s) are clear to everyone, it will be difficult to manage the conflict well. If you are involved in conflict, determine what your goals are. Then, identify your partner's goals. Finally, identify where goals overlap and where there are differences.

Do not confuse a goal with the strategy for achieving what you and your feuding friend want. For example, you may ask the group to make fewer copies on the copy machine. Your goal is to save money, because you are in charge of managing the office. Asking that your colleagues make fewer copies is a strategy that you have suggested for achieving your goal. Clarifying the underlying goal rather than only debating the merits of one strategy for achieving it should help unravel clashes over issues or personalities.

Generate Many Options to Solve Problems.

During negotiation, adamantly holding firm to only one solution results in a competitive climate. Cooperative conflict managers are more likely to use brainstorming, nominal group technique, or other strategies for identifying a variety of options to manage the disagreement; they seek several solutions to overcome obstacles. Sometimes feuding group members may become fixated on only one approach to achieve their goal. When conflict management degenerates into what amounts to a verbal arm-wrestling match, where combatants perceive that there is only one way to win, the conflict is less likely to be managed successfully.

Base Decisions on Objective Criteria.

Criteria are the standards for an acceptable solution to a problem. Typical criteria are such things as a limit to how much the solution can cost or a deadline by which a solution must be implemented. If, for example, group members agree that a solution must decrease the spread of AIDS but also not cost more than $1 million to implement, the group is using criteria to help identify a mutually acceptable solution. If the solution is based on not only whether a person subjectively agrees with an idea but whether the so-

"Let the secretary record the vote as 19 'Ayes' and one 'Not at this college during *my* lifetime.'"

lution achieves a specified outcome, conflict is more likely to be cooperatively resolved.

WHEN PEOPLE ARE NOT COOPERATIVE: DEALING WITH DIFFICULT GROUP MEMBERS

One researcher found that managers spend up to 25 percent of their time dealing with conflict.[30] Another author boldly claims that 98 percent of the problems we face are "people problems."[31] Scholars call them "group deviants"; you may call them a pain in the neck. Even though we hope that you will not have to deal with difficult or cantankerous group members, we are not naive. Not all group members will separate people from the problem, focus on shared interests, be eager to search for more alternatives, or base decisions on objective criteria. Our individualistic cultural traditions often make it challenging to develop collaborative groups and teams. It sometimes takes special "people skills" to deal with some group members. Drawing on the principles and skills of the cooperative conflict-management style, we offer the following tips for dealing with the more obstreperous group members.

1. *Manage your emotions.* When you are emotionally charged, you may find it difficult to practice rational, logical methods of managing conflict. When we become upset, one researcher found that

> Our adrenaline flows faster and our strength increases by about 20 percent.... The veins become enlarged and the cortical centers where thinking takes places do not perform nearly as well.... the blood supply to the problem-solving part of the brain is severely decreased because, under stress, a greater portion of blood is diverted to the body's extremities.[32]

It is normal to feel angry when someone constantly seems to say or do things that make you feel judged or evaluated. If you are emotionally aroused when someone provokes you, you will be less likely to listen well and deal logically with the problem.

To manage your emotions, use such strategies as self-talk. Realize you are upset (become consciously competent) and make an effort to gain control over your feelings. Thoughts are linked to feelings, and your mental messages can affect how you feel. Eleanor Roosevelt said "No one can make you feel inferior without your consent."

Also, help manage the emotional climate by avoiding personal attacks and name calling; such outbursts may make you feel better but will likely lead to a further deteriorating relationship.

2. *Describe what is upsetting you.* Try to avoid lashing back at the offending person; hurling a stinging rebuke may make you feel better momentarily, but it will escalate the conflict. Use a descriptive "I" message to explain to the other person how you are feeling; for example, "I find it difficult to listen to you when you raise your voice at me," or "I notice that is the fourth time you have interrupted me when I was trying to explain my point." The goal is not to increase the conflict. Saying "You shouldn't yell at me," or "You shouldn't interrupt me," are examples of "you" statements. Such statements are evaluative and are likely to increase resentment and anger.

3. *Disclose your feelings.* After describing the behavior that offends or irritates you, disclose how you feel when the behavior occurs. "After being interrupted I feel like you don't think what I have to say is important." or "I become increasingly frustrated when I try to contribute to our meeting but I don't feel you are listening." When disclosing your feelings, try to avoid emotional overstatement such as, "I've never been so upset in all my life." Such hyperbole raises the emotional stakes and can trigger a new volley of retorts.

4. *Return to the issue of contention.* The only way to return to a cooperative style is to get back to the issue that is fueling the disagreement. Sometimes there may be a hidden agenda that makes it difficult to confront the key issues. A wise person once said: Often what we fight about is not what we fight about. While an argument may seem on the surface to be over a substantive issue—such as which solution to adopt or whose research to use— the underlying issue may be about power and control. Only if the underlying issue is exposed and addressed will the conflict be managed.

GROUPTHINK: CONFLICT AVOIDANCE

Frank Baxter, chair of the board of Eastern Microtech Company, was meeting with the board of directors to decide whether Eastern Microtech would merge with Southern Microtech Company. Baxter called the meeting to order. After the reading and approval of the minutes from the last meeting, Baxter stated that he thought the merger would benefit both companies. As soon as Baxter finished speaking, other board members quickly chimed in, offering their support for the merger. No board members stated any objections to the deal; they fully supported Baxter's decision. One member, however, thought that the merger might violate antitrust laws by creating a monopoly in the southeastern United States. He also noted that the government probably would oppose the merger. Other board members quickly tried to gloss over the potential problem, one member confidently stating, "The government should not have any power to affect how we run our corporation. After all, it's our company."

After additional supportive comments from board members, the group voted to approve the merger. After the meeting, one member commented, "I wish all the group meetings I participated in would go as smoothly as our board meetings. We always seem to get along so well together. Baxter does a great job as chairperson." "Yes," observed another member, "he certainly has our respect. We always support what he has to say."

On first analysis of this meeting, you might think it effective. The chairperson appears to have the support of the group, whose members have little uncertainty. Looking at the meeting more closely, however, you see that the group is not functioning as well as it should; it is not taking advantage of the benefits of working together. This board of directors is a victim of groupthink.

Groupthink is the illusion of agreement.[33] It occurs when a group strives to minimize conflict and reach a consensus without critically testing, analyzing, and evaluating ideas. When a group reaches decisions too quickly, it does not properly consider the implications of its decisions. Groupthink results in an ineffective consensus; too little conflict often lowers the quality of group decisions. When a group does not take time to examine the positive and negative consequences of alternative decisions, the quality of its decision is likely to suffer. Sociologist Irving Janis believes that many poor governmental decisions and policies are the result of group-think.[34] After studying minutes of meetings and transcripts of conversations, he concluded that a lack of healthy disagreement contributed to inept decisions, such as the Bay of Pigs invasion in 1962. The Kennedy administration's decision to attack Cuba came from a group of advisers who were reluctant to voice their private doubts about invading Cuba. Janis has also noted that a group plagued by groupthink perpetrated the Watergate break-in in 1972. Members of the Committee to Reelect the President believed that they needed information at Democratic headquarters in the Watergate office complex. Again, even though some members privately thought that breaking into Democratic headquarters was wrong, they did not raise their objections. The decision to launch the flawed space shuttle *Challenger* on that unforgettable January morning in 1986 was also tinged by groupthink.[35] Corporate executives and others did not challenge assumptions in the construction and launch procedures; disaster resulted. The pressure for consensus resulted in groupthink.

Groups with highly esteemed leaders are most prone to groupthink. Since these leaders' ideas are often viewed as sacrosanct, few members disagree with them. A group may also suffer from groupthink if its members consider themselves highly cohesive and take pride in getting along so well with one another in providing support and encouragement to members' ideas.

One research study found that groupthink is most likely to occur when: (1) the group is apathetic about the task, (2) group members have low expectations about their ability to be successful, (3) there is at least one highly qualified, credible group member, (4) one group member is exceptionally persuasive, and (5) there is a norm that group members should conform rather than express negative opinions.[36]

SYMPTOMS OF GROUPTHINK

Can you identify groupthink when it occurs in groups to which you belong? Here are some of the common symptoms of groupthink.[37] See if you can think of some group communication experiences that exemplify this phenomenon.

Critical Thinking Is Not Encouraged or Rewarded   If you are working in a group that considers disagreement or controversy counterproductive, chances are that groupthink is alive and well in that group. One advantage of working in groups is having an opportunity to evaluate ideas so that you can select the best possible solution. If group members seem proud that peace and harmony prevail at their meetings, they may suffer from groupthink.

Members Believe That Their Group Can Do No Wrong   During the 1972 presidential election, members of the Committee to Reelect the President did not consider that they might fail to obtain information from Democratic headquarters. They thought their group was invulnerable. This sense of invulnerability is a classic symptom of groupthink. Another symptom is that members dismiss potential threats to the group as minor problems. If your group is consistently overconfident in dealing with problems that may interfere with its goals, it may suffer from groupthink.

Group Members Are Too Concerned about Justifying Their Actions Members of highly cohesive groups like to feel that they are acting in their group's best interests. Therefore, groups that experience groupthink like to rationalize their positions on issues. A group susceptible to groupthink is too concerned about convincing itself that it has made proper decisions in the past and will make good decisions in the future.

Members Apply Pressure to Those Who Do Not Support the Group Have you ever voiced an opinion contrary to the majority opinion and quickly realized that other members were trying to pressure you into going along with the rest of the group? Groups prone to groupthink have a low tolerance for members who do not "go along". Controversy and conflict injected by a dissenting member threaten esprit de corps. Therefore, a person voicing an idea different from the group's position is often punished. Sometimes pressure is subtle, taking the form of frowns or grimaces. Group members may not socialize with the dissenting member, or they may not listen attentively to the dissident. Usually their first response is to try to convince this member to reconsider his or her position. But if the member still does not agree with the others, he or she may be expelled from the group. Of course, if a group member is just being stubborn, the others should try to reason with the dissenter. Do not, however, be too quick to label someone as a troublemaker simply because he or she has an opinion different from that of other group members.

Group Members Often Believe That They Have Reached a True Consensus A significant problem in groups that suffer from groupthink is that members are not aware of the phenomenon. They think they have reached genuine consensus. For example, suppose you and your friends are trying to decide which movie to rent on Friday night. Someone suggests, "Why don't we see *Gone with the Wind?*" Even though you have already seen the movie on television, you do not want to be contentious, so you agree with the suggestion. Other group members also agree.

After your group has seen the movie and you are returning the tape to the video store, you overhear another one of your friends say, "I enjoyed the movie better when I saw it the first time." After a quick poll of the group, you discover that most of your friends had already seen the movie! They agreed to see it only because they did not want to hurt anyone's feelings. They thought everyone else was in agreement. While the group appeared to reach consensus, only a few people actually agreed with the decision. There-fore, even if you think that the rest of the group agrees and that you are the only person who thinks that a different solution would be better, your group could still be experiencing groupthink. Just because your group seems to have reached a consensus does not necessarily mean that all of the members truly agree.

Group Members Are Too Concerned about Reinforcing the Leader's Beliefs
Leaders of small groups often emerge because they suggest some of the best ideas, motivate group members, or devote themselves to group goals more than others do. If group members place too much emphasis on the credibility or infallibility of their leader, groupthink may occur. Leaders who like to be surrounded by people who always agree with their ideas lose the advantage of working in small groups. Most people do not like criticism and do not like to be told that their ideas are inept or inappropriate. Therefore, group leaders are understandably attracted to those who agree with them. Leaders sensi-tive to the problem of groupthink will solicit and tolerate all group view-points, since testing the quality of solutions requires different opinions.

One researcher has found empirical support for the symptoms of group-think. Rebecca Cline found that groupthink groups do express more agree-ment without clarification and also use simpler and fewer substantiated agreements than nongroupthink groups.[38] She also found that groups that experience groupthink spend about 10 percent more of their discussion time making statements of agreement or disagreement than non-groupthink groups. Groups that experience groupthink perpetuate the illusion of agree-ment by sprinkling in frequent comments such as "Yeah, I see what you're saying," "That's right," or "Sure."

SUGGESTIONS TO REDUCE GROUPTHINK

You may think that groupthink, which is characterized by a lack of conflict or controversy, should not occur in an effective task-oriented group, but

---

REVIEW BOX

Symptoms of Groupthink

Critical thinking is not encouraged or rewarded.

Group members think that their group can do no wrong.

Group members are too concerned about justifying their actions.

Group members apply pressure to those who do not support the group.

Group members often believe that they have reached a true consensus.

Group members are too concerned about reinforcing the leader's beliefs.

what you really want to know is, "How can I reduce the chances of group-think occurring in my group?" You expect theory to do more than just describe what happens; it should also suggest ways of improving communication. In order to help prevent groupthink, consider the following specific suggestions based on Janis's initial observations, as well as on the theories and the research of other small group communication researchers.

The Group Leader Should Encourage Critical, Independent Thinking
One characteristic of groupthink is that members generally agree with a group leader. The leader of a small group can help alleviate groupthink by encouraging members to think independently. The leader should make clear that he or she does not want the group to reach agreement until each member has critically evaluated the issues. Most group leaders want to command the respect of their groups, but a leader's insistence that the group always agree with him or her does not constitute respect; instead, it may demonstrate a fear of disagreement. Thus, if you find yourself a leader in a small group, you should encourage disagreement not just for the sake of argument but to eliminate groupthink. Even if you are not a leader, you can encourage a healthy discussion by voicing any objections that you have to the ideas being discussed. Do not permit instant, uncritical agreement in your group.

Group Members Should Be Sensitive to Status Differences That May Affect Decision Making   Imagine that you are a young architect assigned to help design a new dinner theater for a large futuristic shopping center. When you first meet with the other architects assigned to the project, the senior member of your firm presents the group with a rough sketch of a theater patterned after a nineteenth-century American opera house. While the design is practical and attractive, you feel that it does not fit in with the ultramodern design of the rest of the center. Because of the difference in status between the younger architects and the senior architect, you and your contemporaries are tempted to laud the design and keep your reservations to yourselves. Doing so would result in groupthink. Groups should not yield to status differences when evaluating ideas, issues, and solutions to problems. Instead, they should consider the merits of suggestions, weigh evidence, and make decisions about the validity of ideas without being too concerned about the status of those making suggestions. Of course, this is easier to propose than to implement. Numerous studies suggest that a person with more credibility is going to be more persuasive.[39] Cereal companies know this when they hire famous athletes to sell breakfast food. The message is, "Don't worry about the quality of the product. If this Olympic gold medal winner eats this stuff, you'll like it too." The athlete's fame and status do not necessarily make the cereal good; however, you still might buy the cereal, making a decision based on emotion rather than fact. Group members sometimes make decisions this way, too. Avoid agreeing with a decision just because of the status or credibility of the person making it. Evaluate the quality of the solution on its own merits.

Invite Someone from Outside the Group to Evaluate the Group's Decision-Making Process   Sometimes an objective point of view from outside the group can help avoid groupthink. Many large companies hire consultants to evaluate organizational decision making, but you do not have to be part of a multinational corporation to ask someone to analyze your group's decision-making process. Ask someone from outside your group to sit in on one of your meetings. At the end of the meeting, ask the observer to summarize his or her observations and evaluations of the group. An outside observer may make some members uncomfortable, but if you explain why the visitor is there, the group will probably accept the visitor and eagerly await objective observations. Sometimes an outsider can identify unproductive group norms more readily than group members can.

Assign a Group Member the Role of Devil's Advocate   If no disagreement develops in a group, members may enjoy getting along and never realize that their group suffers from groupthink. If you find yourself in a group of pacifists, play devil's advocate by trying to raise objections and potential problems. Assign someone to consider the negative aspects of a suggestion before it is implemented. It could save the group from groupthink and enhance the quality of the decision.

Ask Group Members to Subdivide into Small Groups (or to Work Individually) and to Consider Potential Problems with the Suggested Solutions   In large groups, all members most likely will not be able to voice their objections and reservations. The U.S. Congress does most of its work in small committees.

Members of Congress realize that in order to hear and thoroughly evaluate bills and resolutions, small groups of representatives must work together in committees. If you are working in a group too large for everyone to discuss the issues, suggest breaking into groups of two or three, with each group composing a list of objections to the proposals. The lists could be forwarded to the group secretary, who then could weed out duplicate objections and identify common points of contention. Even in a group of seven or eight, two subcommittees could evaluate the recommendations of the group. Group members should be able to participate frequently and evaluate the issues carefully. Individuals could also write down their objections to the proposed recommendations and then present them to the group.

One study found that having group members share and test ideas and evidence via a computer network rather than always meeting face to face

REVIEW BOX

Suggestions to Reduce Groupthink

As a group leader, encourage critical, independent thinking.

Be sensitive to status differences that may affect decision making.

Invite someone from outside the group to evaluate the group's decision-making process.

Assign a group member the role of devil's advocate.

Ask group members to subdivide into small groups (or to work individually) and to consider potential problems with suggested solutions.

may facilitate more-extensive testing of ideas and opinions.[40] Another technique which may reduce groupthink is to have groups divide into two teams to debate an issue. The principle is simple: Develop a group structure that encourages critical thinking. As we learned in the last chapter, vigilant thinking fosters quality decisions.

Identifying and correcting groupthink should help improve the quality of your group's decisions by capitalizing on opposing viewpoints. A textbook summary of suggestions for dealing with groupthink may lead you to think that this problem can be corrected easily. It cannot. Because many people think that conflict should be avoided, they need specific guidelines for identifying and avoiding groupthink. In essence, be critical of ideas, not people. Remember that some controversy is useful. A decision-making group uses conflict to seek the best decision everyone can agree on—it seeks consensus. The last section of this chapter will discuss managing conflict in the search for consensus.

CONSENSUS: REACHING AGREEMENT THROUGH COMMUNICATION

Some conflict is inevitable in groups, but this does not mean that all group discussions are doomed to end in disagreement and conflict. Conflict can be managed. **Consensus** occurs when all group members support and are committed to a decision. Even if a group does not reach consensus on key issues, it is not necessarily a failure. Good decisions can certainly emerge from groups whose members do not all completely agree on decisions. The U.S. Congress, for example, rarely achieves consensus; that does not mean, however, that its legislative process is ineffective.

While conflict and controversy can improve the quality of group decision making, it is worthwhile to aim for consensus. A few words about consensus may help you form more realistic expectations about working in small groups. The following sections will also suggest some specific ways to help your group reach agreement.

THE NATURE OF CONSENSUS

Consensus should not come too quickly. If it does, your group is probably a victim of groupthink. Nor should consensus come easily. Sometimes group agreement is built on agreements on minor points raised during the discussion. To achieve consensus, group members should try to emphasize these areas of agreement. This can be a time-consuming process, and some members may lose patience before they reach agreement. Regardless of how long a group takes to reach consensus, consensus generally results from careful and thoughtful communication between members of the group.

Is taking the time to reach consensus worth the effort? Groups that reach consensus (not groupthink) and also effectively use good discussion methods, such as testing and challenging evidence and ideas, achieve a better-quality decision.[41] Evidence also suggests that groups that achieve consensus are likely to continue to maintain agreement several weeks later.[42]

To achieve consensus, some personal preferences must be surrendered for the overall well-being of the group. Group members must decide, both individually and collectively, whether they can achieve consensus. If two or three members refuse to change their minds on their positions, the rest of the group may decide that reaching consensus is not worth the extra time. Some group communication theorists suggest that groups might do better to postpone a decision if consensus cannot be reached, particularly if the group making the decision will also implement it. If several group members oppose the solution, they will be less eager to put it into practice. Ultimately, if consensus cannot be reached, a group should abide by the decision of the majority.

SUGGESTIONS FOR REACHING CONSENSUS

Communication researchers agree that members usually go through considerable effort and patience before reaching consensus in a decision-making or problem-solving small group. However, guidelines may help members foster consensus in small group meetings.[43] Consider these specific suggestions for managing conflict and reaching consensus.

Avoid Always Arguing for Your Own Position   You often defend a solution or suggestion just because it is yours. Here is a suggestion that may help you develop a more objective point of view: If you find yourself becoming defensive over an idea you suggested, assume that your idea has become the property of the group; it no longer belongs to you. Present your position as clearly as possible, then listen to other members' reactions and consider them carefully before you push for your point. Just because people disagree with your idea does not necessarily mean that they respect you less.

Do Not Assume That Someone Must Win and Someone Must Lose
When discussion becomes deadlocked, try not to view the discussion in terms of "us" versus "them" or "me" versus "the group." Try not to view communication as a game in which someone wins and others lose. Be willing to compromise and modify your original position. Of course, if compromising means finding a solution that is marginally acceptable to everyone but does not really solve a problem, then seek a better solution.

To be most effective, a group should try to cooperate and work together. The National Training Laboratories describes this type of group behavior as *integrative*—a group tries to integrate individual goals into the group goal. Group members who strive for integrative approaches to conflict management have the following attributes:

1. They attempt to pursue a common goal rather than individual goals.
2. They openly and honestly communicate with other group members.
3. They do not try to manipulate the group.
4. They do not use threats or bluffs to achieve their goals.
5. They try to understand themselves and the needs of others accurately.
6. They evaluate ideas and suggestions on their own merits.
7. They try to find solutions to problems.
8. They strive for group cohesiveness.[44]

Do Not Change Your Mind Too Quickly Just to Avoid Conflict   While you may have to compromise to reach agreement, beware of changing your mind too quickly just to reach consensus. Groupthink occurs when group members do not test and challenge the ideas of others. When agreement seems to come too fast and too easily, be suspicious. Make certain that you have explored other alternatives and that everyone accepts the solution for basically the same reasons. Beware of the tendency to avoid conflict. Of course, you should not produce conflict just for the sake of conflict, but do not be upset if disagreements arise. Reaching consensus takes time and often requires compromise. Be patient.

Avoid Easy Techniques That Reduce Conflict   You may be tempted to flip a coin or to take a simple majority vote when you cannot resolve a disagreement. Resist that temptation, especially early in your deliberation. If possible, avoid making a decision until the entire group can agree. Of course, at times, a majority vote is the only way to resolve a conflict. Just be certain that the group explores other alternatives before it makes a hasty decision to avoid conflict. When time permits, gaining consensus through communication is best.

It is important to celebrate when a group reaches an agreement after a prolonged conflict.

Seek Out Differences of Opinion   Remember that disagreements may help improve the quality of a group's decision. With a variety of opinions and information, a group has a better chance of finding a good solution. Also remember that complex problems seldom have just one solution. Perhaps more than one of the suggestions offered will work. Actively recruit opposing viewpoints if everyone seems to be agreeing without much discussion. You could appoint someone to play the role of devil's advocate if members are reluctant to offer criticism. Of course, do not belabor the point if you think that (group members genuinely agree) after considerable discussion. Test ideas that a group accepts too eagerly.

Try to Involve Everyone in the Discussion; Frequently Contribute to the Group   Again, the more varied the suggestions, solutions, and information, the greater the chance that a group will reach quality solutions and achieve consensus. Encourage less-talkative members to contribute to the group. Several studies suggest that members will be more satisfied with a solution if they have had an opportunity to express their opinions and to offer suggestions.[45] Remember not to dominate the discussion. Good listening is important, too, and you may need to encourage others to speak out and assert themselves.

Use Group-Oriented Pronouns Rather than Self-Oriented Pronouns Harry liked to talk about the problem as *he* saw it. He often began sentences with phrases like, "*I* think this is a good idea," or, "*My* suggestion is to. . . ." Studies suggest that groups that reach consensus generally use more pronouns like *we, us,* and *our,* while groups that do not reach consensus use more pronouns like *I, me, my,* and *mine.*[46] Using group-oriented words can foster cohesiveness.

Use Metadiscussional Phrases **Metadiscussion** literally means "discussion about discussion." In other words, a metadiscussional statement focuses on the discussion process rather than on the topic under consideration.[47] Metadiscussional statements include "Aren't we getting a little off the subject?" or "John, we haven't heard from you yet. What do you think?" or "Let's summarize our areas of agreement." These statements contain information and advice about the problem-solving process rather than about the issue at hand. Several studies show that groups whose members help orient the group toward its goal by (1) relying on facts rather than opinions, (2) making useful, constructive suggestions, and (3) trying to resolve conflict, are more likely to reach agreement than groups whose members do not try to keep the group focused on its goal.[48]

Avoid Opinionated Statements That Indicate a Closed Mind Communication scholars consistently find that opinionated statements and low tolerance for dissenting points of view often inhibit agreement. This is especially apparent when the opinionated person is the discussion leader. A group with a less-opinionated leader is more likely to reach agreement. Remember that using facts relying on information obtained by direct observation are probably the best ways to avoid being too opinionated.

Make an Effort to Clarify Misunderstandings While not all disagreements arise because conflicting parties fail to understand one another, misunderstanding another's meaning sometimes does create conflict and adversely affect group consensus. Dealing with misunderstanding is simple. Ask a group member to explain a particular word or statement that you do not understand. Constantly solicit feedback from your listeners. For example, repeat the previous speaker's point before you state your position on an issue. This procedure can become time-consuming and stilted if overused, but it can help when misunderstandings about meanings arise. It may also be helpful for you to remember that meanings are in people, not in words. Stated another way, the meaning at a word comes from a person's unique perspective, perception, and experience.

Use a Variety of Methods to Reach Agreement   One researcher has found that groups are more likely to reach agreement if group members try several approaches to resolve a deadlocked situation rather than using just one method of seeking consensus.[49] Consider (1) combining two or more ideas into one solution; (2) building, changing, or extending existing ideas; (3) using effective persuasion skills to convince others to agree; and (4) developing new ideas to move the discussion forward rather than just rehashing old ideas.

Expand the Number of Ideas and Alternatives   One reason a group may not agree is because none of the ideas or solutions being discussed are good ones. Each solution on the table may have flaws. The task should change from trying to reach agreement on the alternatives in front of the group to generating more alternatives.[50] Switching from a debate to brainstorming may help pry group members away from a foolish adherence to existing solutions.

Display Known Facts for All Group Members to See   Consider using a chalkboard, flip chart, or overhead projector to display what is really known about the issues confronting the group. When group members cannot agree, they often retreat to restating opinions rather than advocating an idea based on hard evidence. If all group members can be reminded of what is known, consensus may be more easily obtained.

One way to display facts is to use the is/is not technique. Draw a line down the middle of the chalkboard or flip chart. On one side of the line note what is known about the present issue. On the other side, identify what is unknown or is mere speculation. Separating facts from speculation can help group members focus on data rather than unproven inferences.[51]

Emphasize Areas of Agreement   When the group gets bogged down in conflict and disagreement, it may prove useful to stop and identify the issues and information on which group members do agree. One study found that groups whose members were able to keep refocusing the group on areas of agreement, particularly following episodes of disagreement, were more likely to reach consensus than groups that continued to accentuate the negative.[52]

Do Not Wait until the Very End of the Deliberations to Suggest Solutions
Research suggests that groups that delay identifying specific solutions until the very end of the discussion are less likely to reach consensus than those groups that think about solutions earlier in the deliberations.[53] Of course, before jumping to solutions, groups need to analyze and assess the present situation. But groups that only identify solutions at the tail end of discussions have more difficulty reaching consensus.

REVIEW BOX

Suggestions for Reaching Group Consensus

EFFECTIVE GROUP MEMBERS	INEFFECTIVE GROUP MEMBERS
Avoid always arguing for their own position	Argue for an idea because it is their own
Approach conflict as a problem to be solved rather than a win-lose situation	Assume that someone will win and someone will lose the argument
Do not change their minds quickly just to avoid conflict	Give in to the opinion of group members just to avoid conflict
Avoid easy conflict-reducing techniques	Find easy ways to reduce the conflict, such as taking a quick vote without holding a discussion
Seek out differences of opinion	Do not ferret out a variety of viewpoints
Try to involve everyone in the discussion and make frequent, meaningful contributions to the group	Permit one person to monopolize the discussion or fail to draw out quiet group members
Use first-person plural pronouns to talk about the group	Talk about individual accomplishments rather than group accomplishments
Talk about the discussion process using metadiscussional phrases that help orient the group toward its goal	Do little to help summarize or clarify group discussion
Avoid opinionated statements that are not based on facts or evidence	Are closed-minded and inflexible
Clarify misunderstandings	Do not clarify misunderstandings or check to see whether their message is understood
Use a variety of methods to reach agreement	Use only one or two approaches to reach agreement
Expand the number of ideas and alternatives	Seek a limited number of options or solutions
Display known facts for all members in the group to see	Rely only on oral summaries or no summaries of issues or facts about which members agree
Emphasize areas of agreement	Ignore areas of agreement
Suggest possible solutions throughout the group's deliberation	Wait until time is about to run out before suggesting solutions

PUTTING PRINCIPLE INTO PRACTICE

Conflict can have both positive and negative effects on a group. Conflict occurs because people are different, because they have their own ways of doing things. These differences affect the way people perceive and approach problem solving.

COOPERATIVE CONFLICT MANAGEMENT PRINCIPLES

- Separate the people from the problem.
- Focus on shared interests.
- Generate many options to solve problems.
- Base decisions on objective criteria.

GROUPTHINK

The absence of conflict or a false sense of agreement is called groupthink. It occurs when group members are reluctant to voice their feelings and objections to issues.

To help reduce the likelihood of groupthink, review the following suggestions:

- If you are the group leader, encourage critical, independent thinking.
- Be sensitive to status differences that may affect decision making.
- Invite someone from outside the group to evaluate the group's decision-making process.
- Assign a group member the role of devil's advocate.
- Ask members to subdivide into small groups to consider potential problems with suggested solutions.

CONSENSUS

Consider applying the following suggestions to help reach consensus and to help manage the conflicts and disagreements that arise in groups.

- Avoid always arguing for your own position.
- Do not assume someone must win and someone must lose.
- Do not change your mind too quickly just to avoid conflict.
- Avoid easy conflict-reducing techniques.
- Seek out differences of opinion.
- Try to involve everyone in the group discussion; be a frequent contributor to the group.
- Use group pronouns (e.g., *we, us, our*), rather than self-oriented pronouns (e.g., *I, me, mine*).
- Use metadiscussional phrases.
- Avoid opinionated statements that indicate a closed mind.

- Make an effort to clarify misunderstandings.
- Use a variety of methods to reach agreement.
- Expand the number of ideas and alternatives.
- Display known facts for all group members to see.
- Emphasize areas of agreement.
- Do not wait until the very end of the deliberation to suggest solutions.

PRACTICE

AGREE-DISAGREE STATEMENTS ABOUT CONFLICT

Read each statement once, and mark whether you agree (A) or disagree (D) with it. Take five or six minutes to do this.

_____ 1. Most people find an argument interesting and exciting.

_____ 2. In most conflicts someone must win and someone must lose. That's the way conflict is.

_____ 3. The best way to handle a conflict is simply to let everyone cool off.

_____ 4. Most people get upset at a person who disagrees with them.

_____ 5. Most hidden agendas are probably best kept hidden to ensure a positive social climate.

_____ 6. If people spend enough time together, they will find something to disagree about and will eventually become upset with one another.

_____ 7. Conflicts can be solved if people just take the time to listen to one another.

_____ 8. Conflict hinders a group's work.

_____ 9. If you disagree with someone in a group, it is usually better to keep quiet than to get the group off track with your personal difference of opinion.

_____ 10. When a group cannot reach a decision, members should abide by the decision of the group leader if he or she is qualified and competent.

_____ 11. To compromise is to take the easy way out of conflict.

_____ 12. Some people produce more conflict and tension than others. These people should be restricted from decision-making groups.

After you have marked the above statements, break up into small groups and try to agree or disagree unanimously with each statement. Especially try to find reasons for differences of opinion. If your group cannot reach agreement or disagreement, you may change the wording in any statement to promote consensus. Assign one group member to observe your group interactions. After your group has attempted to reach consensus, the observer should report how effectively the group used the guidelines suggested in this chapter.

CONSENSUS EVALUATION FORM

Respond to the following statements to assess the ability of your group to reach consensus.

	Strongly Agree	Agree	Unsure	Disagree	Strongly Disagree
1. Group members always argued for their own positions.					
2. Group members assumed that someone must win and someone must lose an argument.					
3. Group members did not change their minds to avoid conflict.					
4. As a group, we avoided easy conflict-reducing techniques like flipping a coin or taking a quick vote.					
5. Group members sought out differences of opinion.					
6. All group members were involved in the discussion.					
7. Group members used group-oriented words *(we, us, our)* more than they used self-oriented words *(I, me, mine)*.					
8. Group members used meta-discussional phrases.					
9. Group members tried to orient the group toward its goal.					
10. Group members avoided making opinionated statements and were generally open-minded.					
11. Group members made an effort to clarify misunderstandings.					
12. Group members used a variety of methods to reach agreement.					
13. Group members attempted to expand the number of ideas and alternatives under consideration.					
14. Group members summarized and wrote down known facts.					
15. Group members emphasized areas of agreement.					
16. Group members suggested possible solutions throughout the group's deliberations.					

WIN AS MUCH AS YOU CAN

This activity is designed to explore the effects of trust and conflict on communication.[54] Your instructor will explain how this exercise is to be conducted.

4X's: Lose $1 each
3X's: Win $1 each 1Y: Lose $3
2X's: Win $2 each 2Y's: Lose $2 each
1X: Win $3 3Y's: Lose $1 each
4Y's: Win $1

Directions: For ten successive rounds, you and your partner will choose either an X or a Y. Each round's "pay-off" depends on the pattern made in your cluster.

Strategy: Confer with your partner on each round to make a joint decision. Before rounds 5, 8, and 10, confer with the other pairs in your cluster. There are three key rules:

1. Do not confer with the other members of your cluster unless you are given specific permission to do so. This applies to nonverbal and verbal communication.
2. Each pair must agree on a single choice for each round.
3. Make sure that the other members of your cluster do not know your pair's choice until you are instructed to reveal it.

Round	Time Allowed	Confer with	Choice	$ Won	$ Lost	$ Balance	
1	2 min.	Partner					
2	1 min.	Partner					
3	1 min.	Partner					
4	1 min.	Partner					
5	3 min. 1 min.	Cluster Partner					Bonus round pay is multiplied by 3
6	1 min.	Partner					
7	1 min.	Partner					
8	3 min.	Cluster					Pay is multiplied by 5
9	1 min.	Partner					
10	3 min.	Cluster					Pay is multiplied by 10

The Case of Johnny

Read the following case study about Johnny, a youth with several problems. Following the case study are a range of possible solutions to Johnny's problem. Your task is to decide, as a group, on the best solution. Strive for total group agreement. Your instructor will then lead you in a discussion of your group's ability to reach consensus.

Johnny was born in a large midwestern industrial city. There were already nine other children in Johnny's family when he was born; one more child, David, came after Johnny. Their family lived in one of the worst slums in the city, known for its high crime rate and juvenile delinquency. It was a neighborhood of factories, junkyards, poolrooms, saloons, and broken homes.

By the time Johnny's father died, four of the older children had married and moved away. The rest of the family continued in its dismal course; the children were getting into one difficulty after another, and Johnny's mother, sick and confused, was tired of trudging from school to police station to court, listening to complaints about them. Of the remaining children, only Georgie—the oldest—assumed any responsibility toward the others. However, when the rest of the children got out of hand, he beat them brutally.

Johnny's mother tried to pacify landlords by keeping her screaming children on the streets as much as possible. Five of Johnny's brothers, starting in childhood, ran up police records covering charges of disturbing the peace, breaking and entering, larceny, perjury, assault and battery, and malicious injury.

"I was in the police station, too, plenty," Johnny says. "Saturdays they had kids' day. We'd be in this long corridor, there'd be all little kids sitting down. They'd bring us in and those jerks, the cops, they'd be sitting there and this cop here, he was always insulting us. 'You little creep,' he'd tell me, and he'd belt me."

Johnny was a trial to his teachers. They complained that he was "nervous, sullen, obstinate, cruel, disobedient, disruptive." "Teachers can stand him for only one day at a time," one said. "He talks to himself. He fights. He attempted to kick Ms. Clark. He isn't going to be promoted. He knows this and refuses to study."

With every new failure, Johnny committed some new misbehavior. Once, at the beginning of a new semester, he told his teacher, "I wasn't promoted. Okay! This year I'm going to make plenty of trouble." With every new punishment Johnny's conviction grew that his teachers, like everybody else, were "against him." Johnny had been seeing his parole officer, Mr. O'Brien, for some time now.

During the months of Mr. O'Brien's friendship with Johnny, his teachers found that he was making a tremendous effort to behave himself but that he was "like a kettle of boiling water with the lid about to blow off." Johnny managed to get through that term of school without too much trouble and was promoted, but school had not been out long before he fell into trouble with the police again—this time for breaking into a house and stealing $50 worth of jewelry. Before Johnny appeared in court, Mr. O'Brien visited him. Johnny, O'Brien reported, seemed "unhappy, but stolid and apathetic, though once or twice as we talked, he verged on tears."

Johnny didn't deny the theft and, as his confession poured out, Mr. O'Brien asked, "Even when I thought you were being a good boy, Johnny, were you stealing all the while?" Johnny, verging on tears, replied, "Yes, sometimes. But lots of times I didn't steal because I thought of you."

SUGGESTED SOLUTIONS: LOVE-PUNISHMENT SCALE

1. Love, kindness, and friendship are all that are necessary to make Johnny a better youth. If he can be placed in a more agreeable environment such as a warm, friendly foster home, his trouble will clear up.
2. Johnny should be put into warm and affectionate surroundings where he will be punished if he really gets out of hand.
3. Johnny should be sent into a warm and affectionate environment where discipline and punishment will be frequent if his behavior warrants it.
4. Johnny needs an equal measure of both love and discipline. Thus, he should be placed in an atmosphere where he will be disciplined and punished if he does wrong but rewarded and given affection if he behaves himself, and where equal emphasis will be placed on both love and discipline.
5. Though they should not be too strong and frequent, punishment and discipline should be emphasized more than kindness and affection. Johnny should be placed in an atmosphere where he will be seriously disciplined but where he will also be allowed warmth and kindness.
6. Johnny should be sent into surroundings where he will be disciplined and punished, but where he will receive praise and kindness if he behaves himself.
7. There is very little you can do with a youth like this; put him in an extremely severe disciplinary environment. Only by punishing him strongly can we change his behavior.

EXERCISE: IDENTIFYING YOUR CONFLICT STRATEGIES

Different people learn different ways of managing conflict.[55] The strategies you use to manage conflict may be different from those your friends and acquaintances use. This exercise gives you an opportunity to increase your awareness of what strategies you use and how they compare with the strategies of others.

1. With your classmates, form groups of six. Make sure you know the other members of the group; do not join a group of strangers.
2. Working by yourself, complete the following questionnaire.

3. Working by yourself, read the accompanying discussion of conflict strategies. Then make five slips of paper. Write the names of the other five members of your group on the slips of paper, one name to a slip.

4. On each slip of paper write the conflict strategy that best fits the actions of the person named.

5. After all group members are finished, pass out your slips of paper to the people whose names are on them. In turn you should end up with five slips of paper, each containing a description of your conflict style as another group member sees it. Likewise, each member of your group should end up with five slips of paper describing his or her conflict strategy.

6. Score your questionnaire, using the table that follows the discussion of conflict strategies. Rank the five conflict strategies from the one you use the most to the one you use the least. This will give you an indication of how you see your own conflict strategy. The second most frequently used strategy is your backup strategy, the one you use if your first one fails.

7. After drawing names to see who goes first, one member describes the results of his or her questionnaire. This is a personal view of his or her own conflict strategies. The member then reads each of the five slips of paper on which are written the views of the group members. Next the member asks the group to give specific examples of how they have seen him or her act in conflicts. The group members should use the rules for constructive feedback. The person to the left of the first member repeats this procedure, and so on around the group.

8. Each group discusses the strengths and weaknesses of each conflict strategy.

How You Act in Conflicts

The proverbs listed below can be thought of as describing some of the different strategies for resolving conflicts. Proverbs state traditional wisdom, and these proverbs reflect traditional wisdom for resolving conflicts. Read each one carefully. Using the following scale, indicate how typical each proverb is of your actions in a conflict.

    5 = Very typical of the way I act in a conflict
    4 = Frequently typical of the way I act in a conflict
    3 = Sometimes typical of the way I act in a conflict
    2 = Seldom typical of the way I act in a conflict
    1 = Never typical of the way I act in a conflict

_____ 1. It is easier to refrain than to retreat from a quarrel.

_____ 2. If you cannot make a person think as you do, make him or her do as you think.

_____ 3. Soft words win hard hearts.

_____ 4. You scratch my back, I'll scratch yours.

_____ 5. Come now and let us reason together.

_____ 6. When two quarrel, the person who keeps silent first is the most praiseworthy.

_____ 7. Might overcomes right.

_____ 8. Smooth words make smooth ways.

_____ 9. Better half a loaf than no bread at all.

_____ 10. Truth lies in knowledge, not in majority opinion.

_____ 11. He who fights and runs away lives to fight another day.

_____ 12. He hath conquered well that hath made his enemies flee.

_____ 13. Kill your enemies with kindness.

_____ 14. A fair exchange brings no quarrel.

_____ 15. No person has the final answer, but every person has a piece contribute.

_____ 16. Stay away from people who disagree with you.

_____ 17. Fields are won by those who believe in winning.

_____ 18. Kind words are worth much and cost little.

_____ 19. Tit for tat is fair play.

_____ 20. Only the person who is willing to give up his or her monopoly on truth can ever profit from the truths that others hold.

_____ 21. Avoid quarrelsome people; they will only make your life miserable.

_____ 22. A person who will not flee will make others flee.

_____ 23. Soft words ensure harmony.

_____ 24. One gift for another makes good friends.

_____ 25. Bring your conflicts into the open and face them directly; only then will the best solution be discovered.

_____ 26. The best way of handling conflicts is to avoid them.

_____ 27. Put your foot down where you mean to stand.

_____ 28. Gentleness will triumph over anger.

_____ 29. Getting part of what you want is better than not getting anything at all.

_____ 30. Frankness, honesty, and trust will move mountains.

_____ 31. There is nothing so important that you have to fight for it.

_____ 32. There are two kinds of people in the world, winners and losers.

_____ 33. When someone hits you with a stone, hit him or her with a piece of cotton.

_____ 34. When both give in halfway, a fair settlement is achieved.

_____ 35. By digging and digging, the truth is discovered.   SCORING

WITHDRAWING	FORCING	SMOOTHING	COMPROMISING	CONFRONTING
1. _____	8. _____	15. _____	22. _____	29. _____
2. _____	9. _____	16. _____	23. _____	30. _____
3. _____	10. _____	17. _____	24. _____	31. _____
4. _____	11. _____	18. _____	25. _____	32. _____
5. _____	12. _____	19. _____	26. _____	33. _____
6. _____	13. _____	20. _____	27. _____	34. _____
7. _____	14. _____	21. _____	28. _____	35. _____
Total	Total	Total	Total	Total
_____	_____	_____	_____	_____

The higher the total score for each conflict strategy, the more frequently you tend to use that strategy. The lower the total score for each conflict strategy, the less frequently you tend to use that strategy.

NOTES

1. Joseph P. Folger and Marshall Scott Poole, *Working through Conflict: A Communication Perspective* (Glenview, Ill.: Scott, Foresman, 1984), 4.
2. Michael Burgoon, Judee K. Heston, and James McCroskey, *Small Group Communication: A Functional Approach* (New York: Holt, Rinehart & Winston, 1974), 76.
3. B. Aubrey Fisher, "Decision Emergence: Phases in Group Decision-Making." *Speech Monographs* 37 (1970): 60.
4. Linda L. Putnam, "Conflict in Group Decision-Making," in Randy Y. Hirokawa and Marshall Scott Poole (eds.), *Communication and Group Decision-Making* (Beverly Hills, Calif.: Sage, 1986), 190–91.
5. Victor D. Wall and Lindal L. Nolan, "Small Group Conflict: A Look at Equity, Satisfaction, and Styles of Conflict Management," *Small Group Behavior* 18, no. 2 (May 1987): 188–211.
6. Portions of the following discussion of myths about conflict were adapted from Robert J. Doolittle, *Orientations to Communication and Conflict* (Chicago: Science Research Associates, 1976), 7–9.
7. See Fred E. Jandt (ed.), *Conflict Resolution through Communication* (New York: Harper & Row, 1973).
8. C. R. Franz and K. G. Jin, "The Structure of Group Conflict in a Collaborative Work Group during Information Systems Development," *Journal of Applied Communication Research* 23 (1995): 108–27.
9. Doolittle, *Orientations to Communication,* 8.
10. Gerald R. Miller and Mark Steinberg, *Between People: New Analysis of Interpersonal Communication* (Chicago: Science Research Associates, Inc., 1975), p. 264.
11. Ibid.
12. Miller and Steinberg, *Between People,* 269.
13. See: Donald W. Klopf, *Intercultural Encounters: Fundamentals of Intercultural Communication* (Englewood, Calif.: Morton Publishing Company, 1995).

14. C. Kirchmeyer and A. Cohen, "Multicultural Groups," *Group & Organization Management* 17 (June 1992): 153–70.

15. C. L. Wong, D. Tjosvold, and F. Lee, "Managing Conflict in a Diverse Work Force: A Chinese Pespective in North America," *Small Group Research* 23 (August 1992): 302–21.

16. S. Ting-Toomey, "Toward a Theory of Conflict and Culture," In W. Gudykunst, L. Stewart, & S. Ting-Toomey (Eds.) *Communication, Culture, and Organizational Processes* (Beverly Hills, Calif.: Sage, 1985).

17. S. Ting-Toomey, "A Face Negotiation Theory" In Y. Kim and W. Gudykunst (eds.) *Theories in Intercultural Communication* (Newbury Park, Calif.: Sage, 1988).

18. Ting-Toomey, "Conflict and Culture."

19. Ibid. Also see an excellent review of conflict and culture research in William B. Gudykunst, *Bridging Difference: Effective Intergroup Communication* (Newbury Park, Calif.: Sage, 1994).

20. Ting-Toomey, "A Face Negotiation Theory."

21. For an excellent review of conflict and gender see M. Argyle, *The Psychology of Interpersonal Behavior* (London: Penguin Books, 1994).

22. R. Kilmann and K. Thomas, "Interpersonal Conflict-Handling Behavior as Reflections of Jungian Personality Dimensions," *Psychological Reports* 37 (1975): 971–980.

23. L. L. Putnam and C. E. Wilson, "Communicative Strategies in Organizational Conflicts: Reliability and Validity of a Measurement Scale," in M. Burgoon (ed.), *Communication Yearbook* 6 (Beverly Hills Calif.: Sage, 1982).

24. C. Kirchmeyer and A. Cohen, "Multicultural Groups," (1992); Wong, Tjosvold, and Lee, "Managing Conflict in a Diverse Work Force."

25. Ibid.

26. R. Fisher and W. Ury, *Getting to Yes: Negotiating Agreement without Giving In* (Boston: Houghton Mifflin, 1991).

27. See Joyce L. Hocker and William W. Wilmot, *Interpersonal Conflict Management* (Dubuque, Iowa: Wm. C. Brown, 1991); Fisher and Ury, *Getting to Yes:* Robert Bolton, *People Skills: How to Assert Yourself, Listen to Others and Resolve Conflict* (New York: Simon & Schuster, 1979), 217; Dennis A. Romig and Laurie J. Romig, *Structured Teamwork® Guide* (Austin, Tex.: Performance Resources, Inc., 1990).

28. J. Gottman, C. Notarius, J. Gonso, and H. Markman, *A Couple's Guide to Communication* (Champaign, Ill.: Research Press, 1976).

29. Hocker and Wilmot, *Interpersonal Conflict Management.*

30. K. Thomas and W. Schmidt, "A Survey of Managerial Interests with Respect to Conflict," *Academy of Management Journal* 19 (1976): 315–18.

31. J. M. Juran, *Juran on Planning for Quality* (New York: Free Press, 1988).

32. Boulton, *People Skills*, 217.

33. Rebecca J. Welch Cline, "Detecting Groupthink: Methods for Observing the Illusion of Unanimity," *Communication Quarterly* 38, no. 2 (Spring 1990): 112–26.

34. Irving L. Janis, *Victims of Groupthink* (Boston: Houghton Mifflin, 1973).

35. Randy Y. Hirokawa, Dennis S. Gouran, and Amy Martz, "Understanding the Sources of Faulty Group Decision Making: A Lesson from the *Challenger* Disaster," *Small Group Behavior* 19, no. 4 (November, 1988): 411–33.

36. J. F. Veiga, "The Frequency of Self-Limiting Behavior in Groups: A Measure and an Explanation," *Human Relations* 44 (1991): 877–95.

37. Adapted from Irving L. Janis, "Groupthink," *Psychology Today* 5 (November 1971): 43–46, 74–76.

38. Cline, "Detecting Groupthink," 112–26.

39. See Kenneth Andersen and Theodore Clevenger, Jr., "A Summary of Experimental Research in Ethos," *Speech Monographs* 30 (1963): 59–78.

40. S. M. Miranda, "Avoidance of Groupthink: Meeting Management Using Group Support Systems," *Small Group Research* 25 (1994): 105–36.

41. Randy Y. Hirokawa, "Consensus Group Decision-Making, Quality of Decision and Group Satisfaction: An Attempt to Sort 'Fact' from 'Fiction'," *Central States Speech Journal* 33 (Summer 1982): 407–15.

42. Rolayne S. DeStephen and Randy Y. Hirokawa, "Small Group Consensus: Stability of Group Support of the Decision, Task Process, and Group Relationships," *Small Group Behavior* 19, no. 2 (May 1988): 227–39.

43. Portions of the following section on consensus were adapted from John A. Kline, "Ten Techniques for Reaching Consensus in Small Groups," *Air Force Reserve Officer Training Corps Education Journal* 19 (Spring 1977): 19–21.

44. *1968 Reading Book* of the National Training Laboratories Institute of Applied Behavioral Sciences.

45. See Henry W. Riecken, "The Effect of Talkativeness on Ability to Influence Group Solutions of Problems," *Sociometry* 21 (1958): 309–21.

46. See John A. Kline and James L. Hullinger, "Redundancy, Self Orientation, and Group Consensus," *Speech Monographs* 40 (March 1973): 72–74.

47. See Dennis S. Gouran, "Variables Related to Consensus in Group Discussions of Questions of Policy," *Speech Monographs* 36 (August 1969): 385–91; Thomas J. Knutson, "An Experimental Study of the Effects of Orientation Behavior on Small Group Consensus," *Speech Monographs* 39 (August 1972): 159–65; John A. Kline, "Orientation and Group Consensus," *Central States Speech Journal* 23 (Spring 1972): 44–47.

48. Gouran, "Variables," pp. 385–91; Knutson, "Experimental Study," 159–65: Kline, "Orientation," 44–47.

49. Roger C. Pace, "Communication Patterns in High and Low Consensus Discussion: A Descriptive Analysis," *The Southern Speech Communication Journal* 53 (Winter 1988): 184–202.

50. Ibid.

51. See Hirokawa, "Consensus Group Decision-Making"; Randy Y. Hirokawa, "Discussion Procedures and Decision-Making Performance: A Test of the Functional Perspective," *Human Communication Research* 12, no. 2 (Winter 1985): 203–24; Randy Y. Hirokawa and Dirk R. Scheerhorn, "Communication in Faulty Group Decision-Making," in Randy Y. Hirokawa and Marshall Scott Poole (eds.), *Communication and Group Decision-Making* (Beverly Hills, Calif.: Sage, 1986).

52. Ibid.

53. Ibid.

54. J. William Pfeiffer and John E. Jones (eds.), *A Handbook of Structured Experiences for Human Relations Training*, vol. 2 (La Jolla, Calif.: University Associates, 1974), 62–67.

55. David W. Johnson and Frank P. Johnson, *Joining Together: Group Theory and Group Skills* (Englewood Cliffs, N. J.: Prentice-Hall, 1987), 270.

CHAPTER T·E·N

Leadership

After studying this chapter, you will be able to:

- Discuss three approaches to the study of leadership.

- Describe three styles of leadership.

- Explain the relationship between situational variables and the effectiveness of different leadership styles.

- Analyze a small group meeting and determine which leadership behaviors will move the group toward its goal.

- Describe your own leadership style.

- Determine those situations in which you are most likely to be an effective leader.

- Be a more effective group leader and participant.

- Explain the purpose of simulation in leadership training.

- Manage meetings more effectively as designated leader.

*B*efore beginning this chapter, consider the following statements about leadership:

Leaders are born and not made.

An effective leader is always in control of the group process.

A leader is a person who gets others to do the work.

Leadership is a set of functions distributed throughout the group.

The leader should know more than other group members about the topic of discussion.

An authoritarian leader is better than one who allows the group to function without control.

It is best for a group to have only one leader.

A person who has been appointed leader *is* the leader.

What do you think about these statements? With which ones do you agree? Disagree? If it has not happened already, be assured that one day you will find yourself in a leadership position—on a committee, in an organization, or perhaps in the military. In fact, whenever you participate in a decision-making group your attitudes about leadership will affect your behavior, the behavior of others, and the effectiveness of the group.

This chapter provides information about the nature of leadership in groups to help you become a more effective group participant and offers some specific suggestions to help you become an effective leader.

WHAT IS LEADERSHIP?

When you think about "leadership," what comes to mind? A fearless commanding officer leading troops into battle? The president of the United States addressing the country on national television? The student-body president coordinating and representing student efforts? Perhaps you think of the chairperson of a committee you are on. For our purposes here we shall define **leadership** as behavior that influences, guides, directs, or controls a group.

Traditionally, the study of leadership has centered on people who are successful in leadership positions. Researchers argued that by looking at successful leaders they could identify attributes or individual traits that best predict good leadership ability. Identifying such traits would be tremendously valuable to those in business, government, or the military who are responsible for promoting others to positions of leadership.

TRAIT PERSPECTIVE: CHARACTERISTICS OF EFFECTIVE LEADERS

Over the last several decades, researchers have conducted scores of trait studies. These studies indicated that leaders often have attributes such as intelligence, enthusiasm, dominance, self-confidence, social participation, and equalitarianism.[1] Other researchers found physical traits to be related to leadership ability. Leaders seemed to be larger, more active and energetic, and better looking than others.[2] Still other researchers found that leaders possess tact, cheerfulness, a sense of justice, discipline, versatility, and self-control. One alleged study conducted by a branch of the military determined that leaders love good, red meat and aggressively pursue desserts.

The **trait perspective** of leadership seemed like a good idea at the time but actually yielded very little useful information. While correlations between traits and leadership generally have been positive, they occasionally have been weak.[3] Traits useful in one situation, such as leading troops into battle, are not necessarily the traits required for other leadership positions, such as conducting a business meeting.

A further problem with the trait approach is that it does not identify which traits are important to *become* a leader and which are important to *maintain* the position. These studies also do not adequately distinguish between leaders and followers who possess the same traits and do not prove useful to group participants wishing to improve their leadership skills. After all, people cannot make themselves larger, more energetic, or more aggressive pursuers of desserts. Therefore, we will consider the trait approach to be a "historical perspective" and proceed from there.

FUNCTIONAL PERSPECTIVE: GROUP NEEDS AND GROUP ROLES

The **functional perspective** to studying leadership has proven to be informative to students of small group communication. Rather than focusing on the characteristics of individual leaders, the functional approach examines leadership as behaviors that may be performed by any group member to maximize group effectiveness. Dean Barnlund and Franklyn Haiman identify leadership behaviors as those that guide, influence, direct, or control others in a group.[4] This is a much more fruitful approach for those interested in improving their leadership abilities. While the trait approach might help identify the sort of person who should be appointed to a leadership position, the functional approach describes the specific communicative behaviors a leader needs in order for a group to function effectively. By understanding these behaviors, people can participate more effectively in group discussions.

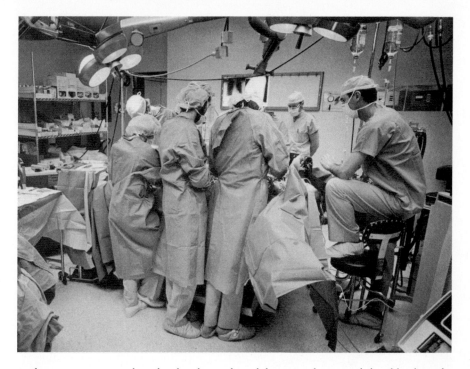

In the operating room, the role of each member of the surgical team is defined by the tasks required.

According to advocates of the functional approach, leadership behaviors fall into two categories. The major distinctions are between **task leadership** and **process leadership** (also called *group building* or *maintenance*). Task-oriented behaviors aim specifically at accomplishing a group goal. Process-oriented behaviors help maintain a satisfactory interpersonal climate within a group. Both types of leadership are essential.

TASK LEADERSHIP

When groups convene to solve problems, make decisions, plan activities, or determine policy, they are frequently hampered by group members' random behavior. Even when they get down to business, group process strays. Discussion becomes tangential, and groups lose track of where they are going. Sometimes one person monopolizes the conversation while others remain silent. Sometimes groups just cannot seem to get started. At such times, members may blame their designated leaders for their failure.

A group leader has a responsibility to keep a group moving, but research in group process has shown that anyone can perform the behaviors that keep a group on track. Just because a person has the title "leader" does not necessarily mean that he or she is best equipped to do the job. If leadership is a set of functions that are often distributed, a group is still quite capable of getting its job done regardless of who is designated leader. If you are a member of a disorganized group, you can provide the leadership the group needs even though you are not the leader.

Chapter 4 listed functional leadership roles. The following sections will look at a few task leadership behaviors and consider ways in which they help a group toward its goal.

Initiating   Task-oriented group discussions need to generate ideas. Sometimes ideas are related to procedural matters; at other times a group needs to generate ideas to solve problems. If, for example, you just finished Chapter 8 on problem solving and can see that your group has not adequately defined its problem before suggesting solutions, you might say: "Listen. I'm afraid that we're all proposing solutions before we've really agreed on the nature of the problem itself. Let's take a few minutes and talk some more about the problem so that we know we're all discussing the same thing."

By proposing a change in the group's deliberations, you are initiating a procedural change—in this case, one that will probably benefit the group. To "initiate" means to "begin." If you say: "Let's get this meeting under way," you have begun a change (assuming the group follows your suggestion). If, later in the meeting, you suggest: "Let's consider an alternate plan" or "Let's generate some more ideas before evaluating what we have here," again you will probably alter the course of the group's action. You are initiating. Without someone who initiates discussion, a group has no direction. The ability to initiate is an important group behavior and one that anyone can contribute.

Coordinating   Different people bring different expectations, beliefs, attitudes, values, and experiences to a group. The contributions of each member are unique, yet all are directed toward a common group goal. Given the diversity in small groups, coordinating is often an important leadership function. Communicative behavior that helps a group explore the contributions of all members is valuable. If, for example, you see a connection between the ideas that two members bring to the group, you should point it out to help focus the group. Coordinating members' efforts can help them see the "groupness" of their activities and reduce their uncertainty about the group, its problem, and its solutions.

Summarizing   Groups can get long-winded. Often, in the middle of a discussion, members cannot tell just where the discussion began and where it is going. It does not take many tangential remarks to get the group off track. Even when the group is on track, it is sometimes useful to stop and assess its progress. Summarizing reduces group uncertainty by showing how far the

discussion has progressed and what it still needs to accomplish. By understanding when a group needs a summary—and then providing it—you can help move the group toward its goal. Even if the group does not accept your summary, you will still reveal discrepancies among group members' perceptions, thus opening the door to more clarification and less uncertainty.

Elaborating Sometimes good ideas are ignored until they are elaborated on enough to be visualized. Suppose you are at a meeting of your fraternity or sorority, which is trying to determine ways of increasing next year's pledge class. Someone in the group suggests that redecorating the recreation room might help. Several things might happen in the discussion: (1) Members might begin to evaluate the idea, some being in favor and some not, (2) another idea might be suggested and recorded, or (3) you (or someone else) might elaborate on the idea by describing how the room might look with new carpeting, a pool table, soft lighting, and a new sofa. Whereas redecoration might have fallen flat by itself, your elaboration gives it a fighting chance. Good ideas are often left unexplored because people fail to elaborate on them.

Initiating, coordinating, summarizing, and elaborating are types of communicative behaviors. While these are some of the more important types of contributions you can make, the list is by no means complete. Task leadership is any behavior that influences group process and helps accomplish the group's task. Making suggestions, offering new ideas, giving information or opinions, asking for more information, and making procedural observations or recommendations are all task-oriented leadership behaviors that can contribute to a group's effort. Viewing leadership from the functional approach, leadership skill is associated with your ability to analyze a group's process and to choose appropriate behaviors.

PROCESS LEADERSHIP

For a group to accomplish its task, members must address themselves to it. For a group to function effectively, it needs to concern itself *with itself!* Groups are composed of people, and people have needs. (In fact, the family is a small group specifically adapted to meeting individual needs.) People do not leave their needs at home when they come to a meeting; they bring them along. Effective group communication must be addressed to the external task of the group and to the needs of its members. Failing to maintain a satisfying group climate can lead to a breakdown in a group's performance. In this respect, small groups resemble automobiles. Cars are great for getting you where you want to go, but they require regular tuning and maintenance in order to run reliably and efficiently. In fact, if an owner does not maintain a car, eventually it will break down. So it is with groups: They, too, need tuning and maintaining.

Leadership research consistently indicates that groups have both task and process needs. The process dimension is often called "group building

Coaching is an activity that requires both task and process leadership skills.

and maintenance." Process leadership behaviors maintain interpersonal relations in a group and facilitate a climate satisfying to members and con-
ducive to accomplishing the group's task. Process leaders are really communication facilitators.

Chapter 5 discussed group climate from the perspective of individual
and interpersonal needs. The following sections look at some specific
process leadership behaviors from the perspective of leadership and group
needs.

Tension Release   Think of times you have studied for exams. You cram
more and more information into your head until you reach a point where it
all seems futile. Everything runs together; ideas blur. You know it is time for
a break. After a cup of coffee and some relaxing conversation, you return to
your books with renewed energy.

Sometimes the most effective leadership you can provide for a group is
suggesting a coffee break. When a group is tired, when its task is difficult,
when the hour is late, when tension and stress are high, a group needs relief.
A joke, a bit of humor, a break, or even a move for adjournment can often
provide just what a group needs—tension release. An occasional break or a
good laugh can renew a group's energy and improve member satisfaction.

Some people seem to be naturally sensitive to a group's need for tension
release. Knowing that tension release is a necessary leadership function can
alert anyone—even the most task-oriented individual—to that need.

Gatekeeping   As we noted in Chapter 1, an advantage of working in small groups is that several heads are better than one. The very diversity that makes group communication so complex also gives it strength. A group possesses more experience and intelligence than does any individual, but experience and individual insight are only useful to a group if they are shared.

Some people like to talk more than others, and in some groups two or three people monopolize the conversation while others remain relatively silent. This fairly common occurrence poses a problem for a group in two ways: First, quiet members are just as likely to possess useful information and ideas as are more vocal group members, and their ideas may never surface unless they say something. Second, people who talk more tend to be more satisfied with a group. Members that do not talk much can have a negative effect on a group in both the task and process dimensions.

Gatekeeping is aimed at coordinating discussion so that members can air their views. It may take the form of eliciting input ("Harvey, you must have given this a lot of thought. What are your views of the problem?") or even of limiting the contributions of more verbal group members ("Can we perhaps limit our comments to two or three minutes so that we can get everyone's ideas before we have to adjourn?"). Gatekeeping is an important leadership function because it insures more input along the task dimension and higher member satisfaction along the process dimension.

Encouraging   People like praise. They feel good when someone recognizes them for their contributions. Encouraging is a leadership behavior aimed at increasing the esteem of group members and raising their hopes, confidence, and aspirations. Improving the morale of a group can increase cohesiveness, member satisfaction, and productivity.

Mediating   Conflict is a normal, healthy part of group interaction. However, mismanaged conflict can lead to hurt feelings, physical or mental withdrawal from a group, reduced cohesiveness, and general disruption. Mediating is aimed at resolving conflict between group members and releasing any tension associated with the conflict. Whenever conflict becomes person-oriented rather than issue-oriented, it is a particularly appropriate time for mediation.

> WANDA: I think that the plan I'm proposing has considerable merit and meets our needs.
>
> HAROLD: That's ridiculous. It'll never work.
>
> WANDA: Get off my case! I don't see you proposing any better solutions.

This potentially volatile situation could easily disrupt the group. You often have to work in groups with people you do not especially like. Obviously, Harold and Wanda do not get along well, but groups can function effectively in spite of personality clashes. They need to focus discussion on issues rather than on personalities. At times, interpersonal difficulties become so severe that they cannot be resolved by simply focusing on a group's task. Such difficulties can be a serious encumbrance to a group and need to be dealt with either within or outside the group; ignoring problems will not make them go away.

The above list of behaviors that contribute to a group's process or maintenance needs is not complete. More complete lists appear in Chapters 4 and 11. The behaviors described above are some of the more essential task and process leadership behaviors. They are included here to illustrate their importance and to help you examine your own leadership behavior in groups.

Both task and process leadership are essential to the success of a small group. If a group does not make progress on its task, members probably will feel frustrated and unsatisfied. In addition, if a group does not maintain a comfortable environment, members tend to focus their attention and energy on their own dissatisfaction with the group rather than on their assigned task.

SITUATIONAL PERSPECTIVE: ADAPTING YOUR STYLE TO THE CONTEXT

So far this chapter has discussed the trait and functional approaches to leadership study and has explored some task and process leadership roles. The **situational perspective** to group leadership accommodates all of these factors—leadership behaviors, task needs, and process needs—but also takes into account leadership style and situation. When you complete the task process leadership questionnaire at the end of this chapter, you may have some new insights about your own leadership behavior in groups. In interpreting the results of that questionnaire, you will find that the degree of your concern for task and for people are related to **leadership style,** an essential concept in the situational perspective.

LEADERSHIP STYLE

Your beliefs and attitudes about leadership will affect your behavior in small groups. Leadership style is a relatively consistent pattern of behavior reflecting a leader's beliefs and attitudes. While no two people act as leaders in precisely the same way, people do lead with three basic styles: authoritarian (or autocratic), democratic, and laissez-faire.

Authoritarian leaders assume positions of intellectual and behavioral superiority in groups. They make the decisions, give the orders, and generally control all activities. Democratic leaders have more faith in the group than authoritarian leaders and consequently try to involve members in making decisions. Laissez-faire leaders see themselves as no better or no worse than other group members. They assume the group will direct itself. Lais-

TABLE 10.1   LEADER BEHAVIOR IN THREE "SOCIAL CLIMATES"

AUTHORITARIAN	DEMOCRATIC	LAISSEZ-FAIRE
1. Leader makes all determination of policy.	1. All policies a matter of group discussion and decision, encouraged and assigned by leader.	1. Complete freedom for group or individual decision; minimum of leader participation.
2. The authority dictates techniques and activity steps one at a time, so that future steps are always largely uncertain.	2. Activity perspective gained during discussion period; general steps to group goal sketched, and when technical advice needed, leader suggests alternative procedures.	2. Leader supplies various materials, making it clear he or she will supply information when asked, but taking no other part in discussion.
3. Leader usually dictates particular work task and work companion of each member.	3. Members free to work with anyone; division of tasks left up to the group.	3. Complete nonparticipation of leader.
4. Dominator tends to be "personal" in praise and criticism of each member's work; remains aloof from active group participation except when demonstrating.	4. Leader "objective" or "fact-minded" in praise and criticism, trying to be regular group member in spirit without doing too much of the work.	4. Leader makes infrequent, spontaneous comments on member activities unless questioned; makes no attempt to appraise or regulate course of events.

sez-faire leaders avoid dominating groups. In one of the earliest studies of the effects of leadership style, researchers compared groups of schoolchildren led by graduate students who had been specifically trained in one of the three leadership styles. The researchers defined the styles as shown in Table 10.1.[5]

Briefly, here are the results of the study:

1. Groups with democratic leaders generally were better satisfied and functioned in a more orderly and positive way.

2. Groups with authoritarian leaders were more aggressive or more apathetic (depending on the group).

3. Members of democratic groups were better satisfied than members of laissez-faire groups; a majority of group members preferred democratic

A leader's effectiveness depends on a proper match of leadership style and situational factors.

to authoritarian, although some members were better satisfied in authoritarian groups.

4. Authoritarian groups spent more time engaged in productive work, but only when the leader was present.

It is tempting to conclude that humanistic, participatory, democratic leadership will invariably lead to greater satisfaction and higher productivity. Unfortunately, the evidence does not warrant such a generalization. Several studies have shown that no one leadership style is effective in all situations. What works at General Motors may not work at a local church. An effective student-body president may be a poor camp counselor. The expectations of one group differ from those of other groups.

Recent research on the effectiveness of different leadership styles has suggested that effective leadership is contingent on a variety of interrelated factors, such as culture, time constraints, group compatibility, and the nature of a group's task. While the functional approach reveals the importance of fulfilling various leadership roles in a group, it does not explain which roles are most appropriate in which situation. It is clear that you need to consider the setting in which leadership behavior occurs.

The situational approach views leadership as an interaction between style and various situational factors. Consider the following case study.

A CASE STUDY

Having been offered some very attractive extra retirement benefits by top management, Arthur agreed to take early retirement at age 62. Once an ambitious and young junior executive for the company, Arthur had, in recent years, taken a rather relaxed, anything-goes attitude as director of his division. As a result, his group had been showing the lowest productivity record in the company, and his subordinates were not receiving attractive salary increments and other rewards from top management. Morale was very low, and employees were discontented.

Hoping to rejuvenate the group, management replaced Arthur with an extremely bright, dynamic, and aggressive young manager named Marilyn. Marilyn's instructions were these: "Get your group's productivity up by 20 percent over the next 12 months or we'll fire the whole group and start from scratch with a new manager and new employees."

Marilyn began by studying the records of employees in her group to determine the strengths and weaknesses of each. She then drew up a set of goals and objectives for each employee and made assignments accordingly. She set a rigid timetable for each employee and made all employees directly accountable to her.

Employee response was overwhelmingly positive. Out of chaos came order. Each person knew what was expected and had tangible goals to achieve. Employees felt united behind their new leader as they all strove to achieve their objective of a one-year, 20 percent increase in productivity.

At the end of the year, productivity was up not 20 percent but 35 percent! Management was thrilled and awarded Marilyn a large raise and the company's certificate of achievement.

Feeling that she had a viable formula for success, Marilyn moved into the second year as she had into the first—setting goals for each employee, holding them accountable, and so forth. However, things went less smoothly the second year. Employees who had been quick to respond the first year were less responsive. While the work she assigned was usually completed on time, its quality was declining. Employees had a morale problem: Those who had once looked up to Marilyn as "Boss" were now sarcastically calling her "Queen Bee" and reminiscing about "the good old days" when Arthur was their manager.

Marilyn's behavior as a manager had not changed, yet her leadership was no longer effective. Something needed to be done, but what?

David Korten has proposed that under certain conditions groups are pressured to have centralized, authoritarian leadership but that as these conditions change, groups often develop a more democratic, participative form of leadership. Korten's work may give us an answer to Marilyn's problem.

Korten says that groups with highly structured goals and high stress move toward authoritarian leadership. The above case study is an example of this. When Marilyn took over as manager, the group was given a very specific goal—to raise productivity by 20 percent. At the same time, employees had a good deal of stress; if they failed, they would lose their jobs. In such situations, groups appreciate an authoritarian style, and it is effective. Think of times when you were in a group with clear goals but with members uncertain of how to achieve them. Remember when a group felt a good deal of stress because of an impending deadline or a group grade. At such times group members will gladly follow any leader who can give direction and show them the means to that goal. When the situation changes—that is, when the group feels less uncertain, has less stress, and has less structured goals—the group has less of a need for authoritarian leadership and instead needs more participative democratic leadership. To clarify this point, return to the case study.

While Marilyn's style of leadership in the first year was appropriate, the situation changed at the end of that year. Employees had reached their goal and replaced it with a much more loosely structured goal—that of continuing what they had been doing. Simultaneously, employees felt less external stress. They no longer operated under the "20 percent ultimatum." Having learned what they had to do as a group to succeed, employees were now ready to attend to their individual needs. They needed a more democratic, people-oriented style of leadership.

Figure 10.1 represents Korten's situational leadership model. The model is applicable even on an international scale. Consider the differences between leadership and goal structure in the Third World and in the United States. Citizens of Third World countries are seeking a new way of life that they as yet have not attained; therefore, their goals are structured, concrete, and operational. By contrast, Americans focus more on maintaining processes than on changing them. The relationship of these goals to leadership styles in the two regions is obvious.

In the case study above, if Marilyn is to lead effectively, she has two basic options. She can either change her leadership style and encourage more participation from her employees (more process, less task); or she can continue her authoritarian style by creating new stress or the illusion of stress. The latter solution may seem unethical, but it is commonly used.

FIGURE 10.1   RELATION OF STRESS, GOAL STRUCTURING, AND LEADERSHIP PATTERNS

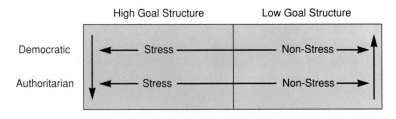

FIGURE 10.2   DETERMINANTS OF SITUATIONAL CONTROL

	1	2	3	4	5	6	7	8
Leader-Member Relations	GOOD				BAD			
Task Structure	HIGH		LOW		HIGH		LOW	
Leader Position Power	Strong	Weak	Strong	Weak	Strong	Weak	Strong	Weak

FIEDLER'S CONTINGENCY MODEL OF LEADERSHIP EFFECTIVENESS

After 15 years of examining over 1,600 hundred small groups. Fred Fiedler developed a theory of leadership effectiveness that relates a group's effectiveness to the situational variables that enable a leader to exert influence. His major finding was that most people are effective leaders in some situations and ineffective in others. Fiedler related two leadership styles ("task-oriented" and "relationship-oriented") to three situational variables (leader-member relations, task structure, and position power). Defining leadership, then, involves looking at a leader's situational control. A good deal of control gives people the feeling that they can get what they want. If they want to accomplish a task, then they need to concern themselves with successfully completing a job. They feel insecure when the task outcome is uncertain. What makes a leader certain that a job will be done? The leader must answer three important questions: (1) "Will group members do what I tell them; are they reliable, and do they support me?" (2) "Do I know what I am supposed to do and how the job is to be done?" (3) "Do I have the support and backing of the 'big boss' and the organization in dealing with subordinates?"[6] Figure 10.2 describes the ways in which situational control may be related to the three situational variables.[7]

Leader-member relations is the most influential dimension of situational control. A leader who group members like, respect, and trust has little trouble exerting influence in that group.

Task structure ranks second in importance. Fiedler observed that organizations form most groups to perform tasks. Since organizations have large stakes in the successes or failures of groups, they can get groups to comply with their objectives by giving group leaders standard sets of operating instructions to follow, or step-by-step ways of tackling problems. According to Fiedler:

> One important feature of the highly programmed or structured task is that the organization through the leader can maintain quality control over the process and over group behavior at every step. This also enables the organization to back up the leader whenever someone gets out of line. In effect, by structuring the task the organization is able to provide the leader with power, irrespective of the power of the position which he may occupy.[8]

Position power is the least influential of Fiedler's three determinants of situational control. He cautions students that they must not view this hierarchy as being "eternally fixed." Large differences in rank or status may outweigh task structure in some situations; however, these situations are considered exceptions to the rule.

The model in Figure 10.2 describes all possible combinations of conditions along these three dimensions. Cell 1, indicating all dimensions high, represents the most situational control. Cell 8, with all dimensions low, represents the least situational control. The intervening cells, particularly 4 and 5, describe situations of intermediate situational control.

Fiedler researched and described the relationship between leadership style and situational control in terms of a leader's motivations. As pointed out earlier in the chapter, most people are primarily motivated by either task concerns or maintenance concerns. Different group members usually perform these two functions. Fiedler identified individuals who were primarily motivated by task concerns and those who were primarily motivated by human relations. Then he studied the different individuals' effectiveness as leaders in situations of varying favorableness. Here is what he found:

> Leaders who are task motivated and task-controlling perform best under conditions that are very favorable or are relatively unfavorable for them. Considerate, relationship-motivated leaders perform best under conditions that are intermediate in favorableness.[9]

In other words, if you are highly task-oriented and authoritarian, you are likely to be most effective as a leader in groups with very favorable or very unfavorable situations. Consider an unfavorable situation such as a fire in a theater. A leader considerate of the feelings and attitudes of the audience, who will not act before discussing decisions with the group, is not going to gain a great deal of esteem from the panicking crowd. Rather, the people need decisive, authoritarian direction: "Let's get out of here! Follow me!" In a highly favorable situation where leader-member relations are strong, the task is clear-cut, and the leader has a position of authority, the task-motivated leader is operating under optimum conditions because the group is ready to work.

In the intermediate range of situational favorableness, a process-oriented democratic leader is most effective. With weak position power, leaders' influence must be based on the respect group members hold for them. Democratic leaders are more likely to gain respect. Groups with poor leader-member relations or confusion over tasks need the confidence and cohesiveness that democratic leadership can foster. Again, when a situation is so bad that it appears hopeless, strong, authoritarian leadership saves a group.

In his contingency model, Fiedler suggests that while people are primarily motivated by task or process concerns, they are secondarily motivated by whichever concern is not their primary concern. If Harold is a real taskmaster as a leader and finds himself with a task that is easily accomplished, he can then be more congenial toward his workers and satisfy both his primary and secondary needs. Harold will be satisfied *and* effective. If Wanda finds herself in a group with relationship problems, she can satisfy her process motivational needs by helping resolve conflicts and then, secondarily, helping accomplish the group's task.

People are motivated by both task and process concerns, but one of the two is a primary motivation. Highly task-oriented individuals seem to function best in highly favorable or unfavorable situations, while more process-oriented individuals are more effective in situations of intermediate favorableness. Matching style to situation allows people to fulfill their motivation needs in order of their primacy.

You can use Fiedler's theory and research to assess the situation in which you are working, to determine the leadership style that will be most effective. Of course, changing your personality is no easy task, but often you can bring about changes in the situation that will help you become a more effective leader. In situations where you know you are not effective, you can lend your support to those in the group who are best equipped to deal with the situation. Furthermore, at times in your life you may have to appoint a group leader. Fiedler's theory can help you select the most appropriate person for the job.

HERSEY AND BLANCHARD'S SITUATIONAL MODEL

Like other situational leadership theories, Paul Hersey and Kenneth Blanchard's model uses various combinations of task and relationship-oriented leadership behavior to describe leadership style as it relates to different situations.[10] In this case, the maturity of the group is the situational variable.

Take a few minutes to examine their model in Figure 10.3. Note that the two axes of the model represent the now-familiar task and relationship (process) dimensions of leadership behavior, reflecting different leaders' orientations. Quadrant S1 represents a leader whose orientation is high task and low relationship; quadrant S2, high task and high relationship, and so on. To these various combinations, Hersey and Blanchard gave the terms *telling, selling, participating,* and *delegating.* A telling style is extremely directive, A selling style is also directive, but a leader is concerned that the group accept and internalize orders given. A participating style is driven primarily by concern for relationships and a need for all group members to share in decision making. In a delegating style, a leader takes a hands-off attitude and allows the group to direct itself.

According to Hersey and Blanchard, these four leadership styles are more or less appropriate depending on a group's maturity. Note across the bottom of the Hersey and Blanchard model a scale labeled M4 (high maturity) to M1 (low maturity). Maturity refers not to chronological age or emotional maturity, but to the degree of experience group members have with one another in that group. When viewed in combination with the rest of the

FIGURE 10.3   HERSEY AND BLANCHARD'S SITUATIONAL LEADERSHIP
MODEL

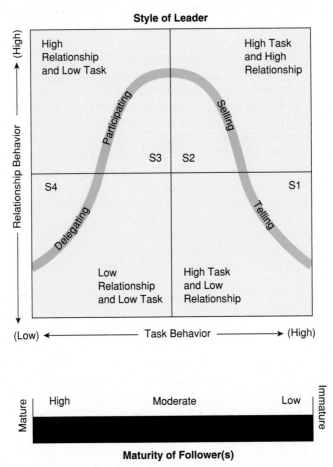

Paul Hersey/Ken Blanchard, *Management of Organizational Behavior: Utilizing Human Resources*, 6e,
© 1982, p. 248. Reprinted by permission of Prentice-Hall, Englewood Cliffs, New Jersey.

model, you can see that a "telling" style is most appropriate with groups
that are just starting out, perhaps in their orientation stage of development.
As groups mature, effective leadership allows for more autonomy. "Just as
parents should relinquish control as a function of the increasing maturity of
their children, so too should leaders share more decision-making power as
their subordinates acquire greater experience with and commitment to their
tasks."[11]

Communication scholar Sarah Trenholm offers the following example of
how the theory might apply to a classroom:

Consider teaching style as a form of leadership. Hersey and Blanchard would suggest that at the beginning of a course of study, with inexperienced students, a highly directive telling style is best. The teacher who tells a freshman class. "You decide what and how you want to learn. It's entirely up to you," is using a delegating style, which will fail, because at this point, students are not yet ready to take full responsibility for their own learning. As the course progresses, however, and as the students feel more comfortable with the course and each other, the teacher might use selling and participating styles, and perhaps end up with a delegating approach. More mature students may be ready for autonomy and may even resent being told what to do.[12]

The Hersey and Blanchard model is widely used in training managers and executives, probably because it shows how managers can change styles according to their subordinates' maturity level. A delegating style can be used with one employee or group and a telling style with another.[13]

SOME OBSERVATIONS ON THE SITUATIONAL APPROACH TO LEADERSHIP

At first glance, the situational approach seems to cover all bases. It looks at the style, task needs, process needs, and situational variables that influence groups. Unfortunately, most research utilizing this approach has focused on the behavior of leaders rather than on leadership as a process of realizing group goals.[14] Thus, while the situational approach is useful, it is, perhaps, not as helpful to the student of small group communication as is the functional approach. Achieving a group goal involves everyone in the group, not just the leader. Consequently, students and scholars continue to be concerned over the influence group members' verbal and nonverbal statements have on group goals.

TRANSFORMATIONAL LEADERSHIP

A relatively new theory of leadership, which describes leadership, in organizations, is called "transformational leadership." As described in manage-

REVIEW BOX

Perspectives on Leadership

Trait approach:	Attempts to identify characteristics common to successful leaders
Functional approach:	Views leadership as a set of behaviors that may be shared by all group members
Situational approach:	Relates effective leadership to interaction between leadership style and the group situation

ment and public administration literature, transformational leadership has four defining characteristics, called the Four I's: idealized leadership, inspirational motivation, intellectual stimulation, and individual consideration.

Contrasted with transactional leaders, who manage within the existing norms of their organizations, the transformational leader changes the organization by realigning its culture with a new vision and a restructuring of its shared assumptions and norms. Transformational leaders have a sense of vision and purpose.

In innovative transformational organizational cultures, we are likely to see assumptions and norms such as these: People can be trusted; everyone has a contribution to make; complex problems should be handled at the lowest possible level. In a transformational culture, norms are flexible to adapt to changing external environments. Superiors serve as mentors, coaches, role models, and leaders.[15]

Transformational leadership is not so much a set of behaviors that one can observe or emulate as it is a philosophy of leadership and change.[16] Small groups everywhere operate within the cultures of larger organizations and thus are affected by and a part of those cultures. Small groups in organizations will be the topic of our next chapter.

EMERGENT LEADERSHIP IN SMALL GROUPS

A fascinating series of leadership studies begun at the University of Minnesota (called the Minnesota Studies) sought the answer to the question: "Who is most likely to emerge as the perceived leader of a leaderless discussion group?" Led by Professor Ernest Bormann, the Minnesota Studies formed and observed "test-tube groups" that engaged in leaderless group discussions.

Most people think of a leader as someone who takes charge and organizes a discussion. Predictably, group members often perceive as leaders those who actively participate in the group and who direct communication toward procedural matters. While studies show a clear correlation between perceived leadership and talkativeness, especially task-oriented talkativeness,[17] those who talk most are not the only ones who become leaders in leaderless groups. In fact, most groups do not select leaders at all. The Minnesota Studies show that leaders emerge through a method of residues in which group members are rejected until only one remains. The first members to go are the quiet ones who do not actively participate in the early stages of a group's discussion. The next to go are the talkative but overaggressive or dogmatic group members who are perceived to be too inflexible for leadership positions.

After this initial phase of elimination, a group enters a second phase, in which roughly half the group members remain in contention for the leadership role. This phase moves much more slowly than the first phase, and it is a good deal more painful and frustrating. One by one, the group rejects contenders until only one or two remain. Often, members reject would-be leaders because their style is perceived as disturbing. In the Minnesota Studies' classroom discussion groups, members often rejected an authoritarian style on the grounds that the person was "too bossy" or "dictatorial." (Of course, some people may consider the authoritarian style inappropriate in a classroom discussion group, but they may consider it highly appropriate in other situations, especially those that involve extreme stress.) In another study, Deborah Baker found that specific communication behaviors increase the likelihood of rejection as leader. Group members who seem unable to contribute to either the group's tasks or organization because they are quiet, vague, tentative, self-effacing, or always asking others for direction are usually rejected.[18] In this second phase of role emergence, the Minnesota Studies also found that, to some extent, groups with two or more men rejected female contenders. Groups containing only one man often selected a female leader and isolated the man—a pattern that may be changing.

Task-motivated group members often rejected a contender who was perceived as too process-oriented—that is, too concerned about everyone's feelings and moods to be decisive. Likewise, process-oriented members tended to reject those they saw as too concerned with the task.

According to Bormann:

> In the final analysis groups accepted the contender who provided the optimum blend of task efficiency and personal consideration. The leader who emerged was the one that others thought would be of most value to the entire group and whose orders and directions they trusted and could follow.[19]

The Minnesota Studies give fascinating insight into the process through which group leaders emerge. While this information does not tell you how to behave in order to rise to leadership positions, it does alert you to the process through which leadership emerges. These studies also highlight the complexity of small groups and explain, to an extent, why a person who assumes a leadership role in one group may not do so in another and why a person who is perceived to be a leader in two groups may not assume the same role in each.

LEADERSHIP AND GENDER

A review of research literature on the subject of gender and leadership reveals that times, indeed, are changing.[20] Research in the 1960s and 1970s found that women were reluctant to assume leadership roles;[21] that group members perceived males as more independent, rational, confident, and influential than females and viewed males as leaders more often than females.[22] In 1979 researchers noted that females exceeded males in being receptive to ideas, fostering interpersonal relations, showing concern, and being attentive to others. Males in the same study in actual organizational settings exceeded females in dominance, being quick to challenge others and controlling the course of conversation. The researchers noted that females' leadership styles were more compatible with human resource theories of how managers should behave.[23]

In 1981, research reported that the influence of gender on leadership emergence was most evident early in the process and dissipated over time.[24] By the late 1980s some studies were reporting no difference in the way males and females are perceived in leadership roles.[25] Also in the 1980s there was a substantial body of research distinguishing *psychological* gender (introduced in Chapter 3) from *biological* gender. This research supported the argument that the most effective leader was that androgynous individual who could draw from a repertoire of both traditionally male and traditionally female behaviors.[26]

In the mid-1990s researcher Katherine Hawkins identified task-relevant communication as being the sole significant predictor in her study of emergent leadership, regardless of the gender of the candidate for leadership. Her study also noted no significant gender differences in the production of task-relevant communication.[27] Such communication, it seems, is the key to emergent leadership in task-oriented group interaction, for either gender.

LEADERSHIP TRAINING

Research consistently indicates that the productivity of a group improves if its members are trained. One team-building intervention among a group of department leaders resulted in a measurable increase in the ability to raise issues and manage conflict; an increase in mutual praise, support and cooperation; clarification of roles and responsibilities; and long-term commitment to teamwork and innovation. The author concluded that there are positive and lasting results of a communication-focused team-building intervention.[28] **Training** involves instruction to develop skills. Most of the instruction you receive in university classrooms involves what and how you *think;* training emphasizes what you can *do*.

The simplest form of leadership training provides members feedback on their performance.[29] Evidence suggests that when members receive such feedback, they tend to work harder, particularly when they are being evaluated by an expert.[30] This technique of observation and feedback is the mainstay of most leadership training programs. Whether other group members provide feedback, or an observer or a video monitor does, people need a more objective eye than their own to see what they are doing and how they can do it better. Beyond the basics, leadership training ranges from the simple and inexpensive to the elaborate and expensive. Given the various definitions of leadership outlined in this chapter, training may justifiably encompass any or all of the principles and skills outlined in this book. Often, training will include a simulation exercise.

A **simulation** is a structured exercise that creates conditions that participants might confront outside of the training environment. It provides a context in which participants can experiment with new behaviors without any risks. The war games that are a part of military training are one example of simulation; the conditions of war are re-created so that trainees can try out new behaviors in a situation that is not life threatening. Likewise, many leadership and management training programs re-create conditions of the work environment—through written reports, financial documents, and background information—in which trainees can experiment. Thus simulations are important to leadership training because they add a context that approximates the actual circumstances for which participants are trained.

While most training focuses more on behavior than it does on cognition, good training is multidimensional; that is, it incorporates more than one level of learning. Good training should provide you an expanded repertoire of behaviors and the understanding and awareness to make judgments about why, how, and when to use those behaviors. To learn effectively, you need to be aware of both principles and practice.

PUTTING PRINCIPLE INTO PRACTICE

All of the theory and research points to the conclusion that the most effective leadership behavior is that which best meets the needs of the group. Groups have both task and process needs; these and other situational variables determine the most appropriate type of leadership behavior for groups. Here are some suggestions on how to apply what you have learned.

If you are the designated leader or chairperson of a group:

- The rest of the group will have certain expectations of you as leader. For example, they probably will expect you to be particularly influential on matters of procedure. You should meet such expectations.
- Prepare a realistic agenda well in advance and distribute it to all group members. At the meeting, help the group stick to its agenda.
- Analyze the group's situation—its time constraints, goal structure, task structure, stress, leader-member relations, position power, and so on.
- Consider your own orientation toward group work. Are you motivated primarily by task concerns or by people concerns? Some situations call for decisive, authoritarian action. Is this what you are good at? If not, you may want to delegate authority to someone who is more task-oriented, at least until the crisis has passed. Does your concern for task outweigh your concern for group-member relations? At times you may want to follow a laissez-faire leadership style and let person-oriented

group members take over for a while. Adapt your style to the situation and use the resources of the group to everyone's advantage.

- In an ad hoc group that meets only once or twice, the style of leadership you choose is not nearly as important as it is in a committee that meets regularly over a long period of time. In most long-term situations, a democratic style of leadership is preferable. Provide procedural structure for the group, but encourage as much participation as possible. Increased member participation can breed a better solution.
- Remember that groups have task and process needs. Members need to get the job done, but they also need encouragement, praise, and thanks.

If you are not the designated leader or chairperson of the group:

- While you have less control in this situation because of the different expectations the group has of you, you are still influential. You can still demonstrate leadership behavior.
- Use your knowledge about small group communication—leadership, problem solving, growth, and development—to analyze what is going on in the group. Consider your own strengths as a group member. What roles do you fulfill best in the group? Use your strengths to provide what the group needs and to support those who have other needed skills.
- Occasionally a group suffers a leadership void. This often occurs when leaders are appointed by an outside source or when leaders are elected at the first meeting before group members have had a chance to evaluate one another as potential leaders. In these cases, rely on the functional approach, since any member of the group (including you) can provide leadership. But watch out for delicate egos. When people do not live up to your expectations, you disapprove of them. In a small group this can result in an attempt to overthrow a leader or in a resentful and ineffectual group climate. Members set aside the group's task while they hassle over who is in charge. Almost invariably, such groups produce unsatisfactory results and bruised egos. For a more effective strategy, work around an ineffectual leader (every rule, of course, has exceptions). Any group member can provide leadership while leaving a leader's self-esteem intact.
- Sometimes a small group contains a wealth of leadership talent. Leadership is not (or *should* not be) a contest for status and power. Individual goals must be placed behind group goals. Good leaders need good followers and supporters.

Usually, the most effective leaders are those who put the group ahead of their own ego needs.[31] In every group the effectiveness of your leadership depends on the situation, your sensitivity to the group's needs, and your ability to adapt your communicative behavior to meet those needs. Effective leaders bring out the leadership in others.

PRACTICE

TASK PROCESS LEADERSHIP QUESTIONNAIRE

The following items describe aspects of leadership behavior. Respond to each according to the way you most likely would act if you were the leader of a group. Circle whether you would most likely behave in the described way, and score your response as follows: always (A), frequently (F), occasionally (O), seldom (S), or never (N).[32]

_____ 1. I most likely would act as the spokesperson of the group.
_____ 2. I would encourage overtime work.
_____ 3. I would allow members complete freedom in their work.
_____ 4. I would encourage the use of uniform procedures.
_____ 5. I would permit members to use their own judgment in solving problems.
_____ 6. I would stress being ahead of competing groups.
_____ 7. I would speak as a representative of the group.
_____ 8. I would prod members to greater effort.
_____ 9. I would try out my ideas in the group.
_____ 10. I would let the members do their work the way they think best.
_____ 11. I would be working hard for a promotion.
_____ 12. I would tolerate postponement and uncertainty.
_____ 13. I would speak for the group if visitors were present.
_____ 14. I would keep the work moving at a rapid pace.
_____ 15. I would turn the members loose on a job and let them go to it.

FIGURE 10.4

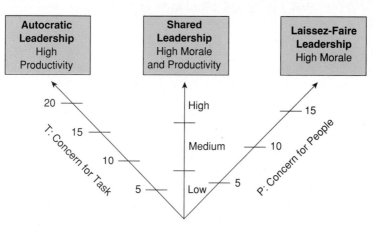

Shared leadership results from balancing concern for task and concern for people.

_____16.   I would settle conflicts when they occurred in the group.
_____17.   I would get swamped by details.
_____18.   I would represent the group at outside meetings.
_____19.   I would be reluctant to allow the members any freedom of action.
_____20.   I would decide what should be done and how it should be done.
_____21.   I would push for increased production.
_____22.   I would let some members have authority which I could keep.
_____23.   Things would usually turn out as I had predicted.
_____24.   I would allow the group a high degree of initiative.
_____25.   I would assign group members to particular tasks.
_____26.   I would be willing to make changes.
_____27.   I would ask the members to work harder.
_____28.   I would trust the group members to exercise good judgment.
_____29.   I would schedule the work to be done.
_____30.   I would refuse to explain my actions.
_____31.   I would persuade others that my ideas are to their advantage.
_____32.   I would permit the group to set its own pace.
_____33.   I would urge the group to beat its previous record.
_____34.   I would act without consulting the group.
_____35.   I would ask that group members follow standard rules and regulations.

P_____   T_____

To score the Task Process Leadership Questionnaire:

A.   Circle the item number for items 8, 12, 17, 18, 19, 30, 34, and 35.
B.   Write the number 1 in front of a circled item number if you responded S (seldom) or N (never) to that item.
C.   Also write a number 1 in front of item numbers not circled if you responded A (always) or F (frequently).
D.   Circle the number 1's which you have written in front of the following items: 3, 5, 8, 10, 15, 18, 19, 22, 24, 26, 28, 30, 32, 34, and 35.
E.   Count the circled number 1's. This is your score for concern for people. Record the score in the blank following the letter P at the end of the questionnaire.
F.   Count the uncircled number 1's. This is your score for concern for task. Record this number in the blank following the letter T.

LEADERSHIP EXERCISES

1.   Observe a working group and analyze the situation from the perspective of Fiedler's contingency model. What type of leadership would be

most appropriate for this situation? What type of leadership is actually taking place?

2. Consider the stages in problem solving that are described in Chapter 7. Identify which leadership functions might be the most appropriate at each stage of development.

3. At some time you probably have been in a position of leadership. How does the style of leadership you choose relate to the way you feel about yourself as a person, a leader, or a discussant? How does it relate to the way you feel about groups? Other people? Do you want to assume leadership?

4. Consider the dialogue between Harold and Wanda presented early in this chapter. List five responses that would help the group, and especially Harold and Wanda, resolve the conflict.

NOTES

1. A. Paul Hare, *Handbook of Small Group Research,* 2nd ed. (New York: Free Press, 1976).

2. Dane Archer, "The Face of Power: Physical Attractiveness as a Non-Verbal Predictor of Small-Group Stratification," *Proceedings of the 81st Annual Convention of the American Psychological Association* 8 (1973): Part 1: 177–78.

3. Hare, *Handbook,* 278.

4. Dean Barnlund and Franklyn Haiman, *The Dynamics of Discussion* (Boston: Houghton Mifflin, 1960), 275–79.

5. Ralph White and Ronald Lippitt, "Leader Behavior and Member Reaction in Three 'Social Climates'," in Dorwin Cartwright and Alvin Zander (eds.), *Group Dynamics,* 3rd ed. (New York: Harper & Row, 1968), 319.

6. Fred E. Fiedler and Joseph E. Garcia, *New Approaches to Effective Leadership: Cognitive Resources and Organizational Performance* (New York: John Wiley & Sons, 1987), 52.

7. Adapted from Fred Fiedler, "Personality and Situational Determinants of Leadership Effectiveness," in Darwin Cartwright and Alvin Zander (eds.), *Group Dynamics.* 3rd ed. (New York: Harper & Row, 1968).

8. Fred Fiedler. *A Theory of Leadership Effectiveness* (New York: McGraw-Hill, 1967), 144.

9. Fiedler, "Personality and Situational Determinants," 372.

10. Paul Hersey and Kenneth Blanchard, *Management of Organizational Behavior: Utilizing Human Resources,* 6th ed. (Englewood Cliffs, N.J.: Prentice-Hall, 1992).

11. Victor H. Vroom and Arthur G. Jago, *The New Leadership: Managing Participation in Organizations* (Englewood Cliffs, N.J.: Prentice-Hall, 1988), 52.

12. Sarah Trenholm, *Human Communication Theory* (Englewood Cliffs, N.J.: Prentice-Hall, 1990).

13. Vroom and Jago, *New Leadership,* 52.

14. Dennis Gorman, "Conceptual and Methodological Approaches to the Study of Leadership," *Central States Speech Journal* 21 (Winter 1970): 217–23.

15. Bernard M. Bass and M. J. Avolio, "Transformational Leadership and Organizational Culture," *International Journal of Public Administration* 17 (1994): 541–54.

16. Francis J. Yammarino and Alan J. Dubinsky, "Transformational Leadership Theory: Using Levels of Analysis to Determine Boundary Conditions," *Personnel Psychology* 47 (1994): 787–809.

17. J. Kevin Barge et al., "Relational Competence and Leadership Emergence: An Exploratory Study." Paper presented at the annual conference of the Central States Speech Association, Schaumberg, Ill., April 14–16, 1988.

18. Deborah C. Baker, "A Qualitative and Quantitative Analysis of Verbal Style and the Elimination of Potential Leaders in Small Groups," *Communication Quarterly* 38 (1990): 13–26.

19. Ernest Bormann, *Discussion and Group Methods,* 2nd ed. (New York: Harper & Row, 1975), 256.

20. See, for example the review of literature in Patricia Hayes Andrews, "Sex and Gender Differences in Group Communication: Impact on the Facilitation Process," *Small Group Research* 23 (1992): 74–94.

21. E. I. Megargee, "Influence of Sex Roles on the Manifestation of Leadership," *Journal of Applied Psychology* 53 (1969): 377–82.

22. C. Nemeth, J. Endicott, and J. Wachtler, "From the 50's to the 70's: Women in Jury Deliberations," *Sociometry* 39 (1976): 293–304.

23. J. E. Baird and P. H. Bradley, "Styles of Management and Communication: A Comparative Study of Men and Women," *Communication Monographs* 46 (1979): 101–11.

24. B. Spillman, R. Spillman, and K. Reinking, "Leader Emergence: Dynamic Analysis of the Effects of Sex and Androgyny," *Small Group Behavior* 12 (1981): 139–57.

25. J. R. Goktepe & C. E. Schneier, "Sex and Gender Effects in Evaluating Emergent Leaders in Small Groups," *Sex Roles* 19 (1988): 29–36. See also E. Kushell and R. Newton, "Gender, Leadership Style, and Subordinate Satisfaction: An Experiment," *Sex Roles* 14 (1986): 203–9.

26. See, for example, V. P. Hans and N. Eisenberg, "The Effects of Sex Role Attitudes and Group Composition on Men and Women in Groups," *Sex Roles* 12 (1985): 477–90.

27. Katherine W. Hawkins, "Effects of Gender and Communication Content on Leadership Emergence in Small, Task-Oriented Groups," *Small Group Research* 26 (1995): 234–49.

28. Susan B. Glaser, "Teamwork and Communication," *Management Communication Quarterly* 7 (1994): 282–96.

29. Rita Spoelde-Claes. "The Effect of Varying Feedback on the Effectiveness of a Small Group on a Physical Task," *Psychologica Belgica* 13, no. 1 (1973): 61–68.

30. Murray Webster, Jr., "Source of Evaluations and Expectations for Performance," *Sociometry* 32, no. 3 (1969): 243–58.

31. Carl E. Larson and Frank M.J. LaFasto, "Teamwork: What Must Go Right, What Can Go Wrong," *Sage Series in Interpersonal Communication,* vol. 10 (Beverly Hills: Sage Publications, 1989).

32. The T-P Leadership Questionnaire was adapted from Sergiovanni, Metzcus, and Burden's revision of the Leadership Behavior Description Questionnaire, *American Educational Research Journal* 6 (1969): 62–79.

CHAPTER
E·L·E·V·E·N

Small Group Communication in Organizations

After studying this chapter, you will be able to:

- Compare and contrast Theory X, Y, and Z assumptions that managers have about workers.

- Describe ways of gathering information using small groups.

- Identify two group approaches to improving quality in an organization.

- List and describe how groups can operate in organizations without meeting face to face.

- Give a meeting structure by preparing an agenda.

- Help facilitate interaction during a meeting.

- Identify what participants and leaders should do during a meeting.

- Lead a formal meeting using parliamentary procedure.

- List and describe the characteristics, skills, and strategies used by an effective team.

Chapter 11 is usually associated with bankruptcy; in this text, Chapter 11 focuses on principles and practices that can enhance organizational effectiveness by developing a better understanding of how groups and teams function in organizations.

Chances are you will earn your living working in an organization. Your career path may lead to a for-profit or nonprofit enterprise; you may work in a business for an educational, medical, or governmental institution. Or you may find yourself working at home with your personal computer, nonetheless networked to other people, involved in a team enterprise. The point is, most likely you will find yourself in an organization. And within this organization, you will undoubtedly work in small groups.

In this chapter we will identify skills and principles that can help you apply the theory and practice of working in groups to organizations. While every chapter in this book includes information and skills that can be applied to organizations, we will present specific formats and ideas that are related to enhancing organizational effectiveness. We will also present skills that are useful in helping you manage the meetings held in organizations. Finally, we will focus on how to build an effective team.

THE ROLE OF SMALL GROUPS IN ORGANIZATIONS

In the latter part of the 20th century, organizations have placed greater emphasis on collaborative work. Roger Mosvick and Robert Nelson report:[1]

- Most business in the United States is accomplished in group meetings.
- The average manager or professional spends almost one-fourth of every work week in group or team meetings.
- Top-level managers spend up to two-thirds of their time in meetings or preparing for meetings.
- People plan to spend more time in meetings. Business organizations expect a 5 to 9 percent increase in the number of meetings they hold.

Organizations are increasingly relying on empowered and involved employees to take a greater lead in shaping the destiny of the organization. Whether selling fast food or fast cars, organizations place workers in groups to help get the job done. But why? Why are corporate human resource development leaders spending millions of dollars teaching their employees principles of collaboration, participative decision making, and teamwork? The short answer is: Teamwork works. Research suggests that there are values to learning principles and skills of working together to achieve a common goal. Most of the same principles and skills being taught to corporate executives and workers are included in this book.

Organizational theories X, Y and Z explain the transformation that is taking place in today's work force from authoritarian to much more participate management styles.[2] These theories describe different assumptions managers have toward workers and how their assumptions affect their approach to collaboration and working in groups and teams.

Theory X is the assumption that people do not like to work and they will not work effectively unless they are motivated with rewards or coerced with threats. A manager with a Theory X style uses authoritarian leadership to enhance productivity. Theory X managers tell rather than ask; they lay out the work that needs to be done, identify how quickly it should be completed, and reward or punish the workers for achieving or failing to achieve the task. While Theory X is associated with managers of the early Industrial Revolution period and sweat-shop service industries, some managers today still hold Theory X assumptions. Theory X managers do not value team collaboration as a strategy to get the work accomplished.

Theory Y managers still want to get as much work done as they can, but they use different strategies to motivate workers. A Theory Y manager is much more sensitive to individual needs and encourages feedback from workers. Workers are assumed to work not just because they are paid, but because they like the sense of accomplishment they experience when a job is done well. While Theory X managers motivate workers with a carrot and stick (reward and punishment), Theory Y managers motivate workers by permitting them to help set the agenda and join with the manager in setting work quotas. Yes, a paycheck is still important to workers, but Theory Y managers also recognize that people work to meet social, esteem, and self-actualization needs. Theory X managers assume workers work primarily to meet their physiological needs—a paycheck is what is important. Theory Y managers encourage increased cooperation between worker and leader.

The latest iteration in the evolution of management thinking is **Theory Z,** proposed by William Ouchi.[3] A Theory Z manager believes workers are motivated by many of the same things that a Theory Y manager believes; workers want to do a good job and enjoy their work. A Theory Z manager gives workers even more autonomy by organizing them into groups and teams to set goals and improve work quality. Many workers attend training seminars to help them become a **self-directed work group.** As the name implies, a self-directed group learns how to govern itself with minimal direction from a higher authority. Theory Z workers need collaboration and group communication skills that will help them work more effectively together. There is evidence that Theory Z may be most effective in cultures that value collaboration and teamwork. Workers should be permitted to structure their own time and set goals working with managers as colleagues. A manager's job becomes much more participative; managers help workers

REVIEW BOX

Assumptions Managers Have about Working with Others[4]

THEORY X ASSUMPTIONS	THEORY Y ASSUMPTIONS	THEORY Z ASSUMPTIONS
People do not like to work.	People like to take pride in their work.	People take pride in their work, especially when working with others.
People work to meet physiological needs—to get a paycheck.	People work to meet social, esteem, and individual self-actualization needs.	People work to meet individual and collaborative needs.
Managers tell workers what to do.	Managers listen to worker feedback.	Managers join with workers in a true collaboration.
Managers set work quotas.	Managers let workers help set quotas.	Workers take the lead in setting team quotas.
Workers do not want to solve problems and must be watched carefully by managers.	Workers have the ability and interest to solve problems creatively.	Workers are encouraged to solve problems in groups and teams.
Managers do not value team collaboration.	Managers will value team collaboration if they receive feedback from workers that team collaboration is valued.	Managers assume team collaboration is effective and highly valued.

receive the necessary resources needed to do a high-quality job. Is Theory Z effective? In dealing with humans, there is no one single theory that can explain and predict how people perform best. There is evidence that participative decision making strategies are effective, especially if group members adopt a collective approach to goal achievement. It is a challenge, however, for some managers to develop a more supportive and less directive strategy of management; managers often manage as they have been managed. When managers are not comfortable with Theory Z, or workers are not committed to a collective effort, Theory Z management strategies are less effective. Also realize that some managers have a blend of Theory X, Y, and Z approaches. For some tasks, they may encourage self-directed work groups, yet for other jobs they may micromanage workers.

USING GROUPS AND TEAMS IN ORGANIZATIONS

Because of the advantages that result when people work together, most managers in organizations rely on a variety of group formats and techniques to get a job done. Groups and teams are used to gather information, improve quality, make decisions, and implement tasks. Principles of group interaction are also used, even when groups of employees work together but do not meet face to face.

GATHERING INFORMATION

As we have noted throughout this book, among the most powerful advantages of working in groups is that groups usually generate more information and creative approaches to accomplish a variety of tasks. This occurs because a group knows more collectively than any single individual in the group. Groups also are helpful in gauging reactions to new ideas and new products.

Focus Groups   One group format used to gather information from others is called a **focus group.** Focus groups are small groups of individuals se-

Most organizations today encourage workers to solve problems and work together in teams.

lected to discuss particular topics so that group leaders can better understand how individuals view these topics. Advertisers often use focus groups for market research. The objective of most focus groups is to gather information and help analyze products or issues. The information gleaned from focus groups helps later on when decisions need to be made about problems related to the topics under discussion.

If a soap company wants to understand how consumers like the soap it sells, it could form a focus group to tap individual attitudes and reactions to the product. Seven to ten people could be invited to discuss what they like and dislike about the soap. The focus group leader, who is trained in group communication skills, engages the group in discussion and listens carefully to members talk about the product. While written questionnaires are used to assess consumer attitudes about the soap, a focus group lets the group leader probe for more detail. The group session can help the company better understand how to sell its product.

A focus group discussion is like a group interview. Universities, large corporations, and political candidates also use focus groups to understand how others perceive their strengths and weaknesses.

Buzz Sessions Have you ever been in an audience during a speech, symposium, or panel discussion and wished that you could contribute more to the discussion? While a large audience inhibits the opportunity to provide feedback and information to presenters, there is one technique that is used to get audience response during a presentation: the **buzz session.** This technique, frequently used in conferences and large group meetings, is quite simple.

To conduct a buzz session, the leader of a large gathering should make sure that everyone present has a general understanding of the problems or issues facing the group. The leader should pose a specific question for the group to address. The audience then divides into small groups of about six people to respond to the question. One member of each small group writes down the suggestions that the group develops. After a specific time period, the recorder of each group reports the results of the discussion to the large group. The results can also be distributed on paper or displayed on a chalkboard for all to see and evaluate.

This method could be used by the CEO or president of an organization when addressing a large gathering of workers or stockholders. It could also be used by department heads of divisions of a company, or in churches, civic groups, or schools. When allowed to participate in sharing information and feedback, listeners are more likely to produce, implement, and support a better decision or solution. Buzz sessions foster involvement when a large group assembles.

IMPROVING QUALITY

TQM, which stands for total quality management, seems to be the management emphasis of the 1990s.[5] Products of high standards from international markets have placed a new emphasis on the importance of quality. Many organizations have found that employees are the best source of ideas and innovations for improving work quality.

One of the principle leaders of the quality movement was the late W. Edwards Deming. He was a professor of statistics who realized that meaningful application of data coupled with empowering team collaboration can enhance work quality. He is often credited with helping Japanese organizations to increase their work quality dramatically. He identified 14 points which, if implemented, he believed would transform an organization into an effective community producing quality goods and services. Many of his ideas emphasize the importance of collaboration and coordinated group effort. A summary of his often-quoted 14 points is given in Table 11.1.

Managers have used a variety of group formats to tap employee expertise to achieve the goal of work quality. Quality circles, and *kaizen* are two team approaches that have been used to improve the quality of goods and services produced.

Quality Circles   A **quality circle** is a group of 5 to 15 employees who meet on a regular basis for the purpose of improving work productivity, morale, and overall work quality.[6] Typical tasks of quality circles include:

Improving the quality of services or products

Reducing the number of work-related errors

Promoting cost reduction

Developing improved teamwork

Developing better work methods

Improving efficiency in the organization

Improving relations between management and employees

Promoting participants' leadership skills

Enhancing employees' career and personal development

Improving communication throughout the organization

Increasing everyone's awareness of safety

The concept of quality circles was an extension of Deming's quality principles. Quality circles were first embraced by Japanese management. Based on their success in Japan, quality circles were eventually implemented in the United States and were especially popular during the 1980s; they remain in use in some organizations today. Quality circles appear to be most successful when members have had training in how to work together as a team and have a clear understanding of the overarching group goal. In an individualistic culture, it remains a challenge for workers to work toward collectivistic goals.

Employees trained in quality circles receive basic information about group communication principles and practices. Many of the concepts presented in this text, such as group relationships, cohesiveness, roles, consen-

TABLE 11.1   HOW TO IMPROVE QUALITY: DR. DEMING'S 14 POINTS

1. Create constancy of purpose toward improvement of product and service, with the aim to become competitive and to stay in business, and to provide jobs.

2. Adopt the new philosophy. We are in a new economic age. Western management must awaken to the challenge, must learn their responsibilities, and take on leadership for change.

3. Cease dependence on inspection to achieve quality. Eliminate the need for inspection on a mass basis by building quality into the product in the first place.

4. End the practice of awarding business on the basis of price tag. Instead, minimize total cost.

5. Improve constantly and forever the system of production and service, to improve quality and productivity, and thus constantly decrease costs.

6. Institute training on the job.

7. Institute leadership. The aim of leadership should be to help people and machines and gadgets to do a better job. Leadership of management is in need of overhaul, as well as leadership of production workers.

8. Drive out fear, so that everyone may work effectively for the company.

9. Break down barriers between departments. People in research, design, sales, and production must work as a team, to foresee problems of production and in use that may be encountered with the product or service.

10. Eliminate slogans, exhortations, and targets for the work force asking for zero defects and new levels of productivity. Such exhortations only create adversarial relationships, as the bulk of the causes of low quality and low productivity belong to the system and thus lie beyond the power of the work force.

11. (a) Eliminate work standards (quotas) on the factory floor. Substitute leadership. (b) Eliminate management by objective. Eliminate management by numbers, numerical goals. Substitute leadership.

12. (a) Remove barriers that rob the hourly worker of his right to pride of workmanship. The responsibility of supervisors must be changed from sheer numbers to quality. (b) Remove barriers that rob people in management and in engineering of their right to pride of workmanship. This means, *inter alia,* abolishment of the annual or merit rating and of management by objective.

13. Institute a vigorous program of education and self-improvement.

14. Put everybody in the company to work to accomplish the transformation. The transformation is everybody's job.

From: A summary of Dr. Deming's 14 points in Peter R. Scholtes, *The Team Handbook,* Joiner® Associates Inc., 1988.

sus, decision making, problem solving, and conflict management, are part of the training of quality circle members. Quality circle group members are also given training in statistics to help them analyze production output and quality.

Leaders of quality circles are given additional training in leading groups and facilitating group interaction. Quality circle facilitators are primarily procedural leaders responsible for developing agendas, scheduling meetings, and ensuring equal participation by all group members.

Participative decision making is one of the most valuable approaches to analyzing, managing, and solving problems in business and industry. Quality circles can be effective if employees have the skills to make quality decisions.

Kaizen   *Kaizen* is a Japanese word that means "continual improvement."[7] Every product, process, and management decision can be improved, according to *kaizen* principles, which can apply not only to groups but to an entire organization. Several large and small companies in the United States use *kaizen* methods when they seek to complete their task more effectively and efficiently. Perhaps you have heard the adage, "If it ain't broke, don't fix it." *Kaizen* operates on the assumption, "If it ain't broke, fix it anyway." According to *kaizen* principles, everything can be improved.

Kaizen groups can be either permanent or temporary. The first task of a *kaizen* group is to identify the areas where work performance can be improved. The group needs to gather statistics that indicate the quality (or lack of quality) of the products or services being produced. Armed with information about how effectively the group is completing its mission, the *kaizen* team can begin suggesting methods for improving the process. *Kaizen* groups usually organize their work around the steps of the decision-making process that we discussed in Chapter 7. Step 1 is to assess the present situation. Step 2 involves creatively expanding alternatives to determine how the group can improve quality. Step 3 is to select the best alternatives by narrowing the list of suggestions to those that will have the most impact. Finally, the group selects action steps and then either recommends that specific action be taken or implements the changes themselves.

Kaizen groups operate on many of the same assumptions as quality circles. The goal, however, is focused on continually assessing how the group can improve. The *kaizen* assumption is that no product or process is ever perfect.

WHEN NOT MEETING FACE TO FACE

It seems oxymoronic to have a group meeting without meeting in person, but there are instances when much can be accomplished if people work individually and then have someone coordinate the information they have gathered or evaluated. These alternatives to an in-person meeting can be useful as preparation for face-to-face gatherings or as a way of following up on ideas that have been discussed in a meeting. We will review one low-tech method of structuring group deliberations when group members do not meet in person, called the Delphi technique, and then review research conclusions about high-tech methods of collaborating when not meeting face-to-face.

Delphi Technique: A Low-tech Method of Not Meeting Face to Face

Named after the ancient oracle, the **Delphi technique** is a method of conducting group business by getting input from group members when group members cannot meet together. Originally used by the Rand Corporation in the 1950s, the technique is a way of seeking agreement from a group when individuals generate ideas anonymously. In many ways, it is like the nominal group technique that we discussed in chapter 8; the key difference is that group members do not assemble and share their ideas in person. The Delphi technique has also been likened to "absentee brainstorming," with individuals sharing ideas and information via memo or letter. Since ideas can be generated without face-to-face interaction, the Delphi technique often is used when conflict within the group inhibits effective group interaction. It also is used when time and distance constraints make it difficult for group members to meet. Here is a step-by-step description of how to implement the Delphi technique.[8]

1. The group leader selects a problem, issue, policy, or decision that needs to be reviewed.
2. The leader corresponds with group members in writing, informing them of the task and inviting their suggestions and input. Often a specific questionnaire is developed or the group members are asked to individually brainstorm suggestions or reactions to the issue confronting the group.
3. The respondents complete the questionnaire or generate a brainstormed list of responses and send them to the leader.
4. The leader then summarizes all the responses from the group and shares the summary with all group members, asking for additional ideas, suggestions, and reactions. Team members are asked to rate or rank the ideas and return their comments to the leader.
5. The leader continues the process of summarizing the group feedback and asking for more input until general consensus emerges and decisions are made. It may take several rounds of soliciting ideas and evaluating ideas before consensus is achieved.

This method often produces many good ideas. All participants are treated equally since no one is aware of who submitted which idea. It is, however, a time-consuming process. And because there is no face-to-face interaction, some ideas worth elaboration and exploration may get lost in the shuffle. Using the Delphi technique in combination with face-to-face meetings can help eliminate some of the disadvantages of the procedure.

Using High-tech Methods when Not Meeting Face to Face

Instead of filing into a room and sitting around a table for a meeting, imagine sitting down at your desk, switching on your computer, keying in your code word, and tapping out your contributions to a meeting on the screen. Increasingly, organizations are having their members use electronic mail, fax machines, video conferences, and other technologies to interact with one another. With today's technological advances it is possible for employees to work on collective tasks while in different locations.

One interesting theory, called **media richness,** seeks to explain and predict why certain types of technologies are effective and others are not effective.[9] Managers today have many choices about how to send and receive messages from workers. Such technologies as e-mail make it possible to connect people for collaborative decision making without meeting face to face. Of course, a manager can also decide to meet with people personally or call them together for a meeting. What is a media-rich method of communicating? The media or method of communication is said to be rich if it has the following four characteristics: (1) potential for instant feedback, (2) several verbal and nonverbal cues that can be processed by senders and receivers, (3) natural rather than formal or stilted language, and (4) a focus on individuals rather than on a mass of people. Face-to-face meetings and personal conferences are highly media-rich; a memo or an announcement posted on a bulletin board is media-lean.[10]

The developers of media richness theory suggest that managers should choose media-rich methods of communicating with employees if the message is ambiguous or potentially ambiguous. If there is less likelihood of misunderstanding, then use a less media-rich method. Group meetings, then, are necessary to discuss issues and ideas where the potential for misunderstanding is high. If the information to be communicated is not ambiguous (people are likely to understand clearly what the message is about) then it is appropriate to use a less media-rich method such as a memo. Table 11.2 shows a continuum of rich and lean communication media.

Electronic Mail   Electronic mail, usually called e-mail, is one of the most prevalent technological methods used to send and receive messages in organizations. Many people use e-mail at home as well if their home computer is connected to their computer at work using a modern connected to a phone line. To send an e-mail message, the sender simply types a message and then electronically "mails" it to one or more people in the organization. Through Internet and the World Wide Web, a network of many computer communication systems, people can communicate with one another from anywhere on the globe. All you need is a telephone, a computer, a modem (which permits your computer to send messages over the phone), and the appropriate software.

Communicating via e-mail can be effective for the discussion of routine business. There is some evidence that groups that make decisions linked only by e-mail are less likely to reach consensus.[11] Other research, in pointing to the value of e-mail meetings, suggests that electronic correspondence minimizes status differences that may be present if people meet face to

Table 11.2   A CONTINUUM OF MEDIA-RICH AND MEDIA-LEAN METHODS OF COMMUNICATION

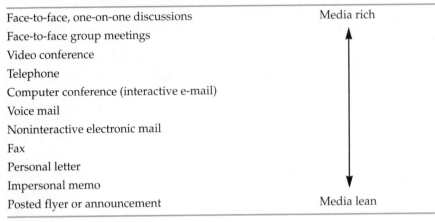

Face-to-face, one-on-one discussions	Media rich
Face-to-face group meetings	
Video conference	
Telephone	
Computer conference (interactive e-mail)	
Voice mail	
Noninteractive electronic mail	
Fax	
Personal letter	
Impersonal memo	
Posted flyer or announcement	Media lean

Adapted from: Katherine Miller, *Organizational Communication: Approaches and Processes* (Belmont, Calif.: Wadsworth, 1995).

face.[12] Another study found that language style has a significant impact on the impression you make when communicating via e-mail. In general, someone who uses a more powerful language style is perceived as more powerful, credible, even physically attractive, than someone whose language style is weak or timid.[13] The research on using e-mail groups, however, is still in its early stages.

Video Conferences   Video conferences are a relatively media-rich use of technology. A video conference occurs when two or more individuals are linked by closed-circuit or satellite-linked TV. The participants meet in specially equipped media rooms where TV cameras broadcast (or in this case "narrow" cast) the meeting to the other participants. The video conference has the obvious advantage of permitting groups to interact over long distances when it may be very expensive to have all members travel to one destination. And the video conference has an advantage over a conference phone call because nonverbal messages—such as facial expressions, eye contact, and posture—which provide more accurate sending and receiving of relational messages, can be seen. Video conferences are expensive, however, and when sensitive decisions and challenging problems need to be solved, individuals prefer a more media-rich method of managing the uncertainty and ambiguity. A software program called *One Touch* is a multimedia system that incorporates electronic voting keypads as well as audio and video systems to structure interaction. This system is especially designed for large corporations in multiple locations. One research team concluded that a video meeting is more likely to be successful if group members have met one another prior to the video meeting.[14] Another study found that video

Video conference technology permits group members to see and hear other group members who are miles away.

conferences are better than face-to-face meetings at handling more structured discussions.[15] Group members also seem to prepare better for a video conference than for a face-to-face meeting; perhaps because of its expense and novelty, group members view a video conference as more important.

Group Decision Support Systems   A new line of software has emerged to help make face-to-face meetings more efficient. As we noted in chapter 2, group Decision Support Systems (GDSS) consist of computer hardware and software that add structure to meetings. This technology is usually used with live interaction. For example, a group may be discussing a particular problem and the facilitator may stop discussion and suggest that each group member do silent brainstorming at a computer terminal. A large screen then projects the results of the brainstorming for all group members to see and evaluate.

Here is a description of some of the newest software programs.[16]

Idea Generator: This program helps users structure problem-solving and brainstorming tasks, as well as organize the ideas generated.

Innovator: Developed by the Wilson Learning Corporation, this system is billed as a meeting-enhancement keypad system that allows participants to vote for specific ideas and provide immediate feedback about the choices of other participants. This system is especially helpful for strategic planning and other tasks where developing consensus is useful.

Option Finder: This program facilitates group decision making by helping groups generate alternatives, evaluate alternatives, identify priorities, and then assess whether consensus is near.

Respondex: This software connects with video and audio equipment to present slides, video, and other multimedia information while also gathering feedback from listeners.

While research on the use of these technologies is relatively new, some conclusions are emerging.[17]

1. The more complex the issue, the more likely that group members will prefer unmediated, face-to-face interaction.
2. Mediated communication (e.g., e-mail, video conferencing) is preferred for sending and receiving information and data to help a group with its task; fewer messages about relationships and group maintenance occur as messages become less immediate.
3. Using media to send and receive messages may contribute to greater polarization of opinions; group members may take more extreme positions when putting information in writing than when communicating orally.
4. Experts recommend that mediated messages will be more effective if participants work from a planned agenda and have a "techno-partner" available to handle hardware and software glitches.
5. Mediated communication seems to work best for more structured, linear tasks.
6. The use of computer technology and more rapid transfer of information does not inherently lead to better solutions and decisions. Problems are solved by people. Technology may simply allow greater access to accurate information, help structure the process, and keep a group focused on facts, but decisions will still be made by people skilled in the art and science of decision making and problem solving. Indeed, technology can help us make mistakes faster.
7. Group members find it more difficult to negotiate relationship issues when the messages are mediated by technology.
8. Use of technology and media increases the amount of information people will have to process. People will need to develop skills in sorting out useful and less useful information.
9. People who develop skills in using technology will become more powerful and important in organizations than people who do not use technology effectively.
10. Researchers have found that cliques and coalitions are more prevalent in mediated meetings than in face-to-face discussions.

11. Group members follow a more rational, structured process when solving problems using Group Decision Support Systems.
12. Group members using GDSS tend to do a poorer job of evaluating the pros and cons of the alternatives group members are considering.

MEETING SKILLS IN ORGANIZATIONS

A committee meeting is a collection of the unfit chosen from the unwilling by the incompetent to do the unnecessary.

"At Electronic Data Systems," said Ross Perot, "when we saw a snake, we'd kill it. At General Motors, when they saw a snake, they'd form a committee."

If you want to get a job done, give it to an individual; if you want to have it studied, give it to a committee.

Sign on conference wall: A meeting is no substitute for progress.

Business meetings are important. They demonstrate how many people the company can do without.

Frankly most people do not like meetings. While this generalization has exceptions, it is safe to venture that few individuals relish the thought of a weekly appointment calendar peppered with frequent meetings. It was President John Kennedy who said, "Most committee meetings consist of 12

REVIEW BOX

Group Methods Used When Groups Do Not Meet Face to Face

Delphi technique	A systematic way to receive ideas from individuals via memo or other written means whereby ideas are then ranked and shared with the entire group
Electronic mail	The use of networked computers to electronically transmit information to others
Video conference	The use of television to link individuals or groups together by use of closed-circuit or satellite technology
Group Decision Support Systems	The use of computer hardware and software to tabulate results of decisions and gather ideas in meetings

people to do the work of 1." Humorist Dave Barry compared business meetings with funerals, in the sense that "you have a gathering of people who are wearing uncomfortable clothing and would rather be somewhere else. The major difference is that most funerals have a definite purpose. Also, nothing is ever really buried in a meeting."[18] Why are meetings held in such low esteem? Probably because many meetings are not well managed either by the meeting leader or the meeting participants. What bothers meeting attendees the most? The list below reports the results of recent studies that ranked meeting "sins."[19]

1. Getting off the subject
2. No goals or agenda
3. Too lengthy
4. Poor or inadequate preparation
5. Inconclusive
6. Disorganized
7. Ineffective leadership/lack of control
8. Irrelevance of information discussed
9. Time wasted during meetings
10. Starting late
11. Not effective for making decisions
12. Interruptions from within and without
13. Individuals dominate/aggrandize discussion
14. Rambling, redundant, or digressive discussion
15. No published results or follow-up actions
16. No premeeting orientation/canceled or postponed meetings

To be effective, a well-run meeting needs to balance two things: structure and interaction. Throughout the book we have talked about the importance of helping a group stay on task by structuring the interaction; following the steps of reflective thinking when solving a problem is one way of helping a group stay on task. As you examine the list above, note how many of the problems associated with meetings stem from a lack of clear structure or agenda. But while structure is important, group members simultaneously need to have the freedom to express ideas and react to the comments of others. If there is too much structure, the meeting is not really a meeting, it is a speech where one person talks and others listen. On the other hand, with too much unstructured interaction, a group meeting bounces along with no clear focus. In unstructured meetings, minimal attention is given to the time it takes to get the job done.[20] In the sections ahead, we offer suggestions for providing both structure and interaction in group meetings. An agenda is the prime tool of structuring a group meeting. Facilitation skills and ways of planning interaction can ensure that meeting participants will be free to interact, yet that their contributions will be relevant and on target.

GIVING MEETINGS STRUCTURE

Getting off the subject and having no goals or agenda are the two most often mentioned complaints about meetings. As we just noted, the principle tool to ensure that meetings are appropriately structured so that the deliberation achieves the intended goal is with a meeting agenda. Uncertainty and lack of an agenda can serve as major barriers to accomplishing a task as a group. An **agenda** is the list of the key issues, ideas, and information that will be presented in the order in which they will be discussed. Consider the steps described below in drafting your meeting agenda.

Determine the Meeting Goal(s)   One cardinal rule of meetings is this: Meet only when there is a specific purpose and when it is advantageous or desirable to discuss issues, solve problems, or make decisions as a group. Before beginning to draft an agenda you need to know the meeting goal. Meeting goals usually fall into one of three categories: (1) information needs to be shared, (2) issues need to be discussed, or (3) action needs to be taken.

As you prepare for a meeting, identify what you would like to have happen as a result of the meeting.[21] A typical goal might be, "At the end of this meeting we will have selected the firm that will produce our new advertising campaign," or, "At the end of this meeting we will have reviewed the applicants for the management position and identified our top three choices." Without a specific goal that is known to both leader and participants, do not be surprised if little is accomplished.

Identify Items That Need to Be Discussed to Achieve the Goal   With the goal in mind, you next need to determine how to structure the meeting to achieve the goal. Consider generating a list of topics that need to be addressed to accomplish the goal: what information needs to be shared, what issues need to be discussed, what action needs to be taken? In the brainstorming phase, do not worry about the order of the items; you can rearrange the items later.

Organize the Agenda Items to Achieve the Goal   After you have a list of items to be addressed, organize them in some logical way. A key constraint in organizing items and determining what to include on a meeting agenda is the amount of time budgeted for the meeting. Many meeting planners underestimate the amount of time discussion will take.

When you have identified potential agenda items, review your meeting goal(s) and eliminate any items that do not help you achieve your goal. Armed with your meeting goal and your list of agenda items, begin drafting your meeting agenda.[22] Consider organizing it around the three meeting goals: information items, discussion items, and action items.

Most meeting experts suggest that your first agenda item should be to ask the group to approve or modify the agenda you have prepared. If meet-

How to Prepare a Goal-Centered Meeting Agenda

1. Determine your meeting goals.
2. Identify what needs to be discussed to achieve the goals.
3. Organize the agenda items to achieve the goals.

FIGURE 11.1 BELL CURVE AGENDA

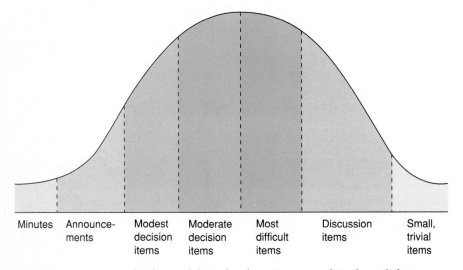

| Minutes | Announce-ments | Modest decision items | Moderate decision items | Most difficult items | Discussion items | Small, trivial items |

Source: *Meetings: How to Make Them Work for You* by John E. Tropman and Gershom Clark Morningstar, p. 56. Copyright © 1985 by John E. Tropman and Gershom Clark Morningstar. Reprinted by permission of Van Nostrand Reinhold.

ing participants make no modifications, you then know that your agenda was on target. Before making final decisions about which items you should cover and the order in which you should cover them, estimate how long you think it might take to deal with each item. You may want to address several small issues first before tackling major ones. Or, you may decide to arrange your agenda items in terms of priority: discuss the most important items first and less important ones later.

John Tropman and Gershom Morningstar recommend using the "bell curve agenda."[23] As indicated in Figure 11.1, the middle of the meeting is reserved for the most challenging or controversial issues. The opening and closing of the meeting include more-routine or less-vital issues.

Many times issues are discussed during meetings but nothing happens afterward. As the following sample meeting agenda shows, one of your last agenda items should be to summarize the action that needs to be taken following the meeting.

Sample agenda
   I. Finalize meeting agenda
  II. Announcements
 III. Information items
         New employee orientation report
         Planning committee report
         Finance committee report
 IV. Action item
         Issue: Should we donate $5,000 to the school volunteer program?
  V. Summarize action that needs to be taken following today's meeting

You are now ready to distribute your agenda to the meeting participants, well in advance of the meeting. Consider using a format like the one Mosvick and Nelson developed, shown below.[24] Meeting participants should come prepared to discuss the issues on the agenda. Obviously, if they do not have an agenda before the meeting, there is no way for them to come prepared for a meaningful discussion.

MEETING DATE	DAY	TIME	PLACE	ATTENDEES
TOPIC				
SCHEDULED BY		TELEPHONE NUMBER		
MEETING OBJECTIVE				
PREPARATION MATERIALS REQUIRED				

Meeting Agenda:

ENSURING THAT MEETINGS HAVE MANAGED INTERACTION

By *interaction* we mean the give-and-take dialogue and contributions that participants make during meetings. Without interaction, meetings become monologues. But with too much interaction, meetings can become disorganized discussions with rambling, redundant, or digressive discussions that waste time and are inconclusive. Meeting leaders and participants can help ensure a balance of structure and interaction by using the skills of gatekeeping, reminding the group of meeting goals, helping the group be sensitive to the time that elapses during discussion, and using strategies that structure group interaction.

As we learned earlier in the book, a gatekeeper encourages less-talkative members to participate and tries to limit lengthy contributions by other group members. Meetings should not consist of a monologue from the meeting leader or be dominated by just a few participants. As a meeting leader, it is your job to make sure that you involve all meeting participants in the discussion.

As also stressed throughout this book, members need to share an understanding of a group's goals. When this is accomplished, the group's agenda for each meeting should provide a road map for moving toward those goals. A leader often has to keep the group on course, and one of the most effective tools for doing so is summarizing. Periodically, use the metadiscussion skill (discussion about discussion) that we talked about in Chapter 9 and review your understanding of the group's progress with brief comments such as, "Okay. Dennis agrees with John that we need to determine how much our project will cost. Are we ready for the next issue?" Such summaries help a group take stock of what it has done and what it has yet to accomplish.

Another job of a meeting leader is to keep track of how much time has been spent on the planned agenda items and how much time remains. Think of your agenda as a map, helping you plan where you want to go. Think of the clock as your gas gauge, telling you the amount of fuel you have to get where you want to go. In a meeting, just as on any car trip, you need to know where you are going and how much fuel you need to get you to your destination. If you are running out of fuel (time), you will either need to fill up the tank (budget more time) or recognize that you will not get where you want to go. Begin each meeting by asking how long members can meet. If you face two or three crucial agenda items, and one-third of your group has to leave in an hour, you will want to make certain to schedule important items early in the meeting.

Another way to ensure that all members participate in the discussion is to use some of the prescriptive decision-making and problem-solving tools and techniques mentioned in Chapter 8. For example, if your meeting goal is to identify new ideas to solve a particular problem, consider using brainstorming or nominal group technique as a way to generate ideas. The is/is

REVIEW BOX

HOW TO GIVE A MEETING STRUCTURE

Prepare an effective agenda by:

- Determining your meeting goals
- Identifying what needs to be discussed to achieve the goals
- Organizing the agenda to achieve the goals.

HOW TO ENSURE MANAGED INTERACTION

- Use effective gatekeeping skills.
- Use metadiscussion to help the group focus on the goals.
- Help the group be sensitive to elapsed time and time remaining for deliberation.
- Use strategies to structure interaction (e.g. write before speaking, nominal group technique, or silent brain-storming).

not, journalist's six questions, and 6M analysis are other tools you could use to invite people to contribute ideas yet structure the interaction so that meeting members do not lose sight of their goals. A key task of the meeting facilitator is to orchestrate meaningful interaction during the meeting so that all meeting participants have the opportunity to give input. Structured methods of inviting involvement (often having group members write individually and then share their ideas with the group) are effective in garnering contributions from all group members.

LEADING MEETINGS

A meeting leader needs to be especially sensitive to balancing meeting structure with interaction. An effective meeting leader should facilitate rather than dictate how the group will conduct the meeting. Different groups accept (or tolerate) different levels of direction from their designated leaders. One simple rule of thumb is this: *When the leader emerges naturally from the group or leads a one-time-only ad hoc group, then the group will allow him or her to be more directive.* Beyond this simple rule, certain tasks are generally expected of leaders. One of the most important leader tasks is to keep the group focused on its agenda during the meeting. Of course, that means the leader needs to *have* an agenda. We strongly urge that agendas be distributed well in advance of a meeting. As we have stressed, give participants a chance to shape the agenda both before the meeting and as the meeting opens. Meeting leaders are often expected to:

- Call the group together, which may involve finding out when participants can meet.
- Call the meeting to order.
- If it is a formal meeting, determine if there is a **quorum**—the minimum number of persons who must be present at a meeting to conduct business.
- Keep the meeting moving; move to the next agenda item when a point is saturated. Use effective gatekeeping skills.
- Use a flip chart, chalkboard, or dry erase board to summarize meeting progress; written notes of the meeting become the "group mind" and help keep the group on track. Give the meeting structure.
- If it is a formal meeting, decide when to take a vote. Make sure the issues are clear before a vote is taken.
- Prepare a committee report (or delegate someone to prepare a report) after one or many meetings. Groups need a record of their progress. Many meetings designate someone to be a secretary and prepare the minutes, or summary of what occurred at the meeting.

PARTICIPATING IN MEETINGS

Even though we have stressed the responsibilities of the meeting leader to give the meeting structure and ensure interaction, meeting participants have similar obligations. In many respects, each meeting participant has leadership responsibilities. Leadership, as noted in Chapter 10, means "to influence." As a meeting participant, you will have many opportunities to influence the group process. Be sensitive to both the level of structure and the interaction in the meeting. Use such skills as metadiscussion (discussion about discussion), which we presented in Chapter 9, to help keep the group on track.

Your key obligation as a meeting participant is to come to the meeting prepared to work. If the leader has distributed an agenda before the meeting (as leaders should), then you have a clear sense of how to prepare and what information you should bring to the meeting. Even if no agenda has been provided, try to anticipate what will be discussed. If you have no clue as to what will be on the agenda, it is appropriate to contact the meeting leader and ask him or her how to prepare.

Mosvick and Nelson, in their book, *We've Got to Start Meeting Like This!*, identify six functions of competent meeting participants.[25]

Organize Your Contributions   Just as a well-organized speech makes a better presentation, well-organized contributions make better meetings. Rambling, disorganized, disjointed ideas increase the likelihood of the meeting becoming sidetracked.

Speak When Your Contribution Is Relevant   Before you make a comment, listen to the person who is speaking. Is your comment useful and helpful? Groups are easily distracted by irrelevant contributions.

Make One Point at a Time   Even though you may be bursting with good ideas and suggestions, your colleagues will be more likely to listen to your ideas if you present them one at a time rather than as a string of unrelated points.

Speak Clearly and Forcefully   No, we are not advocating that you aggressively try to dominate the conversation. Unassertive mumbling, however, will probably get lost in the verbal shuffle of most meetings.

Support Your Ideas with Evidence   One of the key determinants of good decisions and effective solutions is the use of evidence to support your ideas and opinions. Opinions are ubiquitous: Everyone has one. Facts, statistics, and well-selected examples help keep the group focused on the task.

Listen Actively to All Aspects of the Discussion   Group meetings provide one of the most challenging listening contexts. When several people are attempting to make points and counterarguments, you will have to gear up your powers of concentration and listening. Checking your understanding by summarizing or paraphrasing can dramatically improve communication and decrease misunderstanding.

USING PARLIAMENTARY PROCEDURE IN FORMAL MEETINGS

You have, no doubt, participated in groups that followed parliamentary procedure. Often, organizations specify that an authority such as *Robert's Rules of Order* be used to conduct meetings. Parliamentary procedure provides an orderly way for large groups (of 20 or more persons) to conduct business, although it is less useful for small groups (in which it leads to win/lose patterns of decision making rather than consensus).[26] The larger the group and the more unstructured the task, the more likely it is that parliamentary procedure will prove useful.

For a complete guide to parliamentary procedure, consult *Robert's Rules of Order* or the Sturgis *Standard Code of Parliamentary Procedure*. What follows here will be enough to get you started.

TYPES OF MOTIONS

A motion is a proposal for action by the group. Although there are many types, motions can be divided into two groups: main and subsidiary.

Main Motions   A main motion brings an item of business before a group; it is always made when a group is considering no other motion. For example, a member might say, "I move that we reschedule homecoming weekend from the fall to the spring term." Another member seconds the motion by

REVIEW BOX

The Necessary Steps to an Effective Meeting[27]

BEFORE THE MEETING

LEADER

1. Define objective
2. Select participants
3. Make preliminary contact with participants to confirm availability
4. Schedule meeting room and arrange for equipment and refreshments
5. Prepare agenda
6. Invite participants and distribute agenda
7. Make final check of meeting room

PARTICIPANTS

1. Block time on schedule
2. Confirm attendance
3. Define your role
4. Determine what leader needs from you
5. Suggest other participants
6. Know the objective
7. Know when and where to meet
8. Do any required homework

DURING THE MEETING

1. Start promptly
2. Follow the agenda
3. Manage the use of time
4. Limit/control the discussion
5. Elicit participation
6. Help resolve conflicts
7. Clarify action to be taken
8. Summarize results

1. Listen and participate
2. Be open-minded/receptive
3. Stay on the agenda and subject
4. Limit or avoid side conversations and distractions
5. Ask questions to assure understanding
6. Take notes on your action items

AFTER THE MEETING

1. Restore room and return equipment
2. Evaluate effectiveness as meeting leader
3. Send out meeting evaluations
4. Distribute memorandum of discussion
5. Take any action you agreed to
6. Follow up on action items

1. Evaluate meeting
2. Review memorandum summarizing the discussion
3. Brief others as appropriate
4. Take any action agreed to
5. Follow up on action items

saying, "Second" or "I second the motion." Most motions must be seconded and require that at least two members wish to discuss them.

Subsidiary Motions   A subsidiary motion applies to or modifies a main motion. It is in order as long as it outranks (takes precedence over) the motion under consideration. Thus, a motion to refer is in order when a group is discussing a motion to amend, but a motion to postpone indefinitely is not. Any subsidiary motion takes precedence over the main motion.

The six subsidiary motions, in order of preference, are:

1. *The motion to lay on the table,* or simply "to table," is made to put aside the current question before a group. It requires a majority vote. The question may be reintroduced at a later time by a motion to "take from the table."

2. *The motion to call the previous question* is a motion to vote immediately on the question under discussion. As soon as this motion is made and seconded, it must be voted on; it is not debatable. This motion interferes with freedom of discussion and therefore requires a two-thirds vote for passage. If a group does not pass the motion to call the previous question, it continues debate on the motion before it.

3. *The motion to postpone to a certain day* is used to delay a decision or to move discussion to a more convenient time. This motion requires a majority vote and always clearly states where and when the discussion will be resumed.

4. *The motion to refer,* which requires a majority vote, is used to move discussion of an issue to a smaller committee where it can be analyzed in more detail at greater length. The committee then later reports to the larger group. Only the main motion (with or without amendments) can be referred.

5. *The motion to amend* is an effort to add to, delete from, or substitute words, phrases, or paragraphs in the main motion. An amendment must be relevant to the main motion you are amending.

   For example, a member might say, "Mr. Chairman, I move to amend the motion by substituting the words 'October' and 'April' for the words 'fall' and 'spring' in the main motion." If the motion to amend is seconded, discussion follows on the amendment only, and a vote on the amendment is taken. If the amendment carries (a majority vote is required), debate returns to the main motion *as amended;* if the amendment fails, the original motion is considered further.

6. *The motion to postpone indefinitely* is used to kill discussion of the main motion for the duration of a session. It is the lowest-ranking subsidiary motion and requires a majority vote.

A certain amount of faith is involved in successful meeting management—faith in your own ability and, more important, faith in the process you are managing. Meeting management is a skill that can be learned and improved with practice.

TEAM-BUILDING IN ORGANIZATIONS

"Go team!" You can hear this chant at most group sports events. Whether at a touch football game or at the Super Bowl, team members are rewarded for working together. Corporate America has learned that working in teams can enhance productivity, efficiency, and employee satisfaction. In Chapter 1 we identified the advantages that accrue from working collectively on tasks in small groups. Those same advantages occur when employees work together. Whether the task is building cars, developing computer systems, or simply providing a range of services to customers, evidence clearly shows that working in teams enhances effectiveness.

A **team** is a coordinated group of individuals organized to work together to achieve a common goal. The key challenge has been to teach individuals who are used to performing individual tasks how to work together.

CHARACTERISTICS OF AN EFFECTIVE TEAM

President Dwight Eisenhower once said, "It is better to have one person working with you than having three people working for you." A team is a group of people working *with* each other rather than *for* someone. In many ways, this entire book is about teams. Organizations tend to use the word *team* rather than *group* to identify individuals who work together to achieve a common task. Corporate training departments often spend much time and money to train individuals to be better team members. What skills do training programs include? Most of them include the communication principles and practices that we have emphasized: problem solving, decision making, listening, paraphrasing, and conflict management. In addition to communication skills, team members also learn tools that help them set goals, evaluate the quality of their work, and establish team operating procedures.[28] Several researchers have been interested in studying how to make teams function better. One study found that team members find it helpful if their colleagues have compatible work schedules, adequate resources to obtain the information needed to do the work, leadership skills, and help from the organization to get the job done.[29]

Using studies of several real-life teams (such as NASA, McDonald's, and sports teams), Carl Larson and Frank LaFasto identified eight characteristics of an effective team.[30]

A Clear, Elevating Goal   Having a common, well-defined goal is the single most important attribute of an effective team. But having a goal is not enough; the goal should be elevating, important—it should excite team members and motivate them to make sacrifices for the good of the team. Sports teams use the elevating goal of winning the game or the championship. Corporate teams also need an exciting goal that all team members believe is important.

A Results-Driven Structure   Teams need an efficient system or method of organizing how they work together. Team structure is the way in which a group is organized; who reports to whom and who does what are key elements in developing a team structure. It is useful, therefore, for teams to develop a clear sense of the roles and responsibilities of each team member. A team needs individuals who perform both task roles (getting the job done) and maintenance roles (managing the team process) to be high performing. A structure that is not results-driven, one that tolerates ineffective meetings, busywork, and "administrivia," always detracts from team effectiveness.

Competent Team Members   Team members not only need to know *what* their assignment is, but also *how* to perform their job. Team members need to be trained and educated so they know what to do and when to do it. Without adequate training in both teamwork skills and job skills, the team will likely flounder.

Unified Commitment   The motto of the Three Musketeers—"all for one and one for all"—serves as an accurate statement of the attitude team members should have when working together to achieve a clear, elevating goal. Team members need to feel united by their commitment and dedication to achieve the task.

A Collaborative Climate   In Chapter 5 we identified some of the key skills that foster a positive group climate. Those skills and principles are needed to help teams achieve their potential. Effective teams operate in a climate of support rather than defensiveness. Team members should confirm one another, support one another, and listen to one another as they perform their work.

Standards of Excellence   A team is more likely to achieve its potential if it establishes high standards. Goals that cause the team to stretch a bit can serve to galvanize a team into action. Unobtainable or unrealistic goals, however, can result in team frustration. If the entire team is involved in setting goals, the team is more likely to feel a sense of ownership toward the standards it has established.

External Support and Recognition   Teams in any organization do not operate in isolation. They need support from outside the team to help acquire the information and materials needed to do the job. Team members also need to be recognized and rewarded for their efforts by others outside the team. Most coaches acknowledge the "home-field advantage" that flows from the enthusiastic support and accolades of team followers. Corporate teams, too, need external support and recognition to help them function at maximum effectiveness.

Principled Leadership   Teams need effective leaders. This is not to say that a team requires an authoritarian leader to dictate who should do what. On the contrary, teams usually function more effectively when they adopt contingency approaches to leadership. In most effective teams, leadership responsibilities are spread throughout the team.

SKILLS OF COMPETENT TEAM MEMBERS

Team-building seminars do more than just identify the characteristics of an effective team. As we learned in Chapter 1, competence requires more than knowledge of what makes a team effective, it also requires skills and motivation to use one's knowledge and skills. What are those skills? Team members learn how to establish norms and ground rules to design clearly understood team operating procedures. Noncommunication skills include such things as using statistics to evaluate the quality of a team's work and build quality. Team members learn how to use data and plot them on charts and graphs to determine whether or not the team is is achieving its goal. Typical team-building workshops also focus on many of the same communication skills you have learned in your group communication course. Those skills include:

- *Problem solving:* how to overcome obstacles to achieve a goal
- *Decision making:* how to make a choice among several alternatives
- *Listening:* how to select, attend to, comprehend, and evaluate messages
- *Paraphrasing:* how to reflect your understanding of a message to check the accuracy of your understanding
- *Conflict management:* how to manage emotions, clarify misunderstanding, identify conflicting partners' goals, and creatively seek strategies to help achieve the goals
- *Goal setting:* how to identify clear, elevating goals
- *Presentation skills:* how to give a group or individual report to summarize the team's findings to others

STRATEGIES FOR ENHANCING TEAM EFFECTIVENESS

Once you understand the characteristics of an effective team, the challenge—either as team facilitator or team participant—is to ensure that the team achieves its potential. The following strategies may prove useful in helping you develop team strengths.[31]

1. *Develop and clarify the team goal.* As noted above, teams need a clear, elevating goal. Early in the team's history, all team members should have a clear understanding of what the team is attempting to accomplish.
2. *Learn the strengths of each team member.* Before making team assignments, a coach usually takes some time to learn about the players. Team members have different strengths and talents. Learn about team members' abilities to help establish individual roles and responsibilities. Emphasize that all team members' skills are vital to the team's success. Effective teams do not operate on the star system, where only a few members are hailed for their effectiveness.
3. *Clarify group norms and set team ground rules.* Teams function better if team members have an explicit discussion about how the team should

Developing a clear and elevating goal is one of the single most important aspects of forming a high-performing team.

operate. Most team-building sessions include an opportunity for team members to develop a common vision of how the team will function. Discussing such issues as the value of being on time for meetings, reaching consensus, and having everyone's input on all ideas help participants learn how to work together.

4. *Identify barriers that may keep the team from achieving its goal.* Gathering information, reviewing the issues under consideration, and analyzing the current situation are useful steps that help teams identify and overcome difficulties as they proceed.

5. *Use effective communication skills.* Team members need to understand each other accurately. Communicating competently and frequently can enhance team effectiveness. Skills in listening, responding, feedback, conflict management, and awareness of nonverbal messages are important if the team is to operate with a minimum of friction.

6. *Develop a plan to accomplish the goal.* Just as most sports teams have a playbook, any team needs a plan to accomplish a goal. A plan should be designed to help the group overcome obstacles that are keeping it from achieving its goal.

7. *Put the plan into action.* Planning and plotting strategy will not get the job done. Teams need a systematic effort to implement the ideas and suggestions offered. Often the most efficient way is to divide the plan into small, manageable tasks. Frequent communication about progress on completing assignments will reassure group members that they are working together to achieve a goal.

8. *Evaluate the plan and team procedures.* As the team works together, the group needs to evaluate how things are going. Stop and assess whether the group's approach is achieving the desired results. Just like football coaches who look at films of last week's game, the group needs to replay its procedures and examine whether they are appropriate.

PUTTING PRINCIPLE INTO PRACTICE

Most of the work in organizations is accomplished in small groups. This chapter has identified some of the principles and skills that can enhance your effectiveness when working with others on the job. Consider the following methods of accomplishing key tasks in organizations.

- When you want to gather information from others, consider using a focus group.
- When you want to improve work quality, consider two group approaches: quality circles, and *kaizen.*
- When your group does not meet together face to face, use the Delphi technique as well as media and technology to share information.

We also reviewed several principles and skills to help make group meetings efficient and effective.

- Meetings need a balance of structure and information.
- When you lead a group, always prepare an agenda by (1) determining your meeting goal, (2) identifying items to achieve the goal, and (3) organizing the agenda items.
- Find ways to involve all members in the meeting. Draw out quiet members; avoid letting a verbose member dominate a meeting.
- When conducting a formal meeting, use parliamentary procedure to help give the meeting structure and order.
- When you participate in a meeting, make sure your comments are organized, relevant, clear, and supported with evidence. Also make sure you listen to others and monitor your nonverbal messages.

Working together as a team in an organization takes skill, knowledge, and motivation. The key elements that make a team effective include:

- A clear, elevating goal
- A results-driven structure
- Competent team members
- Unified commitment
- A collaborative climate
- Standards of excellence
- External support and recognition
- Principled leadership

PRACTICE

MEETING ASSESSMENT

Attend a meeting on your campus or in your community. Evaluate the meeting by determining which violations of procedures listed on page 336 are evident. Write a report suggesting what changes you would make if you were leading the meeting.

WHAT GROUP SKILLS DO ORGANIZATION MEMBERS HAVE?

Visit an organization in your community. It could be a school, factory, hospital, or any large organization. Interview the individual responsible for training workers to determine what kind of training in small group skills the workers receive. If they have a quality circle program or other participative team format, find out what kind of training group members receive. If the organization has no training program in group communication skills, ask what kinds of skills the organization most values.

THE WORD PROCESSING CASE[32]

John Hager, vice president for operations of Southwest Technical Insurance Company (SWT Insurance), called Bob Morgan, director of human resource development, into his office. Starting the conversation, Hager said, "I know you've been busy grappling with the handicapped employee issue, Bob, but I have another problem that I'd like you to help me with."

"As you know, Bob," Hager continued, "our firm has invested substantial sums of money in word processing centers in our local offices. Right now, I'm not concerned about the larger word processing centers that have replaced the steno pools in the home office. I'm primarily concerned with SWT's 265 local offices. Each workstation, complete with electronic typewriter, computers, and software, costs about $15,000. We took this step to improve our productivity in our branches. But lately, we're wondering what we've bought for our money."

"What are some of your specific reservations?" asked Bob.

"Well, the word processing centers look impressive, but what are they really accomplishing for SWT? Are we investing our money wisely, or are we spending money on a frill? We really don't know whether employees are better satisfied or more productive using the new equipment. Maybe electric typewriters combined with the old dictating equipment were just as good for the amount of work the employees have to produce. We also suspect that younger employees may be more favorably inclined toward word processing than the older employees. Other members of the executive committee and I would like your human resources management team to provide us with some answers to these questions. Our overall goal is to do the work as efficiently as possible, with happy workers."

After thinking for a moment, Morgan replied, "John, those are excellent questions. This is just the kind of problem-solving task the folks in personnel research should be tackling. I'll work with them to develop a preliminary report and share our suggested approach with you in a couple of weeks."

QUESTIONS

1. What is the problem that needs to be solved?
2. What decisions need to be made?
3. How would you recommend that Bob Morgan approach his assignment? Draft a plan that outlines how Morgan's personnel research team should proceed. What should they do first, second, third, and so on?
4. How could Morgan's personnel research group use a teamwork approach to complete its task?

EVALUATE A MEETING[33]

Instructions: Consider the typical meetings you attend. Compare your meetings to the following characteristics of an effective meeting. Check those statements that apply to meetings you normally conduct or attend:

_____ 1. An agenda is prepared prior to the meeting.
_____ 2. Meeting participants have an opportunity to contribute to the agenda.
_____ 3. Advance notice of meeting time and place is provided to those invited.
_____ 4. Meeting facilities are comfortable and adequate for the number of participants.
_____ 5. The meeting begins on time.
_____ 6. The meeting has a scheduled ending time.
_____ 7. The use of time is monitored throughout the meeting.
_____ 8. Everyone has an opportunity to present his or her point of view.
_____ 9. Participants listen attentively to one another.
_____ 10. There are periodic summaries as the meeting progresses.
_____ 11. No one tends to dominate the discussion.
_____ 12. Everyone has a voice in decisions made at the meeting.
_____ 13. The meeting typically ends with a summary of accomplishments.
_____ 14. Participants periodically evaluate the meeting.
_____ 15. People can be depended on to carry out any action agreed to during the meeting.

_____ 16. A memorandum of discussion or minutes of the meeting is provided to each participant following the meeting.

_____ 17. The meeting leader follows up with participants on action agreed to during the meeting.

_____ 18. The appropriate and necessary people can be counted on to attend each meeting.

_____ 19. The decision process used is appropriate for the size of the group.

_____ 20. When used, audiovisual equipment is in good working condition and does not detract from the meeting.

Number of statements checked _____ × 5 = _____ Meeting score

A score of 80 or more indicates that you attend a high percentage of quality meetings. A score below 60 suggests work is required to improve the quality of meetings you attend.

NOTES

1. Roger K. Mosvick and Robert B. Nelson, _We've Got to Start Meeting Like This!_ (Glenview, Ill.: Scott, Foresman, 1987).
2. Several texts offer excellent discussions of management theories X, Y, and Z applied to groups and organizations. See for example: R. W. Pace and D. F. Faules, _Organizational Communication_ (Englewood Cliffs, N.J.: Prentice Hall, 1989); Katherine Miller, _Organizational Communication: Approaches and Processes_ (Belmont, Calif.: Wadsworth, 1995); J. F. Cragan and D. W. Wright, _Communication in Small Groups: Theory, Process, Skills_ (Minneapolis/St. Paul: West Publishing Company, 1995).
3. W. G. Ouchi, _Theory Z_ (New York: Avon Books, 1981).
4. Adapted from: M. Cuffe and J. F. Cragan, "The Corporate Culture Profile." International Association of Quality Circles Annual Conference Transactions. Association of Quality Circles, 1983. Published in J. F. Cragan and D. W. Wright, _Communication in Small Groups: Theory, Process, Skills_ (Minneapolis/St. Paul: West Publishing Company, 1995).
5. For a comprehensive discussion of using groups and teams to enhance organizational quality, see Peter R. Scholtes, _The Team Handbook_ (Madison, Wis.: Joiner Associates Inc., 1988). Also see Michael Argyle, _Cooperation: The Basis of Sociability_ (London: Routledge, 1991), 115–31.
6. _Positive Personnel Practices: Quality Circles' Participant's Manual_ (Prospect Heights, Ill.: Waveland Press, 1982).
7. Masaaki Imai, _Kaizen: The Key to Japan's Competitive Success_ (New York: McGraw-Hill, 1986).
8. Andre L. Delbecq, Andrew H. Van de Ven, and David H. Gustafson, _Group Techniques for Program Planning: A Guide to Nominal Group and Delphi Processes_ (Glenview. Ill. Scott, Foresman, 1975), 7–16.
9. R. H. Lengel and R. L. Daft, "The Selection of Communication Media as an Executive Skill," _Academy of Management Executive_ 2 (1988): 225–32.

10. Ibid.

11. See an excellent review of the effect of technology on group decision making in: M. S. Poole and G. DeSanctis, "Microlevel Structuration in Computer-Supported Group Decision Making," *Human Communication Research* 19 (1992): 5–49.

12. V. J. Dubrovsky, S. Kiesler, and B. N. Sethna, "The Equalization Phenomenon: Status Effects in Computer-Mediated and Face-to-Face Decision-Making Groups," *Human Computer Interaction* 6 (1991): 119–46.

13. M. Adkins and D. E. Brashers, "The Power of Language in Computer-Mediated Groups," *Management Communication Quarterly* 8 (1995): 289–322.

14. See: R. Johansen, J. Vallee, and K. Spangler, *Electronic Meetings: Technical Alternatives and Social Choices* (Reading, Mass.: Addison-Wesley, 1979).

15. P. L. McLeod and J. K. Liker, "Electronic Meeting Systems: Evidence from a Low Structure Environment," *Information Systems Research* 3 (1992): 195–223.

16. Michael Finley, "Welcome to the Electronic Meeting," *Training* (July 1991): 29–32. Also see Marshall Scott Poole and G. Desanctis, "Microlevel Structuration in Computer-Supported Group Decision Making," *Human Communication Research* 19 (1992): 5–49.

17. Starr Roxanne Hiltz, Kenneth Johnson, and Murray Turoff, "Experiments in Group Decision Making: Communication Process and Outcome in Face-to-Face versus Computerized Conferences," *Human Communication Research* 13, no. 2 (Winter 1986): 225; also see: S. M. Farmer and C. W. Hyatt, "Effects of Task Language Demands and Task Complexity on Computer-Mediated Work Groups," *Small Group Research* 25 (August 1994): 331–66; L. M. Jessup, T. Connolly, and D. A. Tanskik, "Toward a Theory of Automated Group Work: The Deindividuation Effects of Anonymity," *Small Group Research* 21 (August 1990): 333–48; C. Aydin, "Occupational Adaptation to Computerized Medical Information Systems," *Journal of Health and Social Behavior* 30 (1989): 163–79; M. S. Poole, M. Holmes, R. Watson, and G. DeSanctis. "Group Decision Support Systems and Group Communication: A Comparison of Decision Making in Computer-Supported and Nonsupported Groups," *Communcation Research* 20 (1993): 176–213; R. E. Rice and D. Case, "Computer-Based Messaging in the University: A Description of Use and Utility," *Journal of Communication* 33 (1983): 131–52. M. W. Aiken, J. S. Martin, J. G. Paolillo, and A. I. Shirani, "A Group Decision Support System for Multilingual Groups," *Information Systems Research* 3 (1994): 155–61; S. G. Strauss and J. E. McGrath, "Does The Medium Matter? The Interaction of Task Type and Technology on Group Performance and Member Reactions," *Journal of Applied Psychology* 79 (1994): 97; J. S. Valacich. A. R. Dennis and T. Connolly, "Idea Generation in Computer-Based Groups: A New Ending to an Old Story, *Organizational Behaviour and Human Decision Processes* 57 (1994); 448–67; J. Morrison and O. R. Lius Sheng, "Communication Technologies and Collaboration Systems: Common Domain, Problems and Solutions," *Information and Management* 23 (1992): 93–112. B. J. Broome and M. Chen, "Guidelines for Computer-Assisted Group Problem Solving: Meeting the Challenges of Complex Issues," *Small Group Research* 23 (1992): 216–36; H. Hwang and J. Guynes, "The Effect of Group Size on Group Performance in Computer-Supported Decision-Making," *Information and Management* 26 (1994): 189–98: L. Chidambaram and B. Jones, "Impact of Communication Medium and Computer Support Group Perceptions and Performance: A Comparison of Face-to-Face and Dispersed Meetings," *Management Information Science Quarterly* 17 (1993); 465–87; J. E. Kottemann, F. D. Davis, and

W. E. Remus, "Computer-Assisted Decision Making: Performance, Beliefs, and the Illusion of Control," *Organizational Behaviour and Human Decision Processes* 57 (1994): 26–37.

18. Dave Barry, *Dave Barry's Guide to Life* (New York: Wings Books, 1991), 311.
19. Mosvick and Nelson, *We've Got to Start Meeting Like This.*
20. Steven A. Beebe and John T. Masterson, "Toward a Model of Small Group Communication: Application for Teaching and Research," *Florida Speech Communication Journal* 8, no. 2 (1980): 9–15.
21. See Dennis A. Romig and Laurie J. Romig, *Structured Teamwork® Guide* (Austin, Tex.: Performance Resources, Inc., 1990); Thomas A. Kayser, *Mining Group Gold* (El Segundo, Calif.: Serif Publishing, 1990).
22. Henry L. Ewbank, Jr., *Meeting Management* (Dubuque, Iowa: Wm. C. Brown, 1968).
23. Suggestions about organizing meeting agendas are based on Michael Doyle and David Straus, *How to Make Meetings Work* (New York: Playboy Press, 1976); Mosvick and Nelson, *We've Got to Start Meeting Like This!;* Gay Lumsden and Donald Lumsden, *Communicating in Groups and Teams: Sharing Leadership* (Belmont, Calif.: Wadsworth, 1993); Dan B. Curtis, James J. Floyd, and Jerry L. Winsor, *Business and Professional Communication* (New York: Harper-Collins, 1992); Romig and Romig, *Structured Teamwork® Guide;* Kayser, *Mining Group Gold.* John E. Tropman and Gershom Clark Morningstar, *Meetings: How to Make Them Work for You* (New York: Van Nostrand Reinhold, 1985) 56.
24. Mosvick and Nelson, *We've Got to Start Meeting Like This,* 238.
25. Mosvick and Nelson, *We've Got to Start Meeting Like This.*
26. Much of this discussion is adapted from an excellent brief guide to parliamentary procedure written by Rufus K. Broadaway, M.D., entitled *How to Run a Medical Meeting,* available from the Advertising and Communication Department of Cedars Medical Center, 1400 NW 12th Avenue, Miami, FL 33136.
27. Marion E. Haynes, *Effective Meeting Skills* (Los Altos, Calif.: Crisp Publications, 1988).
28. Scholtes, *Team Handbook.*
29. R. Y. Hirokawa and J. Keyton, "Perceived Facilitators and Inhibitors of Effectiveness in Organizational Work Teams," *Management Communication Quarterly* 8 (1995): 424–446.
30. Carl E. Larson and Frank M. J. LaFasto, *TeamWork: What Must Go Right/What Can Go Wrong* (Beverly Hills Calif.: Sage Publishing, Inc., 1989).
31. Adapted from David W. Johnson and Frank P. Johnson, *Joining Together: Group Theory and Group Skills* (Englewood Cliffs, N.J.: Prentice-Hall, 1975), 304.
32. Adapted from Raymond S. Ross, *Small Groups in Organizational Settings* (Englewood Cliffs, N.J.: Prentice-Hall, 1989).
33. Haynes, *Effective Meeting Skills.*

APPENDIX

Communicating in Small Groups to an Audience

*T*hroughout this book we have featured principles and skills that can help you communicate with others in groups, meetings, and teams. Most of the groups in which you communicate will be private discussions among you and other members of your group. Some groups, however, are designed so that others can listen to the discussion. Public communication formats help an audience understand all sides of an issue, particularly if individuals with diverse viewpoints are involved in the discussion. The three public communication formats considered in the following sections are panel discussions, symposium presentations, and forum presentations. We will also offer some general guidelines for speaking to an audience.

PANEL DISCUSSIONS

A **panel discussion** is the most frequently used public group discussion format. It is usually selected to inform an audience about a specific issue or problem. A panel discussion is defined as a group discussion that takes place before an audience with the purpose of: (1) informing the audience about issues of interest, (2) solving a problem, or (3) encouraging the audience to evaluate the pros and cons of a controversial issue.

An appointed chairperson or moderator usually organizes a panel discussion. The moderator's job is to keep the discussion on track. The moderator usually opens by announcing the discussion question. Most panel discussions include at least three panelists; if they include more than eight or nine, the panelists have difficulty participating equally. Since the panel is presented for the benefit of an audience, organizers should take care that the audience can see and hear the discussion clearly. Panelists usually sit in a semicircle or behind a table. While they should be informed about the subject they will discuss, they should not rehearse their discussion; the conversation should be extemporaneous. Panelists may use notes to help them remember facts and statistics, but they should not use a prepared text.

After announcing the discussion topic, the moderator briefly introduces the panel members, perhaps noting each one's qualifications for being on the panel. To begin the discussion, the moderator may then direct a specific question to one or more panelists. An effective moderator encourages all panelists to participate. If one panelist seems reluctant, the moderator may direct a specific question to that person. If one panelist tends to dominate the discussion, the moderator may suggest politely that other panel members be given an opportunity to participate. Rather than let the discussion continue until the group has nothing more to say on the issue, a specific time limit should be set on the discussion. Most panel discussions last about an hour, but the time limit can be tailored to the needs of the audience and the topic. At the conclusion of the discussion, the moderator may either summarize comments made by the group members or ask another group member to do so. Often the summary is followed by an invitation to the audience to ask the panel questions.

SYMPOSIUM PRESENTATIONS

A **symposium presentation** is another public discussion format, consisting of a series of short speeches. Usually a central theme or issue unifies all of the speeches. Unlike participants in a panel discussion, participants in a symposium either come with prepared speeches or speak extemporaneously from an outline. The speakers are usually experts who represent contrasting points of view. For example, imagine that your physics instructor has invited four experts in the field of nuclear energy to speak to your class. Each expert has selected a specific aspect of nuclear energy to present. Your instructor probably will briefly introduce the speakers, announce the central topic of discussion, and ask the speakers to address themselves to a discussion question. Then each will speak from eight to ten minutes. The speakers probably will not talk informally between speeches; they most likely will know in advance what general areas the other speakers will discuss. After the speeches, your instructor may summarize the major ideas presented and allow the audience to participate in an open forum.

Technically, a symposium is not really a form of group discussion, because there is little or no interaction among the participants. But a symposium often concludes with a more informal panel discussion or forum. A major advantage of the symposium is that it is easy to organize: Just line up three or four speakers to discuss a designated topic. In addition, when speakers with contrasting viewpoints present their ideas, a lively discussion often follows. Make sure that the speakers know their time limits and address their assigned topics. An able moderator can prevent a symposium from digressing into irrelevant issues. Also announce a time limit for the audience forum following a symposium.

FORUM PRESENTATIONS

Group discussion encourages more interaction and participation than other forms of communication (such as public speaking). A **forum presentation** takes maximum advantage of the principle that when many people participate improved decisions can result. The word *forum* originated with the Romans. The forum was the public marketplace where Roman citizens could assemble and voice their opinions about the issues of the day. A forum discussion generally follows a panel discussion or symposium. It can also come after a single speaker's presentation. A forum permits an audience to get involved in the discussion. Rather than playing a passive role, as in a panel discussion, the audience directs questions and responses to a chairperson or to a group of individuals. When holding a news conference, the president of the United States presents a prepared statement, followed by questions and responses from reporters—a forum. Some talk-radio stations have forum discussions on issues of the day. Many communities conduct town meetings or public hearings in which citizens can voice their opinions about issues affecting the community. The audience in a forum has an opportunity to provide feedback. Comments from audience members sometimes can be used to determine how successfully a speaker or panel has enlightened the audience. The questions and responses also give the featured speakers an opportunity to clarify and elaborate their viewpoints.

Public Communication Group Formats

FORMAT	DESCRIPTION
Panel	An unrehearsed discussion that takes place before an audience to inform, solve a problem, or make a decision
Symposium	A series of short speeches unified by a central theme or issue
Forum	Audience members are invited to question or respond to a group. Forum presentations frequently follow panel or symposium presentations.

PLANNING WHAT TO SAY TO AN AUDIENCE

Speaking to an audience involves skills in planning what you are going to say and presenting your information to your listeners. Your school probably offers a course in public speaking. The discussion that follows highlights some of the essential skills public presenters should master when speaking to an audience whether in a panel, symposium, or forum group presentation.[1] The more formal the presentation (such as in a symposium presentation), the more planning it requires. We will offer some general tips for both planning a presentation and presenting your ideas to others.

Speakers need a plan. Speakers who are part of a group effort to communicate with an audience need a plan that is coordinated with other group members. Central to all of these planning elements is a consideration of your audience. Your first and foremost priority when speaking to an audience is to make sure you consider their needs and backgrounds. A speaking plan also typically involves clarifying and coordinating your topic with other group members, deciding on your specific purpose or objective, identifying your central ideas, and supporting and organizing your ideas.

ANALYZE YOUR AUDIENCE

Analyzing your audience means finding out as much as you can about your listeners. Why will they be listening to you? What are their expectations? What are their attitudes toward you, your group, and your topic? Answers to these questions can help you make choices throughout the planning process. If you are speaking to a captive audience, you need to be especially sensitive to their needs. A captive audience consists of people who have little choice as to whether to attend or not, such as your classmates in small group communication class. Class members may *have to* show up. If that is the case, your group needs to work extra hard to immediately make the information interesting and relevant to the listeners.

Clarify Your Topic Focus

Giving a presentation as part of a group usually means that you are freed from the responsibility of having to select a topic on your own. As we have emphasized, what you contribute to a group discussion or symposium presentation should be coordinated with other group members. Make sure that what you are saying does not duplicate what someone else plans to say. Talk with other group members about your specific topic to avoid unnecessary redundancy.

Clarify Your Overall Objective

Keep your specific presentation objective clearly in mind as you prepare for your public presentation. Is your goal primarily to inform the audience about decisions your group has already made? Or is your goal to persuade your listeners to adopt a solution you are proposing? You might give a public presentation to let the audience eavesdrop on your conversation as you debate issues and share information. If an audience is present, though, you should be keenly aware of the audience's needs and not be lost in conversation that ignores those who came to hear what you have to say. It is a good idea for all group members involved in the presentation to talk explicitly about the overall goal of the group in sharing information and ideas with the audience.

Identify Your Major Ideas

What do you want to say? What are the key points you will make? When you speak in public, do not just start sharing unrelated pieces of information; think about major ideas you want to share. If you were to boil your information down to one, two, or three ideas, what would they be? The major points you want to address flow from the information you have gathered and the discussion that may have taken place in your group.

Support Your Major Ideas

A presentation to an audience does not consist of just asserting points or drawing a conclusion and sharing the conclusion with your listeners. Support your major points with evidence or examples. We discussed the types and tests of evidence in Chapter 7. In addition to using facts, examples, opinions, and statistics, you could also support a point you are making with a hypothetical example or a personal story. Realize, however, that while hypothetical examples and personal experiences can add great interest to your presentation, they are not sufficient to prove a point. Their value lies in illustrating ideas and issues. Again, we urge you to keep your audience in mind as you make choices about how you will support your major points. It is also a good idea to check with other group members to make sure that you are not duplicating information your colleagues plan to share.

ORGANIZE YOUR IDEAS

The last step in developing a presentation plan is to arrange your major ideas and supporting material in a logical way. If you are relating a sequence of steps or discussing the history of an issue, you probably will use chronological order, which means arranging your ideas by telling your listeners what happened first, second, third, and so forth.

Another classic method of organizing ideas is called "topical." In this approach, you simply organize your presentation by topics or natural divisions in your presentation. If you are informing an audience about the functions of your local government, you could arrange your presentation topically by saying: "Our government provides for our safety through the police and fire departments, our education through schools and libraries, and our transportation through funding public transportation and maintaining our roads."

Spatial arrangement, in which you organize information according to location or position, is another approach. In describing your campus to your listeners, you could first talk about the west campus, the central campus, and finally the east campus, rather than hopscotching around a map depicting the layout of your school.

Other ways to organize information include:

Problem solution: First talk about the problem and then the solution

Pro vs. con: Compare advantages and disadvantages

Complexity: Move from simple ideas to more complex ones

Regardless of the specific method you select, make sure your overall organizational strategy makes sense both to you and to your listeners. Most public-speaking teachers strongly urge speakers to develop an outline of their presentation. The introduction to the presentation should, at a minimum, provide an overview of the key ideas and catch and hold the listeners' attention. The body of the presentation presents the key ideas and supporting material. The conclusion's prime function is to summarize and, if appropriate, call for listeners to take specific action.

PRESENTING TO AN AUDIENCE

Armed with your objective, key ideas, and a logical organization of your points, you are ready to consider how to deliver your information to your listeners. As we discussed in Chapter 6, your unspoken messages play a major role in communicating your ideas and feelings to your listeners.

SELECT YOUR METHOD OF DELIVERY

There are four primary methods from which to select: manuscript (reading), memorized, impromptu, and extemporaneous style. Most speech teachers have definite biases about which methods are most and least effective. We do not recommend that you read from a manuscript. Such an approach is stilted and does not permit you to adapt to your listeners. Giving a presentation totally from memory also has its pitfalls, especially if you have many statistics or other forms of evidence that you want to share. You run the risk of forgetting key points. Speaking impromptu means that you speak with minimal or no preparation—you just try to wing it. This has some obvious disadvantages as well. Impromptu speaking negates all of the suggestions we made for planning your presentation. The style of delivery that seems to work best is extemporaneous delivery. You know the major ideas you want to present, you also may have an outline, yet the exact wording of your presentation has not been memorized. This has the advantage of encouraging you to plan your message but gives you the flexibility to adapt to the specific audience to which you are speaking. Your delivery also sounds more natural and interesting when you speak extemporaneously than when you read or memorize your remarks.

USE EFFECTIVE DELIVERY SKILLS

When speaking to an audience, there are several fundamental principles to keep in mind. First and foremost, have eye contact with your audience. Research suggests this is the single most important nonverbal delivery variable.[2]

When speaking in a group presentation, it is not unusual to deliver your message while remaining seated around a table. If your group remains seated, you can still use gestures to emphasize key points and add interest and animation to your talk. Effective gestures should be natural, not overly dramatic, and be coordinated with your verbal message. Usually speakers use fewer gestures when seated than when standing to give a speech. If you are participating in a symposium presentation, more than likely you will be expected to stand when you speak. When standing, ensure that your posture communicates your interest in your listeners.

Besides having eye contact and monitoring your physical delivery, you have a fundamental obligation to speak so others can hear you and to convey interest and enthusiasm in your voice. Speaking with adequate volume and using variations in pitch, rate, and quality are essential to effective speech delivery.

CONSIDER USING VISUAL AIDS

Many groups find that using visual aids helps communicate statistical information and survey results, and can help dramatize the problem the group is attempting to solve. One group, wanting to illustrate the parking problem on campus, made a video to show exactly how overcrowded the parking lots were. Audio and video interviews can also play a role in adding interest and credibility to a group's effort to document problems and solutions. However, we caution you against overusing visual aids. The purpose of most group presentations is to present information, not to entertain. Resist the temptation to spend so much time and energy on visuals, video, and audio material that your overall objective takes a backseat to your method of presentation.

The types of visual aids you can use include objects, models, people, drawings, photographs, slides, maps, and graphs. Bar, pie, and line graphs are especially effective in presenting statistical information to an audience. Other types of visual aids include charts that you make yourself or design on your computer, and videos or audiotapes. Many classrooms and business conference rooms are now furnished with computer-controlled CD-ROM equipment and other high-tech innovations. When using this newer technology, we suggest that you not lose sight of your goal—communicating an idea to your listeners. As we have mentioned, the goal is not to dazzle your listeners with glitzy graphics; it is to communicate clearly.

Among the most effective types of visual aids are overhead transparencies. These are usually inexpensive, yet can be made ahead of time to clearly present information in an effective way. When using an overhead projector and transparency, consider the following suggestions:

- Turn the projector off when you are not showing your visual.
- Do not put too much information on one visual. Many experts recommend no more than seven lines of type, using at least an 18-point type font.
- Consider revealing a transparency one line at a time rather than showing the entire transparency; you are better able to control your listeners' attention.
- Consider using color to add interest.

When using any type of visual aid consider the following guidelines:

- Make sure all audience members can see it easily.
- Give yourself plenty of time to prepare your visual aid before your speak.
- Rehearse with your visual aid.

- Have eye contact with your audience, not your visual aid.
- Talk about your visual aid, do not just show it.
- Do not pass objects among your audience while you are speaking; it distracts from your oral presentation.
- Use handouts during the presentation only if your listeners need to have the information in front of them while you speak.
- Keep your visual aids simple.

The last suggestion we offer when using visual aids is to have a back-up plan if your visual aid is crucial to your presentation. Taking an extra extension cord, making another copy of your homemade video, or making sure the overhead projector has a spare bulb are examples of making back-up plans to ensure that your presentation goes smoothly.

Use other group members to help you manage the visual aids. Consider asking someone to help change the transparencies on the overhead projector or ask for help in displaying charts or graphs. Since you are part of a team, involve other group members to help you present information clearly and effectively.

NOTES

1. Our suggestions for helping you plan and present your speech are adapted from: Steven A. Beebe and Susan J. Beebe, *Public Speaking: An Audience-Centered Approach* (Boston: Allyn & Bacon, 1996).
2. See: Steven A. Beebe, "Eye Contact: A Nonverbal Determinant of Speaker Credibility," *Speech Teacher* 23 (January 1971): 21–25; Steven A. Beebe, "Effects of Eye Contact, Posture, and Vocal Inflection upon Credibility and Comprehension," *Australian Scan Journal of Nonverbal Communication* 7–8 (1979–80): 57–80.

GLOSSARY

Action chart. A grid that lists the tasks that need to be done and identifies who will be responsible for each task.

Activity tracks. Phases of problem solving that do not follow linear, step-by-step patterns.

Adaptor. A nonverbal behavior that helps people respond to their immediate environment.

Ad hoc committee. A committee that disbands when it completes its task.

Affect display. A nonverbal behavior that communicates emotion.

Affection. The human need to express and receive warmth and closeness.

Agenda. The listing of topics or tasks to be discussed or completed in a meeting.

Allness statement. A simple but untrue generalization.

Attitude. A learned predisposition to respond to something in a favorable, neutral, or unfavorable way.

Autonomous work group. A group charged with achieving specific tasks without outside interference.

Belief. The way in which you structure what you believe to be true and false—your reality.

Brainstorming. A problem-solving technique that helps a group generate possible solutions to a problem.

Breakpoint. A point in a group discussion when members shift to a different activity.

Buzz session. A meeting of a few members from a larger group; the smaller group responds to a question or problem and reports back to the larger group.

Bypassing. A barrier to communication that occurs when two people interpret the same word differently.

Category system. A list of terms assigned to determine the frequency of related behaviors.

Closed-ended question. A question that asks a person to choose from among several supplied responses.

Coercive power. The ability to punish people for acting or not acting in a certain way.

Cohesiveness. The degree of attraction members feel toward one another and their group.

Collectivistic. Describes a culture that favors group or team achievement over individual achievement.

Committee. A small group given a specific task by a larger group.

Communication. The vehicle that allows a group to move toward its goals.

Communication competence. Communicative behavior that is both effective and appropriate in a given context.

Communication network. A pattern of interaction within a group; who talks to whom.

Competent group communicator. One who is able to interact appropriately and effectively with others in small groups.

Complementarity. The tendency individuals have to be attracted to others who have knowledge, skills, or other attributes that they themselves do not have but that they admire.

Confirming response. A communication response that allows a person to value himself or herself more.

Conflict. Disagreement over available options caused by seemingly incompatible goals among group members and their thinking that others can keep them from achieving those goals.

Conflict phase. Fisher's second phase of group interaction, in which disagreement and individual differences arise.

Confrontation. The second phase of group conflict, when group members express disagreement openly. Group members may choose sides and form subgroups in opposition to other subgroups.

Consensus. All group members support and are committed to a decision.

Control. The human need for status and power.

Cooperation requirement. The degree to which a group's success depends on its utilizing member resources.

Criteria. Standards for an acceptable solution to a problem.

Culture. A learned system of knowledge, behavior, attitudes, beliefs, values, and norms that is shared by a group of people.

Data splitting. Analyzing information effectively.

Decision making. Making a choice from among several alternatives.

Decision-making group. A group whose purpose is to make a choice from among several alternatives.

Defensive communication. Communicative behavior that arouses in another person the need to protect his or her self-concept.

Delphi technique. Absentee brainstorming. Individuals not meeting face to face share ideas about how to solve a problem or generate ideas by using written messages.

Descriptive problem-solving approach. A method of helping people understand how a group solves a problem.

Disconfirming response. A response that causes another person to value himself or herself less.

Dyad. Two people.

Ego-conflict. Conflict that occurs when individuals become defensive because they feel they are being attacked.

E-mail. Electronic mail. A system using computer terminals to send and receive written messages, and using the computer screen to view messages and the keyboard to encode messages.

Emblem. A nonverbal cue with a specific verbal counterpart—word, letter, or number.

Emergence phase. Fisher's third phase of group interaction, in which a group begins to manage disagreement and conflict.

Expert power. The influence someone has over others because of greater knowledge and information.

Explanatory function. The power theories have to explain things.

Fact-inference confusion. Mistaking a conclusion you have drawn for an observation.

Fantasy. In symbolic convergence theory, the creative and imaginative shared interpretation of events which fulfills a group psychological or rhetorical need.

Fantasy chain. A string of connected stories that revolve around a common theme that occurs when a group is sharing a group fantasy.

Fantasy theme. The common or related content of the stories that the group is sharing during a group fantasy.

Feedback. The response to a message.

Flowchart. A step-by-step diagram of a multistep process.

Focus group. A group of individuals selected to discuss a particular topic so that the group's leaders can better understand how the individuals view that topic.

Force field analysis. A method of structuring the analysis of a problem to assess the driving and restraining forces that contribute to the goal one wishes to achieve.

Forum presentation. A discussion that directly follows a panel discussion or symposium and allows audience members to respond to ideas.

Functional perspective. A view of leadership that assumes that all group members can initiate leadership behaviors.

Functional problem-solving approach. Identifies key communicative behaviors that contribute to effective problem-solving.

Group climate. The emotional environment of a group that affects and is affected by interaction among members.

Group cohesiveness. The degree of attraction members feel toward one another and their group.

Group decision making. The process by which a group arrives at the best decision from among available alternatives.

Group decision support systems (GDSS). Computer hardware and software used to link computer terminals together for purposes of holding an "electronic meeting" without individuals meeting face to face.

Group maintenance role. A behavior that helps a group maintain its social dimension.

Group Support System (GSS). Any computer-based information system used to support intellectual collaborative work.

Group task role. A behavior that helps a group achieve its purpose.

Groupthink. Group members try to minimize conflict and reach consensus without critically testing, analyzing, and evaluating ideas.

Hidden Agenda. A private goal toward which an individual works while appearing to work toward the group's goal.

High-context culture. A culture that emphasizes nonverbal communication.

High-contact culture. Cultures in which people tend to touch others and to require less personal space.

Ideal-solution format. A problem-solving method that helps a group define a problem, speculate about an ideal solution, and identify the obstacles that keep it from achieving its goal.

Illustrator. A nonverbal behavior that accompanies and embellishes verbal communication.

Immediacy. A quality of nonverbal communication that refers to whether an individual likes or dislikes another person.

Inclusion. The human need for affiliation with others.

Individual role. A behavior that calls attention to individual contributions of group members.

Individualism. A tendency to focus on individual accomplishment.

Interaction diagram. A means of identifying and recording the frequency and direction of communication networks in groups.

Interdependence. A relationship among components in a system wherein a change in one component affects all other components.

Interpersonal conflict. An early phase of conflict, in which group members may voice some agreement but may make vague and ambiguous statements.

Interpersonal need. A human need that can be fulfilled by others.

Is/is not analysis. A method of separating the causes from the symptoms of a problem by assessing such issues as: what is/is not the problem, what are/are not symptoms of the problem, when and where did/did not the problem occur.

Johari Window. A model that shows the relationships between self-disclosure, self-perception, and perceptions of others.

Journalist's six questions. Using the six questions of *who? what? when? where? why?* and *how?* to help analyze a problem.

Kaizen. A Japanese term meaning "continuous improvement."

Leadership. Behavior that influences, guides, directs, or controls a group.

Leadership style. A leader's relatively consistent behavior pattern that reflects his or her beliefs and attitudes; classified as authoritarian, laissez-faire, or democratic.

Legitimate power. Power derived from being elected or appointed to control a group.

Listening. An active, complex process of selecting, attending, understanding, and remembering.

Low-contact culture. A culture in which people are uncomfortable being touched and require more personal space.

Low-context culture. A culture that emphasizes verbal expression.

Maintenance roles. Roles that define a group's social atmosphere.

Media richness. The quality of a communication method that has (1) potential for instant feedback, (2) verbal and nonverbal cues to be processed by senders and receivers, (3) natural language, and (4) a focus on individuals.

Metacommunication. An aspect of a message that provides information about how the whole message should be interpreted; communication about communication.

Metadiscussion. A statement about the discussion itself rather than about the discussion's topic.

Method Theories. Special theories that offer prescriptions for behavior.

Monochronic Time. A typically Western view of time as linear and segmented. Contrast: polychronic.

Motivation. An internal drive to achieve a goal.

Mutuality of concern. The degree to which members share the same level of commitment to a group.

Noise. Something in the communication channel or in the mind of the receiver that contributes to an inaccurate understanding of the message intended.

Nominal group technique. A problem-solving method in which members work individually on ideas, rank suggested solutions, and then report their findings for group discussion.

Nonverbal communication. Communication behavior that does not rely on written or spoken words.

Norm. A standard that separates appropriate from inappropriate behavior.

Open-ended question. A question that allows a person to respond freely, since it does not provide suggested answers.

Orientation phase. Fisher's first phase of small group interaction, in which members try to understand one another and the task before their group.

Panel discussion. A group discussion intended to inform an audience about a problem.

Paralanguage. Vocal cues, such as pitch, rate, volume, and quality, which provide information to other people.

PERT. Program Evaluation and Review Technique. A method of developing a chart to structure who should do what tasks at specified periods of time.

Polychronic Time: A view of time in which many things happen simultaneously and there is little emphasis on precision in time. Contrast: monochronic.

Potency. A dimension of nonverbal communication that communicates status and power.

Power. The resources an individual has with which to exert control over others.

Predictive function. The ability theories have to predict events.

Prescriptive problem-solving approach. A problem-solving method that suggests specific agendas or techniques for improving group problem solving.

Primary group. A group that fulfills people's needs to associate with others (such as the family).

Primary tension. Anxiety and tension that occur when a group first meets.

Problem solving. A process that attempts to overcome or manage an obstacle in order to reach a goal.

Problem-solving group. A group that exists to resolve an issue or overcome an obstacle.

Process leadership. Communication directed toward maintaining interpersonal relations and a positive group climate; also called group building and maintenance.

Process Theories. General theories that explain human behaviors across a variety of contexts.

Pseudo-conflict. Conflict that occurs when individuals disagree because of inaccurate communication.

Public communication format. An organized group discussion presented to an audience.

Quality circle. A small group that meets on a regular basis to help with corporate decision making (to improve a product, company morale, or work quality).

Question of fact. A question that asks whether something is true or false.

Question of policy. A question that asks whether a group should change a procedure or behavior.

Question of value. A question that asks the worth or desirability of something.

Quorum. The minimum number of persons who must be present at a meeting to conduct business.

Reasoning. The process of drawing conclusions from information.

Referent power. The power of interpersonal attraction.

Reflective thinking. John Dewey's problem-solving method, which identifies and defines a problem, analyzes it, suggests possible solutions for it, selects the best solution for it, and tests and implements that solution.

Regulator. A nonverbal behavior that helps a group control the flow of communication.

Reinforcement phase. Fisher's fourth phase of group interaction, in which members express positive feelings toward a group and its decision.

Relational activity. An activity dealing with behaviors that sustain or damage relationships among group members.

Responsiveness. A dimension of nonverbal communication that communicates activity, energy, and interest.

Reverse brainstorming. Asking group members to brainstorm ideas or solutions that would make the problem worse. After generating such a list, the group then considers the implications of doing the opposite of what was identified.

Reward power. The power to provide rewards for desired behavior.

RISK technique. A discussion technique designed to assess how group members will respond to and manage a change in policy or procedure.

Role. A consistent behavior pattern resulting from your expectations of yourself, your actual behavior, and the expectations others have of you.

Rolestorming. Asking group members to assume the role of someone other than themselves to help spur creative solutions to a problem during the brainstorming process.

Secondary tension. Conflict over group norms, roles, and differences among member opinions.

Self-concept. The characteristics and attributes an individual believes himself or herself to have.

Self-directed work group. A group that learns how to govern itself with minimal direction from a higher authority.

Self-disclosure. The deliberate communication of information about yourself to others.

Silent brainstorming. Holding a period of individual brainstorming before group members share their ideas with the group. Integral to nominal group technique, or may be used as part of brainstorming.

Similarity. The tendency of individuals with like experiences, beliefs, attitudes, and values to be attracted to one another.

Simple conflict. Conflict that occurs when each of two people knows what the other wants but neither can achieve his or her goal without keeping the other from doing so.

Simulation. A structured exercise that creates conditions for participants that they might encounter outside of the training session.

Single-question format. A problem-solving agenda that helps a group identify key issues and subissues of a problem.

Situational perspective. A perspective that views leadership as the interrelationships among group needs and goals, leadership style, and situation.

6M analysis. An analysis tool that assesses six potential problem obstacles: manpower (human resources), machinery, methods, materials, money, and minutes.

Small group. At least three people interacting with one another.

Small group communication. Interaction among a small group of people who share a common purpose or goal, who feel a sense of belonging to a group, and who exert influence on one another.

Small group ecology. The consistent way in which people arrange themselves in small groups.

Solution multiplicity. The number of available choices that will solve a problem.

Speech communication. The process by which people make sense of their world and share that sense with others; what people say and how they say it.

Standing committee. A committee that remains active for an extended period of time.

Status. An individual's position of importance.

Study group. A group whose primary purpose is to gather information and learn new ideas.

Substantive conflict. The third phase of conflict, in which more-balanced agreement and disagreement occurs; overt conflict decreases and group members offer more constructive and positive comments.

Survey research. A method of sampling several people's attitudes, beliefs, values, behavior, or knowledge.

Symbolic Convergence Theory. The development of a group consciousness and identity through the sharing of fantasies or stories which are often chained together and have a common theme.

Symposium presentation. A series of short speeches unified by a central issue or theme.

System. An organic whole composed of interdependent elements.

Task difficulty. The amount of mental effort required to solve a problem or complete a task.

Task leadership. Communication directed toward accomplishing a group's task or goal.

Task process activity. An activity a group undergoes to manage its task or its reason for convening.

Task role. A role a member assumes to help accomplish the group's task.

Task-contingency theory. The relationship between communication and the type of task before a group.

Task-oriented small group. A group with a specific objective to achieve, problem to solve, or decision to make.

T-chart. A diagram that looks like a large "T" drawn on a board or flip chart, where the "pros" of a particular proposition are listed on one side of the middle line and the "cons" are listed on the other side.

Team. A group of individuals organized to work together to achieve a common goal.

Territoriality. Use of space to claim or defend a given area.

Theory X. The assumption that people do not like to work and they will not work effectively unless they are motivated with rewards or coerced with threats.

Theory Y. The assumption that workers work not just because they are paid, but because they like the sense of accomplishment they experience when they do a job well.

Theory Z. A management model in which workers receive more autonomy by participating in groups and teams to set goals and improve work quality.

Therapy group. A group led by a trained professional whose purpose is to help individuals with personal problems.

Topical focus. An activity at any given time that deals with the issues under discussion by a group.

Training. Instruction emphasizing skill development.

Trait perspective. A view of leadership as the personal attributes or qualities leaders possess.

Transactive process. One in which messages are sent and received simultaneously.

Value. A person's perception of what is right or wrong, good or bad.

Vigilant thinker. A critical thinker who pays attention to the process of how problems are solved.

World view. One's fundamental outlook on reality, one's place in the universe, and how one views one's purpose in life.

X-Y-Z formula. A way to describe feelings by saying: when you do X, in situation Y, I feel Z.

ACKNOWLEDGMENTS

Page 9: © Mark Litzler; 17: © Susan Lapides/Design Conceptions; 21: © K. Straiton/Photo Researchers; 19: © Billy E. Barnes/Stock Boston; 38: © Kathy Sloane/Photo Researchers; 39: © George Bellerose/Stock Boston; 42: © Eastcott/M./The Image Works; 56: © Fredrik D. Bodin/Stock Boston; 57: © Richard Pasley/ Stock Boston; 77: © Michael Siluk/The Picture Cube; 80: "© 1995, Washington Post Writers Group reprinted with permission."; 84: © Collins/Monkmeyer Press Photo Service; 107: © Mark Litzler; 108: © Pickerell/The Image Works; 109: © Mike Mazzaschi/Stock Boston; 113: © David Wells/The Image Bank; 118: © Reprinted by permission: Tribune Media Services; 137: " FRANK & ERNEST reprinted by permission of NEA, Inc."; 138: © Michael Siluk/The Image Works; 146: © Gale Zucker/Stock Boston; 147: Drawing by C. Barsotti; ©1989 The New Yorker Magazine; 149: © Doug Plummer/Photo Researchers; 150: © Reprinted by permission: Tribune Media Services; 156: © Robert A. Isaacs/Photo Researchers; 173: © Superstock; 184: © Bruce Ayres/Tony Stone Images; 226: © Gale Zucker/Stock Boston; 235: © Dan Bosler/Tony Stone Images; 228: © Mark Litzler; 250: © Walter S. Silver/The Picture Cube; 260: Reprinted from the CHRONICLE OF HIGHER EDUCATION. By permission of Mischa Richter and Harald Bakken.; 271: © Skjold/The Image Works; 289: © David E. Kennedy/TexaStock; 292: © Gale Zucker/Stock Boston; 296: © Walter Hodges/Tony Stone Images; 317: © Mark Antman/The Image Works; 325: © Weiss/Jerrican/Photo Researchers; 341: © Carrie Boretz/The Image Works

INDEX